Twenty Years of *European Company Law*

European Company Law Series

VOLUME 20

Editor

Steef M. Bartman, Attorney-at-Law, Emeritus Professor of Company Law at Leiden Law School and Professor of Corporate Group Liability at Maastricht University, the Netherlands.

Introduction

The European Company Law Series is closely linked to the bimonthly journal European Company Law, also published by Kluwer Law International.

Contents/Subjects

The series covers subjects of company law in a broad sense, including insolvency, co-determination and securities law. Topical issues such as merger control, corporate governance, and piercing the corporate veil have been covered.

Objective of Series

Analysis of topical or complex subjects in European company law.

Readership

Academics; regulators; practitioners.

The titles published in this series are listed at the end of this volume.

Twenty Years of *European Company Law*

Developments and Challenges in European Company Law

Edited by

Bastiaan Kemp

Mieke Olaerts

Wolters Kluwer

Published by:
Kluwer Law International B.V.
PO Box 316
2400 AH Alphen aan den Rijn
The Netherlands
E-mail: lrs-sales@wolterskluwer.com
Website: www.wolterskluwer.com/en/solutions/kluwerlawinternational

Sold and distributed by:
Wolters Kluwer Legal & Regulatory U.S.
920 Links Avenue
Landisville, PA 17538
United States of America
E-mail: customer.service@wolterskluwer.com

ISBN 978-94-035-2118-3

e-Book: ISBN 978-94-035-2128-2
web-PDF: ISBN 978-94-035-2138-1

Editors

Bastiaan Kemp is professor of Corporate Governance and Corporate Regulation at the Faculty of Law of Maastricht University and an attorney-at-law at Loyens & Loeff, Amsterdam. In addition, he is co-editor of the journal *European Company Law*, a member of the editorial board of the Dutch corporate law journal *'Maandblad voor Ondernemingsrecht'*, a professorial fellow and vice-academic director at the Institute for Corporate Law, Governance and Innovation Policies and a member of the corporate law advisory council of the Dutch Bar Association and the Royal Association of Dutch Civil Notaries.

Mieke Olaerts is professor of Comparative and National Company Law and Elverding Chair Sustainable Businesss, Culture and Corporate Regulation at Maastricht University. The Elverding Chair is sponsored by DSM Firmenich, DNB, Q-park and ING. She is Of Counsel at DVDW and Academic Director of the Institute for Corporate Law, Governance and Innovation Policies at Maastricht University. She is also co-editor of the journal *European Company Law* and editorial board member of the Dutch journal *'Ondernemingsrecht'*.

Contributors

Victor Burki is an attorney at the Belgian law firm Agio Legal. He specialises in listed companies and advises them on transactions and regulatory topics. In addition, he has published multiple articles on matters of Belgian and European corporate law.

Cees de Groot is an associate professor of Company Law at the Faculty of Law of Leiden University (The Netherlands). He is a member of the editorial board of the journal *European Company Law* and a member of the editorial board of the Dutch corporate law journal 'Onderneming en Financiering'.

Harm-Jan de Kluiver is a professor (emeritus) of corporate law at the University of Amsterdam and a former attorney-at-law and partner at De Brauw. He holds a number of non-executive directorships and is an independent consultant and arbitrator. He is the chairman of the Royal Dutch Commercial Law Association (Koninklijke Vereeniging Handelsrecht).

Tom Dijkhuizen is an attorney-at-law at Finch Dispute Resolution, Utrecht.

Dr Mariia Domina is an associate professor in Business Law at the University of Lorraine (France) and External Research Fellow at the Maastricht European Private Law Institute (University of Maastricht). She holds LLM in International Business Law (University of Manchester), MSc in International Finance (University of Westminster) and PhD in Financial Law (University of Strasbourg).

Philippe Hezer is an attorney-at-law at Loyens & Loeff, Amsterdam, and an external PhD candidate at Erasmus University, Rotterdam. In addition, he is a member of the editorial board of the Dutch corporate law journal '*Maandblad voor Ondernemingsrecht*'. Philippe's research interests are related to corporate governance, with a particular focus on shareholder information rights.

Titiaan Keijzer is an assistant professor of Corporate Law at Erasmus University Rotterdam, the Netherlands, and a member of Young Erasmus Academy. In November 2024, he will also serve as Visting Professor at Turin University. Titiaan is a permanent contributor (vaste medewerker) to *'Ondernemingsrecht'* and an editorial board member of *'Maandblad voor Ondernemingsrecht'*, two Dutch corporate law journals. He is a member of several academic associations, including the European Corporate Governance Institute.

Joti Roest is a professor of Company Law at the University of Amsterdam. She is a member of the European Model Company Act (EMCA) Group, member of the editorial board of the corporate law journal ECCL (European Company Case Law), member of the European Commission's Informal Expert Group on Company Law and Corporate Governance (ICLEG) and a member of the editorial board of the Dutch journal *Rechtspraak Ondernemingsrecht (RO)*.

Prof. Dr. Alexander Schall, M. Jur. (Oxon) holds a chair for German, European and International Private Law, Business Law and Comparative Law at the Law School of the Leuphana University Lüneburg. He was Visiting Fellow at Harris Manchester College, University of Oxford, from September 2018 to August 2019. The resulting research project 'The Principle of Unjust Enrichment' is currently in print. In 2023, he founded the journal ECCL (European Company and Case law) with Prof. Andrea Vicari, University of Milano. He is also co-editor of the ninth edition of the Hachenburg, Commentary on the GmbHG (2024); of the Vicari/Schall, Company Laws of the EU (2020); of the Heidel/Schall, Commentary on the HGB (4th edn 2024) and of the Schall/Theusinger/Pour Rafsendjani, Commentary on the LKSG (2023 – the German Supply Chain Act). Alexander Schall graduated in law at the University of Konstanz (1996), passed the Magister Juris at the University of Oxford (2003), finished his Doctorate at the Ludwig-Maximilians-University Munich (2003) and his Habilitation at the University of Hamburg (2008).

Alexandros Seretakis is an assistant professor of law and Fellow of Trinity College Dublin. His research and teaching interests include alternative investment funds, fintech and financial stability. He has served as a research fellow at the NYU Pollack Centre for Law and Business in New York and the Institute of Advanced Legal Studies in London. He is also a member of Blockchain Ireland Legal Working Group, an expert at the Digital Euro Association and a guest lecturer at the Institute of Bankers in Dublin.

Karsten Engsig Sørensen is a professor at the Department of Law, Aarhus University, Denmark. He holds a Danish law degree, a PhD (on European Union (EU) Company Law), and a Danish Dr. Jur. (on joint ventures). Furthermore, he holds an LLM from the University of Exeter. His research is mainly focused on EU Law and Company Law. He is one of the two editors of the SSRN e-journal on Nordic and European Company Law, member of the management board of ECCL – European Company Case Law and a member of the Nordic Network for Company Law.

Christoph Teichmann holds the Chair for Civil Law, German and European Commercial and Company Law at the University of Wuerzburg (Germany). He graduated at the University of Heidelberg where he also started his academic career with a PhD thesis on labour law in corporate groups and a subsequent habilitation thesis on the interrelationship of company law and the EU rules on the common market. Currently, Christoph Teichmann is a member of the 'Informal Company Law Expert Group' consulting the European Commission in matters of company law.

Constantijn van Aartsen is a postdoctoral researcher at the Private Law Department of Maastricht University. He works on behalf of the Elverding Chair on Sustainable Business, Culture and Corporate Regulation and is specialized in issues of corporate theory, sustainability, and political economy.

Christoph Van der Elst is a professor of Business Law and Economics at Tilburg University (The Netherlands) and at Ghent University (Belgium) and held/holds visiting professorships at different universities including Vanderbilt (US), UAMS (Belgium), European College (Belgium) and Babeş-Bolyai University (Roumania). He is an ECGI research associate and a member of the Belgian Bar (Cottyn) and advised many different government agencies at national and international level. He is also a member of the audit committee of the Ghent University Hospital.

Maarten Verbrugh is a professor of European and Comparative Company Law at Erasmus School of Law and vice dean of education at Erasmus School of Law, Erasmus University Rotterdam.

Andrea Vicari is a professor of Commercial Law and European Company Law at the Faculty of Law of the University of Milan, director of the Advanced Course in Company Law at the University of Milan and an attorney-at-law. He is co-editor of the journal *European Company Case Law Review* and member of the milan board of the journal *Rivista di Diritto Societario*.

Tom Vos is an assistant professor at the University of Maastricht, where he is affiliated with the Institute for Corporate Law, Governance and Innovation Policies (ICGI). In his research, he focuses on corporate law, corporate governance, law and economics, and empirical studies. In addition to that, he is a visiting lecturer at the Jean-Pierre Blumberg Chair of the University of Antwerp, where he teaches a course on international corporate governance and supervises a research project on 'short-termism in European corporate governance'. Finally, Tom is also a (part-time) associate at the Corporate and Finance Practice of Linklaters in Brussels, where he advises clients on corporate and securities laws.

Summary of Contents

Table of Contents

Introduction

Mieke Olaerts & Bastiaan Kemp

The first issue of *European Company Law* appeared in 2004 under the guidance of Steef Bartman (Leiden/Maastricht) as its editor. This book appears exactly 20 years later, in 2024, and is a tribute to the fact that *European Company Law* has been successful in promoting European and comparative company law over those years. Moreover, the book and its authors also rightly focus on the important role of Steef Bartman and Cees de Groot (Leiden), who, as (main) editor and editorial secretary, have played a vital role in making the journal successful. The last contribution to the book is therefore a report of an interview that was held with Steef Bartman and Cees de Groot about the inception of the journal, the development of European company law and the outlook towards the future. One of the interesting aspects is the vision that Steef Bartman had for the format of the journal, which was not only to focus on lengthy academic articles but also to provide more concise publications highlighting developments in the field of European, national and comparative company law. This fits well with the culture of Dutch academia, where most publications are generally shorter (around 10-15 pages) compared to the size of most academic publications in international journals. There was also the focus on how company law was actually applied in practice, with – at the time – even the participation of law firms and their lawyers who contributed to the journal. While the latter is no longer the case, the focus on concise publications that aim to inform both practitioners and be of interest to academics remain key characteristics of the journal today.

The contributions to this book are also a testament to that concise and practice-orientated approach. Many regular contributors to the journal have taken the time to write an interesting contribution to this book, and generally the contributions are written in the style of the journal – concise and focused on current developments in the law. Of course, given its current importance in both corporate practice and legislative approaches, sustainability features in several of the contributions. Next to that, also the more traditional topics in the area of European company law, such as company groups, mergers and shareholder rights, are addressed.

The journal *European Company Law* has not only been successful as a journal but also featured a number of spinoffs. Steef Bartman and his team organised a number of conferences on *European Company Law*, with the first taking place in Leiden (the Netherlands) in 2005. After the success of this conference, six more conferences were organised in – amongst others – Sweden, Italy and Poland. The first conference also led to the first publication in the European Company Law book series, called 'European Company Law in Accelerated Progress.' The second publication was the continuously updated book on European Corporate Law by Adriaan Dorresteijn (Utrecht) and – since the fourth edition (2022) – Mieke Olaerts (Maastricht) and others, which, like the journal, focuses on European and comparative company law. The current book celebrating 20 years of *European Company Law* is the 20th book in that series. Next to conferences and books, *European Company Law*, of course, also focused on students. Over time, *European Company Law* organised various successful summer courses on European company law. With these developments, *European Company Law* has been front and centre in the development of European company law and corporate governance over the past 20 years.

European Company Law was initially set up as an initiative of the University of Leiden, as Steef Bartman was a professor there. In 2019, the journal was transferred to Maastricht University when Steef Bartman was appointed there as a professor of Corporate Group Liability. At the end of 2022, Steef Bartman offered to step down as editor – but remaining a valued member of the editorial board – and Mieke Olaerts and Bastiaan Kemp (both professors at Maastricht University) took over the main editorship. Mieke and Bastiaan are assisted in their task by the members of the editorial board and editorial secretaries Damla Bos (associate professor Maastricht) and Lucia Jeremiasová (PhD, Maastricht). We look forward to taking the journal forward and – hopefully – celebrating another 20 years of *European Company Law* in 2044 and are gratefull for all contributions of the member of editorial board throughout the years.

CHAPTER 1

Shareholders and the Auditor (S)election Process

Christoph Van der Elst

Both in 2006 and in 2014 the European Union reformed the regulatory framework of statutory audits significantly. These new rules also address the auditor's selection process for further enhancing the reliability of the audit and the auditor's position. Before the general meeting of shareholders of listed companies appoints the auditor, the audit committee, exclusively composed of non-executive directors, must prepare the selection process in many details, and inform the general meeting. This chapter analyses and tests how those new European rules of the selection procedure of the auditor influenced the voting results of the auditor appointment. The evidence casts doubts on whether those measures increased the efficacy of the selection process when measured by the voting attitude of the shareholders.

§1.01 INTRODUCTION

Most jurisdictions in the world require an audit of the financial statements of the company:

> An audit is an impartial examination and evaluation of the accounting records of a company by a statutory auditor. The purpose of the audit is to verify that the records are an accurate and fair representation of the company's transactions, and involves obtaining evidence about the financial statements sufficient to give reasonable assurance that the financial statements are free from material misstatement, whether caused by fraud or error. This includes an assessment of: whether the accounting policies are appropriate to the company's circumstances and have

> been consistently applied and adequately disclosed; the reasonableness of significant accounting estimates made by the directors; and the overall presentation of the financial statements.[1]

The audit enhances public confidence in those records. Many people and institutions rely on the quality of the statutory audit for their decision-making process, for example, when deciding whether to loan monies to a company. Obviously, the reliability of the audit depends on the quality of the auditor and the (s)election of this auditor. In this chapter, I address the selection process of the auditor, and I empirically investigate whether the measures that the European Union has provided since the start of the millennium have improved this process. Sections §1.02 to §1.04 briefly give an overview of the selection process and the regulatory innovations in 2006 and 2014. Section §1.05 focuses on the empirical results of the selection process, making use of the voting records of the auditor election in the Netherlands and Belgium. Section §1.06 provides a short conclusion.

§1.02 THE AUDITOR SELECTION PROCESS

Since the start of corporate governance debate, it was emphasized that the external auditor is an integral and important part of the governance set-up of the company. The Cadbury Code states:

The annual audit is one of the cornerstones of corporate governance. … The audit provides an external and objective check on the way in which the financial statements have been prepared and presented, and it is an essential part of the checks and balances required. … The most direct method of ensuring that companies are accountable for their actions is through open disclosure by boards and through audits carried out against strict accounting standards.[2]

In 1996, the European Commission added in its Green Paper:

> The statutory audit is an essential element of the system of corporate governance. In order to put the statutory audit in the right perspective, it is necessary to distinguish the role of the various organs of the company in the field of financial reporting. While the directors are responsible for the preparation of the financial statements, the role of the statutory auditor is to report to the shareholders on the financial statements presented to him by the directors. In doing so, the statutory auditor acts in the interests of the shareholders who have a financial stake in the company. In addition, his report lends credibility to the financial information used by third parties.[3]

1. Office of the Director of Corporate Enforcement, *The Principal Duties and Powers of Auditors under the Companies Act*, 6 (Dublin, 1 October 2018), https://www.odce.ie/Portals/0/Information%20Booklets%202014%20Act/Auditors.pdf.
2. The Committee on the Financial Aspects of Corporate Governance, *The Financial Aspects of Corporate Governance*, 5.1-5.2 (GEE, London, December 1992).
3. European Commission, *Green Paper: The Role, Position and the Liability of the Statutory Auditor within the European Union* (24 July 1996) 23, https://europa.eu/documents/comm/green_papers/pdf/com96_338_en.pdf.

Given the importance of reliable information (streams) in developing good corporate governance, it does not come as a surprise that so much emphasis is placed on the position of the external auditor. The position and role of the external auditor were for a long time only 'lightly' regulated in many jurisdictions.[4] In the European Union, it was only in the 1980s that (large) companies were requested to have their accounts audited (although many Member States already had the audit requirement in their national rules) and confirm that the report is consistent with the accounts.[5] The Eight Company Law Directive added that only persons with appropriate professional qualifications can carry out the statutory audits.[6]

Soon after, the discussion emerged as to the objectivity of the statutory audit services, particularly considering the many other services that auditors provided to the audited companies. Shortly after the implementation of the Eight Company Law Directive, the focus shifted to the independence of the external auditor in order to ensure better audits. The Cadbury Code already noted: 'The framework in which auditors operate, however, is not well designed in certain respects to provide the objectivity which shareholders and the public expect of auditors in carrying out their function.'[7]

In the 1990s, it was recognized that regulatory action is required, guaranteeing that audits can only be performed by independent and qualified professionals.[8] While the Cadbury Code already identified the problem, it could not yet offer a regulatory measure to that effect:

> Although the shareholders formally appoint the auditors, and the audit is carried out in their interests, the shareholders have no effective say in the audit negotiation and have no direct link with the auditors. Indeed the Committee can see no practicable way of establishing one. Auditors do, however, have to work closely with those in management who have prepared the financial statements which they

4. In some jurisdictions, companies have long been familiar with the audit function. The UK Joint-Stock Companies Act of 1844 introduced the requirement for an annual audit for companies formed under it. These audits were performed by accountants, although at the start it was not yet mandatory to have this audit performed by an independent and professional accountant. In the beginning the control was focusing on transactions: 'The object of an audit is a two fold one, the detection of fraud where it has been committed, and its prevention by imposing such safeguards, and devising such means as will make it extremely difficult of accomplishment, even if the inclination is in that direction.' These audit requirements resulted in the establishment of the first organizations of accountants, like the Society of Accountants in Edinburgh in 1854 (Stephan Walker, *The Society of Accountants in Edinburgh, 1854-1914*, 398 p. (London: Routledge, 2020)).
5. *See* Art. 51 of the repealed Fourth Company Law Directive (Fourth Council Directive 78/660/EEC of 25 July 1978 based on Art. 54(3)(g) of the Treaty on the annual accounts of certain types of companies, OJ L 222, 14.8.1978 and Art. 55 providing in a long transition period).
6. Eighth Council Directive 84/253/EEC of 10 April 1984 on the approval of persons responsible for carrying out the statutory audits of accounting documents, OJ L 126, 12.5.1984.
7. The Committee on the Financial Aspects of Corporate Governance, *The Financial Aspects of Corporate Governance*, 5.3 (GEE, London, December 1992).
8. European Commission, *Green Paper: The Role, Position and the Liability of the Statutory Auditor within the European Union* (24 July 1996) 8, https://europa.eu/documents/comm/green_papers/pdf/com96_338_en.pdf.

> are auditing in order to carry out their task, and audit firms, like any other business, will wish to have a constructive relationship with their clients.[9]

In the mid-1990s, the European Commission acknowledged the important role of shareholders in the election process due to their interest in the statutory audit as well as the practical difficulties and conflicting interests. The Commission came up with measures to address and strengthen the independent position of the auditor:

> 4.19 Because the shareholders have the most direct interest in the outcome of the statutory audit, all Member States have given the right to appoint and to dismiss the auditor to the shareholders in the general meeting. However, for the shareholders of most listed companies, as a result of their large numbers and transient nature, there is no effective mechanism for them to do so. It is usually the directors who effectively appoint and dismiss the statutory auditor, with the decision merely being ratified by the shareholders at the annual general meeting. A consequence of this is that statutory auditors are criticised for not being independent of the directors. It is argued that, in disputes between the directors and the statutory auditor on issues such as accounting policy choices, the statutory auditor has an incentive to concede to the wishes of the directors. The statutory auditor may be put in a particularly difficult position in such disputes if the directors have gathered opinions from competing firms of auditors.
>
> 4.20 It is argued that another result of the auditors being effectively appointed by the directors is that, due to cost pressures, both parties have reduced the role of the statutory audit to the minimum necessary to fulfil the legal requirements of company law as interpreted by the auditing firms themselves. It is argued that this has led to less attention being given by the statutory auditors to the assessment of the efficiency and effectiveness of companies' internal control systems, which could lead to an increased incidence of fraud and other illegal acts.[10]

In difference to the Cadbury Council, the European Commission pointed to a number of mitigating instruments that could strengthen the position of the external audit in the corporate governance framework and enhance the independent audit of a company's financial reporting system:

> In order to preserve the independence and objectivity of the statutory auditor, procedures that ensure that the shareholders are able to make a real choice, for instance through a greater use of audit committees and/or reforms of board procedures or through the association of other parties, such as the workers council in the appointment and dismissal of the auditor, have been developed or are currently been examined in certain Member States.[11]

---

9. The Committee on the Financial Aspects of Corporate Governance, *The Financial Aspects of Corporate Governance*, 5.3 (GEE, London, December 1992).
10. European Commission, *Green Paper: The Role, Position and the Liability of the Statutory Auditor within the European Union* (24 July 1996) 23, https://europa.eu/documents/comm/green_papers/pdf/com96_338_en.pdf.
11. European Commission, *Green Paper: The Role, Position and the Liability of the Statutory Auditor within the European Union* (24 July 1996) 24, https://europa.eu/documents/comm/green_papers/pdf/com96_338_en.pdf.

The Commission started to develop a system for the election that can strengthen the auditor's position. As an important safeguard to the indolence threat of the auditor, the Commission recommended that those persons other than the audited entity's own management must be in charge for the appointment of the statutory auditor.[12]

It was soon acknowledged at the European level that a mere recommendation by the Commission was insufficient to provide adequate guarantees for the auditor's independence. A number of corporate collapses in the United States, such as Enron, revealed that the statutory auditor had too close relationships with the audited entity, and when similar debacles were uncovered in the European Union, of which Parmalat is the best known, additional measures were viewed as necessary with an appropriate selection process of the external auditor considered among the best options. Studies provided evidence that management had too large an influence in the auditor selection process[13] and that strengthening the corporate governance standards, including a sufficient number of outside directors on the board and active audit committees can foster the auditor's position (and role in corporate governance).[14] This led to several reports emphasizing the importance of an audit committee in the selection process for both the appointment of the external auditor and the approval of the remuneration and terms of engagement.[15]

§1.03 EUROPEAN DIRECTIVE 2006/43/EC

The aforementioned discussions, reports and findings resulted in a European harmonization process of the audit and the auditor (s)election requirements in European Directive 2006/43/EC.[16] The Directive laid down many independent requirements for

12. Principle 4.1.1.1 of the Commission Recommendation of 16 May 2002 Statutory Auditors' Independence in the EU: A Set of Fundamental Principles, OJ L 191, 19.7.2022, p. 22.
13. *See, e.g.*, Co-Ordinating Group on Audit and Accounting Issues, *Final Report* (29 January 2003) para. 1.67 https://webarchive.nationalarchives.gov.uk/ukgwa/20070603154510/http://www.dti.gov.uk/cld/cgaai-final.pdf, 'In practice it is often the executive management who decide on the auditors. The manner of auditor appointment can itself pose a threat to auditor independence.'
14. Lawrence Abbott and Susan Parker, *Auditor Selection and Audit Committee Characteristics*, 19 (fall) Auditing: A Journal of Practice & Theory, 47-66 (2000); Mark Beasley and Kathy Petroni, *Board Independence and Audit Firm Type*, 20 (March) Auditing: A Journal of Practice and Theory, 97-114 (2001).
15. *See* for instance: Co-Ordinating Group on Audit and Accounting Issues, *Final Report* (29 January 2003) para. 1.5.14 https://webarchive.nationalarchives.gov.uk/ukgwa/20070603154510/http://www.dti.gov.uk/cld/cgaai-final.pdf: We strongly endorse the proposal from the FRC Group chaired by Sir Robert Smith that the audit committee should make recommendations to the board (and thus to the shareholders who formally appoint the auditors) on the appointment of the external auditor and approve the remuneration and terms of engagement of the external auditor (para. 1.67).

    Also legal scholars supported this approach, *see* Anita Anand and Niamh Moloney, *Reform of the Audit Process and the Role of Shareholder Voice: Transatlantic Perspectives*, 5 European Business Organization Law Review 2, 271 (2004).
16. Directive 2006/43/EC of the European Parliament and of the Council of 17 May 2006 on statutory audits of annual accounts and consolidated accounts, amending Council Directives 78/660/EEC and 83/349/EEC and repealing Council Directive 84/253/EEC, OJ L 157, 9.6.2006, p. 87.

statutory auditors and secured a more independent selection. Article 37 of the Directive stipulates that:

1. The statutory auditor or audit firm shall be appointed by the general meeting of shareholders or members of the audited entity.
2. Member States may allow alternative systems or modalities for the appointment of the statutory auditor or audit firm, provided that those systems or modalities are designed to ensure the independence of the statutory auditor or audit firm from the executive members of the administrative body or from the managerial body of the audited entity.

For public-interest entities,[17] the proposed appointment made by the board of directors needs to be based on the recommendation made by the audit committee. Article 41.3 of Directive 2006/43/EC determines:

3. In a public-interest entity, the proposal of the administrative or supervisory body for the appointment of a statutory auditor or audit firm shall be based on a recommendation made by the audit committee.

The audit committee must be independent of management. Members States should determine whether the audit committee shall be composed of non-executive directors, and at least one of the members must be independent and have competence in accounting and/or auditing.[18] It was accompanied by the European Commission's Recommendation of the composition of the (supervisory) board of directors and its committees.[19]

§1.04 STRENGTHENING THE SELECTION PROCESS: REGULATION (EU) NO. 537/2014 AND DIRECTIVE 2014/56/EU

The financial crisis of 2008 signalled to many regulators around the world, including the European Commission, that the regulatory framework for providing independent audits and auditors was flawed. In 2014, the European Union issued additional measures to further strengthen the selection process of the auditor as well as the quality requirements of the audit committee. First, the added third paragraph in Article 37 of Directive 2006/43/EC guarantees the freedom of choice in auditors' selection during the general meeting:

> Any contractual clause restricting the choice by the general meeting of shareholders or members of the audited entity pursuant to paragraph 1 to certain categories or lists of statutory auditors or audit firms as regards the appointment of a particular statutory auditor or audit firm to carry out the statutory audit of that entity shall be prohibited. Any such existing clauses shall be null and void.

17. It includes stock exchange listed companies, credit institutions, insurance companies and other entities that the national Member States identify as public-interest entities.
18. Article 41.1 of Directive 2006/43/EC.
19. Commission Recommendation of 15 February 2005 on the role of non-executive or supervisory directors of listed companies and on the committees of the (supervisory) board, OJ L 52, 25.2.2005, 51.

The position of the audit committee of public-interest entities, the pivotal body in the auditor's selection process, was further strengthened.[20] The audit committee must be a stand-alone committee or part of the administrative or supervisory body and composed exclusively of non-executive members elected by the shareholders. The committee must have sufficient competence of relevance to the sector, and the majority of the members must be independent board members. The chairman must always be an independent member, and the committee can elect its chairman. Conversely, Directive 2014/56/EU softened the expertise requirement. It is no longer necessary for an independent member to be competent in accounting and/or auditing. It can be any member, hence also one of the non-executive directors.

The amendments to the Directive were accompanied by the issuance of an Audit Regulation. The Regulation is prescriptive in the role and the position of the audit committee in the selection process of the auditor.[21] The audit committee must prepare a recommendation for the (supervisory) board for the appointment of the auditor. It must offer at least two choices for the audit engagement, and the committee must justify its preference for one of them. Unless it is about a renewal, the company has to invite audit firms for applying to provide the audit. Audit firms that 'received less than 15% of the total audit fees from public-interest entities in the Member State concerned in the previous calendar year'[22] shall not be precluded in a selection procedure, boosting the competition among different types of audit firms.

The audit committee must make explicit that there was no influence by any third party nor any clause directing to one of the choices. The Regulation does not define who it considers as third parties.[23] Indeed, in some countries, other parties are involved in the selection process of the auditor. For example, under Belgian law, the employees' council has the right to recommend the auditor to the general meeting based on a proposal of the board which is, if an audit committee is established, proposed by that committee.[24] In Belgian law, the auditor has been provided with specific duties vis-à-vis the employees' council,[25] and hence, it is considered of relevance that the council is involved in the selection process of the auditor. The employees' council will recommend the selection of the auditor only after the audit committee has performed its duties in that perspective. Although this signalling should not be qualified as influencing the choice of the auditor,[26] I am of the opinion that the employees' council should not be considered as a third party.

20. Amendment 32 of Directive 2014/56/EU of the European Parliament and of the Council of 16 April 2014 amending Directive 2006/43/EC on statutory audits of annual accounts and consolidated accounts, OJ L 158, 27.5.2014, 196.
21. Article 16.
22. Article 16, §3 (a) of Regulation (EU) No. 537/2014.
23. Also in other European legislations 'third parties' is not identified. This is, for instance, the case in the Environmental Liability Directive 2004/35/EC (*see* for an analysis, *The Study Evaluating the Status Quo and the Legal Implications of Third Party Liability for the European Security Industry*, 23 (Lucas Bergkamp et al., eds., Maastricht, October 2013), https://op.europa.eu/en/publication-detail/-/publication/be8395c5-6272-4cdc-b2a9-906e1f9b7d5f).
24. Article 3:88 Belgian Companies Code.
25. Article 3:83 juncto 3:87 Belgian Companies Code.
26. An assessment of the meaning of influence is outside the scope of this chapter.

The problem of undue influence might arise, for example, when an audit committee is operating in a subsidiary that has not (yet) been derogated from this requirement for having its financial statement audited according to Article 39, §3, (a) of Directive 2014/56/EC. For instance, after an acquisition, the parent company of that subsidiary could, for reasons of efficiency, support the selection of the group auditor.

Further, the company must provide in the tender documents information about the business and type of expected audit and transparent and non-discriminatory selection criteria for the assessment of the received audit firm proposals. The conclusions of the assessment must be validated by the audit committee, which is also responsible for the process. The process can be monitored by the regulatory supervisory body of the Member State. The supervisory body of the Member State carries the responsibility for publishing a list of statutory auditors and audit firms that are eligible.

The general meeting of shareholders must be informed of the recommendation and preference of the audit committee. If the proposal of the board for the election of the auditor by the general meeting is different from the preference of the audit committee, the proposal must justify its reasons for deviating from the recommendation of the audit committee.

Finally, the Audit Regulation provides specific guidelines for the duration of the audit engagement.[27] The term of engagement should be at least one year and can be renewed. However, renewing the audit appointment shall not exceed the maximum of 10 years, a term to which a large number of the Member States opted in their transposed legislation. Indeed, the Regulation provides a number of exceptions that allow for an extension of the duration to a maximum of 24 years. However, the key audit partners of the appointed statutory audit firm must be changed at least every seven years from the date of their appointment and can only be reinstalled after a cooling off period of at least three years.

§1.05 ASSESSING THE REGULATORY AUDITORS' (S)ELECTION FRAMEWORK

These developments raise the question of what the effects of the regulatory strengthening of the procedures for the (s)election of the auditor during the first two decades of the century are. I hypothesize that the signalling effect of the vote of the shareholders on the election of the auditor should have decreased over time. All process measures, terms of engagement and transparency rules that the European Union introduced should have enforced the confidence of the shareholders that the auditor will perform an adequate audit and hence lower the opposition rates for the election of the auditor.

[A] Data Collection and Methodology

In order to test this hypothesis, I collected voting data of the Dutch AEX-25 companies and Belgian BEL-20 companies that are stock exchange listed since at least 2013 and

27. Article 17 of the Audit Regulation.

have their registered seat in the Netherlands or Belgium. The companies were only retained when the general meeting of shareholders (AGM) elected at least one time an external auditor between 2013 and 2015 and again between 2021 and 2023. Fourteen of the 25 AEX-companies as well as 18 of the BEL-20 companies were retained. For Belgian companies, I also collected these data for the period 2006-2008.[28] As not all companies provided the minutes of the meetings in 2006-2008 – being only a best practice and not a statutory requirement in those years – and not all companies were stock exchange listed, only 12 BEL-20 companies disclosed the voting results at those AGMs during which the auditor was (re)elected.

For each of these companies, the audit firm and auditor election voting data have been collected in the three periods 2021-2023, 2013-2015 and 2006-2008 based on the minutes of the meetings of the AGMs or on the published voting results. These elections were taking place under the national regime (2006-2008), the European audit committee selection process (2013-2015) and the advanced audit committee selection process (2021-2023). As the European rules regarding the establishment of audit committees and its role vis-à-vis the selection process of the auditor of Directive 2006/43/EC entered Belgium by the law of 17 December 2008,[29] the selection of the external auditor applies only from 2009 onwards requesting the intervention of the audit committee.

The period of study is three times three years. I included a three-year time period because the Belgian Companies Code requires the (re)election of the statutory auditor one time every three years. The statutory term of the external auditor is mandatorily set at three years.[30] No similar rule exists in the Netherlands, and a wide variety of terms are used by Dutch firms. In two cases, the auditor was elected in 1995 for an indefinite term. In 2012, the companies changed their auditor election policy and started to re-elect the auditor at every AGM. In another company, the auditor was elected for the current accounting period, and another auditor was elected at the same AGM for the following three accounting years. Since following the election of the external auditor in 2014, the next election is scheduled to take place only in 2024 in another company, the maximum term that is provided in the Dutch law after the transposition of the European Directives and Regulation. For the companies in the sample used, the AGMs voted for the election of the auditor at least once during 2013-2015 and during 2021-2023. In addition, only one company in the sample opted for a committee of two external auditors. Elia's AGM elected in 2008 and 2014 KPMG and EY as its external auditors, and in 2023, it elected EY and BDO. The electricity transmission group is indirectly controlled by a number of local cities and villages.

Next to the votes for the election, I also collected the voting results of the agenda item with the highest approval rate and the highest opposition rate. This enables a comparison of the election of the auditor – given the idiosyncratic voting in many companies – in the voting spectrum of all voting items at the AGMs. When the

28. For Dutch companies, these data were not (or no longer) publicly available.
29. Wet 17 December 2008 inzonderheid tot oprichting van een auditcomité in de genoteerde vennootschappen en de financiële ondernemingen, Belgian OJ 29.12., 65568.
30. Article 3:61 Belgian Companies Code.

difference between the item with the highest approval and the lowest approval is set at 100%, the external auditor election is positioned between these two voting items as a percentage above the item with the lowest votes. When this percentage changes over the years, it signals that relatively more or less shareholders are monitoring the auditor election given the regulatory developments.

[B] Findings

Table 1.1 provides information on the voting results for the auditor elections of the companies in the sample over the periods 2006-2008, 2013-2015 and 2021-2023. Over these years, the shareholders overwhelmingly approved the selected auditor. This agenda item was always approved, and the lowest approval rate was 88%. The average approval rate was each year greater than 98%, and in most years, even greater than 99%, resulting in an overall average approval of 99.2% of all the votes. During 2021 and 2023, the average was modestly lower, with approval rates of 98.7% in 2023, resp. 98.9% in 2021. This small difference in more recent years is also noticeable for the maximum approval rates. Overall, the results show that since 2021 the unanimous approval of the auditor election is history. The only 100% approval in 2023 stands as an exception as the company merged with another company with the (new) parent company supporting all agenda items.

There are no major differences between the approval rates of auditors in Belgian and Dutch companies. Shareholders of Dutch companies approved the selected auditor with a mean of 98.5% of the votes, and in Belgium with an average of 98.7%. Only in some Belgian companies, sometimes a larger group of shareholders opposed the selection. The largest opposition of more than 12% of the votes was found in a Belgian company, and in two other Belgian companies, a larger group of shareholders opposed the election of the external auditor with nearly 12% and 9% opposition. Shareholders are under no obligation to disclose the reasons for voting against an agenda item. Nevertheless, institutional investors do regularly disclose the reasons for their voting behaviour. Records show that in one case the opposition against the (re)election of the auditor was based on the large proportion of non-audit services that were provided in the former auditing term, which is considered an independence impediment, and consequently a number of institutional investors voted against the re-election. In another case, the reason disclosed by some institutional investors was the change of the external auditor, which was not documented appropriately.

Dutch companies never experienced opposition of the shareholders with more than 5% of the votes.

I also collected the voting results of all other agenda items for all the meetings where the auditor election was approved. The last columns of Table 1.1 provide information on the dispersion of the voting results for all voted items. As the case is, in many of the years where the auditor election is unanimously approved by all shareholders, there are voting items that all shareholders agree with, which is not surprising. Nevertheless, disagreement with agenda items is not uncommon. In 2013, 2022 and 2023, there were agenda items that received a majority opposition. In 2013, one Belgian company experienced a disapproval of its remuneration report by 95% of all votes, where even the majority shareholder opposed the report. Similarly, in 2022, the voting items that the shareholders rejected were agenda items that were related to the remuneration of the executive officers. In 2023, the shareholders of a Dutch company refused the discharge of the management board because the company experienced serious shortcomings in its marketed products. The CEO and his team were considered accountable, and the shareholders refused to discharge the management board. Overall, a majority vote against an agenda item at the meeting of shareholders is the exception.

The data will be used to locate the relative position of the vote for the auditor and the other voting items and to empirically investigate the evolution of the votes for the external auditor.

Table 1.1 Overview of the Approval Rates for the Election of the Auditor and Other Voting Items

	Vote Auditor Election			*All Voting Items*		
	Minimum	*Mean*	*Maximum*	*Minimum*	*Maximum*	*N*
All	87.99	99.18	100	5.07	100	118
Belgian	87.99	98.72	100	5.07	100	48
Dutch	95.39	98.48	100	20.62	100	70
2006		99.99		98.01	100	1
2007	99.97	99.98	100	96.86	100	6
2008	97.85	99.47	100	79.53	100	5
2006-2008	97.84	99.77	100	79.53	100	12
2013	95.39	99.02	100	5.07	100	19
2014	96.51	99.17	100	52.61	100	18
2015	97.89	99.69	100	70.15	100	13
2013-2015	95.39	99.25	100	5.07	100	50
2021	88.66	98.87	99.99	63.66	100	17
2022	97.09	99.57	99.99	20.62	100	15
2023	87.99	98.68	100	23.58	100	24
2021-2023	87.99	98.98	100	20.62	100	56

Source: Own research based on minutes of the AGM.

Table 1.2 gives an overview of the relative vote of the external auditor compared to the other voting items. It is calculated as follows. The vote for the auditor at the specific AGM lies between or is equal to the voting item with the highest opposition rate and the lowest opposition rate. If the difference between the highest opposition and lowest opposition is set at 100%, the vote of the auditor is measured as the percentage deviation relative to the highest opposition vote. If this result is close to 0, it means that the auditor election is relatively contested a lot. If the vote for the auditor is calculated similarly to that with the highest opposition, if it is close to 100, it means that it is the voting item that received the least opposition.

Both the mean and the median relative vote for the auditor are very high, with a 99 median and a 92 mean. It signals that the shareholders consider the auditor election, given the opposition at the AGM, not as a voting item that must be contested. Very frequently, the auditor election is the voting item that received the lowest number of opposition votes, resulting in a score of 100, or closest to the voting item that received the lowest number of opposing votes, which is frequently the vote on the distribution of the dividend. In Belgium, in more than 25% of the cases, the auditor election was the agenda item with the highest approval rate (Q75%). In a few cases, the auditor election is relatively contested. In 2007, in a Belgian company, the auditor election was the agenda item experiencing the highest opposition rate, and in 2013, an auditor election experienced the same result in a Dutch AGM. In the AGM meeting of the Dutch company, the auditor election was the agenda item with the lowest opposition after 2016. The voting results of the Belgium company show a mixed picture. In 2013, the election of the auditor was among the items that received relatively high support; however, in 2023, the agenda item was again relatively highly contested.

Table 1.2 The Relative Vote of External Auditor Vis-à-Vis the Other Voting Items

	Relative Vote Rate					
	Minimum	*Q 25%*	*Median*	*Q 75%*	*Maximum*	*Mean*
All	0	91.93	98.92	99.95	100	92.25
Belgian	0	92.34	98.81	100	100	89.28
Dutch	0	91.34	98.98	99.51	100	92.71
2006			99.997			
2007	0	93.46	100	100	100	78.69
2008	89.49	99.85	99.997	100	100	97.87
2006-2008	0	96.66	99.99	100	100	89.35
2013	0	90.68	96.95	98.99	100	86.31
2014	63.81	93.25	97.07	99.49	100	94.01
2015	51.49	98.23	99.45	100	100	94.01
2013-2015	0	91.88	98.21	99.71	100	91.09
2021	66.63	91.51	99.17	99.9	100	93.79
2022	86.68	93.1	99.46	99.97	100	96.32
2023	15.93	95.39	99.1	99.88	100	92.37
2021-2323	15.93	91.82	99.16	99.92	100	93.86

Source: Own research based on minutes of the AGM.

Table 1.3 shows that the market of external audit services is very concentrated. More than 95% of all elected auditors belong to one of the Big-4 audit firms. Only six times and for six different Belgian companies the shareholders elected an auditor who is not a member of the Big-4. All Dutch companies are audited by a Big-4 audit firm. The mean approval rates are 98% to 99% of all votes, signalling no significant differences between the different audit firms. In one Belgian company that installed a committee of auditors, the shareholders elected twice two Big-4 audit firms with approval rates close to 100%. One time, a combination of a Big-4 firm and another audit firm was elected, and this agenda item received more negative votes of approximately 5%.

Table 1.3 Elected Audit Firms

	Deloitte	*EY*	*PWC*	*KPMG*	*Others*
Minimum	91.48	99.07	88.66	95.39	88.00
Mean	98.97	99.54	99.17	99.38	97.96
Maximum	100	100	99.99	100	100
N	30	29	24	26	6

Source: Own research based on minutes of the AGM.

Finally, I also empirically tested whether the election of the auditor received more or less opposition before or after a major regulatory change in the selection process. As aforementioned, there were three periods defined. However, for the exam period before 2008, only a number of Belgian companies disclosed the voting results. Therefore, I first tested whether the European changes to the selection procedure of the external auditor in 2014 significantly influenced the auditor election voting results. As the process was further strengthened with the intervention of the audit committee that must meet stringent requirements, I hypothesized that the process should increase shareholders' confidence and, consequently, positively affect the voting results.

A paired samples *t*-test was performed to evaluate whether there was a difference between the voting results for the external auditor in the period 2013 to 2015 and the period 2021 to 2023 for all companies in the sample. In Belgium, for both time periods, there is exactly one observation per company. In the Netherlands, some companies yearly organize a (re)election of their external auditor. The sample contains 49 paired observations.

The results indicated that there was no significant difference between the two time periods (mean 99.23% and 98.84%, SD = [1.06/2.62], $t([df\ (48)])$ = [0.957], p = [0.344]). The same holds when controlling for the relative approval rates (*see* Table 1.2). Again, there is no significant difference between the two time periods (mean 90.90% and 93.19%, SD = [20.12/14.06], $t([df\ (48)])$ = [−0.638], p = [0.527]).

For 12 Belgian companies, the voting data available for the time period 2006-2008 can be used to study the evolution over three time periods. Thereto, a one-way repeated measured analysis of variance (ANOVA) was conducted to assess the hypothesis that the development of the regulatory framework of auditor selection would positively affect the voting results of the shareholders' auditor election. The results of the ANOVA indicated some significant effects ($F(2,12) = 8.35$, $p = 0.007$), but these should be carefully read. The effect is negative, meaning that over time, the opposition rates increased, and stronger opposition of shareholders was registered over the three periods. Especially between the first and the second period, approximately 1% more opposition showed significance at the 5% level ($p = 0.033$). However, the significance of this effect completely disappeared in the relative setting of the external auditor data. There are indications that overtime all agenda items received more opposition from the shareholders, including the election of the auditor. Measured in isolation, the stricter rules did not have the expected effect on the shareholders' vote. However, when considering all voting items, the effect of the regulatory measures on the selection of the auditors does not show any significant change. In sum, the expected effects of the new European selection procedures were not visible when measured as the number of opposing votes for the election of the auditors.

§1.06 CONCLUSION

Since the late nineties of the previous century, it was acknowledged that the framework within which the external auditor and the audited entities were (s)elected showed weaknesses. Especially the independence of the auditor and the combination of offering audit and non-audit services were considered problematic. The European Union strengthened the selection process in the new millennium in several steps. In 2002, the European Commission issued a recommendation aiming to bolster the independence of the external auditor. With Directive 2006/43/EC, the audit committee was introduced as a monitoring agent for the selection of the auditor. In 2014, the selection process was strengthened with more audit committee requirements and maximum terms of election. In this chapter, I have tested whether the enhanced selection criteria affected the shareholders' vote for the selected auditor.

I hypothesized that the stringent selection process results in lower opposition of the shareholders when electing the auditor. However, my findings do not support the hypothesis. Overall, the shareholders gradually criticize all the AGM agenda items, including the election of the auditors. When considering this increased monitoring of the shareholders and the relative position of the auditor election amidst all voted items remaining the same, the evidence casts doubt on whether all new (and costly) selection measures increased the efficiency of the (s)election process. Time for a new selection process?

CHAPTER 2

Architectural Design Meets Corporate Law: The Listing Act Proposal on Multiple Voting Shares

*Titiaan Keijzer & Maarten Verbrugh**

§2.01 INTRODUCTION

The European Commission (EC) has presented a proposed Directive to create a basis in European law for multiple voting shares (MVS). In this chapter, we discuss the EC proposal as well as the counter-proposals by the Council and the EP, and the eventual (provisional) compromise. Corporations, in particular SMEs, may be more likely to go public if controlling shareholders can retain their decision-making power post-listing, and MVS are considered an effective mechanism in this regard. The question is however what MVS will actually be able to achieve. The proposal does, for instance, by its very nature not address the structural differences with the US (one of the EU's main competitors) in terms of regulatory fragmentation, market size and liquidity and valuation. From a legal-economic perspective, it can be said that MVS have both advantages and disadvantages. Even when acknowledging that the benefits can outweigh the costs, the arguments raised for creating a level playing field, and moreover doing so via a Directive, may not be fully convincing. The same can be said of the somewhat restrictive and occasionally vague safeguards that ought to benefit minority shareholders. The proposed MVS Directive thus presents a paradox, in fact on multiple levels. While several Member States are

* The final changes to this chapter were made on February 25, 2024.

actively pursuing legislation to enable MVS, the Directive claims there is insufficient initiative, offering a highly discretionary framework instead. The proposed MVS Directive moreover focuses on small companies and considers this size a viable policy criterion, disregarding other, potentially relevant factors such as industry and shareholder structure. And whereas the proposed MVS Directive seeks to stimulate EU capital markets, its level of ambition is actually rather lackluster.

[A] Form Follows Function

In 1896, the well-known architect and rationalist Louis Sullivan, sometimes considered the father of the American skyscraper, stated the following:

> It is the pervading law of all things organic and inorganic, of all things physical and metaphysical, of all things human and all things superhuman, of all true manifestations of the head, of the heart, of the soul, that the life is recognizable in its expression, that form ever follows function. *This is the law.*[1]

After 1930, Sullivan's maxim, which in the meantime had been distilled to its shorter form, became a battle cry for modernist architects. The modernist view emphasized the importance of aligning a structure's design and architecture with its intended function—"Does it work?" —rather than focusing on the merits of visual aspects. Decorative elements and ornaments were not considered a source of beauty but rather seen as supplementary or even superfluous.[2]

[B] The Proposed Listing Act

In this chapter, we will apply a modernist perspective and, in doing so, critically analyze the Listing Act proposal of the European Commission (EC). The draft EC Listing Act, which is part of the capital markets union legislative package and was published by the EC on December 7, 2022, seeks to further stimulate and develop the European (public) capital markets and access thereto, especially for small and medium-sized enterprises (SMEs).[3] As such, the draft EC Listing Act proposes sweeping changes to the Prospectus Regulation,[4] the Market Abuse Regulation

---

1. L.H. Sullivan, "The Tall Office Building Artistically Considered," *Lippincott's Magazine* 1896, pp. 403-409.
2. Ironically, Sullivan himself often covered the surfaces of the buildings he designed with Celtic Revival and Art Nouveau decorations, which would in fact later become his trademark. We will turn a blind eye to this transgression for the remainder of our chapter.
3. Other aspects of the EC's capital markets legislative package, in addition to the Listing Act, include proposals aimed at clearing services and to harmonize insolvency rules. For an overview of the various projects, *see* http://www.europarl.europa.eu/RegData/etudes/BRIE/2023/747111/EPRS_BRI(2023)747111_EN.pdf/.
4. Regulation (EU) 2017/1129 of the European Parliament and of the Council of June 14, 2017 on the prospectus to be published when securities are offered to the public or admitted to trading on a regulated market, and repealing Directive 2003/71/EC.

(MAR)[5] and the Markets in Financial Instruments Directive (MiFID II)[6] while also repealing the Listing Directive,[7] all with a view to simplifying the listing process and streamlining obligations for corporations once they are listed.

For our analysis, we will focus on another element of the draft EC Listing Act, one that may give rise to considerable controversy:[8] the proposal to create a basis in European law for multiple voting shares (the MVS proposal).[9] The idea behind the MVS proposal is that founders and families are currently being discouraged from conducting an IPO—in the EU, that is[10]—for fear of losing control. Therefore, corporations (in particular SMEs) may be more likely to go public if such controlling shareholders can retain their decision-making power post-listing.[11] Multiple voting shares are viewed as an effective mechanism to achieve this.[12] Hence, the EC has proposed to allow such instruments for corporations that list their securities on an SME Growth Market, i.e., a dedicated Multilateral Trading Facility (MTF).[13]

This is a striking development for several reasons. First, the MVS proposal intervenes in national systems of corporate law on a topic that has not yet been harmonized and for reasons that differ from those traditionally invoked to coordinate corporate laws. Second, the MVS proposal complicates the distinction between securities law and corporate law. This distinction has considerable policy implications, as securities laws are mostly mandatory in nature, whereas corporate law is more enabling.[14] Third, the MVS proposal constitutes a 180° turnaround compared to the

5. Regulation (EU) No. 596/2014 of the European Parliament and of the Council of April 16, 2014 on market abuse (market abuse regulation) and repealing Directive 2003/6/EC of the European Parliament and of the Council and Commission Directives 2003/124/EC, 2003/125/EC and 2004/72/EC.
6. Directive 2014/65/EU of the European Parliament and of the Council of May 15, 2014 on markets in financial instruments and amending Directive 2002/92/EC and Directive 2011/61/EU (recast).
7. Directive 2001/34/EC of the European Parliament and of the Council of May 28, 2001 on the admission of securities to official stock exchange listing and on information to be published on those securities.
8. P. Davies et al., "The European Proposal to Open up Multiple-Vote Share Structures to Listing Companies: A Simplification in Trompe L'oeil" (September 5, 2023), available at http://blogs.law.ox.ac.uk/oblb/blog-post/2023/09/european-proposal-open-multiple-vote-share-structures-listing-companies/ ("It will thus have exhausted its useful effect before it is even enacted...").
9. Proposal for a Directive of the European Parliament and of the Council on multiple-vote share structures in companies that seek the admission to trading of their shares on an SME growth market, COM (2022) 761.
10. EC draft MVS proposal, p. 9.
11. *Ibid.*, pp. 2, 16.
12. Other securities, including loyalty shares and non-voting (preference) shares, may (to some degree) act as a functional equivalents of multiple voting shares. These alternatives are however considered rigid and a constraint to the amount of funds that can be raised. EC draft MVS proposal, p. 3. Note that the EP, as part of the review of the Shareholder Rights Directive, proposed to create a legal basis for loyalty voting shares.
13. EC draft MVS proposal, pp. 2-3, 16. On SME Growth Markets, *see* Arts. 4(1)(12) and 33 of Directive 2014/65/EU.
14. *See* J. Lau Hansen, "A Harmonising Step Too Far—A Comment on the Proposal for a Directive on Multiple Voting Rights in SME," 24 *Nordisk Tidsskrift for Selskabsret* 1 (2023); *see also* L. Enriques et al., "Corporate Law and Securities Markets," in: J. Armour et al., *The Anatomy of Corporate Law: A Comparative and Functional Approach* 246-247 (Oxford University Press, 2017): "Recent empirical literature supports the conventional view that publicly traded firms under-report information—and especially negative information—if disclosure is not mandated."

views that were dominant in European policymaking at the start of the twenty-first century, which perceived multiple voting shares and other deviations from the one share, one vote principle more negatively.[15]

There have been numerous policy developments in connection with the publication of the MVS proposal by the EC on December 7, 2022. For instance, on April 14, 2023, the Council of the European Union (the Council) circulated its negotiating mandate.[16] Subsequently, having taken stock of the (draft and finalized) opinions of the European Parliament's Committee on Legal Affairs (the EP LA Committee),[17] the Committee on Economic and Monetary Affairs (the EP EMA Committee) published its (draft and finalized) reports.[18] The EP EMA Committee then also finalized its negotiating mandate and, on November 9, 2023, announced its intention to enter into inter-institutional negotiations.[19] On February 14, 2024, it was announced that the Council and the EP had reached a (provisional) agreement.[20]

[C] Outline

The contents of this chapter are as follows. To obtain the proper perspective and to fully consider the challenges which the EC is attempting to address, we start with a high-level analysis of the structural differences between the EU and the U.S. economies in §2.02. As the EC's draft for the MVS proposal states, the key reason for high-tech, high-growth issuers to list outside the EU, mainly the U.S., is the latter's flexible corporate law system with respect to multiple voting shares.[21] However, other market characteristics are relevant as well in understanding why U.S.-listed firms—which are, in important part, actual American businesses—can develop more advanced and faster-growing technologies than their EU counterparts. We continue, in §2.03, by discussing some of the potential advantages and disadvantages of multiple voting shares. Such securities can, in short, mitigate information asymmetries, which may hamper younger businesses but may also give rise to agency costs. This observation, in turn, brings us to the MVS proposal and the main subsequent policy developments in

15. *See* Shearman & Sterling, ISS & ECGI, *Report on the Proportionality Principle in the European Union* (2007), available at http://ec.europa.eu/docsroom/documents/14881/attachments/2/translations/en/renditions/pdf/. In the meantime, the EC has commissioned a new study. *See* Oxera Consulting LLP, *Primary and secondary equity markets in EU* (2020), available at http://www.oxera.com/wp-content/uploads/2020/11/Oxera-study-Primary-and-Secondary-Markets-in-the-EU-Final-Report-EN-1.pdf/.
16. *See* http://data.consilium.europa.eu/doc/document/ST-8192-2023-INIT/en/pdf/.
17. For the draft opinion of the EP LA Committee dated July 3, 2023, *see* http://www.europarl.europa.eu/doceo/document/JURI-PA-750107_EN.pdf/; for the final version of September 20, 2023, *see* http://www.europarl.europa.eu/doceo/document/JURI-AD-750107_EN.pdf/.
18. *See* http://www.europarl.europa.eu/doceo/document/ECON-PR-749139_EN.pdf/ for the draft report of the EP EMA Committee of June 14, 2023 and https://www.europarl.europa.eu/doceo/document/A-9-2023-0300_EN.html for the final version dated October 26, 2023.
19. An overview of the respective (EC, EP and Council) proposals can be found at https://eur-lex.europa.eu/legal-content/EN/TXT/PDF/?uri=CONSIL:ST_15371_2023_INIT/.
20. *See* https://www.consilium.europa.eu/en/press/press-releases/2024/02/01/multiple-vote-share-structures-council-and-parliament-adopt-provisional-agreement-to-ease-smes-access-to-finance/.
21. EC draft MVS proposal, p. 9.

relation thereto, which we describe in §2.04 and evaluate critically in §2.05. As we show, the MVS proposal complicates the relationship between national and EU corporate law, aims for an ill-defined group of target businesses, and is insufficiently ambitious. We then conclude, in §2.06, that whereas the MVS proposal could not have aspired to remedy the market structure gap between the EU and the U.S., it could have mitigated or even offset the corporate law gap, yet in its current form, it fails to do so.

§2.02 MARKET STRUCTURE: COMPARING THE EU AND THE U.S.

[A] Regulatory Fragmentation

First, and despite the continued and noble efforts of the European Union (EU), it should be noted that the European market suffers from greater regulatory fragmentation than its U.S. counterpart.[22] This becomes apparent when just considering applicable corporate laws. Whereas in the EU, corporate law has become somewhat of an amalgamation of national statutes and EU Directives and Regulations,[23] most large U.S. businesses are, due to their choice of (re)incorporation, governed by the same set of laws, being those of Delaware.[24] The Delaware General Corporation Law, for the avoidance of doubt, readily allows multiple voting shares (§151 and §212 DGCL). In other important areas of regulation, such as corporate taxation and social security, differences between the frameworks applied by Member States have persisted as well.

[B] The Size of Home Markets

Second, and building on the first point, the size of corporations' home markets differs across the EU and the U.S. For instance, a start-up in Germany—the largest economy in the EU—may aspire to serve approximately 85 million people (i.e., excluding Austria and Switzerland) before encountering regulatory and language barriers. By contrast, a U.S. start-up might be able to target up to 340 million customers just by serving its

22. Cf. P. van Asperen, *Controle over grenzeloos financieren: Een onderzoek naar efficiëntie van financiering van internationale concerns in de EU en de VS; een rechtenbenadering* 125-162 (Universiteit van Amsterdam, 2023).
23. *See* L. Enriques, 'A Harmonized European Company Law: Are We There Already?', 66 *International and Comparative Law Quarterly* 763 (2017); *see also* M.A Verbrugh, 'Naar een beter Europees ondernemingsrecht', 22 *Ondernemingsrecht* 99 (2020). Note that in the last few years, a number of new and important Directives have been adopted, e.g., in relation to cross-border restructurings and digitalization. On 14 December 2023, it was moreover announced that the EU had reached a political agreement on the CSDDD, although subsequent developments have given rise to doubts with respect to the viability of the mechanism.
24. More than 66% of the Fortune 500 corporations have chosen Delaware as their legal home. *See* S.M. Bainbridge et al. (eds), *Can Delaware Be Dethroned? Evaluating Delaware's Dominance of Corporate Law* (Cambridge University Press, 2018). Furthermore, most state corporate laws in the US are similar due to the widespread use of the Model Business Corporation Act (MBCA). *See* J.M. Gorris, L.A. Hamermesh & L.E. Strine, "Delaware Corporate Law and the Model Business Corporation Act: A Study in Symbiosis," 74 *Law and Contemporary Problems* 107 (2011).

primary market.[25] As such, U.S. corporations are potentially more scalable and could benefit from lower (variable) costs than their European competitors. This is relevant, particularly in the digital age, where markets are increasingly divided according to the winner-takes-all principle and barriers for new entrants may be prohibitively high.[26] The foregoing may also explain why some start-ups, after having successfully penetrated the market in one Member State, immediately shift their focus to entering the U.S. rather than another Member State.

[C] Liquidity and Valuation

Third, and again following up on the first two points, it should be acknowledged that, although the availability of funding from private investors is dependent on the interest rates set by central banks, liquidity and valuation in EU and U.S. capital markets are not identical. The EU model is traditionally said to be based on bank finance, whereas the U.S. approach has been more oriented towards stock exchanges.[27] The U.S. system is typically considered more liquid.[28] In addition, the U.S. may benefit from the presence of more (concentrated and better-connected[29]) VC investors with a larger risk appetite due to the wealth of experience gained during decades of start-up funding.[30] Perhaps, therefore, U.S. investors are usually willing to pay higher valuations compared to their European fellow investors.[31] Specifically in the Netherlands, the number of listed SMEs has decreased markedly in recent years, with commentators citing low valuations and complex reporting obligations.[32]

---

25. Data according to the CIA World Factbook as per November 22, 2023. (Of course, population size is only a crude proxy for potential revenues and profits.)
26. *See* T. Eisenmann, G. Parker & M.W. Van Alstyne, "Strategies for Two Sides Markets," 84 *Harvard Business Review* 92 (2006), discussing how market characteristics such as network effects, economies of supply, specialization, and multihoming can give rise to winner-take-all markets.
27. *See* F. Allen, "Stock Markets and Resource Allocation," in: *Capital Markets and Financial Intermediation* 84 (C. Mayer & X. Vives eds, Cambridge University Press 1993).
28. *See, e.g.*, M. Arnold, "Europe Needs Its Own SEC, Says Christine Lagarde," *Financial Times* November 17, 2023. ("The problem Europe has is the fact that it has [so many] exchanges. Liquidity concentration is a problem for European capital markets.")
29. N. Patel, *Global VC Ecosystem Rankings* (October 10, 2023), available at https://pitchbook.com/news/reports/, noting that of the top-20 global VC hubs, only 1 is located in the EU (with another one in London).
30. Cf. I. Levingston, "Funding for European Technology Companies Plunges by Nearly Half," *Financial Times* November 28, 2023. ("One reason for the shortfall this year was due to reduced funding from US investors. [...] Venture capital investment in the US continues to dwarf spending in Europe, with nearly triple the level of tech investment this year.")
31. K. Martin & N. Asgari, 'Why Europe's Stock Markets Are Failing to Challenge the US', *Financial Times* April 25, 2023 (discussing the "massive outperformance of the US in recent years—both in terms of listing numbers and in the valuations that companies there can command.").
32. Cf. E. Schram & P. van Engen, "Amsterdamse beurs wordt steeds onaantrekkelijker voor kleine bedrijven," *Het Financieele Dagblad* October 18, 2023. For financial years starting on or after January 1, 2026, the CSRD will also apply to listed SMEs (assuming these are not micro-sized companies). By contrast, the reporting obligations for a number of non-listed SMEs have recently been relaxed with the implementation of the amended Accounting Directive, which adjusts size categories of businesses to account for inflation.

§2.03 ADVANTAGES AND DISADVANTAGES OF MULTIPLE VOTING SHARES

[A] Advantages

The EC's draft for the MVS proposal posits that businesses should be able to adopt a "governance structure that suit best their development stage."[33] The main advantage of multiple voting shares, according to the EC's draft for the MVS proposal, is that such instruments permit founders and other controlling shareholders to continue the execution of their strategic vision without being excessively burdened by market fluctuations.[34] Indeed, multiple voting shares mitigate the potential adverse effects of information asymmetries between insiders and outsiders (i.e., the controlling shareholder is more insulated from the whims of less-informed parties). Such asymmetries relate both to the costs of assessing the operational activities of the corporation as well as the corporation's financial valuation (i.e., the understanding of the business and the appropriate share price in view thereof).[35] Thus, multiple voting shares may be especially (although not exclusively) useful for younger, less understood firms[36]—currently mostly technology firms, but in the future, potentially businesses from other industries as well. By insulating insiders from the pressures of capital markets, multiple voting shares could facilitate a long-term instead of a short-term perspective, stimulating innovation.[37]

[B] Disadvantages

As economists have traditionally stressed, multiple voting shares can be a source of agency costs.[38] In this regard, two potential agency conflicts can be identified.[39] First,

33. EC draft MVS proposal, p. 16. Thus, the EC essentially adopts a life cycle perspective. On this concept, *see* T.A. Keijzer, *Vote and Value: An Economic, Historical and Legal-Comparitive Study on Dual Class Equity Structures* (Wolters Kluwer, 2020).
34. EC draft MVS proposal, pp. 2-5, 16. For important contributions in this regard, *see* Z. Goshen & A. Hamdani, "Corporate Control and Idiosyncratic Vision," 125 *Yale Law Journal* 560 (2016); *see also* Z. Goshen & R. Squire, "Principal Costs: A New Theory for Corporate Law and Governance," 117 *Columbia Law Review* 767 (2017).
35. *See* A.A. Alchian & H. Demsetz, "Production, Information Costs, and Economic Organization," 62 *The American Economic Review* 777 (1972); *see also* F. Black, "Noise," 41 *Journal of Finance* 528 (1986); H.W. Jung & A. Subramanian, "Capital Structure under Heterogeneous Beliefs," 18 *Review of Financial Studies* 1617 (2014).
36. *See* M. Cremers, B. Lauterbach & A. Pajuste, "The Life-Cycle of Dual Class Firms" (2018), available at http://www.ssrn.com/; *see also* H. Kim & R. Michaely, "Sticking Around Too Long? Dynamics of the Benefits of Dual-Class Structures" (2019), available at http://www.ssrn.com/, both observing that dual class equity structures initially command a premium valuation which evaporates with the lapse of time.
37. *See* T. Chemmanur & X. Tian, "Do Antitakeover Provisions Spur Corporate Innovation? A Regression Discontinuity Analysis," 53 *Journal of Financial and Quantitative Analysis* 1163 (2018); *see also* (somewhat more nuanced) J. Atanassov, "Do Hostile Takeovers Stifle Innovation? Evidence from Antitakeover Legislation and Corporate Patenting," 68 *Journal of Finance* 1097 (2013).
38. Notably since the publication of M.C. Jensen & W.H. Meckling, "Theory of the Firm: Managerial Behaviour, Agency Costs and Ownership Structure," 3 *Journal of Financial Economics* 305 (1976).

an individual shareholder may be able to exercise control without a correspondingly large equity stake.[40] As a result, that investor might be tempted to enter into transactions which benefit himself but harm minority investors. For instance, the controlling shareholder could sell himself a valuable asset at a significant discount and force the decision upon the General Meeting of Shareholders (GMS).[41] Second, a dual class equity structure could strengthen the position of the board and render it less accountable, which may affect minority shareholders as well. For example, the use of non-voting shares might constrain investors from voicing their concerns about the corporation's strategy or its remuneration policy.

§2.04 THE EC's DRAFT FOR THE MVS PROPOSAL AND THE RESPONSES OF THE COUNCIL AND THE EP

[A] Creating a Level Playing Field

The legal basis of the MVS proposal is twofold. It rests on Article 50 of the Treaty on the Functioning of the European Union (TFEU), which pertains to the freedom of establishment, as well as Article 114 TFEU, which enables measures in relation to the internal market and the removal of disparities between national legal systems.[42] The EC observed that there currently exists an uneven playing field for corporations across different Member States. Indeed, entrepreneurs and firms from Member States that (to a certain extent) prohibit multiple voting shares are at a competitive disadvantage in terms of going public and obtaining access to capital compared to Member States that (fully) permit such mechanisms.[43] For the sake of completeness, we note that if the main argument for harmonization were to just achieve a level playing field, the EC could also have drawn the opposite conclusion—as the (cultural) situation is that only some Member States have, historically, allowed multiple voting shares—and propose an EU-wide prohibition on these instruments. Such an approach would, however, not have been very realistic from a policy perspective (cfr. §2.01[B]) and would moreover have eliminated the advantages of multiple voting shares in the Member States that do allow them.

The EC thus preferred to remedy this situation—and introduce multiple voting shares—by means of minimum harmonization. Such an approach was claimed to implement uniform standards while also leaving flexibility to the Member States and

39. Cf. J. Armour, H. Hansmann & R. Kraakman, "Agency Problems and Legal Strategies," in: J. Armour et al. (eds), *The Anatomy of Corporate Law: A Comparative and Functional Approach* 29 (Oxford University Press, 2017).
40. On the issues this can give rise to, *see* L.A. Bebchuk & K. Kastiel, "The Perils of Small-Minority Controllers," 107 *Georgetown Law Journal* 1453 (2019).
41. *See* S. Johnson et al., "Tunneling," 90 *American Economic Review* 22 (2000); *see also* S. Djankov et al., "The Law and Economics of Self-Dealing," 88 *Journal of Financial Economics* 430 (2008).
42. EC draft MVS proposal, pp. 7-8.
43. EC draft MVS proposal, pp. 4, 17.

respecting different legal cultures.[44] The EC's draft to the MVS proposal also discussed the alternative of maximum harmonization, in which case a detailed and rigid set of rules would be provided, including for the protection of minority shareholders. This approach was not favored, however, also because some Member States are already familiar with multiple voting shares.[45]

The MVS proposal brings about questions of subsidiarity (Article 5 TFEU). In this regard, the EC's draft noted that it would be unlikely that "Member States, which currently do not allow these share structures, would unilaterally and without external incentive amend their rules in the near future."[46] This was attributed to "historical reasons, opposition from stakeholders in those countries and the fact that changing company law [...] is often difficult."[47] This argument for a top-down approach, 65 years after the start of the harmonization project and in relation to such a fundamental aspect of corporate law, is, however, not very convincing.[48] Another option could have been to leave the introduction of multiple voting shares to the Member States. This would have constituted more of a bottom-up approach, whereby Member States are stimulated to amend their national laws.

[B] Safeguards for Minority Investors

The EC recognized the potential disadvantages of multiple voting shares (cfr. §2.03[B]) and the concerns that institutional investors may possibly have over these instruments.[49] Therefore, the MVS proposal considers, by means of harmonization, various mechanisms to safeguard the interests of minority shareholders and of the corporation.[50] These safeguards are described below.

44. EC draft MVS proposal, p. 8. For an appeal to take cultural differences in the Member States more into account when drafting new proposals for harmonization, *see* M.A. Verbrugh, "Naar een beter Europees ondernemingsrecht," 22 *Ondernemingsrecht* 99 (2020).
45. EC draft MVS proposal, p. 13, mentioning Denmark and Sweden as examples (at p. 4). The EC has invoked similar arguments for not presenting its policies in the form of a Regulation. EC draft MVS proposal, p. 9.
46. EC draft MVS proposal, p. 8. A similar statement can be observed on p. 19 ("the objectives of this Directive, namely to increase funding options for businesses and make SME growth markets more attractive, cannot be sufficiently and timely achieved by Member States.").
47. EC draft MVS proposal, p. 8.
48. *See* critically, J. Lau Hansen, "A Harmonising Step Too Far—A Comment on the Proposal for a Directive on Multiple Voting Rights in SME," 24 *Nordisk Tidsskrift for Selskabsret* 1 (2023): "The necessary empirical and legal basis on which to adopt a harmonising instrument as the one suggested has not been presented by the Commission."
49. EC draft MVS proposal, p. 10. One organization to express its doubts regarding the proposal, touching upon a variety of topics such as proportionality and subsidiarity, voting weight, sunset provisions and GMS agenda items, was Dutch institutional investor association Eumedion. *See Eumedion Position on the Proposal*, available at https://www.eumedion.nl/clientdata/215/media/clientimages/Statement-proposal-for-a-directive-on-multiple--vote-share-structures-DEF.pdf?v=230327144256/.
50. EC draft MVS proposal, p. 5.

[1] SME Growth Markets Only (?)

First, the possibility of issuing multiple voting shares existed, based on Article 4 of the EC's draft for the MVS proposal, only for corporations that become listed on an SME Growth Market for the first time. Therefore, corporations whose shares are already traded on any other venue (such as a different type of MTF or a Regulated Market) would not, again based on the EC's draft for the MVS proposal, have the possibility to issue multiple voting shares.[51] For the avoidance of doubt, it should be noted that this would not prejudice the Member States from introducing or maintaining national provisions of corporate law, which would also allow corporations to use multiple voting shares in other circumstances.[52]

The SME Growth Market itself is a somewhat hybrid concept. These markets and their regulatory framework were designed for listing smaller corporations (defined as firms with an average market capitalization of less than EUR 200 million[53]). However, not all corporations with their securities listed on an SME Growth Market are, in fact, SMEs. For MTFs to qualify as an SME Growth Market, just over half of the issuers need to be an SME.[54] Thus, the MVS proposal would effectively not only enable SMEs but also permit large established corporations to issue, subject to the terms of the Directive, multiple voting shares.

Whereas the Council subscribed to the EC's approach of focusing on SME Growth Markets, the EP intended to enable the use of multiple voting shares beyond SME Growth Markets, i.e., also for companies seeking admission to a different type of MTF or a Regulated Market.[55] According to the (provisional) Council-EP agreement, the use of multiple voting shares would be expanded to MTFs but not to Regulated Markets.[56] This approach actually makes sense. Broadening the MVS proposal's scope to include Regulated Markets could, at first sight, have greatly increased its usefulness. However, when considered jointly with some of the proposal's more problematic aspects (cfr. §2.04[B][2], §2.04[B][3] and §2.04[B][5]), the effects would have possibly been quite the opposite.

51. EC draft MVS proposal, p. 18. The Member States moreover may provide that the casting of the enhanced voting rights is conditional upon the corporation's shares actually being admitted to trading at the SME Growth Market.
52. EC draft MVS proposal, p. 18. As such, the Member States may also provide that corporations listed on a Regulated Market can issue multiple voting shares, or that corporations may also do so in the midstream phase rather than as part of the IPO only.
53. Article 4(1)(13) Directive 2014/65/EU.
54. EC draft MVS proposal, p. 1. Such markets actually welcome larger issuers, as these corporations generally have more liquid securities and hence their listing allows the SME Growth Market to generate higher trading fees.
55. Article 4(1) of the final report of the EP EMA Committee dated October 26, 2023. Of course, the change would have affected the entirety of the wording of the proposed Directive.
56. Article 4 Council-EP Agreement.

[2] *Mandatory Qualified Majority Requirement for Adoption or Modification*

Second, Article 5(1)(a) of the EC's draft for the MVS proposal stipulated that the decision of the GMS to adopt or modify an equity structure involving multiple voting shares should be subjected to a qualified majority.[57] The size (i.e., voting percentage) of this qualified majority was not determined by the EC's draft for the MVS proposal itself; rather, it was to be specified in national law. The Council and the EP both aimed to relocate this provision while keeping it substantively intact.[58] The (provisional) Council-EP agreement, which reinstated the requirement in Article 5(1)(a), intends to do the same.[59]

In a general sense, it can be observed that the use of qualified majority requirements across the Member States varies. Some systems of corporate law, for instance, that of Germany, are quite familiar with qualified majorities (in the case of Germany, 75%[60]). The European Model Companies Act (EMCA) requires a 66% majority.[61] According to the Mobility Directive,[62] Member States shall subject (draft) cross-border conversions to a majority of not less than 66% but not more than 90% of the votes (of the shares or of the represented share capital), which majority shall, in any event, not exceed the one laid down in national law for the approval of cross-border mergers. Other systems of corporate law of Member States, for instance, that of the Netherlands, are based on shareholder decision-making by absolute majority,[63] potentially in combination with other safeguards, such as the use of a Special Committee.[64] For these Member States, Article 5(1)(a) of the MVS proposal would entail a change in (potentially longstanding) national practices.

[3] *Mandatory Limit of the Voting Weight*

Third, the EC's draft for the MVS proposal sought to limit the decision-making power that could be attributed to the multiple voting shares (Article 5(1)(b)).[65] The EC's draft for the MVS proposal provided the Member States with two alternatives (of which at least one had to be adopted) on how to achieve this. First, the Member States had the option of setting a maximum voting ratio and a ceiling on the percentage of the outstanding share capital, which the multiple voting shares could represent (Article

57. EC draft MVS proposal, pp. 18, 21.
58. Article 4(1) of the Council negotiating mandate; Art. 4(3a) of the final report of the EP EMA Committee dated October 26, 2023.
59. Article 5(1)(a) Council-EP Agreement.
60. *See* § 179 Aktiengesetz (governing modifications of the articles of association in general) and § 141 (3) Aktiengesetz (regarding changes to the rights of non-voting preference shares).
61. Articles 5.09 and 11.29 EMCA.
62. Directive (EU) 2019/2121 of the European Parliament and of the Council of November 27, 2019 amending Directive (EU) 2017/1132 as regards cross-border conversions, mergers and divisions.
63. Article 2:120 Dutch Civil Code.
64. On which B. Kemp, "Het special committee in de Nederlandse (overname)praktijk bij beursvennootschappen," 3 *Maandblad voor Ondernemingsrecht* 257 (2017).
65. EC draft MVS proposal, pp. 5, 18, 21.

5(1)(b)(i)). Second, the Member States could subject the shareholder votes in which the multiple voting shares participate to a qualified majority, which majority could pertain to either the votes cast or the share capital represented at the GMS (Article 5(1)(b)(ii)). Notably, in each of these cases, the EC's draft for the MVS proposal did not itself impose any substantive standards. Thus, whether these requirements would, in practice, facilitate or constrain the effectiveness of the multiple voting shares mechanism—consider, e.g., a maximum voting ratio of 1:2 versus a maximum voting ratio of 1:5,000—would, in this approach, largely have depended on the decisions of the Member States. Such an approach would fit with the freedom which the Member States currently enjoy in addressing multiple voting shares, but it could also effectively perpetuate the existing situation of—potentially material—regulatory differences across the EU. This element of the EC's draft for the MVS proposal was, therefore, not fully in line with the aim of creating a level playing field.

As far as the first item, i.e., the voting ratio, was concerned, the Council did not propose any changes. The EP, by contrast, did do so, seeking to adopt a more top-down approach. Accordingly, the Member States would be required (this would no longer be optional) to impose a maximum voting ratio of, at most, 1:12 (and also a ceiling on the outstanding share capital which the multiple voting shares could represent).[66] Furthermore, the additional voting rights vested in the multiple voting shares would be (mandatorily) excluded from resolutions tabled by the shareholders, especially where it concerned humanitarian or environmental matters.[67] With respect to the second item, i.e., the qualified majority for shareholder votes in which the multiple voting shares participate, both the EP and the Council sought to reduce the relevance of this requirement by making a carve-out for director appointments and dismissals. In the approach of the Council, however, the use of a qualified majority remained optional (as long as the Member State had set a maximum voting ratio), whereas in the proposal of the EP, this would have become mandatory.[68] The (provisional) Council-EP agreement fully follows the approach of the Council for both points while further specifying that the qualified majority carve-out applies to "members of the administrative, management and supervisory bodies."

[4] Possibility to Implement Sunset Clauses in National Law

Fourth, the EC's draft for the MVS proposal permitted—but did not require—the EU Member States to implement further safeguards in their national systems of corporate law (Article 5(2)(a)-(c)).[69] Such measures, according to the EC's draft for the MVS proposal, could have especially included sunset provisions. These mechanisms, in

66. Article 5(1)(a) of the final report of the EP EMA Committee dated October 26, 2023. Note this was actually a more lenient approach than the one adopted by the draft opinion of the EP EMA Committee of June 14, 2023, which suggested a maximum voting ratio of 1:5.
67. Article 5(1)(ba) of the final report of the EP EMA Committee dated October 26, 2023.
68. Article 5(1)(b)(ii) of the Council negotiating mandate; Art. 5(1)(b) of the final report of the EP EMA Committee dated October 26, 2023.
69. EC draft MVS proposal, pp. 4, 10, 21.

short, entail that the increased voting rights are discontinued following a predetermined trigger, for instance, after a transfer of shares, the lapse of a certain period of time or otherwise (e.g., the controlling shareholder's equity stake decreasing below a certain threshold).[70] The Council aimed to retain (the substantive contents of) Article 5(2)(a)-(c) of the EC's draft for the MVS proposal, yet in the form of a Preamble, whereas the EP sought to retain these provisions outright.[71] The (provisional) Council-EP agreement has retained the (optional) sunset provisions of Article 5(2)(a)-(c).

Prior studies have shown that firms with multiple voting shares typically command a stock market premium compared to their one share, one vote peers, which premium then on average (!) evaporates over a six- to nine-year period.[72] Whether this finding can, in and by itself, justify a (mandatory) sunset provision, in the time-based variant or otherwise, may be debated. For instance, firms with multiple voting shares can be controlled by a founder, i.e., a natural person, who may age and hence lose his edge over the markets over time. However, when a professionally managed firm (rather than a natural person) serves as the controlling shareholder, that investor may be able to retain its edge over extended periods of time. Similarly, a corporation may effectively be a composition of multiple enterprises, each with different growth paths and product development timelines. In that case, applying a single sunset mechanism for the corporation in its entirety could be an overly blunt instrument.[73]

[5] Possibility to Require No Adverse ESG Impact in National Law

Fifth, the EC's draft for the MVS proposal stipulated in Article 5(2)(d) that Member States could provide—but again were not required to implement—further safeguards to ensure that the enhanced voting rights could not be used to block GMS decisions aimed at "preventing, reducing or eliminating adverse impacts on human rights and the environment related to the company's operations."[74] According to the EC, this provision was expected to have an indirect positive environmental impact, as companies that receive funding from public markets could engage in the development of new, environment-friendly technologies.[75] The impact of the MVS proposal on the environment and ESG in general is, however, difficult to predict. Once companies are taken public, they may, for instance, also be more subject to hedge fund activism, which could negatively impact corporate sustainability, as CSR activities can be perceived as

70. On these measures, *see* A.W. Winden, "Sunrise, Sunset: An Empirical and Theoretical Assessment of Dual-Class Stock Structures," 2018 *Columbia Business Law Review* 852 (2019).
71. Preamble 12 of the Council negotiating mandate; Art. 5(2)(a)-(c) of the final report of the EP EMA Committee dated October 26, 2023.
72. Cf. Cremers, Lauterbach & Pajuste 2018; *see also* Kim & Michaely 2019.
73. *See* Keijzer 2020, pp. 139-142.
74. EC draft MVS proposal, pp. 7, 13, 18, 22.
75. EC draft MVS proposal, p. 13.

a signal of wasteful spending that distracts companies from maximizing short-term shareholder value.[76]

The exact meaning of Article 5(2)(d) of the EC's draft for the MVS proposal was unclear[77]—yet the matter could be highly relevant, given the intense focus of policy-makers on ESG. Firms with multiple voting shares may indeed be susceptible to certain specific ESG issues. For instance, the controlling shareholder could induce the corporation to pursue a specific social cause ("frolics"), which may or may not be desirable for large parts of society, or use his influence to forestall public policies ("exploits," e.g., via political donations).[78] It could well be argued that, in such cases, the additional layer of complexity warrants a further debate on the social desirability of multiple voting shares. At the same time, an overly strict approach could effectively render multiple voting shares useless, given that many items on the agenda of the GMS, including those pertaining to the corporation's strategy, may potentially relate to or be intertwined with human rights and the environment. Nonetheless, the EP aimed to have the additional voting rights vested in the multiple voting shares mandatorily excluded whenever a resolution "related to the impact of the company's operations on human rights and the environment" is tabled by the shareholders (cf. §2.04[B][3]).[79] By contrast, the Council was more deferential towards the Member States and sought to strike Article 5(2)(d) of the EC's draft for the MVS proposal. As a compromise, the (provisional) Council-EP agreement stipulates, in Preamble 13c, that the enhanced voting rights should not prevent "compliance with any applicable EU environmental or fundamental rights law." Whether a safeguard ends up in the final Directive as (part of) a Preamble or as a concrete Article can, in practice, make a big difference, as Preambles are not directly implemented in national laws.

[6] Detailed Capital Structure Disclosure Requirements

Sixth, the EC's draft for the MVS proposal required Member States to ensure that corporations shall be sufficiently transparent and provide detailed information on their capital structure (Article 6).[80] This would include the different classes of shares and the rights and obligations vested therein, restrictions on the transfer of shares and the

76. *See* M.R. DesJardine, E. Marti & R. Durand, "Why Activist Hedge Funds Target Socially Responsible Firms: The Reaction Costs of Signaling Corporate Social Responsibility," 64 *Academy of Management Journal* 851 (2020).
77. Cf. Davies et al. 2023.
78. *See* G.H. Shill, "The Social Costs (and Benefits) of Dual-Class Stock" (2023), available at https://corpgov.law.harvard.edu/2023/10/16/the-social-costs-and-benefits-of-dual-class-stock/. In similar vein, *see* V. Battocletti, L. Enriques & A. Romano, "Dual-Class Shares in the Age of Common Ownership," 48 *Journal of Corporation Law* 541-576 (2023), noting that multiple voting shares may enable just a few natural persons to impose enormous externalities on society (but failing to substantiate a difference in the externalities imposed by dual class corporations compared to other firms).
79. Article 5(1)(ba) of the final report of the EP EMA Committee dated October 26, 2023. Note that in Art. 5(2)(d), the EP furthermore permitted the Member States to exclude the applicability of the additional voting rights vested in the multiple voting shares in "matters relating to executive remuneration and dividend policy or to the approval of related party transactions."
80. EC draft MVS proposal, pp. 5, 19, 22.

exercise of voting rights, and the identity of the holders of the multiple voting shares. Such information must be provided when the shares of the corporation are being admitted to trading as well as periodically via the annual financial statements. These periodic disclosure obligations can typically be observed in legal systems where the use of multiple voting shares is permitted.[81] To this, the EP sought to add a Preamble stating that corporations with multiple voting shares may publish a report on the usefulness of these shares for all stakeholders.[82] By contrast, the Council aimed to have the periodic disclosure obligation removed.[83] The (provisional) Council-EP agreement distinguishes, for reporting purposes, between companies listed on an SME Growth Market and those listed on an MTF while also requiring ESMA to develop technical standards specifying how to identify companies with multiple voting shares.[84]

§2.05 A MODERNIST ASSESSMENT

[A] A Peculiar View on the Relationship Between European and National Corporate Law

[1] *Prohibiting Multiple Voting Shares as a Violation of the Fundamental Freedoms?*

The legal basis of the MVS proposal rests, in part, on Article 114 TFEU, which enables measures to address disparities between the national legal systems of the Member States (§2.04[A]). In this regard, the EC's draft for the MVS proposal noted the following:

> The objective of the proposed Directive is to remove obstacles to the exercise of fundamental freedoms, such as the free movement of capital and freedom of establishment. [...] [S]ome Member States prevent their companies from accessing public markets through multiple-vote share structures. This restricts their access to capital.[85]

The foregoing may be interpreted as entailing that Member States whose national system of corporate law prohibit the use of multiple voting shares violate EU law. This approach, which can also be observed in the (provisional) Council-EP agreement,[86] is remarkable from a historical perspective and would involve a thorough rebalancing of powers from the Member States to the EU (cf. §2.01). The position of the Council, which stated that differences between the Member States *can* create barriers to the free movement of capital, would have appeared more nuanced in this regard.[87]

81. For the Netherlands, *see e.g.*, Art. 2:378(2) Dutch Civil Code.
82. Preamble 11a of the final report of the EP EMA Committee dated October 26, 2023.
83. Article 6 of the Council negotiating mandate.
84. Article 6 Council-EP Agreement.
85. EC draft MVS proposal, pp. 7-8.
86. Council-EP Agreement, p. 5.
87. Preamble 6 of the Council negotiating mandate.

Similarly, one can question the internal consistency of the MVS proposal. Indeed, the proposal allows the Member States to implement rather distinct legal regimes regarding the permissibility of multiple voting shares (cfr. §2.04[B][3], §2.04[B][4] and §2.04[B][5]). Thus, it apparently presumes that such—potentially material—differences will not pose any obstacles to fundamental freedoms. However, their presence might effectively perpetuate the existing situation,[88] in which firms redomicile from one Member State to the other, (also) with a view to being able to issue multiple voting shares.

[2] Member States Being Unlikely to Enable Multiple Voting Shares?

The EC's subsidiarity assessment, i.e., that the Member States are unlikely to implement the necessary regulatory changes on their own initiative (§2.04[A]), is moreover difficult to reconcile with recent events.[89] Just in the last few years, important Member States (such as France[90]) have been studying legislative changes or have even put forward the proposals required to create a legal basis for multiple voting shares (Germany[91]). As such, Member States are actually actively working towards creating more enabling corporate legal systems.

In this regard, the potential effects of the Mobility Directive of 2019 should be considered as well.[92] The Directive, which had to be implemented by the Member States on January 31, 2023, intends to set a uniform legal framework for cross-border legal mergers, divisions and conversions.[93] As such, corporations that seek to adopt an equity structure involving multiple voting shares may find it easier to redomicile towards a jurisdiction which supports such a mechanism. This possibility, in turn, may further incentivize the Member States to amend their respective legal systems with a view to enabling multiple voting shares.[94] The Netherlands, for instance, has, due to its flexible corporate laws which, *inter alia*, allow for multiple voting shares, attracted several (large) companies from Italy (e.g., Exor, Campari and MFE) and Spain (Ferrovial). This, in turn, has led to proposals to amend the statutes of these respective

88. Cf. the scenario mentioned in § §2.04[B][3], in which Member State A subscribes to a maximum voting ratio of 1:2 and Member State B applies a maximum voting ratio of 1:5,000.
89. For a concise overview, *see* C. Clottens, "Meervoudig stemrecht in genoteerde vennootschappen—een kwestie van tijd?," 10 *Tijdschrift voor Rechtspersoon en Vennootschap—Revue pratique des sociétés* 525 (2023).
90. On these developments, *see* A. Pietrancosta, "Propositions françaises et européennes pour ouvrir le vote multiple aux sociétés entrant en bourse," 37 *Bulletin Joly Sociétés* 63 (2022).
91. *See* S. Mock & J. Mohamed, "Goodbye One Share One Vote?—Welcome Dual-Class Shares! Ein komparativer Überblick zu rechtspolitischen Reformüberlegungen," 25 *Neue Zeitschrift für Gesellschaftsrecht* 1275 (2022). In addition, Belgium and Spain have implemented regulatory reforms to permit the use of loyalty voting shares.
92. Directive (EU) 2019/2121 of the European Parliament and of the Council of November 27, 2019 amending Directive (EU) 2017/1132 as regards cross-border conversions, mergers and divisions.
93. *See* M.A. Verbrugh, "De Mobiliteitsrichtlijn en het Hof van Justitie EU: belangrijke impuls voor actie van ondernemers en wetgevers," 152 *Weekblad voor Privaatrecht, Notariaat en Registratie* 2 (2021).
94. That would, of course, improve the internal consistency of the MVS proposal and, as such, reduce the relevance of the criticisms voiced in §§2.05[A][1].

countries. A similar effect of regulatory competition has, in the past, emerged with respect to the laws for private companies (such as the Dutch *Besloten Vennootschap*, the German *Gesellschaft mit beschränkter Haftung* and the (also) French *Société à responsabilité limitée*) after the landmark cases of the European Court of Justice on the freedom of establishment, such as *Centros* in 1999. One might, of course, argue that the resulting statutory frameworks need not be identical across Member States—but that is not the presumption of the MVS proposal.

[B] A Diffuse Audience and Objective

[1] Small Firms as a One-Size-Fits-All Category?

The EC's draft for the MVS proposal referenced "smaller family-owned companies, start-ups and businesses with long-term projects."[95] All these firms might appear largely interchangeable due to their perceived similarity in size—but on closer inspection, there also exist considerable differences between them. Such differences, combined with the fact that the MVS proposal fails to target a well-defined type of corporation, impair the imperative for policy making.

For instance, the products and services delivered by a family-owned corporation may be of a more conventional nature than those of a start-up or a business focusing on a long-term project, resulting in smaller information asymmetries between insider shareholders and outside investors. Then, the possible benefits of multiple voting shares would be smaller as well (§2.03[A]). Moreover, family-owned corporations may have a more concentrated ownership structure compared to start-ups,[96] for instance, if the latter has experienced several funding rounds in which many different VC funds participated. Such variations in ownership structure could also translate into diverging shareholder preferences which can, occasionally, be challenging to overcome.

Start-up investors, for instance, may be more understanding if the controlling shareholder decides to retain and reinvest profits as much as possible. In case of a mature and listed family-controlled business, however, outside investors might be quite rightfully eying frequent dividend payments.[97] Both such companies could be taken public using a governance structure provided by the MVS proposal (and might, for illustrative purposes, have stayed private in the absence thereof). Only in the first scenario, however, the argument to prevent distributions (using the additional voting rights granted by the multiple voting shares) would be more convincing. In the second scenario, precisely as a result of the company becoming listed, differences of opinion between insiders and outsiders could arise, possibly increasing the risk of shareholder litigation. Indeed, outside investors may be much more inclined to litigate than

95. EC draft MVS proposal, p. 2.
96. On governance arrangements in closed situations, *see* J.A. McCahery & E.P.M. Vermeulen, *Corporate Governance of Non-listed Companies* (Oxford University Press, 2008).
97. On the phenomenon of dividend-oriented investors flocking to dividend-paying firms (and vice versa), *see* M. Baker & J. Wurgler, "A Catering Theory of Dividends," 59 *Journal of Finance* 1125 (2004).

members of a (close-knit) family. In the Netherlands, for example, the (envisaged) Article 2:346(1)(d) of the Dutch Civil Code posits that investors just holding 1% of the shares will be able to launch specific corporate governance-focused legal proceedings at the Enterprise Chamber of the Amsterdam Court of Appeals.

[2] Small Firms Will Become Successfully Listed Firms?

One cannot create vibrant equity markets at will by making a great number of small firms go public, which then, over time, just develop into corporate behemoths. Indeed, research has shown that it may be difficult for smaller corporations, such as those that could be listed on an SME Growth Market or MTF, to "trade up" and become established constituents of the premium ("blue chip") segment of the stock exchange.[98] Of the firms with a comparatively more modest market capitalization at the time of their stock market debut, many continue to struggle over time, with only a handful of exceptions. In this regard, it should also be noted that in the twentieth century, only a few firms have been responsible for the entirety of (U.S.) stock market returns.[99]

In fact, the structure of the MVS proposal could create roadblocks on the corporate growth trajectory (also when disregarding its substantive drawbacks) as Member States would not be required to accommodate the use of multiple voting shares on all trading venues. These instruments would, according to the EC's draft for the MVS proposal, only be permitted on SME Growth Markets and, pursuant to the (provisional) Council-EP agreement, also on other MTFs but not on Regulated Markets. The loss of control which the switch from an MTF towards a Regulated Market would entail could prevent issuers from making such a move, thus creating a lock-in at a less developed stock market.[100]

[C] A Generally Insufficient Level of Ambition

The MVS proposal seeks to strengthen public markets rather than banks (cf. §2.02[C]). There is something to be said for this approach. Partly due to the rise of private equity, fewer and fewer corporations are being listed, while established firms are increasingly delisting. As a result, significantly less corporations are listed than one would expect

98. *See* U. Brüggeman et al., "The Twilight Zone: OTC Regulatory Regimes and Market Quality," 31 *Review of Financial Studies* 898 (2018), showing that over time, only 7% of corporations "trade up."
99. H. Bessembinder, "Wealth Creation in the U.S. Public Stock Markets 1926 to 2019," 30 *Journal of Investing* 47 (2021), observing that almost 60% of the stocks reduced shareholder value, with US markets nonetheless appreciating in value by more than USD 47.4 trillion.
100. A similar point was raised in relation to the Belgian legal reforms of 2019, where the use of multiple voting shares was confined to non-listed corporations. *See* J. Delvoie & S. Declercq, "De invoering van meervoudig stemrecht en loyauteitsstemrecht in bestaande vennootschappen," 4 *Tijdschrift voor Rechtspersoon en Vennootschap—Revue pratique des sociétés* 129 (2019).

based on the size of the economy.[101] The decision to list is, as the EC's draft for the MVS proposal correctly notes, "a complex one and is influenced by a multitude of factors."[102] As such, the use of a single governance mechanism, even where it concerns multiple voting shares, cannot be expected to serve as a panacea.

However, if the idea would indeed be to actually make multiple voting shares work for the EU, the objective would be simple: create a simple, effective—and, in fact, potent—instrument. By contrast, the MVS proposal sets requirements (including the qualified majority and maximization of the voting weight) and optional provisions (such as sunset clauses and the no adverse ESG impact standard) that may hamper, perhaps seriously so, the usefulness of the multiple voting shares instrument. The amendments proposed by the EP would, if they had been implemented, probably put the EU even further on the back foot, as is already illustrated by the fact that a shareholder-tabled resolution could simply eliminate the additional voting rights vested in the multiple voting shares.

§2.06 CONCLUSION

In this chapter, we have reviewed the MVS proposal. As the EC correctly noted, there currently exists a corporate law gap between the U.S. and the EU. However, there also exists a market structure gap between the two economic blocs. Indeed, the U.S. market is more attractive in certain key areas, including regulatory fragmentation, size, liquidity and valuation. The MVS proposal could not have aspired to remedy the market structure gap, yet it could have mitigated or even offset the corporate law gap. This would have required a more facilitative system of corporate law, in terms of multiple voting shares, than what is currently available across the pond.

Our analysis has, however, illustrated that the MVS proposal, while undoubtedly well-intended, does not cover the existing deficit. In its present form, the MVS proposal muddies the relationship between securities law and corporate law (and between European and national systems of corporate law), aims for a diffuse audience and sets unrealistic objectives, whereas the restrictions imposed entail that multiple voting shares will likely not be a useful and potentially even a counter-effective mechanism.

In the spirit of Louis Sullivan's modernism, it would be best to leave superfluous decorations aside. This would involve reviewing, perhaps once the MVS proposal has been enacted, the necessity of many of its (mandatory) safeguards and simply focusing on the core issues at hand. Doing so might just contribute to creating a new generation of skyscrapers, but rather in Europe than in the U.S. and of an economic nature rather than those consisting of brick and mortar.

101. This is true even for the US, where valuations are typically higher. *See* M. Jensen, "Eclipse of the Public Corporation," 67 *Harvard Business Review* 61 (1989); *see also* C. Doidge et al., "Eclipse of the Public Corporation or Eclipse of the Public Markets?," 30 *Journal of Applied Corporate Finance* 8 (2018). For the Netherlands, *see* Schram & Van Engen 2023.

102. EC draft MVS proposal, p. 2.

Chapter 3
Civil Liability for Human Rights Violations under Article 29 of the CSDDD

Alexander Schall

Under the Belgian presidency, the Corporate Sustainability Due Diligence Directive was agreed upon in a last-minute compromise. It will impose various obligations on large corporations to prevent human rights violations and environmental damage in their supply chains. Article 29 CSDDD (Art. 22 in the previous versions throughout the legilösative process) obliges the Member States to introduce a civil liability for due diligence breaches that contribute to the causation of such violations. The Article presents the genesis of the rule and critically evaluates its implications. For example, the duty of Member States to procure 'overriding mandatory application' under Article 29(7) CSDDD raises complicated issues, as do the duties to introduce preliminary procedures and pre-trial discovery under Article 29(3). The core criticism is, however, directed against the scope of the liability. It is too wide as responsibility for the acts of independent third parties (suppliers) transgresses the traditional boundaries of tort law. The safe harbour proposed by the Commission has been rejected in the Trilogue. However, the alternative restraints that have been put in place are not fit for the purpose. Civil liability for oversight failures at the far end of the supply chains should be restricted to serious harms ('les atteintes graves'), as is the case under the French loi de vigilance (Article L. 225-102-4).

§3.01 INTRODUCTION

The Directive on Corporate Sustainability Due Diligence (CSDDD) will set a milestone for the enforcement of human rights and environmental duties. Since the UN Guiding Principles on Business and Human Rights were published in 2011, this purpose has become generally accepted across the Western world, and rightly so, although it is also true that not all steps the Directive takes to reach it will be welcomed by everyone. This paper will focus on Article 29 CSDDD.[1] This provision obliges the Member States to order civil liability of companies violating the human rights due diligence under Articles 7 and 8 CSDDD. This rule sounds self-evident because the violation of legal obligations will normally trigger damages claims. But on closer look, this case is not clear-cut.

The main reason is that the duties of human rights due diligence reach far beyond the usual headings of tort liability. For example, if producers of goods are liable for harm that their products cause to customers or bystanders, this is justified by their control over the production process. This control allows us to hold them accountable for the risks of their products. By contrast, supply chain due diligence is not restricted to human rights violations caused by dangerous or unlawful conduct of the enterprises themselves. Rather, it obliges them to use their economic bargaining power to enforce human rights compliance against their business partners. This oversteps the usual boundaries of tort law. The principle at work is not '*neminem leadere*' but not to benefit from another's injury or loss – the principle of unjust enrichment according to Sextus Pomponius (D.50.17.206): '*Iure naturae aequum est neminem cum alterius detrimento et iniuria fieri locupletiorem.*'

Some might argue this. They would say that 'buying cheap' in the Global South makes Western enterprises tortfeasors because by doing so, they make an active contribution to the widespread human rights violations.[2] To this, I would answer that a market economy is based on the free play of forces. That is why bargaining for the lowest possible price cannot be deemed dangerous or illegal per se – which is, of course, not to say that the business conduct of producers sourcing their supply in the Global South can *never* amount to any misfeasance in itself.

But be this as it may. The establishment of a civil liability for human rights violations is fraught with legal and factual problems. The paper will first introduce the new Article 29 CSDDD before analysing the hurdles that will have to be overcome. When going through the genesis of the rule, it should be borne in mind that it had been Art. 22 in all previous drafts and all stages of the legislative process before it became Art. 29 after a renumbering of the provisions in the final CSDDD. Furthermore, the

1. Papers with a specific focus on Art. 22 CSDDD in the earlier versions were written by Loes Lennarts, *Civil Liability of Companies for Failure to Conduct Corporate Sustainability Due Diligence throughout their Value Chains – Is Art. 22 CSDDD Fit for Purpose?*, 5(36) Ondernemingsrecht 257 (2023); Kathrin Buhmann, *Confronting Challenges to Substantive Remedy for Victims: Opportunities for OECD National Contact Points under a Due Diligence Regime Involving Civil Liability*, 8(3) Business and Human Rights Journal 403 (2023) DOI: 10.1017/bhj.2023.9; Alessio Pacces, *Civil Liability in the EU Corporate Sustainability Due Diligence Directive Proposal: A Law & Economics Analysis*, ECGI Law Working Paper No. 691/2023, March 2023, available at https://papers.ssrn.com/sol3/papers.cfm?abstract_id=4391121; cf. also Harm-Jan de Kluiver, *Towards a Framework for Effective Regulatory Supervision of Sustainability Governance in Accordance with the EU CSDD Directive. A Comparative Study*, 20(1) ECFR 201, at 211 et seq. (2023).
2. Take for example Marc-Philippe Weller & Laura Nasse, *„Menschenrechtsarbitrage als Gefahrenquelle* 107 (Bergmann et al eds, 2020).

paragraphs (2a) and (2b) that were inserted in the version after the Trilogue became paragraph (3) and (4), pushing the following paragraphs further up: (3) - (5); (4) - (6); (5) - (7). When talking about the process, I will therefore stick to the original denominations. When talking about the CSDDD, I will adapt.

§3.02 THE CONTENT OF ARTICLE 29 CSDDD (FORMERLY ARTICLE 22)

[A] The Text of the Commission

Article 29 is not a liability rule itself. It merely obliges the Member States to implement one. Even if the CSDDD turned into a 'CSDD-Reg' in the foreseeable future, this would probably remain so because it is doubtful whether EU law could directly enshrine a civil liability rule. Nevertheless, Article 29 CSDDD is well aware of the issues that a liability rule for breaches of the human rights due diligence obligations will face. They are reflected in the texts of the competing drafts by the Commission and the Council. The Commission's draft of what was originally Art. 22 reads as follows:

> Art. 22 CSDDD (Commission draft):
>
> 1. Member States shall ensure that companies are liable for damages if:
>   (a) they failed to comply with the obligations laid down in Articles 7 and 8 and;
>   (b) as a result of this failure an adverse impact that should have been identified, prevented, mitigated, and brought to an end or its extent minimised through the appropriate measures laid down in Articles 7 and 8 occurred and led to damage.
> 2. Notwithstanding paragraph 1, Member States shall ensure that where a company has taken the actions referred to in Article 7(2), point (b) and Article 7(4), or Article 8(3), point (c), and Article 8(5), it shall not be liable for damages caused by an adverse impact arising as a result of the activities of an indirect partner with whom it has an established business relationship, unless it was unreasonable, in the circumstances of the case, to expect that the action actually taken, including as regards verifying compliance, would be adequate to prevent, mitigate, bring to an end or minimise the extent of the adverse impact.
>   In the assessment of the existence and extent of liability under this paragraph, due account shall be taken of the company's efforts, insofar as they relate directly to the damage in question, to comply with any remedial action required of them by a supervisory authority, any investments made and any targeted support provided pursuant to Articles 7 and 8, as well as any collaboration with other entities to address adverse impacts in its value chains.
> 3. The civil liability of a company for damages arising under this provision shall be without prejudice to the civil liability of its subsidiaries or of any direct and indirect business partners in the value chain.
> 4. The civil liability rules under this Directive shall be without prejudice to Union or national rules on civil liability related to adverse human rights impacts or to adverse environmental impacts that provide for liability in situations not covered by or providing for stricter liability than this Directive.
> 5. Member States shall ensure that the liability provided for in provisions of national law transposing this Article is of overriding mandatory application in cases where the law applicable to claims to that effect is not the law of a Member State.

[B] The Text of the Council

The Council accepted the text in principle but proposed several material and editorial changes that are highlighted in bold print below. Like throughout the Directive, the Council replaced the Commission's 'value chain' with 'chain of activities', thus cutting the (dubious) ties to the taxonomy of economics and creating an original legal term. In the first paragraph, it added that the damage had to be caused 'to a natural or legal person'. This may seem self-evident. But it connects with the subsequent restriction that failure in the human rights due diligence under Articles 7 and 8 only triggers damages 'when the right, prohibition or obligation listed in Annex I is aimed to protect the natural or legal person'. In addition, the liability standard was made explicit. The company would be liable if it 'intentionally or negligently' failed to comply with Articles 7 and 8. There were two further restrictions added. First, it was inserted that the damage had to be done to 'the natural or legal person's legal interest protected under national law' (in more detail below, §3.04[B][1]). Second, the company cannot be held liable if the damage was caused only by its business partners in its chain of activities (*see* §3.04[B][1]).

The second paragraph was completely re-written, now ordering full compensation but prohibiting punitive damages – two veritable *quisquilia* for European jurisdictions that are generally hostile to the concept of punitive damages. The third paragraph was extended by a second sentence ordering joint and several liability in case of a multitude of tortfeasors. It may be surprising why the European regulator thought it worthwhile to insert an explicit provision to that end. The answer is found in debates on the French *loi de vigilance* where legal writers have argued that the loss caused by an insufficient *plan de vigilance* of the parent company was merely the loss of an opportunity to avoid the damage, whereas the final harm will only be caused by the subsidiary or the business partner.[3] I have difficulties subscribing from this point of view, though. The negligent guardian sets a contributory cause for the theft itself, not merely for the loss of the opportunity to avoid the theft. This has been so since the days of Roman law.[4] He is therefore liable for the same damage. The lower grade of culpability does not save him under the general rules of joint and several liability. However, with respect to the special French problems probably stemming from the 'directness requirement' that comes on top of causation,[5] the European regulator may have been well advised to spell this out clearly.

3. Iris Barsan, *Scope and Enforcement of Corporate Sustainability Due Diligence Requirements – A Comparative Approach*, 1 ECCL 31, at 44-45 (2023), referring to Anne Danis-Fatôme/Geneviève Viney, *La responsabilité civile dans la loi relative au devoir de vigilance des sociétés mères et des entreprises donneuses d'ordre*, Receuil Dalloz 1610 (2017).
4. In D.12.7.2. (Ulpian ad ed.) a bleacher ('*fullo*') had lost a toga. Ulpian answers the follow-up question what happens if the toga was retrieved: 'The fullo can claim back the damages in unjust enrichment' (*condictio sine causa*). That seems to be the solution of Dutch law, too, cf. Lennarts, *supra* n. 1, at 263.
5. Barsan, *supra* n. 3, at 44 et seq. *See also* Constitutional Council, C. Const. No. 2017-750 DC du 23 March 2017, at § 17.

The fourth paragraph remained completely unchanged, whereas the wording of the fifth paragraph underwent a minor editorial change with no consequence:

Art. 22 CSDDD (Council proposal)

1. Member States shall ensure that a company can be held liable for damage caused *to a natural or legal person*, provided that:
   (a) the company *intentionally or negligently* failed to comply with the obligations laid down in Articles 7 and 8 *when the right, prohibition or obligation listed in Annex I is aimed to protect the natural or legal person*; and
   (b) as a result of a failure, as referred to in point (a), a damage *to the natural or legal person's legal interest protected under national law* was caused.

   A company cannot be held liable if the damage was caused only by its business partners in its chain of activities.
2. *Where the company was held liable in accordance with paragraph 1, a natural or legal person shall have the right to full compensation for the damage occurred in accordance with national law. Full compensation under this Directive shall not lead to overcompensation, whether by means of punitive, multiple or other types of damages.*
3. The civil liability of a company for damages arising under this provision shall be without prejudice to the civil liability of its subsidiaries or of any direct and indirect business partners in the *company's chain of activities.*

   When the damage was caused jointly by the company and its subsidiary, direct or indirect business partner, they shall be liable jointly and severally, without prejudice to the provisions of national law concerning the conditions of joint and several liability and the rights of recourse.
4. The civil liability rules under this Directive shall be without prejudice to Union or national rules on civil liability related to adverse human rights impacts or to adverse environmental impacts that provide for liability in situations not covered by or providing for stricter liability than this Directive.
5. Member States shall ensure *that the provisions of national law* (editorial change instead of: that the liability provided for in provisions of national law) transposing this Article *are* of overriding mandatory application in cases where the law applicable to claims to that effect is not the law of a Member State.

[C] The Amendments Proposed by Parliament: Article 22(2a) and (2b)

The European Parliament proposed some amendments to the Commission draft as a basis for the Trilogue. Apart from some editorial changes, it wanted the civil liability under Article 22 CSDDD to cover all violations of the Directive. That would have, *inter alia*, meant a liability for violations of the climate protection rules under Article 15 CSDDD. Also, it added a second sentence to Article 22(3) where it demanded a parent liability in the case of a dissolution of a liable subsidiary. But these changes were eventually rejected, and are not followed up any more. The successful point of the Parliament's position paper for the Trilogue was two completely new and very extensive paragraphs, Article 22(2a) and (2b). Paragraph 2a contained several procedural provisions in order to facilitate, or at least prevent the obstruction of liability suits by the victims of human rights violations, namely:

- long limitation period of 10 years (a);
- prohibition of too high costs (a);
- availability of injunctions (b);
- standing to sue on behalf of the victims for NGOs (c);
- availability of pre-trial discovery (d).

Paragraph 2b explicitly rejected any safe harbour through compliance with the due diligence provisions, in open contradiction to the Commission's Article 22(2):

2a. Member States shall ensure that:

(a) the limitation period for bringing actions for damages is at least ten years and measures are in place to ensure that costs of the proceedings are not prohibitively expensive for claimants to seek justice;
(b) claimants are able to seek injunctive measures, including summary proceedings. These shall be in the form of a definitive or provisional measure to cease an action which may be in breach of this Directive or to comply with a measure under this Directive;
(c) measures are in place to ensure that mandated trade unions, civil society organisations or other relevant actors acting in the public interest can bring actions before a court on behalf of a victim or a group of victims of adverse impacts and that these entities have the rights and obligations of a claimant party in the proceedings, without prejudice to existing national law;
(d) when a claim is brought that a claimant provides elements substantiating the likelihood of a company's liability under this Directive and has indicated that additional evidence lies in the control of the company, courts are able to order that such evidence be disclosed by the company in accordance with national procedural law, subject to the Union and national rules on confidentiality and proportionality.

2b. Companies that have participated in industry or multi-stakeholder initiatives or used third-party verification or contractual clauses to support the implementation of specific aspects of their due diligence obligations *can still be held liable* in accordance with this Article.

[D] The Final Version

The current version of Article 29 corresponds in all material aspects with the final version of Article 22 CSDDD after the Trilogue. That is why it is shown here in the final version without highlighting the minor editorial changes of that final step. Instead, it highlights how the Trilogue compromises Article 22 diverged from the previous draft versions. It was mainly based on the amendments in the Council proposal. But Article 29(3) and (4) [previously Article 22(2a) and (2b)] essentially followed the version proposed by Parliament. While the explicit exclusion of the safe harbour in (4) was adopted *tel quel*, the text of (3) underwent several modifications that led to a considerable extension. They are highlighted in italics below. While some of the changes are merely editorial, as will be indicated in brackets, others interfere with the substance of the Parliament's proposal. *Inter alia*, the limitation period was reduced from ten to a minimum of five years and a massive extension was added to subparagraph (e) in order to specify *en detail* the scope of the possible restrictions that could be ordered by National Courts to limit pre-trail discovery:

1. Member States shall ensure that a company can be held liable for damage caused to a natural or legal person, provided that:
   (a) the company intentionally or negligently failed to comply with the obligations laid down in Articles 10 and 11 when the right, prohibition or obligation listed in the Annex to this Directive is aimed at protecting the natural or legal person; and
   (b) as a result of the failure referred to in point (a), damage to the natural or legal person's legal interests that are protected under national law was caused.

   A company cannot be held liable if the damage was caused only by its business partners in its chain of activities.
2. Where a company is held liable in accordance with paragraph 1, a natural or legal person shall have the right to full compensation for the damage, in accordance with national law. Full compensation under this Directive shall not lead to overcompensation, whether by means of punitive, multiple or other types of damages.

3.[2a.] Member States shall ensure that:
   (a) *national rules on the beginning, duration, suspension or interruption of limitation periods do not unduly hamper the bringing of actions for damages and, in any case, are not more restrictive than the rules on national general civil liability regimes;*

   the limitation period for bringing actions for damages under this Directive shall be at least *five years and, in any case, not shorter than the limitation period laid down under national general civil liability regimes;*

   limitation periods shall not begin to run before the infringement has ceased and the claimant knows, or can reasonably be expected to know:
   (i) of the behaviour and the fact that it constitutes an infringement;
   (ii) of the fact that the infringement caused harm to them; and
   (iii) the identity of the infringer;
   (b) the cost of proceedings is not prohibitively expensive for claimants to seek justice;
   (c) claimants are able to seek injunctive measures, including summary proceedings; *such injuctive measures* shall be in the form of a definitive or provisional measure to cease *infringements of the provisions of national law adopted pursuant to this Directive by performing an action or ceasing a conduct;* [editorial change instead of: an action which may be in breach of this Directive, or to comply with a measure under this Directive]
   (d) *reasonable conditions are provided for under which any alleged injured party may authorise a trade union, non-governmental human rights or environmental organisation or other non-governmental organisation, and, in accordance with national law, national human rights' institutions, based in a Member State to bring actions to enforce the rights of the alleged injured party, without prejudice to national rules of civil procedure;* [complete editorial overhaul of Art. 22 (2a) (c) as proposed by Parliament]

   a trade union or non-governmental organisation may be authorised under the first subparagraph of this point if it complies with the requirements laid down in national law; those requirements may include maintaining a permanent presence of its own and, in accordance with its statutes, not engaging commercially and not only temporarily in the realisation of rights protected under this Directive or the corresponding rights in national law.

(e) when a claim is brought, and a claimant *presents a reasoned justification containing reasonably available facts and evidence sufficient to support the plausibility of its claim for damage* [editorial change instead of: provides elements substantiating the likelihood of a company's liability under this Directive] and has indicated that additional evidence lies in the control of the company, courts are able to order that such evidence be disclosed by the company in accordance with national procedural law;

national courts shall limit the disclosure of the evidence sought to that which is necessary and proportionate to support a potential claim or a claim for damages and the preservation of evidence to that which is necessary and proportionate to support such a claim for damages; in determining whether an order for the disclosure or preservation of evidence is proportionate, national courts shall consider the extent to which the claim or defence is supported by available facts and evidence justifying the request to disclose evidence; the scope and cost of disclosure as well as the legitimate interests of all parties, including any third parties concerned, including preventing non-specific searches for information which is unlikely to be of relevance for the parties in the procedure; whether the evidence the disclosure of which is sought contains confidential information, especially concerning any third parties, and what arrangements are in place for protecting such confidential information;

Member States shall ensure that national courts have the power to order the disclosure of evidence containing confidential information where they consider it relevant to the action for damages; Member States shall ensure that, when ordering the disclosure of such information, national courts have at their disposal effective measures to protect such information.

4.[2b.] Companies that have participated in industry or multi-stakeholder initiatives, or used *independent* third-party verification or contractual clauses to support the implementation of due diligence obligations *may nevertheless* be held liable in accordance with this Article.

5.[3.] The civil liability of a company for damages arising under this provision shall be without prejudice to the civil liability of its subsidiaries or of any direct and indirect business partners in the chain of *activities of the company*.

When the damage was caused jointly by the company and its subsidiary, direct or indirect business partner, they shall be liable jointly and severally, without prejudice to the provisions of national law concerning the conditions of joint and several liability and the rights of recourse.

6.[4.] The civil liability rules under this Directive shall not limit companies' liability under Union or national legal systems and shall be without prejudice to Union or national rules on civil liability related to adverse human rights impacts or to adverse environmental impacts that provide for liability in situations not covered by or providing for stricter liability than this Directive.

7.[5.] Member States shall ensure that the provisions of national law transposing this Article are of overriding mandatory application in cases where the law applicable to claims to that effect is not the law of a Member State.

§3.03 THE META-PURPOSE OF ARTICLE 29 CSDDD: REMOVING HURDLES FOR CIVIL LIABILITY IN MEMBER STATES' LAWS

The overall purpose of Article 29 CSDDD is to overcome various hurdles that currently stand in the way of a civil liability of European enterprises at the top of the value chains. The most obvious example is the explicit bar to a civil liability for human rights due diligence violations under the German *Lieferkettengesetz* (sub. 1). But it is also true for Article 29(7) CSDDD that aims to override the connecting factor of Article 4 I Rome II Regulation: 'the law of the country in which the damage occurs' (sub 2). And it applies to the procedural provisions inserted by Article 29(3) and (4).

However, it is also true that Article 29 CSDDD orders liability also in cases that would not normally be covered by national law. This extension is less obvious because one would normally assume that human rights violations always trigger tort liability. But it nevertheless holds true – and poses considerable problems regarding the width of potential liability.

While direct human rights violations by enterprises lead to civil liability under all national laws, a different picture emerges with a view to subsidiaries and business partners. The reason is that under European private laws, there is generally no liability for the acts of independent third parties. Now, it is surely a matter of debate whether subsidiaries may always be counted as independent third parties.[6] But there is little doubt that business partners at arm's length do not qualify as such. Nevertheless, the due diligence requirements of Articles 10 and 11 CSDDD aim at holding enterprises accountable for the conduct of their direct and even indirect business partners. This is an obvious extension of the general principles of tort law under both common and civil law. Common lawyers would deny attribution in cases of a '*novum actum interveniens*'. The same restrictive approach to liability for third parties is found in civil law jurisdictions like France[7] and Germany.[8]

This shows that Article 29 CSDDD does not merely purport to overcome formal legal hurdles for meritorious damages claims. It extends substantive tort law in the Member States. That being so, it is understandable that both the Commission and the Council also proposed restrictions. While the Commission's approach to a safe harbour was rejected in the Trilogue, the Council's proposals were adopted. However, it will be shown that they are not persuasive and will not lead to the appropriate level of liability for human rights violations, but they will leave businesses out in the cold.

6. For a critical view, e.g., Alexander Schall, *Die Mutterverantwortlichkeit für Menschenrechtsverletzungen ihrer Auslandstöchter*, ZGR 479 (2018).
7. Cf. Barsan, *supra* n. 4, at 44 et seq.
8. Jan Lieder & Sarah Meyer, *Supply Chain Act and Liability under German Law*, 1 ECCL 55, at 63 et seq. (2023).

[A] The Liability Bar of § 3 III LkSG in Germany

The first national liability obstacle that Articl 29 CSDDD aims to overcome is the explicit prohibition of a civil liability in the German *Lieferkettengesetz* (LkSG). The *Lieferkettengesetz* entered into force on 1 January 2023. It contains specific provisions on human rights (and environmental) due diligence in the supply chains of enterprises (§§ 3-10 LkSG). They are of a similar nature to the rules of the French *loi de vigilance* of 2017. Both Acts served as a kind of blueprint for Articles 10 and 11 CSDDD. But despite their structural similarity, the question of civil liability for breaches of human rights due diligence duties was decided quite differently by France and Germany. While Article L. 225-102-5 (1) C.com. explicitly states that breach of duties under the *loi de vigilance* would trigger liability under Article 1240 C.civ.,[9] § 3 III LkSG orders to the contrary that civil liability could not be based on the violation of the newly instated due diligence provisions of the LkSG but only on the pre-existing provisions of general tort law (§§ 823 BGB et seq.). Compliance with the new duties of the *Lieferkettengesetz* is solely to be enforced by the competent supervisory body, the BAFA (*Bundesamt für Wirtschaft und Ausfuhrkontrolle*).

The German solution was a compromise after a long and hard-fought battle over the LkSG that took place in the legislative period of 2017-2021. It was the last term of Chancellor Angela Merkel. Her party, the Christian Democratic Union (CDU), was with two minor partners in a coalition government: the Social Democrats (SPD) and the Christian Social Union (CSU), the small Bavarian sister party of the Christian Democratic Union (CDU). Somewhat surprisingly, the traditionally conservative CSU joined the SPD in the push for the LkSG though their ministers Hubertus Heil (SPD) and Gerd Müller (CSU), while the *Wirtschaftsministerium* (ministry of economic affairs) under Peter Altmaier (CDU) tried to block the enactment because he wanted to prevent new burdens for German businesses. The conflict was carried out until the very last minute of the old legislative period. Shortly before the initiative of the LkSG would have failed completely, a compromise was reached. The major concession to Altmaier was that there should be no civil liability. This was hailed by business representatives but lamented by NGOs and other commentators who felt that compensation for the victims should have been at the centre of a supply chain law.

§ 3 III LkSG turned out to be a short-lived 'Pyrrhic' victory. When the Commission published its proposal, Article 22 CSDDD was inserted to 'overrule' the decision of the German legislator. That was backed by all parties of the Trilogue. After the strongest opponent of civil liability in Europe, the CDU of former chancellor Angela Merkel had been ousted in the general election of 2021, § 3 III LkSG has become a lost cause.

[B] The Obstacle of Article 4 Rome II Regulation (EC) No. 864/2007

Another well-known obstacle for human rights claims in Europe has been erected by Article 4 Rome II Regulation (EC) No. 864/2007. It prescribes that the tort law 'of the

9. Cf. Barsan, *supra* n. 4, at 31, 43 with fn. 73.

country in which the damage occurs' is to be applied (*lex loci damni; Erfolgsortprinzip*). This rule replaced the old *favor laesi* (*Günstigkeitsprinzip*) of International Private Law that granted the tort victim the choice between the law of the country 'in which the damage occurs' and law of the country 'in which the event giving rise to the damage occurred' (*lex loci actus; Tatortprinzip*). If human rights violations by a subsidiary were caused by breaches of the parent's due diligence duties, the *Tatortprinzip* would have allowed the victim to sue at the place of the parent's business under the laws of that country. But the old rule of choice has been abandoned. The *Tatortprinzip* only survived in a number of special cases, most notably in Article 7 Rome II Regulation for environmental damage. In all other cases of human rights violations, Article 4 Rome II Regulation points to the law of the country in which the damage occurs, i.e., the foreign law of the country in the Global South. This is a major impediment to claims against the parent companies because the actors before the Court will normally not be familiar with the local law in the Global South. This makes such trials prone to errors like those that occurred in the *Kik* case. It concerned a fire in the textile factory Ali Enterprises in Karachi where more than 250 people burned alive. A contributory cause was insufficient fire protection. The case was rejected because of the short limitation period of two years under Pakistani common law.[10]

Ways to get around the rule under Article 4 Rome II Regulation have been discussed since the issue of civil liability was put on the agenda by the Ruggie principles. But no proposition proved persuasive.[11] That is why Article 22(5) CSDDD was inserted. It requires Member States to 'ensure that the provisions of national law transposing this Article is of overriding mandatory application in cases where the law applicable to claims to that effect is not the law of a Member State'.

From a regulatory perspective, this is a remarkable approach, or as Lennarts puts it, 'a creative solution'. Article 4 Rome II Regulation is directly applicable to EU law. If the EU wanted to reinstate the *Tatortprinzip* for all human rights violations, it should simply have extended Article 7 Rome II Regulation accordingly. Of course, changing a Regulation is a daunting procedure. However, it would be the right way to go. By contrast, it looks odd that the EU should oblige the Member States via its Directive to manoeuvre around its Regulation.

This criticism weighs even heavier since the outcome is far from easy to achieve. Take the example of Germany. Without the said Article 3 III LkSG, civil liability for damages arising from the violation of the LkSG would be based on the general tort law rule of § 823 II BGB. This rule grants damages in case of a *Schutzgesetzverletzung*, i.e., 'if someone violates a law purporting to protect another' (*welcher gegen ein den Schutz eines anderen bezweckendes Gesetz verstößt*).[12] It might be assumed that the LkSG

10. LG Dortmund, BeckRS 2019, 388.

11. *See* the accounts by Heinz-Peter Mansel, *Internationales Privatrecht de lege lata wie de lege ferenda und Menschenrechtsverantwortlichkeit deutscher Unternehmen*, ZGR 439 (2018); Axel Halfmeier, Zur *Rolle des Kollisionsrechts bei der zivilrechtlichen Haftung für Menschenrechtsverletzungen* in *Zivil- und Strafrechtliche Unternehmensverantwortung für Menschenrechtsverletzungen* 33 (Krajewski, Oehm & Saage-Maß eds, 2017).

12. This is also the underlying notion enshrined in the new text of Art. 22(1) CSDDD. We will come back to that below, §3.03[B][2].

qualified as a *Schutzgesetz* in the sense of § 823 II BGB.[13] Also, many writers argued before Article 3 III LkSG was inserted that the *Lieferkettengesetz* extended the so-called *Verkehrssicherungspflichten*, i.e., the general duty of care that is owed to anyone who comes within the 'zone of danger' created one's negligent behaviour, beyond the own sphere of the enterprise. That being so, violations of the due diligence duties would also have resulted in liability under the general tort law provision of § 823 I BGB.[14]

General tort law would be the basis for damages for human rights due diligence violations in other Member States. In France, violations of the *Loi de Vigil*ance lead to damages claims under Article 1240 C.civ. This is explicitly stated in Article L. 225-102-5 (1) C.com.[15] The same result may well be reached under the Dutch Code[16] after the CSDDD will be implemented:[17]

> Article 6:162 Dutch Civil Code (DCC)
>
> –1. A person who commits a tortious act (unlawful Act) against another person that can be attributed to him must repair the damage that this other person has suffered as a result arguably thereof.
> –2. As a tortious act is regarded as a violation of someone else's right (entitlement) and an act or omission in violation of a duty imposed by law or of what according to unwritten law has to be regarded as proper social conduct, always as far as there was no justification for this behaviour.
> –3. A tortious act can be attributed to the tortfeasor [the person committing the tortious Act] if it results from his fault or from a cause for which he is accountable by virtue of law or generally accepted principles (common opinion).

As soon as the duties of Articles 10 and 11 CSDDD are transposed into Dutch law, breaches could be seen as 'violation of a duty imposed by law' in the sense of the second section of Article 6:162.

The problem is, however, that none of the aforementioned tort liabilities would be of 'overriding mandatory application', as required by Article 29(7) CSDDD. This is because the basis of the damages claims is always found in general tort law. But general tort law cannot be qualified as 'overriding mandatory provision', *lois d'application immédiate* or *Eingriffsnorm*, as Germans would call it. This could only be assumed for the underlying human rights due diligence duties that will be transposed into national law. But those duties do not carry the damages awards.

From the legislative perspective, the only way out of this dilemma seems to be the inclusion of the damages claim directly in the national provisions, transposing the

13. Anna Beckers, *Globale Wertschöpfungsketten: Theorie und Dogmatik unternehmensbezogener Pflichten*, ZfPW 220, 249 (2021).
14. Gerhard Wagner, *Haftung für Menschenrechtsverletzungen in der Lieferkette*, ZIP 1095, 1103 (2021): '*... das wirklich Neue am Sorgfaltspflichtengesetz [sei] die Ausweitung der Sorgfaltspflichten über den Organisationsbereich der jeweiligen Unternehmung hinaus*'. Likewise: Walter Paefgen, *Haftung für die Verletzung von Pflichten nach dem neuen Sorgfaltspflichtengesetz*, ZIP 2006, 2011 (2021).
15. Cf. Barsan, *supra* n. 3, at 31, 43 with fn. 73.
16. English version available at: http://www.dutchcivillaw.com/legislation/dcctitle6633.htm
17. Concurring view by Loes Lennarts. *See* Lennarts, *supra* n. 2, at 267.

human rights due diligence of the CSDDD. For example, the *Lieferkettengesetz* would have to be supplemented by a provision prescribing, 'If violations of the duties under this Act cause damage to legal or natural persons protected by those duties, compensation can be claimed.' A similar rule would have to be inserted into the *loi de vigilance* within the Code de commerce. It would have to replace the current reference to the general tort law claim under Article 1240 C.civ. The same point was made by Eva-Maria Kinienger in her presentation 'Private Enforcement of Human Rights Due Diligence from a German and PIL point of view' at the ECCL-Symposium *CSDDD, Sustainability and Corporate Law* on 31 May 2024 in Ghent.

The problem is not merely theoretical. If the priority of the liability under Member States' laws is not achieved, there is a severe risk that the CSDDD will have a damaging, counterproductive effect. This is because the violation of legally imposed duties of care does not give rise to damages claims under common law but excludes them.[18] The reason is that a common law duty of care is doctrinally attached to a one-sided, voluntary assumption. There is no scope for such assumption where the law obliges a person to act. The leading case to show this adverse effect is *Gorringe v. Calderdale Council*.[19] It has been confirmed in *HMCE v. Barclays*[20] where Lord Hoffmann said:

> The question … is comparable with the question of whether a statutory duty can generate a common law duty of care. The answer is that it cannot: see *Gorringe v. Calderdale Metropolitan Borough Council* [2004] 1 WLR 1057. The statute either creates a statutory duty or it does not. … But you cannot derive a common law duty of care directly from a statutory duty.

Because of the danger that existing tort liability under local (common) law is excluded by the statutory duty created in implementing the Directive, it is understandable that Member States are to override the application of local law. But as Lennarts already pointed out, a solid legal solution could better be achieved by amending the Rome II Regulation.

[C] The (Excessive) Removal of Procedural Hurdles by Article 29(3)

Article 29(3) CSDDD follows a line of European regulatory tradition that draws from experiences of legal problems in prior cases and attempts to decide those issues *pro futuro*. This is normally a good way to draft legislation. For example, after the European institutions had been watching for years the proceedings in the *Daimler/Geltl* case[21] on (allegedly belated) ad-hoc disclosure of insider information extending over seven legal

18. *See* already Alexander Schall, *Die erhöhten Haftungsrisiken für Menschenrechtsverletzungen nach King Okpabi v Royal Dutch Shell – und die überraschende Enthaftungswirkung des Lieferkettengesetzes*, ZIP 1241 (2021).
19. *Gorringe v. Calderdale Metropolitan Borough Council* [2004] 1 WLR 1057.
20. *Her Majesty's Commissioners of Customs and Excise v. Barclays Bank plc* [2006] UKHL 28, at para. 39.
21. ECJ C-19/11 *Daimler/Geltl*. The total of three BGH-decisions were BGH NZG 2008, 300; NZG 2011, 109 and NZG 2013, 708. The ECJ was only involved after the case came up to the BGH for the second time.

instances (!), they took considerable care to clarify the contentious issues around protracted processes in the new text of Article 7 MAR.

On principle, this regulatory approach deserves praise. However, in the case of the CSDDD, one cannot help that the European Parliament took a lopsided view of the issues at stake and got carried away in its adamant intent to pave the way for claimants. In doing so, it displayed an attitude towards Member State laws that amounts to disrespect and does not sit well with the general requirements of proportionality and subsidiarity. It overlooks that the typical obstacles to victims' access to judicial remedies stem from the procedural and substantive law of the countries where the human rights violations occur.

For starters, the first subsection on limitation periods appears to be inspired by the failure of the *Kik* case before the LG Dortmund.[22] That was indeed a heart-breaking case that made it difficult to accept a rejection on a 'formality' like limitation. However, the main problem in that case was the very short limitation period of two years under the applicable law of Pakistan combined with the unique feature that it would not be stalled by negotiations. As the LG Dortmund said in paragraph 23 of the judgment: '*Anders als in den meisten anderen Rechtsordnungen hätten bloße Verhandlungen über den Anspruch weder verjährungshemmende noch sonst die Verjährung berührende Wirkung.*' [Unlike in most other legal systems, mere negotiations about the claim would have neither dilatory nor any other effect on the limitation period]. This problem will already be solved by the overriding mandatory application of Member State laws under Article 29(7) CSDDD. It is hard to see why it would be necessary on top of that to interfere with the general rules on the limitation periods of the European Member States – none of which would presumedly have barred the claim. Article 29(3)(a) reads like a vote of no confidence in the laws of the Member States.

The same is true for Article 29(3)(b) forbidding prohibitive costs. This rule seems unnecessary because of the provision Article 29(3)(d) granting NGOs and other entities standing to sue on behalf of the victim. The model for that latter rule is found in § 11 LkSG.[23] The sound idea of this approach is well proven and tested, e.g., in consumer law.

Also, hefty criticism must be directed against the rules in Article 29(3)(c) and (e) CSDDD because the Directive forces two standard elements of alien common law procedure, pre-trail discovery and summary proceedings to strike out claims, upon the mostly civilian jurisdictions of the EU. Some of these elements may be known to some EU Member States. For example, the Dutch Courts seem to have ordered the surrender of far more and specific documents of Shell by way of pre-trial discovery than the English Courts.[24] However, for many other Member States, such procedures are in part

22. LG Dortmund, BeckRS 2019, 388.
23. On this provision, *see*, *e.g.*, the commentary by Axel Halfmeier in Alexander Schall/Ingo Theusinger/Mansur Pour Rafsendjani (eds), LkSG, 2023, § 11 marginal note 1-44.
24. Cf. *Okpabi v. Shell*, at para. 137: 'The appellants were and are able to identify specific internal documentation which is likely to be material to the claims made. The most obvious example is *the documentation which the Dutch Court of Appeal ordered RDS and SPDC to produce in related proceedings*. These include the annual Assurance Letters submitted to the CEO confirming the level of compliance with the RDS Control Framework; internal Asset Integrity Audits evaluating

or totally alien. For example, German procedural law knows neither full-scale pre-trial discovery[25] nor summary judgments to strike out claims.[26]

Admittedly, there is a problem gathering evidence in cases against businesses because the decisions taken are internal affairs that cannot be accessed by outsiders. But that does not necessarily lead to a *déni de justice*. For example, in the German legal tradition, this issue is dealt with by modifying or reversing the burden of proof, as happened in the famous *Hühnerpestfall* with respect to the distribution of faulty goods.[27] To give a hypothetical example of human rights due diligence: As soon as it is established that the fire protection in a factory was insufficient and that the enterprise was a supplier of a German enterprise obliged to conduct human rights due diligence, German lawyers would readily accept a presumption that the enterprise was in default. Then, it would be up to the enterprise to produce all the necessary internal documents to exonerate itself by showing compliance with its due diligence duties. Otherwise, it would be held liable.

Under this approach, the enterprise's 'duty to disclose' turns into a mere 'duty against itself' to disclose. German lawyers would speak of an *Obliegenheit* as opposed to a *Pflicht*. This approach makes all the burdensome balancing exercises required for the duty to disclose under Article 29(3)(e) obsolete. If the enterprise does not want to disclose confidential information to exonerate itself, so be it. Liability follows suite. This is a neater and more time-efficient approach than the complicated balancing exercise prescribed by lit. (e).

So, how did the procedural rules of common law sneak into the CSDDD? I can only imagine that the *Okpabi* Case was the culprit. The 2021 judgment *Okpabi v. Royal Dutch Shell* of the Supreme Court concerned summary proceedings on the issue of jurisdiction in which Shell – unsuccessfully – sought to strike out the claim brought against it. In addition, some of the successful claimant's arguments stemmed from findings in the pre-trial discovery, notably also from (much broader) discovery ordered by the Dutch Court.[28] The eventual successful outcome of the case (but only on the preliminary stage!) may have induced the European Parliament to call for similar procedures to be put in place all over Europe.

However, on closer looks, the Okpabi Case is far from being a blueprint for ideal human rights proceedings. The judges of the English Supreme Court openly expressed

the technical integrity and the operational integrity of the pipelines; HSE audits evaluating SPDC's Emergency and Oil Spill response procedures applying to the pipelines; and the audit results and remedial action plans (findings, recommendations and approval and closeout of actions) documented on the basis of those audits.'

25. The rule in § 142 ZPO has a far more limited scope, *see* Tobias Lüpke & Robert Müller: 'Pre-Trial Discovery of Documents und § 142 ZPO – ein trojanisches Pferd im neuen Zivilprozessrecht?', NZI 588 (2002).
26. For sake of accuracy, it should be noted that there is a kind of equivalent procedure under § 114 ZPO if a plaintiff or a defendant requires public funding. Presumably, similar 'mini-trials' on issues like jurisdiction can be found in many jurisdictions of the EU. But that is not to say that they replicate in any way the broad approach of common law that aims to strike out in advance every unmeritorious claim.
27. BGHZ 104, 323 = NJW 1988, 2611.
28. *Okpabi v. Shell*, at para. 137.

their frustration about the abuse of the 'summary proceedings' that they felt because of the exorbitant scope of materials put forward. To make this point, Lord Hamble in *Okpabi*, at paragraphs 20-21 and before him Lord Briggs in Vedanta, at paragraph 9 referred to the speech of Lord Hope of Craighead in *Three Rivers District Council v. Governor and Company of the Bank of England (No 3)* [2003] 2 AC 1:

> 94. For the reasons which I have just given, I think that the question is whether the claim has no real prospect of succeeding at trial and that it has to be answered having regard to the overriding objective of dealing with the case justly. But the point which is of crucial importance lies in the answer to the further question that then needs to be asked, which is – what is to be the scope of that inquiry?
>
> 95. I would approach that further question in this way. The method by which issues of fact are tried in our courts is well settled. After the normal processes of discovery and interrogatories have been completed, the parties are allowed to lead their evidence so that the trial judge can determine where the truth lies in the light of that evidence. To that rule there are some well-recognised exceptions. For example, it may be clear as a matter of law at the outset that even if a party were to succeed in proving all the facts that he offers to prove he will not be entitled to the remedy that he seeks. In that event a trial of the facts would be a waste of time and money, and it is proper that the action should be taken out of Court as soon as possible. In other cases, it may be possible to say with confidence before trial that the factual basis for the claim is fanciful because it is entirely without substance. It may be clear beyond question that the statement of facts is contradicted by all the documents or other material on which it is based. The simpler the case, the easier it is likely to be to take that view and resort to what is properly called summary judgment. But more complex cases are unlikely to be capable of being resolved in that way without conducting a mini-trial on the documents without discovery and without oral evidence. As Lord Woolf said in *Swain v Hillman* [[2001] 1 All ER 91], at paragraph 95, that is not the object of the rule. It is designed to deal with cases that are not fit for trial at all.
>
> 96. In *Wenlock v Moloney* [1965] 1 WLR 1238 the plaintiff's claim of damages for conspiracy was struck out after a four day hearing on affidavits and documents. Danckwerts LJ said of the inherent power of the Court to strike out, at paragraph 1244B-C: 'this summary jurisdiction of the court was never intended to be exercised by a minute and protracted examination of the documents and facts of the case, in order to see whether the plaintiff really has a cause of action. To do that is to usurp the position of the trial judge, and to produce a trial of the case in chambers, on affidavits only, without discovery and without oral evidence tested by cross-examination in the ordinary way. This seems to me to be an abuse of the inherent power of the court and not a proper exercise of that power.

These statements clearly show that summary proceedings are prone to mistakes that force appeals. And this is exactly what happened in *Okpabi v. Shell*:

> Paragraph 120: 'Being drawn into conducting a mini trial led to the court making determinations in relation to contested factual evidence that were not appropriate on an interlocutory application.'
> Paragraph 126: 'Conducting a mini-trial also led to the court making inappropriate determinations in relation to the documentary evidence. Since the court was making a decision on the evidence, it effectively had to conclude that the prospect of there being further relevant evidence on disclosure could and should be discounted.'

Against this background, it must be asked why the European regulator obliges the Member States to copy malfunctioning common law procedures even though venerable common lawyers do not hold those procedures fit for purpose. Moreover, Article 29(3)(c) and (e) amount to a massive interference with the procedural laws that belong to the sovereign domain of the Member States. Where is the justification to do that?

§3.04 THE EXTENSION OF SUBSTANTIVE TORT LAW AND THE FUTILE ATTEMPTS OF RESTRAINT

[A] The Extension of Liability for Other Person's 'Danger Zones'

The establishment of civil liability for breaches of human rights due diligence provisions like those of the *loi de vigilance*, the *Lieferkettengesetz* or Articles 10 and 11 CSDDD faces a major problem. The actual tortfeasors are not normally the European companies at the top of the supply chain but local business partners and subsidiaries. It is a general rule of tort law that natural persons and entities are responsible for their own conduct but not for the acts of independent third parties. There is the notable exception of 'vicarious liability' for acts of agents and employees. But the contractors of the supply chain do not usually tick this box.[29] The mere fact of a contractual relation is not enough to render one business partner accountable for the acts of another under general tort law. This principle is valid both under common law and civil law.[30]

The same basic rule is traditionally applied to subsidiaries. It is the law in major jurisdictions like France, Germany or the UK. However, it must be questioned whether it is really right to equate 100%-held subsidiaries to independent businesses. In my opinion, this view is based on a fallacy. While it is evidently true that corporate entities have *separate* legal personality distinct from their shareholders, this is not to say that they are *independent* third parties. Employees are individual persons as well. But still, they are dependent. That is why the employer can be held accountable for their acts on the premise of '*qui facit per alium facit per se*'. A similar rule should in my opinion apply to legal persons. Only if they are truly independent because the parent does not control their business but takes on the role of a passive investor may the equation with independent third parties become appropriate. But in most jurisdictions, this is not the law yet. If anything, we are seeing a slow movement in this direction. The most advanced jurisdiction in this respect may be England where the Supreme Court held that the separate legal personality of the subsidiaries does not exclude the assumption of a group-wide duty of care by the parent company.[31] Similar arguments have been

29. Barsan, *supra* n. 3, at 44 et seq.; Jan Lieder & Sarah Meyer, *Supply Chain Act and Liability under German Law*, 1 ECCL 55, at 63 et seq. (2023).
30. As to Germany, *see* Mathias Habersack & Max Ehrl, *Verantwortlichkeit inländischer Unternehmen für Menschenrechtsverletzungen durch ausländische Zulieferer – de lege lata und de lege ferenda*, 219(2) AcP 155 (2019); Holger Fleischer & Stefan Korch, *Zur deliktsrechtlichen Verantwortlichkeit von Auftraggebern in der Lieferkette*, ZIP 2181 (2019).
31. *Vedanta Resources Ltd v. Lungowe* [2019] UKSC 20; *King Emre Okpabi v. Royal Dutch Shell* [2021] UKSC 3. Substantive hearings in the Shell Case are expected to take place in 2024. After

made in Germany, too.[32] But unlike in the UK, they remained in the realm of academia and have not found clear support by the Courts yet.

The legal situation changes profoundly with the introduction of civil liability for mistakes in the supply chain due diligence. The original aim of the supply chain due diligence was to energise the bargaining power of large enterprises within their supply chains for the enforcement of human rights improvements. This follows the masterplan of the UN Guiding Principles. In order to compensate for the failure of international politics, John Ruggie aimed to activate the power of international businesses in order to achieve private enforcement of human rights. But this oversteps the traditional boundaries of tort law. Normally, we would require that a company engaged in unlawful or at least dangerous conduct to hold it accountable for damages. There have been attempts to brand doing business in the Global South generally as dangerous. Learned colleagues argued that seeking the benefits of 'human rights arbitrage' [33] gave rise to the danger of human rights violations. That may sometimes be the case. But generally, it seems closer to the truth that the only act linking the company to the human rights violation is the entertainment of a business relation with the delinquent. That is per se neither illegal not dangerous. It is only the imposition of human rights due diligence, for the purposes just set out, that obliges the company to procure compliance by its business partner. That is why the company becomes responsible for overseeing the human rights efforts of its business partners. By that mechanism, the law creates duties to oversee independent third parties that would otherwise not have existed. Only after these duties have been established can tort liability for violations follow.

However, it cannot be overlooked that Article 29 CSDDD creates a liability for the misconduct of others. The actual delinquents in case of human rights violations will usually be third parties in the Global South: local employers and business people eventually aided and abetted by (or aiding and abetting) state representatives. From a formal perspective, the human rights due diligence may not base the liability on the misdeeds of third persons. Unlike in the case of vicarious liability, the company is not held responsible for another person's tort on principle '*qui facit per alium facit per se*' but for its own violation of the human rights due diligence. That works as a duty of oversight. But in essence, it is a responsibility for the acts of others. This is difficult to

a group litigation order had been rejected by the High Court (*Okpabi v. Royal Dutch Shell* [2022] EWHC 989), several thousand individual claims have been filed.

Cf. further Holger Fleischer & Stefan Korch, *Okpabi v Royal Dutch Shell und das Deutsche Deliktsrecht in Konzernlagen*, ZIP 709 (2021); Alexander Schall, *Die erhöhten Haftungsrisiken für Menschenrechtsverletzungen nach King Okpabi v Royal Dutch Shell – und die überraschende Enthaftungswirkung des Lieferkettengesetzes*, ZIP 1241 (2021).

32. Mathias Habersack & Peter Zickgraf, *Deliktsrechtliche Verkehrs- und Organisationspflichten im Konzern*, ZHR 182, 252 (2018); Marc-Philippe Weller & Laura Nasse, *Menschenrechtsarbitrage als Gefahrenquelle* in *Vom Konzern zum Einheitsunternehmen* 107 (Bergmann et al. eds, 2020); Alexander Schall, *supra* n. 6; *See also* the accounts in the paper by Holger Fleischer & Stefan Korch, *Konzerndeliktsrecht: Entwicklung und Zukunftsperspektiven*, DB 1944 (2019) and the book by Leonhard Hübner, *Unternehmenshaftung für Menschenrechtsverletzungen* (2022) (based on his habilitation thesis).
33. *See* Weller & Nasse, *supra* n. 3.

establish because, generally, all torts must be attributed to the person to be held answerable for the tort.[34] But malicious acts of independent third parties are difficult to attribute because of what common lawyers call '*novus actus interveniens*'. That was a major hurdle in the UK cases. It was held that the Act of the third party must pass the tests of 'proximity' and 'foreseeability' (i.e., very likely to happen).[35] It is therefore not clear yet whether the claimants in the *Okpabi* case will be able to show in the upcoming main proceedings that this requirement is fulfilled. Also, in France, attribution is subject to a heated debate because of the requirement of a 'direct causal link'.[36]

The justification for a tort liability is even weaker since the reason to impose the responsibility on the companies under the CSDDD is not clearly connected with one's own wrongdoing nor with one's own control over third parties or a 'danger zone'.[37] Entering into contractual relations as such is not wrong. Moreover, it does not give actual *control* over the other party of the contract but only influence. Only a majority of votes do. In the contractual context, there is nothing but bargaining power. This was enough for the regulator to attach the human rights due diligence to it. But it is feebler than control. If the other party does not budge, you cannot stop the wrong. You can only walk away.

As a consequence, while the human rights due diligence under Articles 10 and 11 bears some resemblance with typical tort law duties, it is essentially different, at least as far as it concerns the oversight of contractual relations.[38] It consists of 'best efforts duties' or 'obligations of means'. The company has to do its best to mitigate adverse impacts on human rights caused by independent third parties. It may even have to cut ties with its business relations. But it does not have to stop the violation unconditionally because that is beyond its influence. This contrasts with the situation under tort law where a 'best efforts defence' would be as inconceivable as escaping liability by 'cutting the legal ties' simply through relinquishing the property (dereliction) to the gas leaking plant or the oil spilling platform. The different nature of the human rights due diligence duties has also been recognised by the European regulator in *Recital 19 of the CSDDD*:

> This Directive should not require companies to guarantee, in all circumstances, that adverse impacts will never occur or that they will be stopped. For example,

34. *See* only Art. 6:162 section 3 of the Dutch Code above.
35. *See* the leading case *Dorset Yacht Co Ltd. v. Home Office* [1970] AC 1004: 'These cases shew that, where human action forms one of the links bet- ween the original wrongdoing of the defendant and the loss suffered by the plaintiff, that action must at least have been something *very likely to happen* if it is not to be regarded as novus actus interveniens breaking the chain of causation.' This case was referred to by Lord Briggs in *Vedanta Resources Ltd v. Lungowe* [2019] UKSC 20, at para. 54. The law was confirmed in *King Emre Okpabi v. Royal Dutch Shell* [2021] UKSC 3, at para. 151 (per Lord Hamblen).
36. *See* Constitutional Council, C. Const. No. 2017-750 DC du 23 March 2017, at § 17; Barsan, *supra* n. 3, at 31 and 45 et seq.
37. Cf. Art. 1242 C.civ.: '*On est responsable non seulement du dommage que l'on cause par son propre fait, mais encore de celui qui est causé par le fait des personnes dont on doit répondre, ou des choses que l'on a sous sa garde.*'
38. For this argument, *see also* Alexander Schall & Sebastian Merkel in Alexander Schall/Ingo Theusinger/Mansur Pour Rafsendjani, Anhang Art. 3 marginal notes 88-99.

with respect to business partners, where the adverse impact results from State intervention, the company might not be in a position to arrive at such results. Therefore, the main obligations in this Directive should be obligations of means. The company should take appropriate measures which are capable of achieving the objectives of due diligence by effectively addressing adverse impacts, in a manner commensurate to the degree of severity and the likelihood of the adverse impact. Account should be taken of the circumstances of the specific case, the nature and extent of the adverse impact and relevant risk factors, including, in preventing and minimising adverse impacts, the specificities of the company's business operations and its chain of activities, sector or geographical area in which its business partners operate, the company's power to influence its direct and indirect business partners, and whether the company could increase its power of influence.

The CSDDD approach to force the use of economic power by enterprises to implement regulatory purposes is nouvelle and legally challenging. Both the Commission and the Council seem to be aware of this because they have made proposals to ameliorate the liability risk. We will have a look at those before discussing alternative solutions.

[B] Safe Harbour (Commission)

To mitigate the liability risk for misconduct of remote business partners in the value chain, the Commission proposed a safe harbour for companies complying with the requirements of the human rights due diligence under Articles 10 and 11 (in the previous versions: Articles 7 and 8] of the CSDDD:

Art. 22(2) CSDDD [Commission Proposal]:

> Notwithstanding paragraph 1, Member States shall ensure that where a company has taken the actions referred to in Article 7(2), point (b) and Article 7(4), or Article 8(3), point (c), and Article 8(5), it shall not be liable for damages caused by an adverse impact arising as a result of the activities of an indirect partner with whom it has an established business relationship, unless it was unreasonable, in the circumstances of the case, to expect that the action actually taken, including as regards verifying compliance, would be adequate to prevent, mitigate, bring to an end or minimise the extent of the adverse impact.

Art. 7(2) [Commission Proposal]: Companies shall be required to take the following actions, where relevant:

...

(b) seek contractual assurances from a business partner with whom it has a direct business relationship that it will ensure compliance with the company's code of conduct and, as necessary, a prevention action plan, including by seeking corresponding contractual assurances from its partners, to the extent that their activities are part of the company's value chain (contractual cascading). When such contractual assurances are obtained, paragraph 4 shall apply.

Art. 7(4): The contractual assurances or the contract shall be accompanied by the appropriate measures to verify compliance. For the purposes of verifying

> compliance, the company may refer to suitable industry initiatives or independent third-party verification. ...
>
> Art. 8(3): Companies shall be required to take the following actions, where relevant:
>
> ...
>
> (c) seek contractual assurances from a direct partner with whom it has an established business relationship that it will ensure compliance with the code of conduct and, as necessary, a corrective action plan, including by seeking corresponding contractual assurances from its partners, to the extent that they are part of the value chain (contractual cascading). When such contractual assurances are obtained, paragraph 5 shall apply.
>
> Art. 8(5): The contractual assurances or the contract shall be accompanied by the appropriate measures to verify compliance. For the purposes of verifying compliance, the company may refer to suitable industry initiatives or independent third-party verification. ...

The long and short of it is that companies are exempt from liability if they (a) seek contractual assurances of human rights compliance by their business partners and (b) have them verified by industry initiatives or independent third parties. The concept of a safe harbour had been discussed for the German LkSG, too, but did not materialise in the final version of the Act. One reason may have been the exclusion of any civil liability under § 3 III LkSG that made the case for additional safeguards less urgent. But there is a criticism on the more general level, too. Safe harbours create a danger of box-ticking exercises instead of actual due diligence. This is aggravated by eventual flaws in the certification processes. From a doctrinal perspective, 'safe harbours' are at fundamentally odds with the structure of a negligence rule. The duty of care works like Bentham's 'dog's law': If you want to teach your dog not to do something, you wait till he does it and then beat it out of him. Bentham's scathing criticism was directed at common law. But on closer look, it neatly describes the functioning of the duty of car. Tort law would not work without a generic standard along the lines of 'acting with due care'.[39] It is necessary to establish whether the acts or omissions of the company contributed to the human rights violation because the company acted without taking good care. For that purpose, the standard is applied *ex post* to the known facts of the case. Then, the Court will determine whether the alleged tortfeasor is in default or whether what happened was a tragic accident that could not have been avoided with due care.

This system does not work if specific duties are stated in compliance which leads to a safe harbour. The company only needs to focus on this duty. Other lines of contribution will not be investigated. That militates against the functioning of the duty of care. It is a better fit with the US-American duty of oversight after *Caremark*[40] and *Stone v. Ritter*.[41] This duty is not understood as a negligence rule any more, but as a part

39. *See* only Lord Atkin's *Donoghue v. Stevenson* [1932] AC 562 for the UK and Judge Cardozo's *MacPherson v. Buick Motor Co.*, 217 N.Y. 382, 111 N.E. 1050 (1916) for the US.
40. *In re Caremark International Inc Derivative Litigation* 698 A.2d 959 (1996).
41. *Stone ex rel. AmSouth Bancorporation v. Ritter*, 911 A.2d 362 (Del. 2006).

of the duty of loyalty which is subject to a good faith standard.[42] According to *Caremark*, the aim of this classification is to relax liability for omissions in a similar way as the business judgment rule does with regard to active business decisions[43] in order to avoid constant second-guessing of director's conduct:[44]

> In re Caremark International Inc Derivative Litigation 698 A.2d 959 (1996), at 967 et seq.: '*Director liability for a breach of the duty to exercise appropriate attention may, in theory, arise in two distinct contexts. First, such liability may be said to follow from a board decision that results in a loss because that decision was ill advised or "negligent". Second, liability to the corporation for a loss may be said to arise from an unconsidered failure of the board to act in circumstances in which due attention would, arguably, have prevented the loss. The first class of cases will typically be subject to review under the director-protective business judgment rule, assuming the decision made was the product of a process that was either deliberately considered in good faith or was otherwise rational. ... Thus, the business judgment rule is process oriented and informed by a deep respect for all good faith board decisions.*
>
> The second class of cases in which director liability for inattention is theoretically possible entail circumstances in which a loss eventuates not from a decision but, from unconsidered inaction. ... Financial and organizational disasters such as these raise the question, what is the board's responsibility with respect to the organization and monitoring of the enterprise to assure that the corporation functions within the law to achieve its purposes? ... But it is important that the board exercise a good faith judgment that the corporation's information and reporting system is in concept and design adequate to assure the board that appropriate information will come to its attention in a timely manner as a matter of ordinary operations, so that it may satisfy its responsibility.'

42. Cf. *e.g.*, Claire Hill & Brett McDonnell, *Stone v. Ritter and the Expanding Duty of Loyalty*, 76 Fordham Law Review 1769, 1773 (2007); Stavros Gadinis & Amelia Miazad, *The Hidden Power of Compliance* (2018), available at: https://papers.ssrn.com/sol3/papers.cfm?abstract_id=3123987; Dauner-Lieb, *25 Jahre In re Caremark – der Grundgedanke der Compliance-Pflicht* in *Festschrift für Thomas Heidel* 187 (Gehle & Hirte/Lochner eds, 2021); Alexander Schall, *Compliance-Pflicht als Loyalitätspflicht – weist Delaware einen Weg zur Haftungsbegrenzung ohne Übernahme des arbeitsrechtlichen Haftungsprivilegs?* in *Festschrift für Eberhard Vetter* 659, 668 et seq. (Barbara Grunewald, Jens Koch & Jörgen Thielmann eds, 2019); *See generally* Melvin A. Eisenberg, *The Duty of Good Faith in Corporate Law*, 31 Del. J. Corp. L. 1 30-31 (2006); Melvin A. Eisenberg, *The Duty of Good Faith in American Corporate Law*, 1 ECFR 2006, 1 ff.
43. *See generally* Stephen M. Bainbridge, *The Business Judgment Rule as Abstention Doctrine*, 57 Vand. L. Rev. 83 (2004).
44. *Stone ex rel. AmSouth Bancorporation v. Ritter*, 911 A.2d 362 (Del. 2006), at 373: 'With the benefit of hindsight, the plaintiffs' complaint seeks to equate a bad outcome with bad faith. The lacuna in the plaintiffs' argument is a failure to recognize that the directors' good faith exercise of oversight responsibility may not invariably prevent employees from violating criminal laws, or from causing the corporation to incur significant financial liability, or both, ... '; *see also* Jennifer Arlen, *The Story of Allis-Chalmers, Caremark, and Stone: Directors' Evolving Duty to Monitor*, NYU L&E Working Papers, 11-19-2008, https://papers.ssrn.com/sol3/papers.cfm?abstract_id=1304272, at 3: 'Chancellor Allen had two goals in mind when he issued Caremark. First, he wanted to induce directors to play a more active oversight role, especially over corporate legal compliance. Second, he wanted to ensure that directors remained free to exercise their own judgment about how best to satisfy this duty, free from court oversight of whether their decisions were objectively reasonable.'

For the directors to be in good faith, it is principally enough to put the 'corporation's information and reporting system in place.[45] In other words: the installation of an appropriate compliance system provides a safe harbour. The company does not permanently have to check and search actively for eventual misconduct, as would be the case under a negligence rule. The good faith is only destroyed by a 'sustained or systematic failure to exercise oversight'.

> *In re* Caremark International Inc Derivative Litigation 698 A.2d 959 (1996), at 971: *'Since it does appear that the Board was to some extent unaware of the activities that led to liability, I turn to a consideration of the other potential avenue to director liability that the pleadings take: director inattention or "negligence". Generally, where a claim of directorial liability for corporate loss is predicated upon ignorance of liability creating activities within the corporation, as in Graham or in this case, in my opinion only a sustained or systematic failure of the board to exercise oversight — such as an utter failure to attempt to assure a reasonable information and reporting system exist — will establish the lack of good faith that is a necessary condition to liability.'*

The new approach has been criticised as overly lenient towards managers.[46] But that may not hold true because good faith can also be destroyed by red flags.[47] Again, this is reflected in the Commission's proposal. The last part of Article 22(2) CSDDD says that compliance with the 'safe harbour' due diligence will exonerate from liability '*...unless it was unreasonable, in the circumstances of the case, to expect that the action actually taken ... would be adequate to prevent, mitigate, bring to an end or minimise the extent of the adverse impact*'.

Unlike fiduciary duties, tort law duties of care are not based on the standard of good faith or best efforts but on a negligence rule. A safe harbour does not sit well with

45. *In re Caremark International Inc Derivative Litigation* 698 A.2d 959 (1996), at 970: 'Thus, I am of the view that a director's obligation includes a duty to attempt in good faith to assure that a corporate information and reporting system, which the board concludes is adequate, exists ...'.
46. *See, e.g.*, Jennifer Arlen, *The Story of Allis-Chalmers, Caremark, and Stone: Directors' Evolving Duty to Monitor*, NYU L&E Working Papers, 11-19-2008, https://papers.ssrn.com/sol3/papers.cfm?abstract_id=1304272; Stephen M. Bainbridge, Star Lopez & Benjamin Oklan, *The Convergence of Good Faith and Oversight*, 55 UCLA L. Rev. 559, 600 (2008): 'Perhaps ignorance is really a bliss.'; Sean J. Griffith, *Corporate Governance in an Era of Compliance*, 57 WM. & Mary L. Rev. 2075, 2111 (2016); Kimberly D. Krawiec, *Cosmetic Compliance and the Failure of Negotiated Governance*, 81 Wash. U. L. Q. 487, 491 (2003); Eric J. Pan, *Rethinking the Board's Duty to Monitor: A Critical Assessment of the Delaware Doctrine*, 38 Fla. St. U. L. Rev. 209 (2011); Megan W. Shaner, *The (Un)Enforcement of Directors' Duties*, 48 U.C. Davis. L. Rev. 271, 304 (2014). Contrast for a positive view Claire Hill & Brett McDonnell, *Stone v Ritter and the Expanding Duty of Loyalty*, 76 Fordham Law Review 1769, 1788 (2007); Stavros Gadinis & Amelia Miazad, *The Hidden Power of Compliance* (2018), https://papers.ssrn.com/sol3/papers.cfm?abstract_id=3123987.
47. *Stone ex rel. AmSouth Bancorporation v. Ritter*, 911 A.2d 362 (Del. 2006), at 373: 'In the absence of red flags, good faith in the context of oversight must be measured by the directors' actions "to assure a reasonable information and reporting system exists"'...; *see* in detail on red flags Stavros Gadinis & Amelia Miazad, *The Hidden Power of Compliance* (2018), https://papers.ssrn.com/sol3/papers.cfm?abstract_id=3123987; Alexander Schall, *Compliance-Pflicht als Loyalitätspflicht – weist Delaware einen Weg zur Haftungsbegrenzung ohne Übernahme des arbeitsrechtlichen Haftungsprivilegs?* in *Festschrift für Eberhard Vetter* 659, 668 et seq. (Barbara Grunewald, Jens Koch & Jörgen Thielmann eds, 2019).

that, as has been shown above. However, doctrinal consistency is not an end in itself. The US-approach under *Caremark* and *Stone v. Ritter* at least accepts that the duty of oversight materially differs from duties of care for one's own conduct. It deserves a more lenient standard – which the classification as a part of the duty of loyalty is supposed to guarantee. It allows the company and its directors to avoid liability by showing that they put a viable compliance system in place. The Commission's approach was right to follow a similar path because the civil liablity under Article 29 is primarily concerned with insufficient oversight over others, too. It is deplorable that the sound justification for mitigating the liability risk akin to the business judgment rule has been overlooked by the other parties of the Trilogue.

[C] The Restrictions in Article 29 CSDDD (as Proposed by the Council)

The Council did not subscribe to Article 22(2) of the Commission draft, but proposed three different ways to restrict the liability risk. Unfortunately, none of them seems fit for purpose.

[1] Article 29(1)(b) Sentence 2: 'A Company Cannot Be Held Liable If the Damage Was Caused Only by Its Business Partners in Its Chain of Activities'

This sentence was inserted in the Council proposal. The law only targets damages that could be avoided.[48] But that is self-evident. There is no tort law in Europa (or anywhere) holding someone liable who did not cause the damage. That being so, this sentence is both superfluous and inept to restrict liability. If anything, it could serve as a reminder that there can be no liability in the case of the *omnimodo facturus*, that is: If the business partner is prepared to commit violations of human rights anyway, a failure of the duty of oversight (e.g., not to have inserted human rights covenants) will not be causative and cannot lead to liability. But the requirement of causation cannot restrict the attribution any further.[49]

However, it is a rule of interpretation in many laws that the text of a provision must not be interpreted in a way that would render the provision basically useless. Therefore, an argument could be made that liability can also be restricted if the damage was caused 'almost only', i.e., *predominantly* by the business partner. This would translate into an actual restriction instead of a self-evident statement of existing law, as must surely have been intended by the Council when inserting this sentence. But would it produce

48. With a view to the loid de vigilance, *see* Barsan, *supra* n. 3, at 45.
49. The situation is more difficult in France because the causal link must be direct, cf. Iris Barsan, *supra* n. 3, at 45 et seq. This corresponds with general tort law and was emphasised by the Constitutional Council, C. Const. No. 2017-750 DC du 23 March 2017, at § 17. But at the end of the day, even direct causation can be established.

acceptable results? In the example of the textile factory case, it would probably have relieved Kik from liability. The grave violation of fire protection that caused the high number of fatalities was primarily to be blamed on the local business partner. In addition, it was alleged that the reason for the fire was arson in the context of a protection racket. If that was so, any failure of Kik's oversight would have been a minimal contributing factor in comparison to the gross misfeasance and crimes of the other. Under an interpretation that 'only' means 'almost only', Kik may well have escaped liability. Such an outcome seems hard to reconcile with the aim of Article 29 CSDDD.

[2] *The Restriction of Damages for the Violation of 'Protected Interests' in Article 29(1) CSDDD*

Taken in context, the protected interest restrictions under Article 29(1) read as follows:

> 'Member States shall ensure that a company can be held liable for a damage caused to a natural or legal person, provided that ... the right, prohibition or obligation listed in the Annex of this Directive is aimed to protect the natural or legal person ... and a damage to the natural or legal person's legal interest protected under national law was caused.'

These restrictions are useless. This will be demonstrated by reference to the German tort law that apparently inspired it. But before that, it should be observed that the provision contains a strange twist. First, it requires that the *human rights law* under the Annex protects the natural or legal person, but then it requires that the natural or legal person's legal interests are protected under *national law*. That seems to imply that damages claims based on violations of human rights that are aimed to protect a person may still be barred if the interest of that person is not recognised by national law. It might follow that any violation of ILO-rules demanding fair wages could be irrelevant if a national tort law does not compensate pure economic losses. Apart from the fact that this would allow the Member States to outflank human rights protected by the Directive and drive a coach and horses through the harmonisation purpose, it would not even work, at least not under German law that may well be regarded as the spiritual mother of this restriction.

The great natural law codifications of France (Code Civil) and Austria (ABGB) both contained a general tort claim that compensates for pure economic loss caused intentionally or negligently. The underlying principle was '*neminem laedere*'. A century later, the German BGB rejected that concept of tort law. It deemed pure economic loss as an insufficient basis to claim damages because it would give rise to too many claims. The example used in German lectures is the accident on the motorway causing a huge traffic jam causing innumerable economic losses to the people caught in the jam who, e.g., miss their holiday flights, prebooked trains, work, etc. Another fitting example would be the recent destruction of the Key Bridge by the cargo ship 'Dali' and the subsequent closure of Baltimore harbour. German law only wants to compensate the direct victims of the accident who suffered injuries or damages to their personal property.[50] In order to achieve this, Germany established a threefold system of basic tort claims: *Rechtsgutsverletzung* (§ 823 I BGB), *Schutzgesetzverletzung* (§ 823 II BGB) or *Vorsätzliche sittenwidrige Schädigung* (§ 826 BGB).

The restriction in Article 29(1) CSDDD seems to pick up the German notion of banning damages for pure economic loss. But this does not work for the CSDDD, as can be shown by reference to German tort law where damages are granted if:

- a natural or legal person's life, body, health, freedom, property or any other (comparable) right was violated intentionally or negligently (§ 823 I BGB, *Rechtsgutsverletzung*);
- a law purporting to protect another was violated (§ 823 II BGB, *Schutzgesetzverletzung*);[51]
- damage was done to another intentionally and unconscionably.

Under this system, the main cases for compensation are the *Rechtsgutsverletzungen* under § 823 I BGB. Such violations doubtlessly qualify as the natural or legal person's interest protected by national law (e.g., health and property of the victims of the accident). However, compensation for pure economic loss is not excluded completely. It is only restricted to the cases of § 823 II and § 826 BGB. That is why personal wealth also qualifies as a (partially) protected interest under German law. Pure economic loss will be compensated in cases of intent and unconscionability (§ 826 BGB). And it will be compensated if it results from the violation of a law purporting to protect another's wealth (§ 823 II BGB).[52] To demonstrate that latter requirement: if the accident was caused by speeding in violation of a speed limit, a law purporting to protect others was violated. However, the speed limit only purports to protect the health and property of the victims, not the financial interests of the people in the traffic jam. By contrast, fraud (*Betrug*) under § 263 *Strafgesetzbuch* / StGB or embezzlement (*Untreue*) under § 266 StGB are laws purporting to protect the wealth of others. If their violation causes damage to another, compensation can be demanded by that other even though it is a pure economic loss. Insofar as the human rights laws of the Annex protect pure economic interests of natural or legal persons (like, e.g., all fair wage laws of the ILO), they will be qualified as a *Schutzgesetz* in the sense of § 823 II BGB. As a result, the pure economic loss resulting from the violation will be a protected interest under German law and compensation will be awarded. This is why the restriction in Article 29(1) CSDDD is of no consequence.

---

50. An alternative way to achieve this outcome is the requirement of direct causal link under French law, *see supra* n. 34. But this way is fraught with the difficulty that we will very often have longer chains of causation (e.g., product liability) that must nevertheless lead to a liability of the originator (e.g., the manufacturer). Whatever solution is found, it will necessarily militate against the directness requirement.
51. *See* already above, text with (*supra*) n. 11. Note that even if the violation of the law did not require default, damages could only be claimed if it happened intentionally or negligently according to § 823 II BGB.
52. *See also* Barsan, *supra* n. 3, at 46.

[3] The Prohibition of Overcompensation under Article 29(2) CSDDD

Finally, the prohibition of overcompensation under Article 29(2) CSDDD is superfluous. It is a self-evident principle of European private laws that is closely connected with the prohibition of unjust enrichment (*schadensrechtliches Bereicherungsverbot*). The European regulator did not have to enshrine it. On the contrary, if Member States, maybe induced by findings of Law and Economics literature, feel the need to introduce US-style punitive damages in their national jurisdictions, it would be an unbearable discrimination to exclude the victims of human rights violations. Let us listen to Gerhard Wagner:[53]

> There is no European legislation specifically authorizing courts to award punitive damages. However, where a particular national legal system acknowledges the deterrence function of damages and allows for supra-compensatory remedies, it must not discriminate between breaches of national law and European Union law. Therefore, the European Court of Justice (ECJ) has held that it is the duty of the English courts to award exemplary damages in cases involving the liability of the state for a breach of EU law, as long as they would also order the same damages if national law had been breached (ECJ Joined Cases C-46/93 and C-48/93 – *Brasserie du pêcheuer and Factortame III* [1996] ECR I-1029 paragraph 90 f).

§3.05 ARE ALTERNATIVE RESTRICTIONS OF DAMAGES POSSIBLE ('SERIOUS HARM')?

The analysis has shown that the only effective restriction of damages claims under Article 22 CSDDD would have been the safe harbour proposed by the Commission but rejected by the other parties of the Trilogue. By contrast, the restrictions put in place following the Council proposal have no consequences. Moreover, by explicitly determining the liability standard 'intentionally or negligently' in Article 22(1)(a), the Council barred any option for reduction, e.g., by subjecting the human rights due diligence to the good faith standard of the American duty of oversight (above §3.04[A]). That leaves open the question of whether alternative ways to restrict the potential liability risks are available.

One way might be the application of the 'Business Judgement Rule' (BJR). This rule aims to protect directors from liability for business judgments. It cannot normally be used to protect businesses from liability towards third parties. But it might be applied to specify the standard of 'negligence' in this context, always bearing in mind that it is the directors and officers who have to run the compliance management and make the relevant decisions and that the business decisions of these persons *are* protected by the BJR. Moreover, the liability of the company will normally be passed on – at least in part – to the managers under their directors' duties.[54] However, it should

53. Gerhard Wagner, *Punitive Damages*, Max-EuP 2012, https://max-eup2012.mpipriv.de/index.php/Punitive_Damages.
54. *See also* Barsan, *supra* n. 3, at 47 et seq.; Jan Lieder & Sarah Meyer, *Supply Chain Act and Liability under German Law*, 55 ECCL, at 70 et seq. (2023).

also be noted that in the context of corporate compliance/the duty of oversight by the directors, the majority of German legal writers reject the application of the business judgment rule because the issues at stake are *legal judgments* that allow for less leeway.[55]

In my opinion, it would be appropriate to restrict liability under Article 29 CSDDD to severe cases of human rights violations, like what happened in the textile factories of Karachi and Rana Plaza, in the chemical plant in Bhopal or in the Niger Delta. This is in line with the *loi de vigilance* that only targets serious harms under Article L. 225-102-4 C.com. ('*les atteintes graves envers les droits humains et les libertés*').[56] As it happens, I have presented a liability provision of such limited scope during the discussions on the German *Lieferkettengesetz* that will be attached in the Annex. I think that this restrictive proposal would be a fairer and more balanced approach to creating a tort liability under Article 29 CSDDD. European Courts need not be called for every other workplace accident, tragic as it always will be for every victim. They need to provide justice in cases where the victims lack access at home and where this situation is unbearable. It might be argued that the wording Article 29 CSDDD does not contain leeway to reduce civil liability to severe cases. But I beg to disagree. The wording is only the starting point of interpretation, not the final stop. The purpose of the Ruggie Principles has never been to erect international tort law or labour law courts to enforce Western health and safety standards or to pave a broad way to distant but deep pockets for the crimes of Southern delinquents. The 'best efforts' duty shall initiate changes from within to improve the human rights situation in the Global South. To achieve this, enforcement of human rights due diligence by public supervisory bodies like the German BAFA is sufficient. Civil liability is a far bigger burden and exposes enterprises to unpredictable risks. The principle of proportionality demands that this is applied restrictively in the sense of an *ultima ratio*. These teleological arguments are supported by the explanations in Recital 19 as well as by the visible but failed attempt of the European regulator to insert meaningful restrictions.

§3.06 CONCLUSION

Article 29 CSDDD obliges Member States to introduce a civil liability for violations of the human rights due diligence required by Articles 10 and 11 CSDDD. This liability will be based on the violation of a 'best efforts duty' – which is currently only known to contract law but alien to tort law. Moreover, the liability will exceed the traditional scope of tort liability under both civil law and common law because it will establish a duty to supervise independent third parties merely on the basis of contractual relations at arm's length. This is at odds with basic principles of tort law that have been established over centuries in the European legal tradition.

55. For an account *see, e.g.*, Alexander Schall, *„Compliance-Pflicht als Loyalitätspflicht – weist Delaware einen Weg zur Haftungsbegrenzung ohne Übernahme des arbeitsrechtlichen Haftungsprivilegs?* in *Festschrift für Eberhard Vetter* 659 (Barbara Grunewald, Jens Koch & Jörgen Thielmann eds, 2019).

56. Barsan, *supra* n. 3, at 45.

The European regulator was aware of that. To counter-balance the extension, the Commission proposed a safe harbour. But this proposal was rejected in the course of the Trilogue because neither the Council nor the European Parliament warmed to it.[57] It is now expressly prohibited under Article 29(3) CSDDD. However, the alternative restrictions proposed by the Council have proven to be of no consequence after the foregoing analysis (§3.04[B]). This is the main criticism directed at Article 29 CSDDD. The answer therefore has to be a restrictive interpretation that civil liability only needs to cover severe cases (§3.05). This corresponds with the current law in France under the *loi de vigilance* where the *plan de vigilance* must only address the prevention of serious human rights violations (‘*atteintes graves envers les droits humains*’).

The Parliament-driven Article 29(3) CSDDD is overstepping the competences of the Union by far (§3.03[C]). With the notable exception of Article 29(3)(c), none of the rules is proportionate nor even necessary to secure effective implementation of the civil liability by states that belong to – and are legally obliged to – the EU and its values.[58] The Parliament did not only act like the central legislator of a federal state that it is not. It also acted as a bad legislator because it proposed a completely one-sided set of rules for the benefit of the victims without even testing their necessity – that is lacking throughout, as has been shown.

Finally, Article 29(7) CSDDD is dangerous (§3.03[B]).[59] The aim of making the civil liability under Article 29 CSDDD applicable under the conflict rules of the Rome II Regulation is important. But it can only be achieved in a solid manner via amending that Regulation. For the benefit of the victims of human rights violations, the previous choice between the law of the country ‘in which the damage occurs’ (*lex loci damni, Erfolgsortprinzip*) and law of the country ‘in which the event giving rise to the damage occurred’ (*lex loci actus, Tatortprinzip*) must be re-introduced, ideally by extending Article 7 Rome II Regulation form environmental damages to all human rights violations.

To sum up, even if one shares the view (as I do) that human rights violations by subsidiaries should give rise to damages claims by the parent companies at home (*Shell Nigeria*) and that no one should cynically benefit from severe human rights violations of business partners in the Global South, it is inevitable to conclude after thorough analysis: Article 29 CSDDD is to a large extent lopsided, unbalanced and drafted without sufficient consideration of the proportionality vis-à-vis Member States as well as enterprises and their officers. It should not have become law,[60] but since it did, it is

57. Also critical Lennarts, *supra* n. 2, at 260.
58. For a more positive view, *see* however Lennarts, *supra* n. 1, at 266.
59. Also critical Lennarts, *supra* n. 1, at 263 et seq.
60. In the same direction Harm-Jan de Kluiver, *Towards a Framework for Effective Regulatory Supervision of Sustainability Governance in Accordance with the EU CSDD Directive. A Comparative Study*, ECFR 201, at 211 et seq. (2023), with following heading 4: ‘The CSDDD Is in Need of a Strong Policy Framework and Effective Policy Instruments. Liability Rules are not that Instrument’; In the opposite direction, favoring strong civil liability of enterprises *see, e.g.*, Lennarts, *supra* n. 3, at 257; also Alessio Pacces, *Civil Liability in the EU Corporate Sustainability Due Diligence Directive Proposal: A Law & Economics Analysis*, ECGI Law Working Paper No. 691/2023, March 2023. But Pacces introduces his conclusion with the sentence: ‘Corporations have been using limited liability to avoid tort liability and externalise damages to society, as

best interpreted in a restrictive way that is reduced to violations that cause serious harm (*'atteints graves'*). It could be implemented into national laws by a provision like that in the Annex.

ANNEXE: PROPOSAL FOR A § 823A BGB IMPLEMENTING ARTICLE 29 CSDDD

(1) Ein Unternehmer (§ 14), der im Rahmen seiner internationalen Geschäftstätigkeit eine **bewusste und schwerwiegende Missachtung der international anerkannten Menschenrechte (Menschenrechtsverletzung)** verschuldet, haftet den Opfern auf Ersatz des daraus entstehenden Schadens.

(2) Die gleiche Verpflichtung trifft den Unternehmer, wenn im Rahmen seiner internationalen Geschäftstätigkeit ein abhängiges Unternehmen (§§ 16, 17 AktG) / beherrschtes Unternehmen (§ 17 AktG) / abhängiges Konzernunternehmen (§ 18 Abs. 1 AktG) eine Menschenrechtsverletzung verschuldet. Die Ersatzpflicht tritt nicht ein, wenn der Unternehmer seine menschenrechtliche Sorgfaltspflicht gewahrt hat, indem er die abhängigen Unternehmen zur Wahrung der Menschenrechte verpflichtet, die Einhaltung angemessen überwacht und etwaigen Verstößen unverzüglich abgeholfen hat.

(3) Abhängigen Unternehmen i.S. des Absatz 2 stehen Unternehmen gleich, die vom Unternehmer in der Weise wirtschaftlich abhängig sind, dass er ihnen seinen Willen aufzwingen kann, sofern sie die Menschenrechtsverletzung im Zusammenhang mit der geschäftlichen Beziehung zum Unternehmer verschulden.

(4) Ein Unternehmer haftet den Opfern einer Menschenrechtsverletzung, die durch einen Dritten begangen wird, auf Ersatz ihres Schadens, wenn er im Sinne des § 830 mit dem Dritten zusammengewirkt hat oder wenn er wusste oder wissen musste, dass der Dritte die Menschenrechtsverletzung im Zusammenhang mit den gemeinsamen Geschäftsbeziehungen begangen hat und er dadurch in nicht unerheblichem Maße profitiert hat.

Translation by Deep-L

(1) An entrepreneur (Section 14) who is responsible for a deliberate and serious violation of internationally recognised human rights (human rights violation)

confirmed by economic theory and empirical evidence.' This suffers from a general bias against limited liablity. Law and economics literature imports this thesis into European law without recognising the different legal framework. For example under German law, unlike under US law, directors will be personally held liable for violations of the duty of care of their corporations, *see* BGHZ 107, 297; Andreas Diekmann, *30 Jahre 'Baustoff-Entscheidung' und ihre Relevanz für die Organaußenhaftung von heute*, ZGR 1039 (2020). Also, while I fully agree with liability for subsidiaries, why should enterprises have to 'internalise' the detrimental acts of independent third parties, contrary to legal rules that have existed for centuries.

in the course of his international business activities is liable to compensate the victims for the resulting damage.

(2) The same obligation applies to the entrepreneur if a dependent company (Sections 16, 17 AktG)/controlled company (Section 17 AktG) / dependent group company (Section 18 (1) AktG) is responsible for a human rights violation in the course of its international business activities. The obligation to pay compensation does not apply if the company has complied with its human rights due diligence obligations by obliging the dependent companies to respect human rights, monitoring compliance appropriately and remedying any violations without delay.

(3) Companies that are economically dependent on the business operator in such a way that the business operator can impose its will on them shall be deemed equivalent to dependent companies within the meaning of paragraph 2, provided that they are responsible for the human rights violation in connection with the business relationship with the business operator.

(4) An entrepreneur shall be liable to compensate the victims of a human rights violation committed by a third party for their damages if he has cooperated with the third party within the meaning of Section 830 or if he knew or should have known that the third party had committed the human rights violation in connection with the joint business relationship and that he had benefited from it to a not insignificant extent.

CHAPTER 4

EU Law under Construction: Sustainability, Stakeholders and the Relevance of Employee Consultation

Harm-Jan de Kluiver & Joti Roest

Stakeholder consultation is rapidly becoming a buzzword in recent EU legislation including the CSDDD. This concept is often described in rather broad terms and therefore it is left to companies how this can best be realised. In this chapter, we examine various ways to realise stakeholder consultation and how to arrange such consultation. We argue that even where stakeholder consultation is to be understood broadly, the consultative structures and whistleblowing mechanisms that are already available for workers' consultation can play a crucial role. Workers, whether employed by the company, its subsidiaries or its business partners, are often the first to become aware of potential adverse impacts in terms of sustainability, human rights or the environment and are the eyes and ears on the ground. Therefore, it is important to ensure that all workers in the chain of activities, not only those employed by the company but also by its subsidiaries and business partners, will have access to consultation platforms and at least be able to share relevant information with worker representatives. The European Works Council (EWC) offers an example in point of such a representative forum which can play a significant role in this regard. As the European Works Council Directive (EWC Directive) is currently under review, this is a good time to make necessary changes to reflect the above. Some examples of national law are discussed to illustrate potential amendments which could be made to the Directive. Perhaps the most important takeaway from our analysis is that workers are not only a vital category of stakeholders in their own right but also can play a crucial role through already existing mechanisms and platforms in ensuring that human and environmental rights of others are respected.

§4.01 INTRODUCTION

Sustainable long-term value creation has become a key term in corporate circles nowadays. This is primarily an issue and a challenge for companies and their shareholders. However, actions by companies are almost by definition affecting related parties like employees, suppliers and customers as well as unrelated third parties, including communities where the company has set up production facilities, who sustain adverse environmental or social consequences of company actions. Generally, this wide group is denoted *as 'stakeholders'*. Parallel to the realisation that third parties are being affected by company actions, there is increasingly the notion that such stakeholders also in some way should have a say, or at least should be heard, when the policies of companies are being determined.

However, even if one subscribes to the abstract idea of consulting stakeholders, it is not easy to put this idea into practice. How should the company identify its stakeholders and how should those stakeholders be consulted? The sheer number of stakeholders makes it impossible to consult with all of them in person. This may mean that generally consultation partners will be representative organisations. But by what criteria should the company decide which persons or organisations can be deemed representative and is this really the best approach to get a clear picture of the interests of the various stakeholders?

Above we already referred to employees as an important segment of stakeholders. In relation to engaging with employees, the organisational challenges are easier to overcome. First, they can be more easily identified as there will be a formal relationship with the company, its subsidiaries, or suppliers.[1] Second, in many countries, structures have been developed and institutionalised that facilitate consultation of employees in works councils and the like which bodies are in a position to influence corporate policies. Hereafter, we will explore whether and to what extent one can draw on the rules, structures and traditions related to workers' involvement to bring stakeholder concerns to the fore and improve due diligence policies and practices and thereby minimise human rights violations and environmental adverse impacts.

1. Of course we acknowledge that employees of suppliers do not have a direct relationship with the group and/or group companies which are being supplied, and therefore under current law are not represented in consultative bodies such as a European Works Council (*see hereafter* 'paragraph 11'). Having said that however, workers of suppliers certainly may qualify as identifiable stakeholders for group companies that are being supplied and may be very important in identifying violations of human rights and/or the environment for example through whistleblowing mechanisms (*see infra* §4.05).

§4.02 CATEGORIES OF 'STAKEHOLDERS' DISTINGUISHED

In an increasing number of corporate law instruments, stakeholders are being referred to as a relevant category that should be included in corporate decision-making. At the same time, it is far from clear who actually are deemed to be stakeholders. This is further complicated by the various fundamentally different categories of stakeholders that can be distinguished and the aims that stakeholder consultation is supposed to achieve. A distinction can be made along the lines of legal or factual proximity to the company. In view of the latter, relevant elements may be whether there is a specific legal duty of the company towards the stakeholders or whether from a legal point of view the legal position is more open.

The first category of stakeholders are the employees of a company, which we understand broadly and for our purposes; it also includes employees of group companies and other companies that are closely related to the company in question (e.g., established suppliers). In general, one could say that employees, both in physical and legal terms, work in proximity to the company. They tend to work at sites owned by the company, live near its premises and have close legal ties in terms of an employment contract with the companies. However, there may also be considerable differences. The person that only works for a company on a temporary basis on a digital assignment from home will likely experience a greater distance to the company than the person who is not an employee of the company but happens to live near its premises and experiences hindrance caused by the company. In Part. II of this paper, we will focus on whether and how these differences between the various categories of employees are taken into account and which lessons may be drawn from that. Clearly, employees may also fall into various categories, e.g., if they live near company operations and sustain hindrance of such operations.

The second category of stakeholders with a clear (factual) proximity to the company is local residents living in the vicinity of its production and/or other facilities. Although there is no legal relation with the company, they may be directly affected by the company, for example, if the company releases hazardous substances or causes noise or other hindrances or facilitates such hindrance. An example is to set up a consultative council to be consulted by a company that operates an airport. Since 1 July 2023, Amsterdam Schiphol Airport has established such a body consisting of and elected by local residents, representatives of organisations and experts.[2] In this category, one could also think of plans to develop new production facilities or close existing ones (which may also include the transfer of operations to other locations in the EU or abroad).

The *third category of stakeholders* is customers of the company. They may not be affected by the operation of the company as such, but may experience detrimental effects caused by the products of the company. In principle, they may rely on their legal position as a contracting party of the company – and the ensuing contractual claims –

2. *See* https://maatschappelijkeraadschiphol.nl. This council does not have formal decision powers but may advise the company and the relevant ministry of infrastructure. The minister is bound to at least respond if advice is rendered.

and the relatively well-developed principles of product liability. Over the last few years, there have been many examples to choose from, but from a sustainability perspective, maybe the 'Dieselgate' claims against German automakers (including Volkswagen and Mercedes) stand out the most.

The fourth category of stakeholders is the wider group of persons that are affected by company operations without being in proximity to the company. One may think of situations in which actions by the company only cause a negative effect at a distance from the company operations. An example is pollution of a river which only affects the environment at downstream locations many miles away. Another example is the disproportionate emission of CO_2, methane or other greenhouse gasses which may have consequences in places far from business locations. In relation to this category, it will generally not be possible to organise direct consultation. In this case, there may be a role to play for non-governmental organisations that focus on protecting human rights and the environment.

The *fifth category of stakeholders,* which may overlap with the other categories, may be distinguished as the category of persons affected by company actions or of its subsidiaries or suppliers, which qualify as *a violation of human rights.* Clear examples are child labour, forced labour in general and evidently unsafe and/or unhealthy working conditions. Other examples include causing pollution which substantially affects the life of people in certain regions like farmers whose lands are being polluted by oil spills from pipelines, as was the case in the well-known *Shell Nigeria* case. In the literature, the latter category is frequently referred to as *'right holders'* with the implication that their position is of a special nature compared to other categories of stakeholders (who may be confronted with adverse effects which do not amount to violations of human rights).[3] Legal cases in relation to this category tend to receive quite some attention from lawyers as well as from the general public. Apart from the *Shell Nigeria* case, well-known examples are the *Kalina and Lokono People v. Suriname* case[4] and the decision of the Columbia Constitutional Court regarding the claim of a local Awá community in view of oil and gas exploration on their stewarded lands.[5] *See also* the case decided by the Constitutional Court of South Africa in *Occupiers of 51 Olivia Road v. Johannesburg.* In this case, the court ruled that the occupiers and the municipality were expected to enter into a meaningful dialogue to resolve the situation.[6]

---

3. This raises the pertinent question when adverse effects do or do not amount to human rights violations. Sometimes one may get the impression that all adverse effects are deemed human rights violations if such violations are not covered by other legal doctrines (like tort law).
4. IACTHR (2015) Series C, No 309 and *inter alia,* Fergus MacKay, *The Case of the Kaliña and Lokono Peoples v. Suriname and the UN Declaration on the Rights of Indigenous Peoples: Convergence, Divergence and Mutual Reinforcement,* Erasmus Law Review April, 1 (2018).
5. Decision SU-123/18 re the claim of the Awá community "La Cabaña" in view of oil and gas exploration and mandatory prior consultation with indigenous communities in their stewarded lands. *See*: Report of Constitutional Court of Columbia, *Notable Judgements on vulnerable and disadvantaged groups* (2021), www.corteconstitucional.gov.co/english/.
6. [2008] ZACC 1:2008. *See, inter alia,* Gustav Muller, *Conceptualising 'Meaningful Engagement' as a Deliberative Democratic Partnership,* Stellenbosch Law Review 22, 3, (2011), 742-758.

In this chapter, we will not analyse and elaborate on these categories and the associated cases further. For what we aim to discuss in this article, it suffices to illustrate that when discussing consultation of stakeholders, there are a variety of categories of stakeholders with different characteristics. All these categories call for a different approach to organizing stakeholder engagement and dialogue. The choice of the instruments may also depend on the objectives of stakeholder consultation.

§4.03 OBJECTIVES OF STAKEHOLDER ENGAGEMENT AND CONSULTATION

Parallel to the categories of stakeholders distinguished above, a relevant question may be what consultation of stakeholders actually aims to achieve.

In the first and second categories distinguished above, the aim of consultation will ideally be to be informed about the negative impacts of company operations and concerns workers and residents may have in that respect. Subsequently, it will be on the company to explain which options it may develop to alleviate such concerns and explain to workers and/or residents what may and may not be feasible. This may take the form of an ongoing and structured consultation, including meetings with (representatives of) workers and residents.

In relation to the third category, customers, the aim will be to become aware of customer satisfaction on the one hand and, on the other hand, make sure that products do not and will not have adverse negative effects. The first aim (information on customer satisfaction) will relate to a vast group and will generally have to rely on surveys, etc. The second objective (product safety) will generally not be something to be assessed by customers, but it will need input from experts. Setting up a structure to facilitate a dialogue with customers will generally not be possible or feasible as customers will generally meet the company in a one-off situation and may be spread all over the globe. If products do have adverse effects, this will generally lead to legal (class) actions led by consumer organisations and legal action. In the previous paragraph, we noted, as an example, the 'Dieselgate' matter.

The fourth and fifth categories seem to have taken front and centre over the last few years and may count on wide public interest. This has strongly been reinforced by fairly recent EU initiatives such as the Company Sustainable Reporting Directive (CSRD)[7] which came into effect on 5 January 2023, and the draft Corporate Sustainability Due Diligence Directive (CSDDD).[8] We will discuss these instruments in the next paragraph. For now, we note that in respect of these categories, it is crucial that the company will be informed of (potential) violations of human rights and (potential) environmental adverse impacts in its supply chain. In case of new projects, this will call for a fairly traditional due diligence effort, i.e., mapping all relevant aspects and

7. Directive (EU) 2022/2464 of the European Parliament and of the Council of 14 December 2022 amending Regulation (EU) No. 537/2014, Directive 2004/109/EC, Directive 2006/43/EC and Directive 2013/34/EU, as regards corporate sustainability reporting, OJ L 322, 16.12.2022.
8. Proposal for a Directive on Corporate Sustainability Due Diligence and amending Directive (EU) 2019/1937 (COM(2022) 71 final), 23.02.2022.

consequences of a new business operation including its economic, social, and environmental impact. As far as existing operations are concerned, one may probably have to rely more heavily on information provided by stakeholders.

§4.04 ENVISAGED STAKEHOLDER CONSULTATION IN THE PROPOSED EU CSDD DIRECTIVE AND THE ROLE OF EMPLOYEES

As is well known by now, the EU has embarked on an ambitious journey to promote sustainability in business. As set out in the so-called Green Deal, corporate sustainability is made the subject of two Directives which respectively relate to detailed reporting and due diligence obligations. As noted in the previous paragraph, the reporting obligations have been laid down in the Corporate Sustainability Reporting Directive (CSRD) EU 2022/2464 that is in force since 5 January 2023.[9] As far as due diligence obligations are concerned, the draft Corporate Sustainability Due Diligence Directive has been the subject of difficult negotiations between the EU Council of Ministers and the EU Parliament.[10] Only after several rounds of amended proposals, an agreement between representatives of both bodies was reached on 15 March 2024 which was approved by the EU Parliament (April 2024) and EU Council on 24 May 2024. The EU CSDDD proposal will add a new layer of due diligence obligations related to the operations of EU companies (and other companies in case of a turnover of EUR 450 million or more in the EU), its subsidiaries and specifically suppliers outside the EU if the number of workers employed exceeds 1000.

According to the March 2024 agreement,[11] the CSDDD anticipates intense consultations with stakeholders, specifically employees. Recital 39 and Article 7 (2) provide explicitly: 'The due diligence policy should be developed in prior consultation with the company's employees and their representatives.' And where Article 3(1)(n) CSDDD defines stakeholders, it is no coincidence that employees of the company but also of affected companies are put first: '"stakeholders" means the *company's employees, the employees of its subsidiaries, trade unions and workers' representatives,* consumers; and other individuals, groups, communities or entities whose rights or interests are or could be affected by the products, services and operations of that company, its subsidiaries and its business partners, *including the employees of the company's business partners, trade unions and workers' representatives*'. According to a new Article 13(1): 'Member States shall ensure [...] effective engagement with

9. Directive (EU) 2022/2464 of the European Parliament and of the Council of 14 December 2022 amending Regulation (EU) No 537/2014, Directive 2004/109/EC, Directive 2006/43/EC and Directive 2013/34/EU, as regards corporate sustainability reporting, OJ L 322/60, 16.12.2022.
10. *See further, inter alia*, with many more references to literature, Harm-Jan de Kluiver, *Towards a Framework for Effective Regulatory Supervision of Sustainable Governance in Accordance with the EU CSDDD Directive. A Comparative Study*, ECFR 20(1), (2023), 203-239.
11. *See* Proposal for a DIRECTIVE OF THE EUROPEAN PARLIAMENT AND OF THE COUNCIL on Corporate Sustainability Due Diligence and amending Directive (EU) 2019/1937 - Analysis of the final compromise text with a view to agreement dated 13 March 2024 no. 7327/1/24 Rev 1, a consolidated text was published 15 April 2024, https://www.europarl.europa.eu/doceo/document/A-9-2023-0184-AM-430-430_EN.pdf.

stakeholders, in accordance with this article and in all steps of the due diligence process including (3)(a) to gather the necessary information on actual or potential adverse impacts, [...]; (b) the development of prevention and corrective action plans [...]; (c) the decision to terminate or suspend a business relationship [...]; (d) the adoption of appropriate measures to remediate adverse impacts [...].' And in addition to the above, Recital 65 provides: 'effective engagement should cover providing consulted stakeholders with relevant and comprehensive information, as well as ongoing consultation that allows for genuine interaction and dialogue at the appropriate level, such as project or site level and with appropriate periodicity'.

§4.05 ON THE OVERRIDING IMPORTANCE OF EMPLOYEE CONSULTATION: WHISTLEBLOWING AS AN EXAMPLE

Although the position of distinguished stakeholder groups are quite different, the objectives of stakeholder engagement and consultation are pretty straightforward and unequivocal. The main objective, as illustrated in Article 8d, will always be to gather information about potential and actual negative impacts on human rights and the environment. In gathering such information, different tools may be used, depending on the characteristics of the various categories of stakeholders discussed above.

However, there is generally one group of stakeholders involved in one way or another, i.e., workers employed either by the company, its subsidiaries or its suppliers. All actions undertaken by these entities will either be instigated or at least witnessed by employees. They are also best placed to note whether adverse effects on human rights and environmental policies occur. An example in point goes back to the tragic Rana Plaza disaster which has played a significant role in devising stricter legislation and increased awareness of detrimental practices offered by the Bangladesh Accord for Fire and Building Safety between companies and trade unions to further a fair and safe textile industry. After the collapse of the Rana Plaza Building, this agreement has set out specific steps to prevent such disasters from happening again and improve working conditions in the textile industry. To oversee the efforts and monitor that the goals are being achieved, a steering committee is set up in which companies and *worker organisations* are represented *in equal numbers* and worker organisations have a crucial say in setting policies and deciding on measures to be taken.[12] Obviously, worker organisations will be able to rely on information they receive from employees all over the industry.

The Rana Plaza situation is, of course, not unique. In many, if not all situations, workers, either employed by the company, its subsidiaries or suppliers, will be involved or at least have knowledge of actions or situations which may be threatening human rights or the environment. In general, this will be the case in relation to all rules and regulations applicable to companies.

12. *See* https://internationalaccord.org/updates-overview/ for all information up to now as well as reports of its Secretariat. On 24 April 2023 the Rana Plaza disaster was officially commemorated by this organisation. *See* https://internationalaccord.org/10-years-rana-plaza-bangladesh-accord/.

This is exactly why, over the last twenty years, whistleblowing procedures have been promoted and have become mandatory in various EU Member States. In 2019, EU Directive 2019/1937[13] (as amended[14]) mandated that in all EU Member States, whistleblowing statutes will have to be introduced. The principal aim thereof (according to Article 1 of the Directive) is 'to enhance the enforcement of Union law' and 'policies in specific areas' which include product safety, consumer protection and protection of the environment.

According to Article 4, the Directive applies 'to persons working in the private or public sector who acquired information on breaches in a work-related context'. This definition includes persons with a 'self-employed status' and 'any persons working under the supervision and direction of contractors, subcontractors and suppliers' (Article 4(1)(b) and (d)) as well as (Article 4(4)) third persons who are connected with the reporting persons and who could suffer retaliation in a work-related context, such as colleagues or relatives of the reporting persons and legal entities that the reporting persons own, *work for or are otherwise connected within a work-related context.* Article 4(3) Directive extends the scope to persons whose work-based relationship is yet to begin in cases 'where information on breaches has been acquired during the recruitment process or other pre-contractual negotiations'. Every company (Article 8) will have to 'establish channels and procedures for internal reporting and for follow-up, following consultation and in agreement with the social partners where provided for by national law'.

If the CSDDD comes into force, *compliance with the CSDDD will fall under the scope of the Whistleblower Directive* as Article 32 of the CSDDD provides for an Amendment to that effect to the Directive (EU) 2019/1937. In Point E.2 of Part I of the Annex to Directive (EU) 2019/1937 ('Rules on the environment and climate'), the CSDDD will be explicitly designated as one of the statutory instruments which will be covered by the Whistleblower Directive. Although it is somewhat curious that in defining the material scope (Article 2 of Directive 2019/1937), the area of the protection of human rights is not mentioned, we think there is little doubt that also the CSDDD obligations to respect human rights are covered by the Directive.

§4.06 STAKEHOLDER CONSULTATION IN THE UN GUIDING PRINCIPLES ON BUSINESS AND HUMAN RIGHTS

The CSDDD can be regarded as a culmination point of the development of the due diligence concept introduced and elaborated in the UN Guiding Principles on Business

13. Directive (EU) 2019/1937 of the European Parliament and of the Council of 23 October 2019 on the protection of persons who report breaches of Union law, OJ L 305, 26.11.2019.
14. *See* Regulations EU 2020/1503 of 7 October, 2022/1925 of 14 September 2022 and 2024/573 Of 7 Februari 2024 and for the Consolidated version: www.eur-lex.europa.eu/legal-content/EN/TXT/HTML/?uri=CELEX:02019L1937-20240311.

and Human Rights (2011), hereafter 'UNGP',[15] and the OECD Guidelines for Multinational Enterprises on Responsible Business Conduct (most recently updated on 8 June 2023) hereafter 'OECD Guidelines'.

The UNGP Principle 18 requires, 'in order to gauge human rights risks', that business enterprises 'should identify and assess any actual or potential adverse human rights impacts with which they may be involved either through their own activities or as a result of their business relationships'. This assessment should: (a) 'draw on internal and/or independent external human rights expertise' and (b) '*involve meaningful consultation* with potentially affected groups and other relevant stakeholders, as *appropriate to the size of the business enterprise and the nature and context of the operation*' (italics added).

The Commentary to this Principle, as well as the UN Guiding Principles Reporting Framework,[16] underlines that an important aim of due diligence as envisaged by the UNGP should be 'to enable business enterprises to assess their human rights impacts accurately'. In order to achieve this, 'business enterprises should seek to understand the concerns of potentially affected stakeholders by consulting them directly in a manner that takes into account language and other potential barriers to effective engagement. In situations where such consultation is not possible, business enterprises should consider reasonable alternatives such as consulting credible, independent expert resources, including human rights defenders and others from civil society'.

The overriding goal that can be inferred from the commentary is that consultation of stakeholders is meant to obtain a better understanding of whether and which human rights may be at stake. In other words, a consultation is not primarily aiming to reach an agreement on how a company should conduct its business but to gather information on whether human rights might be infringed and therefore provide an opportunity to remediate the situation. In the Reporting Framework (p. 59), the 'supporting guidance' puts it even more strongly, noting that 'a key purpose of engagement with stakeholders is *to ensure a full understanding* of how the company's actions and decisions can affect individuals and groups'. As we already noted in paragraph 2 of this Chapter, this may include specific actions as well as more 'permanent arrangements' ('e.g., dialogue tables, stakeholder advisory councils, consultative groups').

UNGP Principle 16 provides that a company should embed its intentions in 'a statement of policy' that is 'reflected in operational policies and procedures'. In the Reporting Framework (2015) p. 57, it is explained that relevant information for the company to formulate such policies may come from 'any internal or external consultative processes' including 'who is expected to implement the policy/policies (e.g., employees, contractors, suppliers)' and 'whose human rights the policy/policies relate to (e.g., employees, contract workers, communities, consumers)'. Such implementation is obviously crucial in realizing the overriding goals of identifying, mitigating and terminating human rights violations.

---

15. *See* www.ohchr.org/sites/default/files/documents/publications/guidingprinciplesbusinesshr_en.pdf.
16. *See* www.ungpreporting.org.

That raises the question of who actually would be on the frontline to implement such policies. The Reporting Framework (2015) p. 58 is quite clear that an important role in this respect in any case is to be played by '*employees, contract workers,* suppliers, business customers, joint venture partners'. These parties will also be very important in assessing the effectiveness of the policies in mitigating human rights violations. By way of example, the UNGP Reporting Framework p. 65 refers to 'an engagement with a business partner to mitigate a risk of impacts *in light of feedback from employees*' or a decision 'not to proceed with a project based on inputs from communities and relevant experts'.

§4.07 THE (2023) OECD GUIDELINES AND THE (2018) OECD DUE DILIGENCE GUIDANCE

A relevant push for stakeholder consultation over the last 20 years has been given by the *OECD*. The most recent version of the *OECD Guidelines for Multinational Enterprises on Responsible Business Conduct (2023)*, hereafter 'OECD Guidelines', was adopted on 8 June 2023.[17] Chapter II of the OECD Guidelines emphasises the importance of respecting general policies applicable in the countries in which they operate but also to 'consider the views of other *stakeholders*' and '*engage meaningfully with relevant stakeholders* or their legitimate representatives' (sub A.15). The commentary explicitly refers to OECD Due Diligence Guidance for Responsible Business Conduct (2018) and summarises the OECD position on p. 20 (sub 28) where it reads:

> *Meaningful stakeholder engagement* is a key component of the due diligence process. In some cases, stakeholder engagement may also be a right in and of itself. Stakeholder engagement involves interactive processes of engagement with relevant stakeholders through, for example, meetings, hearings or consultation proceedings. Relevant stakeholders are persons or groups, or their legitimate representatives, who have rights or interests related to the matters covered by the Guidelines that are or could be affected by adverse impacts associated with the enterprise's operations, products or services. Enterprises can prioritise the most severely impacted or potentially impacted stakeholders for engagement. The degree of impact on stakeholders may inform the degree of engagement.

Meaningful stakeholder engagement refers to ongoing engagement with stakeholders that is a two way process conducted in good faith by the participants on both sides and responsive to stakeholders' views. To ensure that stakeholder engagement is meaningful and effective, it is important that it is timely, accessible, appropriate and safe for stakeholders to participate, as well as identify and remove potential barriers to engaging with stakeholders in positions of vulnerability or marginalisation. Moreover, it is emphasised that companies should provide 'the public, *workers, and other relevant stakeholders with adequate, measurable, verifiable [..] and timely information*' (p. 34).

17. *See* https://read.oecd-ilibrary.org/finance-and-investment/oecd-guidelines-for-multinational-enterprises-on-responsible-business-conduct_81f92357-en#page1.

These general notions in respect of stakeholder engagement are further elaborated on in the OECD Due Diligence Guidance for Responsible Business Conduct (2018)[18] which also underlines that companies should strive to realise 'meaningful stakeholder engagement'. On p. 18, it is stipulated that Due Diligence should be informed by engagement with stakeholders, i.e., 'persons or groups who have interests that could be affected by an enterprise's activities' including '*workers, workers' representatives, trade unions (including Global Unions)* community members, civil society organisations, investors and professional industry and trade associations'. Annex Q8 distinguishes between *impacted stakeholders (workers, communities, consumers)* and '*relevant stakeholders*' (NGOs, human rights defenders, business partners, governments, investors/shareholders). The Guidelines note that '*not all interests are of equal importance and it is not necessary to treat all stakeholders in the same way*. Where the interest is individual human rights or collective rights [...] the stakeholders whose human rights are or may be affected can be referred to as *"rightsholders"*'. In situations where these amount to a vast number, 'an enterprise may engage with credible stakeholder representatives'. 'Enterprises can prioritise the most severely impacted or potentially impacted stakeholders or rightsholders for engagement. The degree of impact on stakeholders or rightsholders may inform the degree of engagement.'

As indicated above, 'meaningful stakeholder engagement' is deemed a key component of the due diligence process (p. 50). What does 'meaningful stakeholder engagement' entail? Annex Q9 on p. 49 identifies as relevant elements that it is an '*interactive process*' ('through meetings, hearings or consultation proceedings'), 'two-way communication' (which presupposes to be able to 'freely express opinions', 'share perspectives' and 'listen to alternative viewpoints' as well as providing timely information needed by stakeholders 'to be able to make an informed decision' on 'possible adverse impacts') and 'good faith of the participants on both sides' (which should include a 'genuine intention to understand' and the enterprise being 'prepared to address adverse impacts' and that stakeholders 'honestly represent their interests, intentions and concerns'), 'responsive and on-going' and, in principle, 'before decisions have been made'. It also means that 'relevant stakeholders' have the opportunity to design engagement activities themselves' and that there is 'follow-through on implementation of agreed commitments'. For employees, stakeholder engagement or consultation may even be deemed closely related to the fundamental right to form or join trade unions and their right to bargain collectively. That is an additional argument why it '*is important to engage with trade unions or workers' representatives*' when engaging with workers on these issues. Moreover, it is noted that already in itself 'industrial relations is a form of stakeholder engagement'.

18. *See* www.oecd.org/daf/inv/mne/due-diligence-guidance-for-responsible-business-conduct.htm.

§4.08 REGULATION OF 'STAKEHOLDER CONSULTATION' ON THE NATIONAL LEVEL IN STATUTORY PROVISIONS

When compared to the non-binding instruments devised by international organisations discussed above, the role of stakeholder engagement and consultation on the national level, and the question of whether any duties for companies exist, becomes more blurred. As far as there is relevant regulation, the national approaches are formulated in general terms and are rather unspecific.

An example is the French *Loi de Vigilance*, Article L. 225-102-4.[19] The law requires French companies (of a certain size) to draw up a 'vigilance plan' which should include 'measures to allow for risk identification and for the prevention of severe violations of human rights and fundamental freedoms, serious bodily injury or environmental damage or health risks'. The statutory provision holds that the plan shall be drafted '*in association with the company stakeholders* involved, and where appropriate, within multiparty initiatives that exist in the subsidiaries or at territorial level'. However, no further guidelines are provided on how that 'involvement of stakeholders' should be organised and what it actually would entail. A notable exception is that some form of 'alert mechanism' should be developed 'in *working partnership with the trade union* organizations representatives'. In light of our earlier analysis, this once again underlines that when discussing the role of stakeholders, *workers/employees actually play a much more important role* than sometimes is anticipated.

Also, the probably most detailed human rights/environmental due diligence Act to date, the German *Lieferkettensorgfaltspflichtengesetz*, does not explicitly provide for a mechanism of stakeholder consultation.[20] What it does provide for – in section 11 of the German Act – is that any person claiming to have been violated in a legal position pursuant to section 2(1) of that Act 'may authorise a *domestic trade union or non-governmental organisation* to bring proceedings to enforce his or her rights in its own capacity' provided the trade union or non-governmental organisation maintains a permanent presence of its own and is not engaged commercially and not only temporarily in the realisation of human rights or corresponding rights in the national law of a state. However, this role in proceedings on behalf of stakeholders obviously is very different from stakeholders being *consulted prior* to the development of business policies.

Even the far-reaching Proposal for a Dutch Act on responsible business conduct,[21] although acknowledging the relevance of stakeholder consultation (Article 2.2.1), only requires companies to draw up *a policy document* in which it commits to due diligence obligations set out in the draft Bill and the OECD Guidelines for multinational companies, '*in consultation with, in any case, stakeholders*, experts and business relations'. Stakeholders also should be consulted when prioritising which

19. Loi relative au devoir de vigilance des sociétés mères et des entreprises donneuses d'ordre, www.legifrance.gouv.fr/jorf/id/JORFTEXT000034290626/.
20. www.gesetze-im-internet.de/lksg/.
21. *See* Dutch parliamentary papers: *Kamerstukken II* 2022/23, 35 761 no. 9.

situations should be addressed in which order (Article 2.3.1(4)(b)). How this consultation should take place is, however, not addressed. The parliamentary papers (no. 10 p. 21) only note it should be 'meaningful' ('betekenisvol') and that consultation could take place in round table meetings, symposia or expert meetings (p. 72). As far as monitoring of its policy is concerned, it is mentioned that consultation may take place through meetings or surveys (p. 86). Again, it is interesting that in defining the principal stakeholders (Article 1.1(b)) *employees explicitly* are named as such. And in mapping (potential) adverse effects on human rights and the environment, the company is explicitly expected to take account of information provided by 'representatives of employees' and 'trade-unions' (Article 2.3.1 (c)).

All in all, we may conclude that the level of regulation of 'stakeholder engagement' and 'stakeholder consultation' in national (binding) statutory law in relation to human rights and adverse environmental impacts is limited. Where statutory provisions have been enacted, such provisions are very general in nature and mainly indicate that companies are expected to develop policies in relation thereto which basically echo the OECD Guidance discussed above. Of course, this is not surprising. It is one thing to set out broad obligations in a *non-binding instrument* and something else to enshrine such obligations in *binding legislation*. Therefore, it might be interesting to see how ideas around stakeholder engagement and consultation have fared in other non-binding instruments, such as national corporate governance codes.

§4.09 REGULATION IN NATIONAL CORPORATE GOVERNANCE CODES

Where statutory binding law, understandably, does not provide much guidance in relation to stakeholder engagement and stakeholder consultation, another layer of regulation which may shed light on what stakeholder engagement and consultation may entail is constituted by national governance codes. These codes have over time come to include much broader notions of sustainability and the role of and responsibility vis-à-vis stakeholders. Specifically, after the 2008 financial crisis, the code movement has gained momentum in this respect. After a short wave of documents which were dubbed 'Stewardship Codes',[22] the attention has shifted to growing concerns in respect of sustainability, ESG and climate change in particular, and the importance of integrating this in business strategies and policies. This is reflected in many national corporate governance codes.

An example is offered by the Dutch Corporate Governance Code. In the first 2003 version of that Code, the key principle was that the management board was responsible 'for achieving the company's aims, strategy and policy, and results'. The board was expected to also consider 'the interests of the company's stakeholders' (provision II.1), but the emphasis was on compliance, risk management, etc. According to its most

22. *See* Harm-Jan de Kluiver, *An unresolved issue: the role and responsibility of institutional investors in view of ESG matters in corporate governance and stewardship codes, in: De beursvennootschap en de institutionele belegger: naar een nieuwe balans*, 21-54 (Rients Abma et al. eds, 2023).

recent revision, the Dutch Corporate Governance Code in 2022,[23] the basic principle has become '*sustainable* long-term value creation' (principle 1.1 and provision 1.1.1), and to achieve this, the company should take into account (principle 1.1) 'the impact the actions of the company and its affiliated enterprise have on people and the environment and *to that end weighs the stakeholder interests* that are relevant in this context'. Code provision 1.1.5 prescribes that 'to ensure that *the interests of the relevant stakeholders* of the company are considered', the company should draw up a 'policy for effective dialogue with those *stakeholders*'. The company should publish the policy on its website. 'Subsequently, the company (Provision 1.1.4 of the *Dutch Code*) is expected to report 'how the interests of stakeholders have been considered'. For our current purposes, it is important to note that the Explanatory Notes to the Dutch Code emphasise that the 'consultation policy' in any case should describe how '*the company's employee participation body forms part of this* [stakeholder; HJdK/JR] *dialogue* and how this relates to the other *consultations between the management board, the supervisory board and the employee participation body'*. Once again, this emphasises the special position of employees and employee participation when discussing stakeholder consultation.

Although the Dutch Code still leaves open many questions on how employee engagement and consultation in practice may be designed, almost all corporate governance codes in EU Member States do even give less guidance than the Dutch Code. The Danish and Spanish Corporate Governance Codes are, apart from the Dutch Code, probably the most extensive in addressing the importance and the aim of stakeholder engagement and stakeholder consultation. The *Danish Code,* officially Recommendations on Corporate Governance (2020),[24] underlines that it is 'important that the *interaction* between management and shareholders, as well as with the company's investors *and other stakeholders, including society, is well-functioning*'. In this respect, it recommends 'openness and transparency' (1.1.1) through 'ongoing dialogue and interaction ensures' with the aim that also 'stakeholders' gain the 'relevant insight into the company's affairs' and that the board has the 'possibility of hearing and including their views'. How this should be achieved is left (*see* 1.1.2) to the company which should, however, adopt '*policies on the company's relationships* with its shareholders, investors and *if relevant other stakeholders*' to ensure that 'the various interests are included in the company's considerations'. In the *Spanish Corporate Governance Code (2020)*,[25] recommendation 12 in Chapter III.3 notes that 'in pursuing the corporate interest', the company should 'strive to reconcile its own interests with the legitimate interests of *its employees*, suppliers, clients and *other stakeholders*, as well as with the impact of its activities *on the broader community* and the natural environment'. Recommendation 54 sub c expects that the board is 'catering, as appropriate, to the legitimate interests of remaining stakeholders'. Recommendation 55 under d refers in that respect to the importance of '*channels for stakeholder*

23. *See* www.mccg.nl/publicaties/codes/2022/12/20/corporate-governance-code-2022.
24. *See* https://corporategovernance.dk/sites/default/files/2023-08/Danish-recommendations-corporate-governance-02122020.pdf.
25. *See* www.cnmv.es/DocPortal/Publicaciones/CodigoGov/CBG_2020_ENen.PDF.

communication, participation and dialogue'. How such channels would look is, however, not elaborated in the *Spanish Code*.

Other national corporate governance codes are even less specific on whether and what is expected in relation to stakeholder engagement and consultation. The *German Corporate Governance Code (2022)*[26] recommends in paragraph A.1 that the management board should 'systematically identify and assess the risks and opportunities associated with social and environmental factors, as well as the ecological and social impacts of the enterprise's activities' but the role of 'stakeholders' in general is not mentioned although employees are. According to Recommendation A.4: '*Employees* shall be given the opportunity to report, in a protected manner, suspected breaches of the law within the enterprise.' Although 'third parties should also be given this opportunity', it is telling that only employees are explicitly mentioned. The recent *Portuguese Corporate Governance Code (revised in 2023)*[27] notes in principle 1.C that in its 'decision-making process, the management body' also should consider the interests of '*employees, suppliers and other stakeholders* in the activity of the company', but further guidance is not provided. The *Italian Corporate Governance Code (2020)*[28] is somewhat more specific in adding the element of 'dialogue' in principle IV, prescribing that: 'The board of directors *promotes dialogue* with shareholders *and other stakeholders which are relevant for the company*, in the most appropriate way.' The *Swiss Code of Best Practice for Corporate Governance (2023)*[29] in paragraph 9 acknowledges that the duty of the board of directors is to 'also take account of the interests of *employees*, business partners, customers, *society* and the environment'. Under 12, it is specifically highlighted that '*employees can report the suspected irregularities they have identified in the company*'.

The *French Corporate Governance Code (2022)*[30] only requires that the board establishes 'multi-annual strategic guidelines on social and environmental responsibility' (5.1), as does the *Swedish Corporate Governance Code (2020)*[31] by simply stating in 3.1 that the principal tasks of the board include that it should define 'appropriate guidelines to govern the company's conduct in society'. Finally, the *UK Corporate Governance Code* (revised in 2023[32] and published by the FRC on 22 January 2024[33]) also reflects a limited view on stakeholder consultation. Although section 1 of the Code under D determines that the 'board should ensure effective engagement with, and encourage participation from' shareholders and stakeholders, Provision 5 provides very little guidance in relation to stakeholders other than stipulating that the board

26. *See* www.dcgk.de/en/home.html.
27. *See* https://www.ecgi.global/node/10556.
28. *See* www.borsaitaliana.it/comitato-corporate-governance/codice/2020eng.en.pdf.
29. *See* https://economiesuisse.ch/en/publications/swiss-code-best-practice-corporate-governance.
30. *See* https://hcge.fr/wp-content/uploads/2022/12/Code_AFEP_MEDEF_decembre_2022.pdf.
31. *See* www.bolagsstyrning.se/Userfiles/Koden/Dokument/Eng/SvenskKodBolagsstyrn_justerad_ENG_211220.pdf. We note that the Swedish Code is under revision. Proposed changes have been made in October 2023. *See* https://www.bolagsstyrning.se/news/proposed-changes-to-the-code-submitted-f__439.
32. *See* https://www.frc.org.uk/consultations/corporate-governance-code-consultation/.
33. www.frc.org.uk/library/standards-codes-policy/corporate-governance/uk-corporate-governance-code/.

'should understand the views of the company's key stakeholders and describe in the annual report how these and the matters set out in section 172 of the Companies Act 2006 have been considered in board discussions and decision-making'. As far as the engagement with the workforce is concerned, the company is, according to the Corporate Governance Code, not required to do more than either: (i) have a director appointed from the workforce, or (ii) institute a 'formal workforce advisory panel', or (iii) have a 'designated non-executive director'. The company may even decide: (iv) not to make a choice from these options provided it clarifies what alternative arrangements are in place 'and why it considers that they are effective'.

To be fair, of course, the limited references to workers' participation in the various corporate governance codes should not be taken as evidence that employee participation as such is of limited importance. In many countries, employee participation has a statutory basis and/or has evolved in established practices. Therefore, the above should not be understood as making the point that the regulation of worker participation in itself would be unsatisfactory. *The point that we do want to make* is that *employee participation does not yet seem to be regarded as a crucial instrument to gather the relevant information in relation to negative impacts of company actions and policies in relation to stakeholders*, including potential and actual environmental and human rights violations.

§4.10 EMPLOYEE INVOLVEMENT AND STAKEHOLDER ENGAGEMENT

All in all, we can conclude that in abstract terms, there is a broad consensus in the EU that when determining the policies of the company, the board and management thereof should take account of all relevant interests, including the interests of a broad spectrum of stakeholders. It is, however, less clear what that actually should imply and how that is to be achieved.

What is clear is that to take account of other stakeholder interests, the company will need to start by gathering relevant information on the negative impacts of company policies on the various stakeholders. In relation to certain categories of stakeholders, as distinguished in paragraph 9 above, it is feasible to realise some form of engagement and hear directly or at least indirectly from stakeholders what they experience and what their concerns may be; however, in respect of other categories that will be difficult to organise. Moreover, even if stakeholder engagement and consultation are taking place, it may not necessarily be so that, for example, the impact and seriousness of environmental adverse effects are fully appreciated by stakeholders. It may require considerably more 'inside knowledge' to really assess such impact.

To really become aware of the negative impacts of company actions, the most reliable source of knowledge will be the workers employed by the company, its subsidiaries or its suppliers, who will necessarily, in both a legal and a practical sense, operate in close proximity to the relevant company. Reflecting on stakeholder engagement and stakeholder consultation, we therefore conclude that it is fundamental to optimise the engagement with and consultation of workers in the company, its subsidiaries and/or companies in the supply chain. Hereafter, we therefore will explore whether current mechanisms of worker consultation as established in EU and national law already facilitate such consultation and whether, and if so, how such structures and mechanisms can be improved.

§4.11 EMPLOYEE INVOLVEMENT: THE EU PERSPECTIVE

Various types of participation rights are distinguished in the European context. The umbrella term 'involvement of employees' is defined as: 'any mechanism, including information, consultation and participation, through which employees' representatives may exercise influence on decisions to be taken within the company'.[34] *Information and consultation rights* are usually exercised (at the national or European level) by a body representing employees (such as a [European] Works Council).

Employee participation refers to the influence of employee representatives in the composition of the supervisory board (two-tier governance structure) or administrative body (one-tier model). Employee participation, also referred to as board-level employee representation (BLER), should thus be clearly distinguished from other forms of co-determination.[35] Obviously, through representation in the (supervisory) board of the company, employees can influence the corporate sustainability policy of the company since the strategy and policy in this respect are determined by the management board (and supervisory board). Because this contribution focuses on mechanisms for employee consultation, employee *participation is less relevant* and will therefore not be addressed in this chapter.

In this chapter, we focus on employee *consultation*. Particularly important in that respect is, at the European level, the European Works Council Directive ('EWC Directive'), as adopted in 1994 and amended in 2009 ('Recast Directive).[36] The objective of the EWC Directive is 'to improve the right to information and to consultation of employees in Community-scale undertakings and Community-scale groups of undertakings' (Article 1(1)). The scope of the directive includes transnational undertakings and groups with at least 1,000 employees within the European Union while at least 150 employees are employed in at least two Member States.[37]

To clarify the distinction between the competences of national representative bodies of employees (hereinafter: 'works council') and the European Works Council (EWC), Article 1(3) stipulates that information and consultation of employees must

34. Article 2(h) SE Directive.
35. *See further*: Joti Roest, *Corporate Mobility – The Involvement of Employees*, ECFR 16(1-2), § 2 (2019). Protection of existing employee participation rights is particularly relevant when establishing European legal persons such as a European Company and in cross-border restructurings.
36. Council Directive 94/45/EC of 22 September 1994 on the establishment of a European Works Council or a procedure in Community-scale undertakings and Community-scale groups of undertakings for the purposes of informing and consulting employees, OJ L 254, 30.09.1994, reenacted by Directive 2009/38/EC of the European Parliament and of the Council of 6 May 2009 on the establishment of a European Works Council or a procedure in Community-scale undertakings and Community-scale groups of undertakings for the purposes of informing and consulting employees (Recast), OJ L 122, 16.05.2009.
37. In the following we will refer to the 'undertaking' as 'company'.

occur at the relevant level of management and representation; in order to achieve that, the competence of the EWC and the scope of the information and consultation is therefore limited to transnational issues. Matters are considered to be transnational where they concern the transnational company as a whole or at least two companies/ establishments of the transnational company in two different Member States (Article 1(4) EWC Directive). In our opinion, the transnational company's obligations under the CSDDD qualify as transnational matters, so the EWC has a competence therein.

The framework of the EWC Directive has been referred to as a system of 'regulated self-regulation'.[38] The establishment of an ECW (or an alternative system of information and consultation) is to be negotiated 'in good spirit' (Article 6(1)) between the management of the transnational company and a special negotiating body (SNB) consisting of employee representatives from the transnational company or group. The management of the transnational company is responsible for establishing the SNB.

The EWC Directive gives the negotiating parties considerable freedom as to the content of the agreement to be concluded so that it can be tailored to the company or group in question, but Article 6(2) includes specific topics that must be included in the agreement. Subjects to be covered are, for example, the composition of the EWC, the powers of the EWC, the relationship of the EWC to national employee representative bodies, frequency and location of the EWC's meetings, its financial and material resources, and the term of the agreement and rules for adjustment, termination or renegotiation. If the management and the SNB fail to reach an agreement on transnational participation of employees within three years, then so-called Subsidiary Requirements (Article 7) apply, which are attached as Annex I to the Directive.[39] In practice, these binding requirements obviously have a major impact on the outcome of negotiations.

§4.12 INFORMATION AND CONSULTATION RIGHTS AND THE EWC

In principle, the remit of the EWC is to facilitate consultation of employees on matters with 'transnational character' that could have an impact on jobs and working conditions of the workforce in Europe. More especially, '[t]he information and *consultation of the EWC* shall relate in particular to the situation and probable trend of *employment, investments, and substantial changes concerning organisation, introduction of new working methods or production processes, transfers of production, mergers, cut-backs or closures of undertakings, establishments or important parts thereof, and collective redundancies*' (1(a) Subsidiary Requirements).

The EWC meets with the management of the transnational company at least annually to be informed and consulted on the basis of a report prepared by the

38. Stan De Spiegelaere, *Too Little, Too Late? Evaluating the European Works Councils Recast Directive*, ETUI Report 138 (2016), 15.
39. These requirements also apply if management and SNB so decide or if management refuses to initiate negotiations within a period of 6 months after a request to do so (Art. 7(1) EWC Directive).

management containing information on the progress of the business and its prospects (1(2) Subsidiary Requirements). In case of exceptional circumstances or if decisions are being considered that may have far-reaching consequences for employees (e.g., relocations, plant closures or collective dismissals), the EWC may form from among its members a 'select committee' consisting of five members. The select committee (or the EWC if no committee has been established) has the right to meet in session and express an opinion on a management report in which the contemplated decision is explained.

Although a diverging EWC opinion does not affect the prerogatives of central management (1(3) Subsidiary Requirements), Article 11(2) EWC Directive stipulates that the Member States shall provide for appropriate administrative or judicial procedures in the event the management of the transnational company or group does not comply with the provisions of the Directive. In the Netherlands, the Enterprise Chamber of the Amsterdam Court of Appeal is the competent court (Article 5 Dutch European Works Council Act).

The Commission published a report in 2018 on the implementation of the 2009 EWC Recast Directive and an accompanying Evaluation Report.[40] One of the findings is that it is estimated that half of all eligible companies have not yet established an EWC. The Commission further concluded that the requirement that matters should have a 'transnational' character should be better defined in Article 1(4) of the Recast Directive as the interpretation of this requirement has proven to be difficult in practice. In our opinion, in the case human rights or the environment in third countries are not respected, such issues will, in light of the CSDDD proposal, have a 'transnational' character. The evaluation also observed that the lack of dedicated means for the EWCs to enforce their rights and the lack of dissuasive and proportionate sanctions are a barrier to the effectiveness of the EWC Directive.[41]

The European Parliament adopted a resolution in February 2023 calling on the Commission to carry out the long-awaited revision of the EWC Directive.[42] The resolution contains concrete recommendations for revising the Directive; in the context of this contribution, the following recommendations are particularly important. The Directive should ensure 'timely and meaningful consultation' as 'EWC's still face major difficulties to enforce their rights, especially on timely information and prior and effective consultation on matters of transnational character that could have an impact on jobs and working conditions of the workforce in Europe, *including changes deriving from the green and digital transitions*' [italics added].[43] The European Parliament also recommends that the concept of the 'transnational character of a matter' should be clarified: the definition needs to be precise and comprehensive and the scope of

40. Implementation Report EWC 2018 (SWD(2018) 187 final). The Implementation Report is accompanied by a Commission staff working document 'Evaluation' (COM(2018) 292 final).
41. *See* for more details: Evaluation (COM(2018) 292 final), 45-46.
42. P9_TA(2023)0028, European Parliament resolution of February 2, 2023 with recommendations to the Commission on Revision of European Work Councils Directive (2019/2183 (INL)).
43. *Supra* n. 42, at 9.

possible effects as well as the relevant level of management and representation it involves need to be considered.[44]

Following the EP's resolution, the Commission launched a first-stage consultation with the European social partners on the revision of the EWC Directive in April 2023. After reviewing the replies, a second stage consultation on a revision of the Directive followed from July to October 2023.[45] On 24 January 2024, the Commission presented its Proposal for the amended Directive.[46] The Proposal clarifies the definition of 'transnational matters' to ensure legal certainty for both management and employee representatives (Article 1(4)). A matter shall be considered transnational not only when the measures considered are expected to affect workers in undertakings or establishments in more than one Member State but also when the envisaged measures affect workers in one Member State while workers in another Member State can expected to be affected by the *consequences* of such measures. The preamble under 18 considers that this extension of the definition is necessary as proposed measures (such as collective redundancies) may be targeted at establishments in one Member State but nevertheless can be expected to have effects on workers in other Member States due to, for instance, changes in the cross-border supply chain or production activities. The Proposal aims to strengthen the position of the EWC by specifying that consultation of the EWC shall take place at such time, in such fashion and with such content that it enables the EWC to express an opinion and is entitled to a written response by the management prior to the adaption of the decision by the management (Article 9).

The Proposal furthermore includes provisions on financial and material resources allocated to the EWC, strengthening gender balance in the composition of the EWC and/or the SNB (Article 6 (2a)), confidentiality of information (Articles 8, 8a) and effective enforcement of the Directive through sanctions and access to justice (Article 11).

§4.13 THE ROLE OF THE EWC IN IDENTIFYING HUMAN RIGHTS AND ENVIRONMENTAL VIOLATIONS AS MEANT BY THE CSDDD

For our current purposes, it is important to note that although the Commission's Proposal to amend the EWC Directive does not specifically address the role of the EWC as a 'stakeholder' in the context of corporate sustainability and the duty to address and mitigate human rights and environmental violations, the Explanatory Memorandum to

44. *Supra* n. 42, at 10. The EP further recommends, *inter alia*, to strengthen the Subsidiary Requirements, clarify the scope of confidentiality of information, introduce effective and proportionate penalties for non-compliance with the Directive and ensure EWC's access to justice.
45. The relevant documents COM(2023) 2330 final (Consultation Document) and COM(2023) 5054 final (the Accompanying Analytical Document dated 26 July 2023) can be accessed at https://ec.europa.eu/commission/presscorner/detail/en/ip_23_3922.
46. Proposal for a Directive of the European Parliament and of the Council amending Directive 2009/38/EC as regards the establishment and functioning of European Works Councils and the effective enforcement of transnational information and consultation rights, COM(2024) 14 final, *see* https://eur-lex.europa.eu/legal-content/EN/TXT/?uri=COM:2024:14:FIN ('Proposal').

the Proposal does explicitly address the role of employees and their representatives. First, this Document underlines that the focus on sustainability will inevitably have substantial consequences for society, including how the world of work will develop and how social dialogue will evolve:

> In the ongoing *transformation* of the world of work driven by environmental, economic and social *sustainability* and the deployment of new technologies, *a meaningful involvement of workers and their representatives at all levels* can help *anticipate and manage change*, diminish job losses, maintain employability, and ease effects on social welfare systems and related adjustment costs. In multinational undertakings or groups, the information and consultation of employees at transnational level can make an important contribution to such involvement.[47] [italics added]

Second, it is recognised that although the scope of information and consultation of EWCs under the Directive only relates to 'transnational matters', the subject matter is not limited to specific topics or issues and may include various EU policies including sustainability, human rights and environmental issues as the Commission sets out in its Explanatory Memorandum:[48]

> Transnational matters are not defined by reference to specific topics or issues, but rather their ability to affect employees in several Member States. EWCs thus have the potential to enhance the implementation of various EU policies in multinational companies, by providing a forum for dialogue between central management and employee representatives. *Synergies can thus occur between this initiative and any EU policy field that stands to benefit from the effective involvement of EWCs, in particular in the context of the twin transitions.* [italics added][49]

Although the Explanatory Memorandum does not explicitly refer to the role the EWC can play in channelling information on potential and actual violations of human rights and environmental adverse impacts as covered by the CSDDD, the Commission did emphasise this role earlier in the *Analytical Document* (to the second stage consultation in 2023):

> *the Commission's proposal for a Directive on Corporate Sustainable Due Diligence (CSDDD), adopted in February 2022, provides that, where relevant, companies should also carry out consultations with potentially affected groups including workers and other relevant stakeholders to gather information on actual or potential adverse impacts.* In this context, EWCs could be informed and consulted on the due diligence policy and other due diligence actions of multinational corporations.

47. Explanatory Memorandum to the Proposal, p. 1, Impact Assessment Report (SWD(2024) 10 final), at 1.
48. *Supra* n. 45, at 4.
49. *See also* the Impact Assessment Report (*supra* n. 47) at 22: 'The proposed Directive on Corporate Sustainable Due Diligence (CSDDD) is likely to be adopted during the baseline period. It would set out obligations for large companies regarding the information and consultation of employees in relation to adverse environmental and human rights impacts in their global value chains. The CSDDD has the potential to achieve synergies with the Directive, as EWCs' opinions can contribute to the development and dissemination of the due diligence policy of multinational corporations. However, that Directive would not affect the legal framework for the operation of EWCs.'

> *EWCs' opinions on transnational matters relating to corporate due diligence* can potentially help central management to *identify and mitigate adverse impacts on workers' rights, other fundamental rights and the environment.* Furthermore, EWCs can play an important role in *disseminating information about sustainability due diligence matters amongst the employees they represent* and can *submit complaints using the complaints procedures under the proposed CSDDD.*[50]

In light of the foregoing, we fully subscribe to these views expressed by the Commission. We do agree that the EWC, as a 'transnational' representative body of employees, could and should play a fundamental role in corporate sustainability issues.[51]

It is clear that the proposed revision of the EWC Directive will strengthen its role. In order to ensure that decisions of a transnational company on corporate sustainability, human rights and environmental impacts are recognised as 'transnational issues', we would strongly recommend that in the Directive (or its preamble and recitals) this is made explicit. Furthermore, we would suggest that the requirements outlined in Annex I be amended to align with this objective.

It is worth noting in this respect that the list of matters in which the EWC has competence (notably nos 1(a) and 3 of the Subsidiary Requirements) dates back to its inception in 1994. Thirty years later, it certainly is about time to update this catalogue with topics which have become of great importance and will remain so in decades to come. Corporate sustainability and addressing adverse impacts on human rights and the environment certainly are such topics.

§4.14 EMPLOYEE INVOLVEMENT ON THE NATIONAL LEVEL: THE DUTCH WORKS COUNCIL BY WAY OF EXAMPLE

At the national level, Member States' co-determination law is harmonised only to a very limited extent. The Directive on Information and Consultation of Employees in the EU, created in 2002, only requires Member States to provide legislation giving employees specific information and consultation rights in various areas.[52] These rights concern general developments of the company and the economic situation, (a threat to) employment and (intended) decisions of the company leading to substantial

50. *Supra* n. 45, at 14.
51. We note that in the view of the European Trade Union Confederation (ETUC) the consultation on the EWC missed an opportunity to specify the role of EWCs in the due diligence process: 'The ETUC strongly believes that involvement of workers' and trade unions representatives are necessary for the company to build a strong and effective due diligence process. Thus EWCs must be fully involved in all steps of companies' due diligence plans and policies. This includes the involvement in mapping potential risks on human rights and the environment across the company operations as well as its supply and subcontracting chains, *see* https://www.etuc.org/en/document/etuc-reply-first-phase-social-partner-consultation-possible-revision-european-works, *see also* the Impact Assessment Report (*supra* n. 47), at 59.
52. Directive 2002/14/EC of the European Parliament and of the Council of 11 March 2002 establishing a general framework for informing and consulting employees in the European Community, OJ L80, 23.03.2002.

changes in work organisation or in contractual relations. In the national laws of the Member States, these information and consultation rights may be granted to works councils or to trade unions.

For the Netherlands, this Directive did not require substantial legislative changes because the Works Councils Act (Wet op de Ondernemingsraden (WOR)) already grants participation rights to the works council on these matters,[53] such as a right to information (Article 31 WOR) and a consultation and initiative right (Article 23 WOR). These rights offer the works council the opportunity to obtain information about the company's corporate sustainability initiatives and to discuss them with the management. These rights also are a stepping stone for the works council to discuss any policy concerns or related developments.

The right to render a (written) advice (Article 25 WOR) on certain (proposed) board decisions of the company is one of the most powerful participation rights of the Works Council. Article 25(1) WOR contains an exhaustive list of company resolutions that are subject to the (prior) advisory right of the works council. Such resolutions include, *inter alia*, mergers, acquisitions, major investments of the company and raising substantial financing for the benefit of the company. For the purpose of the advice being sought, the works council must be furnished with a summary of the reasons for the decision. If the decision of the company is not in accordance with the advice of the works council, the works council may lodge an appeal against the decision with the Enterprise Chamber of the Amsterdam Court on the ground that the decision is evidently unreasonable. If the Enterprise Chamber grants the appeal, it can order the company to rescind its decision in whole or in part (Article 26(5) WOR).

In 1998, the advisory right of the Works Council was expanded to include a specific provision dealing with environmental matters. According to Article 25(1)(l), WOR '[t]aking an important measure in connection with the company's concern *for the environment,* including taking or changing a policy, organisational and administrative provision in connection with the environment' is subject to advice of the works council. According to the parliamentary notes, this should be understood in a relatively broad fashion and may include (in our informal translation HJdK/JR):

> drawing up a *company environmental plan* or taking substantial environmental measures, such as installing technical facilities, [...] introducing or modifying an environmental care system [...], a coherent system of policy, organisational and administrative provisions aimed at [...] managing and, where possible, reducing the effects of business operations on the environment. Policy-related provisions may include the establishment of environmental plans and environmental programs [and] [...] other important measures relating to the company's responsibility for the environment. One might think of implementing a company transportation plan, a waste collection system, a waste prevention plan, or applying for an Environmental Permit ['Hinderwetvergunning'] with significant environmental consequences (...).[54]

53. Official Gazette of the Kingdom of the Netherlands 2004, 652.
54. *See* Dutch Parliamentary Papers: *Kamerstukken II* 1995/96, 24615, 3, 42.

In academic literature, the position has been taken that policy *objectives*, provided they have a sufficient degree of concreteness in them, would also fall within the scope of the advisory right of Article 25(1)(l) WOR.[55]

In our opinion, the provision included in Article 15 of the CSDDD obliging companies to adopt a climate plan falls within the scope of Article 25 (1)(l) WOR.[56] We note that corporate sustainability due diligence obligations of the company as contained in the CSDDD are 'as such' and are not explicitly covered by the Works Council Act. However, as such obligations are expected to require substantial investments by the company, decision-making to this end may be subject to advice by the works council as such under Article 25(1)(h) WOR (according to which substantial investments are subject to works council advice).

In addition to Article 25(1)(l) WOR, the 1998 amendment of the WOR assigned to the works council a role in monitoring the impact of the company on the environment. Since then, Article 28(4) WOR reads: '[t]he works council shall encourage to the best of its ability that the company discharges its responsibility for the environment, including setting and amending policies, and taking organisational and administrative measures in relation thereto'. The explanatory parliamentary documents emphasise the '*desirability of involving employees in the responsibility for the environment' and provide the works council with the right to use its powers to encourage companies regarding their environmental responsibility*.[57] This article provides the works council with a legal basis to discuss the impact of the company on the environment, the policies of the company in this respect and the right to receive all relevant information pertaining to these matters.[58]

This raises the question of whether corporate sustainability due diligence, within the meaning of the CSDDD, is covered by this provision and therefore subject to the right of advice of the works council. One could argue that the due diligence obligation basically only amounts to a fact-finding exercise. However, in light of the obligations enshrined in the CSDDD to explicitly address any adverse impacts, that would be a very restrictive interpretation and, in our view, certainly too restrictive. This is even more so as setting up an adequate structure to monitor whether human rights and the environment are respected will require substantive investments and, as already explained above, substantial investments themselves are subject to the right of advice of the Works Council (*see* Article 25(1)(h) WOR).[59]

---

55. Loe Sprengers & Annette Terpstra, *De ondernemingsraad en het adviesrecht over milieumaatregelen: het terra incognita van de WOR*, ArbeidsRecht 10, 27-28 (2023).
56. The proposal for the Responsible and Sustainable International Business Act (in Dutch: Wet verantwoord en duurzaam internationaal ondernemen) includes a similar obligation in Art. 2.4.2.
57. *See* Dutch Parliamentary Papers: *Kamerstukken II* 1995/96, 24615, 3, 44.
58. *See also* Eline Snijders & Margot Hoving, *Het arbeidsrecht kleurt groen*, Tijdschrift Arbeidspraktijk 8 (2022), 17.
59. We note that Art. 27 Works Council Act grants the works council a right of consent relating to proposed decisions regarding the adoption, amendment or repeal of regulations concerning the enterprise's social policy. This includes a regulation on working conditions (Art. 27(1)(d) Works Council Act). Since such regulations are strongly intertwined with Dutch labour law, we believe

A restrictive interpretation would in any case not be in line with the much broader view taken by the Commission in view of the proposed amendments to the EWC Directive (discussed in the previous paragraph). Finally, in light of the nowadays widely accepted view that companies should pursue not only their own interests but also those of all stakeholders, we believe the WOR should be understood as also offering a legal basis for taking into account the interests of not only employees but also other stakeholders and corporate sustainability in general.[60]

Considering all this, we do think it would be good to clarify, for example, at the occasion of the implementation of the CSDD Directive in Dutch law, this issue and amend the WOR to the effect that it explicitly stated that all actions related to the CSDDD, and corporate sustainability, be presented to the works council for advice.

§4.15 CONCLUSION

The purpose of this chapter was to clarify what is actually expected from companies with regard to stakeholder consultation where such consultations are prescribed in statutory law or other legal instruments, without, however, being very clear on what this should comprise. We have noted that in almost all definitions of stakeholders employees and workers in general feature prominently. In this chapter, we have examined the role of workers not only as stakeholders but also as a vital link between companies and their ability to identify and address potential and actual negative adverse impacts on human rights or the environment whether nearby or in remote locations.

Nearly always workers employed by the company or its group companies or suppliers will have knowledge of negative adverse effects. Therefore mechanisms open for all workers, such as whistleblower procedures, which may also be used by employees of suppliers (*see* above §4.04), and mechanisms for employee consultation can be utilised to facilitate the upward flow of information. This can be instrumental in achieving the objective of ensuring that the ultimate parent company and its group companies are well informed and able to take account of a broad array of stakeholder interests, as well as develop specific stakeholder engagement and consultation mechanisms where appropriate.

Such stakeholder consultation mechanisms may take inspiration from employee consultation structures that have been developed over the last few decades both at the EU level (such as the European Works Council; EWC) and in the national arena. This may include setting up regular consultation meetings to discuss sustainability policies and practices of the company and the group as a whole. However, different from consultation in works councils, the membership of broader stakeholder meetings does not have to be fixed, but it could depend on the issues at hand in light of the specifics of the industry. Works councils could however provide inspiration for drawing up rules

section 25 Works Council Act provides a broader basis for the works council's involvement in the context of corporate sustainability due diligence.

60. *See also* Loe Sprengers & Annette Terpstra, *De ondernemingsraad en het adviesrecht over milieumaatregelen: het terra incognita van de WOR*, ArbeidsRecht 10 (2023), 28.

of procedure for stakeholder consultation bodies including who may propose agenda items, how information will be disseminated, the structure of meetings, and which parties may be invited. This will not only enable the company to receive input from relevant organisations but also provide information to them in a structured manner.

Overall, we believe that when it comes to further developing stakeholder consultation as is increasingly mandated by laws and regulations, such as, but not limited to, the CSDDD, there is much to be learned from the development of workers' consultation in recent decades, as discussed in this chapter. One important lesson learned would seem to be that workers are not only a crucial category of stakeholders in their own right but also can play a crucial role in ensuring that human and environmental rights of others are respected.

§4.16 CONGRATULATIONS ON THE TWENTIETH ANNIVERSARY OF THE JOURNAL *EUROPEAN COMPANY LAW*

We are honoured to have the opportunity to contribute to this book on the occasion of the 20th anniversary of the *European Company Law* Journal. The Journal has successfully established itself as a platform for information, analysis and debate on trends and developments in company law in Europe in all its
aspects, both at the EU level and from a comparative perspective. That is quite an accomplishment for all involved. However, it should also be acknowledged that this accomplishment was ultimately made possible thanks to the founder and longstanding editor-in-chief of the Journal, Prof Steef Bartman. He not only had the vision to start the Journal but also the energy and enthusiasm to involve a wide range of scholars and encourage their contributions to the Journal. Among many other things, this book is a token of appreciation and admiration for the work of Steef Bartman and his contribution to European company law both in the Journal and the subject itself.

CHAPTER 5

Corporate Purpose and Sustainable Decision-Making: Examples from Dutch Corporate Practice

*Mieke Olaerts & Constantijn van Aartsen**

In this contribution, we examine the state of the art of purpose statements in Dutch corporate practice. We discuss the general debate on corporate purpose, explore differences between purpose and related terms such as mission and vision, and outline the legal qualification and effects of purpose statements. We also review the Dutch legal background against which purpose statements are used, present empirical findings on the use of these statements over the past decade, and reflect on their value for the sustainable future of companies in a Dutch and European corporate law setting.

Overall, we identify that discussions on corporate purpose have influenced Dutch corporate practice. We demonstrate a notable increase in such statements over the past decade and show that they have become increasingly oriented towards sustainability and extrinsic aims. We do not, however, infer from these developments that purpose statements have had a standalone, positive effect on the sustainability of companies since they are often vaguely formulated, seldom included in articles of association, and are typically formulated as a voluntary act by the board. Ultimately, we conclude that the effectiveness of corporate purposes depends on how companies implement them within the regulatory context that is provided by society.

§5.01 INTRODUCTION

Twenty years ago, Professor Bartman founded the journal *European Company Law*. Over the past years, the journal has played an important role in providing authors with

* This contribution will also be published in European Company Law in the course of fall 2024.

an audience for several contemporary debates in the area of European company law. Bartman himself also made notable contributions to the development of (European) company law over the course of his rich career. These contributions and reaching the landmark of 20 years of *European Company Law* both call for a celebration and an evaluation of the developments over these 20 years in European company law.

Twenty years ago, Europe, especially European company law, looked different from what it is today. Towards the end of the 2000s, the agenda in the area of European company law was mainly dominated by empowering shareholders.[1] The current debate and legislative initiatives in the area of European company law are, on the contrary, largely influenced by the European sustainability agenda and the desire to make corporate decision-making long-term oriented by incorporating the interests of not only shareholders but also all other stakeholders. Many potential solutions and instruments have been suggested with this aim in mind.[2] One is to change directors' duties and reformulate how companies should be managed. In general, it has been suggested that, within the European Union (EU), all Member States require directors to protect and promote the interests of the company.[3] However, national laws differ in the interpretation of this interest. Furthermore, it is evident from discussions surrounding the Corporate Sustainability Due Diligence Directive (CSDDD) that there is not much consensus yet on a harmonised approach to the fiduciary duties of directors. This implies, by extension, that there is not yet a consensus view on how companies should be sustainably managed.

In the absence of such a harmonised European view, one way to stimulate directors to take a wide range of interests into account is by formulating a corporate purpose which includes stakeholder interests and is oriented towards a broader societal goal rather than only striving for financial gain.[4] According to some scholars,

1. Reference can be made to the Shareholder Rights Directive as regards the encouragement of long-term shareholder engagement) enhancing shareholder rights in the EU (Directive 2007/36/EC of the European Parliament and of the Council of 11 July 2007 on the exercise of certain rights of shareholders in listed companies, OJ L 184, 14.7.2007).
2. Directive (EU) 2009/125/EC of the European Parliament and of the Council of 21 October 2009 Establishing a Framework for the Setting of Ecodesign Requirements for Energy-Related Products, OJ L 285, 31.10.2009. Directive (EU) 2022/2464 of the European Parliament and of the Council of 14 December 2022 amending Regulation (EU) No 537/2014, Directive 2004/109/EC, Directive 2006/43/EC and Directive 2013/34/EU, as regards corporate sustainability reporting, OJ L 322, 16.12.2022. Regulation (EU) 2020/852 of the European Parliament and of the Council of 18 June 2020 on the establishment of a framework to facilitate sustainable investment, and amending Regulation (EU) 2019/2088, OJ L 198, 22.6.2020.
3. Ernst & Young, *Study on Directors' Duties and Sustainable Corporate Governance*, Annex I, 89 (2020).
4. Mayer, for example, explains that 'Purpose is ... about finding ways of solving problems profitably where profits are defined net of the costs of avoiding and remedying problems. By defining purpose and profits in this way, purpose is associated with enhancing the wellbeing and prosperity of shareholders, society and the natural world. It does not disadvantage any party because profits are only legitimate if they are not earned at the expense of other parties and corporate purposes are only valid if they are profitable in this sense' (Colin Mayer, *The Future of the Corporation and the Economics of Purpose*, 58 Journal of Management Studies 3, 889 (2021).

such a purposeful company can 'contribute to a more inclusive form of capitalism' because it allows companies to reorder their priorities and shift away from short-term shareholder gain.[5] Whether this is true is still under discussion.[6] Nonetheless, it is clear that the topic of corporate purpose is gaining in popularity due to a general societal concern about the impacts of corporations on social and environmental issues such as human rights, climate change, and biodiversity loss.[7] Increasing attention to the corporate purpose is also visible in corporate practice. This is evidenced by our research findings, explored below in more detail. We investigated the purpose statements of Dutch companies between 2013 and 2021. We found, for example, that the use of purpose statements has increased over this time period and that an increasing number of companies adopt an external (socially and environmentally) oriented purpose statement rather than one which focuses solely on improving their own activities.

In this contribution, we will discuss the development and state of the art with regard to purpose statements in Dutch corporate practice. We will also look into the question of how to legally qualify purpose statements and whether they can have legal effects. Even though our empirical research does not answer the question of whether purpose statements are indeed effective, it does show that at least the academic debate regarding purpose statements has had an influence on corporate practice. We will therefore also reflect on what the legal and practical value of purpose statements can be from a theoretical perspective in the Netherlands as well as in a broader European context. The contribution will have the following outline. In §5.02, we first discuss the general contours of the corporate purpose debate. We then discuss, in §5.03, the different perspectives on the use of mission/vision/purpose terminology and explore the differences, if any, between these terms. We also discuss the legal qualification of purpose statements in that section. Subsequently, we look in §5.04 at the Dutch legal background against which these purpose statements are used. We also present our empirical findings on the use of corporate purpose statements by Dutch-listed companies over the past decade. In §5.05, we reflect on whether purpose statements can have value for the sustainable future of companies in a Dutch as well as a European corporate law setting. Lastly, §5.06 concludes.

5. David Kershaw & Edmund Schuster, *The Purposive Transformation of Corporate Law*, 40 American Journal of Comparative Law 3, 480 (2022).
6. Colin Mayer, *What Is Wrong with Corporate Law? The Purpose of Law and the Law of Purpose*, 18 Annual Review of Law and Social Science (2022). Mayer, *supra* n. 4. Alex Edmans, *Grow the Pie: How Great Companies Deliver Both Purpose and Profit* (Cambridge University Press 2020). Lucian A. Bebchuk & Roberto Tallarita, *The Illusory Promise of Stakeholder Governance*, 106 Cornell L. Rev. 91 (2020). Lucian A. Bebchuk & Roberto Tallarita, *Will Corporations Deliver Value to All Stakeholders?*, 75 Vand. L. Rev. 1031 (2022).
7. Michael E. Porter & Mark R. Kramer, *Creating Shared Value: How to Reinvent Capitalism—And Unleash a Wave of Innovation and Growth*, 1 Harvard Business Review (2011). Colin Mayer, *What Is Wrong with Corporate Law? The Purpose of Law and the Law of Purpose*, 18 Annual Review of Law and Social Science (2022).

§5.02 THE CORPORATE PURPOSE DEBATE

The topic of corporate purpose is not new – in fact, it has surrounded the corporation since its inception.[8] However, it has recently received a lot of renewed attention.[9] One way to understand the contemporary debate on corporate purpose is as a reaction to the 1970s 'Friedmanite' view[10] on the role of corporations which suggests that they only have one responsibility, which is to make profits for their shareholders.[11] This view was leading in academic and business circles for many decades, and its narrow focus on profits has long been criticised for contributing towards corporate short-termism and social and environmental issues. Sjåfjell and Mahonen, for example, note that 'the economics based social norm of shareholder primacy is in the heart of the unsustainability of business'.[12] Mayer, another leading proponent of a shift in corporate purpose, explains that shareholder primacy has led to a divergence between private and public interests and that we need to close this gap to ensure that business operates once again in the public interest.[13] Some finance scholars have also come to endorse the shift in corporate purpose. Edmans, for example, explains that 'a company's purpose cannot be to earn profits – instead, profits are a by-product of serving a purpose'.[14] In general, there is an identifiable consensus, woven throughout the work of these and other proponents, that a shift in corporate purpose away from shareholder primacy and towards the interests of other stakeholders will contribute towards more ethical and sustainable business activities.[15]

To understand the purpose debate, it is important to point out that this debate currently concerns two different levels.[16] The first level is the *level of society*. At this level, the purpose debate focuses on the role of corporations in society. Relevant questions in this respect are, for example, what is the role of companies in society, in whose interest should the board of directors manage the company, and what does this then entail for corporate regulation? To provide examples of this debate, we can start

8. David B. Guenther, *Of Bodies Politic and Pecuniary: A Brief History of Corporate Purpose*, 9 Mich. Bus. & Entrepreneurial L. Rev. 1 (2019). Leonardo Davoudi, Christopher McKenna & Rowena Olegario, *The Historical Role of the Corporation in Society*, 6 Journal of the British Academy s1 (2018). Dorothy S. Lund & Elizabeth Pollman, *Corporate purpose*, ECGI Law Working Paper no. 711/2023 (2023). Kershaw & Schuster, *supra* n. 5.
9. Holger Fleischer, *Corporate Purpose: A Management Concept and Its Implications for Company Law*, 2 European Company and Financial Law Review, 169 (2021) mentions that for example in Germany all Dax30 companies *see* a recognizable purpose and inner drive as crucial for the company's future success, and refers to a survey by B. Fröndhoff & M. Scheppe, *Die Frage nach dem Warum: Was unserer Arbeir Bedeutung verleiht*, Handelsblatt online (18 April 2019).
10. Paul L. Davies, *Shareholder Voice and Corporate Purpose: The Purposelessness of Mandatory Corporate Purpose Statements*, ECGI Law Working Paper no. 666/2022 (2023).
11. Milton Friedman, 'The Social Responsibility of Business Is to Increase Its Profits', *The New York Times Magazine* (13 September 1970).
12. Beate Sjåfjell & Jukka Mähönen, *Corporate Purpose and the Misleading Shareholder vs Stakeholder Dichotomy*, 22 Nordic & European Company Law LSN Research Paper Series 8, 12 (2022).
13. Mayer, *supra* n. 6.
14. Edmans, *supra* n. 6.
15. Colin Mayer, *Prosperity: Better Business Makes the Greater Good* (Oxford University Press 2018). Edmans, *supra* n. 6.
16. *See, e.g.*: Lund & Pollman, *supra* n. 8.

with the British Academy which suggests that 'the purpose of business is to solve the problems of people and planet profitably, and not profit from causing problems'.[17] Next, Sjåfjell and Mahonen contend that business should be tasked with 'sustainable value creation within planetary boundaries'.[18] Lastly, the World Economic Forum's *Davos Manifesto 2020* proposes that:

> The purpose of a company is to engage all its stakeholders in shared and sustained value creation. In creating such value, a company serves not only its shareholders, but all its stakeholders – employees, customers, suppliers, local communities and society at large.[19]

These purposes are generally concerned with the role and acceptable boundaries of corporate activities in society and are not focused on particular companies.

The second level of debate on corporate purpose is the *level of individual companies* and is concerned with how individual companies formulate or should formulate their own corporate purposes. There is a range of different opinions on how to do this. Again, to provide several examples, the British Academy advises that:

> A properly formulated purpose statement is neither purely descriptive about what a company does nor aspirational in saving the planet or society. Instead, it identifies how companies assist people, organisations, societies and nations to address the challenges they face, while at the same time helping companies to avoid or minimise the problems they might cause.[20]

This suggests that a company's purpose should explain the problems that it is trying to solve while outlining a limit on the kinds of profit that it is willing to generate. Edmans, by contrast, proposes that individual company purposes should focus on a particular activity in which the company has a comparative advantage and should be dedicated to the welfare of one or more specified groups of material stakeholders.[21] Fisch and Solomon, for their part, suggest that a purpose statement should 'be sufficiently concrete [so] that stakeholders can ascertain whether the corporation is operating in a manner that is consistent with that purpose' and so that it can subsequently be enforced through market-based mechanisms such as product sales or the market for corporate control.[22]

It is widely argued by proponents of corporate purpose that a shift in corporate purpose can help to promote corporate and director accountability,[23] address

17. British Academy, *Principles for Purposeful Business: How to Deliver the Framework for the Future of the Corporation*, Future of the Corporation Project (2019).
18. Sjåfjell and Mahonen, *supra* n. 12.
19. World Economic Forum, *Davos Manifesto 2020* (2019).
20. British Academy, *supra* n. 17.
21. Edmans, *supra* n. 6.
22. Jill E. Fisch & Steven Davidoff Solomon, 'Should Corporations Have a Purpose?', 99 Tex. L. Rev. 1344 (2021).
23. 'Corporate purpose could also enhance the functioning of markets and promote competition in tackling the most challenging issues of our time. It could encourage a race to the top, not to the bottom in delivering the greatest societal benefits in the most profitable way. It significantly strengthens accountability to all stakeholders impacted by the firm, including but not exclusively to its shareholders' (British Academy, *supra* n. 17, at 16).

short-termism,[24] and 'enhance financial performance and business resilience' in the long run.[25] It is not, however, suggested that a mere change in purpose will be enough to change the nature of business. Instead, the argument is that a shift in purpose is a necessary but not a sufficient condition to ensure the sustainability of company operations.[26] In this regard, corporate purpose can only ever be as effective as its implementation by companies within the regulatory context provided by society.[27]

Against these proponents, there are scholars such as Bebchuk and Tallarita who argue that the promise of purpose is overstated and that there are better ways to promote sustainability, for example, through government regulation.[28] As evidence, the authors point out that an influential statement from the US Business Roundtable (BRT),[29] which claims a shift in purpose away from shareholder primacy towards stakeholders, has had no discernible influence on the activities of its signatories. As they put it, 'in spite of the stakeholderist rhetoric of the BRT Statement, BRT Companies are not planning to deliver value to all stakeholders'.[30] If these authors are correct, then purpose statements may be little more than a distraction from more important issues.[31]

Notwithstanding these critiques, the overall development in practice is that companies are adopting socially minded purpose statements and that they are broadly appreciated as an important part of corporate identity and governance.[32] Meanwhile, the purpose concept is also finding its way into corporate regulation. The UK Corporate Governance Code 2018, for example, requires the board to establish the company's purpose, values and strategy and satisfy itself that these and its culture are aligned.[33] We

24. Sjåfjell & Mahonen, *supra* n. 12.
25. Mayer provides an outline and critical analysis of this common argument (Mayer, *supra* n. 6, at 4).
26. Vino Timmerman, *Purpose in de managementleer en het vennootschapsrecht*, Bestuursbesluiten (IVOR no. 123) 2021/4 (2021). As Edmans puts it, 'A purpose statement is meaningless unless it translates into action … . A company's purpose should shape the activities it's involved in" (Edmans, *supra* n. 8, at 208).
27. Lund and Pollman explain that 'the flexibility provided under law to self-determine a particular corporation's purpose is effectively modified or constrained by the cultural, legal, and institutional environment that fiduciaries operate in' (Lund & Pollman, *supra* n. 8, at 18).
28. Bebchuk & Tallarita, *supra* n. 6.
29. From the statement: 'Since 1978, Business Roundtable has periodically issued Principles of Corporate Governance that include language on the purpose of a corporation. Each version of that document issued since 1997 has stated that corporations exist principally to serve their shareholders. It has become clear that this language on corporate purpose does not accurately describe the ways in which we and our fellow CEOs endeavor every day to create value for all our stakeholders, whose long-term interests are inseparable … . While each of our individual companies serves its own corporate purpose, we share a fundamental commitment to all of our stakeholders' (Statement on the Purpose of a Corporation, Business Roundtable (2019), https://opportunity.businessroundtable.org/ourcommitment/).
30. Bebchuk & Tallarita, *supra* n. 6, at 1086.
31. Fisch & Solomon, *supra* n. 22.
32. Rob Bauer et al., *Sustainability Embedding Practices in Dutch Listed Companies*, Report Commission on Behalf of Eumedion (2021). Luc K. Audebrand, *Sustainability in Strategic Management Education: The Quest for New Root Metaphors*, 9 Academy of Management Learning & Education 3 (2010).
33. Corporate Governance Code (UK) 2018.

also see purpose appearing in new company law rules, with some national legislators inviting companies to voluntarily adopt purpose statements in their articles of association to make explicit what their intended role in society is and what they aim to achieve. France, for instance, has adjusted its legislation in this respect by introducing the *Loi Pacte*.[34] As mentioned in the introduction, the renewed attention to the corporate purpose is also visible in corporate practice. This is evidenced by our research findings which we will discuss further in §5.04 below.

§5.03 QUALIFYING CORPORATE PURPOSE

[A] Mission, Vision, and Purpose

Companies use different terms to formulate their ambitions and identities, with their websites and annual reports variously referring, for example, to missions, visions and/or purposes. This variation makes it interesting to consider the relationship between corporate purpose and these other terms also to help clarify what a company's purpose could entail. In general, there are at least two perspectives.

First is the suggestion that mission, vision, and purpose are distinct terms that serve different functions. Vision is often seen as what the company is aiming at for the foreseeable future, say, the next five to ten years.[35] Fitzsimmons et al. elaborate further and propose that: 'a mission statement explains what a corporation does... a vision statement explains what a company desires to become in the future ... [and] a purpose statement is a unifying principle that guides a corporation; it explains why a corporation does what it does'.[36] Overall, they argue that companies should use all three kinds of statements for both internal and external reasons (organisational branding, employee motivation, etc.).

Second, it has been argued that the metaphors which companies use to think about their activities have long been rooted in military metaphors (such as mission, engage, deploy, defend, and target)[37] and that sustainability issues may require a new, less combative and competitive kind of metaphor.[38] This perspective suggests that the shift towards corporate purpose may be part of a rhetorical change which more closely aligns the values, ideas, and language that companies use with the changing needs of society. In our empirical research, we also checked the development of the use of the terms mission, vision and purpose over the years in Dutch-listed companies, as will be explained in §5.04.

34. Loi n° 2019-486 du 22 mai 2019 relative à la croissance et la transformation des entreprises. *See* about this law amongst others J.M. de Jongh, Onderneming en maatschappij: naar een nieuw sociaal contract?, *Ondernemingsrecht* 2020/80 (2020). Fleischer, *supra* n. 9.
35. Fleischer, *supra* n. 9, at 9.
36. Alexis B. Fitzsimmons et al., *Purpose vs Mission vs Vision: Persuasive Appeals and Components in Corporate Statements*, 26 Journal of Communication Management 2, 207 (2022).
37. Audebrand, *supra* n. 32, at 416.
38. Audebrand, *supra* n. 32.

[B] Legal Qualification of Corporate Purposes

The question has also been raised as to how purpose statements should be qualified from a legal perspective. Fleisher, for example, points to the fact that purpose is a concept from management studies which does not necessarily have a legal connotation.[39] It should be noted, however, that many national company laws in the EU do recognize so-called object clauses. For instance, Dutch and German company law respectively allow and even require companies to include an object clause in their articles of association.[40] These clauses in theory come close to giving the managerial concept of purpose statements a legal connotation insofar as they require companies to set out their objectives and main activities.

Most of the purpose statements that we found in our research do not have a statutory basis, i.e., in the articles of association. However, if they would be given such a basis through incorporation in the articles of association, then it would be most logical to do this as part of the object clause. Arguably, this kind of incorporation would represent a stronger commitment on the side of the company since it is a change which requires approval of the general meeting of shareholders.[41] In this regard, it is not simply part of the strategy section in the annual report which can be adjusted on a yearly basis with the consent of the board of directors and, if applicable, the supervisory board. It can also be argued that the incorporation of a purpose in the articles of association can have further legal consequences. Whether or not this is the case will be discussed in §5.05. For now, in order to make the distinction between purpose statements with a basis in the articles of association and those without, we will use the terms statutory and non-statutory purposes, respectively.

§5.04 CORPORATE PURPOSE FROM A DUTCH PERSPECTIVE

As mentioned in the introduction, we researched the use of purpose statements in Dutch-listed companies over approximately the past decade. We did so by examining the purpose statements that they included (or not) in their annual reports for 2013, 2017 and 2021. Before we discuss our findings, we briefly outline the background of the Dutch governance model against which these purpose statements operate.

[A] The Dutch Governance Model

In defining the role of the board of directors and the purpose of corporations in general, the Dutch governance model views the company as an institute with its own interest. This interest is not derived from that of the shareholders, nor is it a combination of all

39. Fleischer, *supra* n. 9, at 16. For a UK perspective, *see*: Kershaw & Schuster, *supra* n. 5, at 9.
40. Fleischer, *supra* n. 9, at 16.
41. Corporate Governance Code (NL) Art. 2:121.

stakeholder interests. Instead, Dutch company law uses a holistic view. The board of directors is obliged to serve the interests of the company which is defined as promoting the lasting success of the company and its affiliated enterprise.[42] The company therefore has an interest of its own.

The stakeholder orientation is further emphasised by the most recent version of the Dutch Corporate Governance Code (DCGC) which is applicable to listed companies. The DCGC stipulates that the board of directors is responsible for the continuity of the company and its affiliated enterprise and for sustainable long-term value creation. It is required, moreover, to take into account the impact of the actions of the company and its affiliated enterprise on people and the environment. For this aim, it has to set specific targets and report on their attainment. In setting these targets, the board has to weigh the relevant stakeholder interests and the company has to develop a policy for its stakeholder dialogue.[43] This pluralistic view grants the board of directors of Dutch companies a considerable discretion in defining the corporate strategy and how to achieve it. The DCGC also addresses shareholders and requires them to '(...) recognise the importance of a strategy focused on sustainable long-term value creation for the company and its affiliated enterprise.'[44] This may also be relevant in light of the corporate purpose debate. Kershaw and Schuster argue that the effective implementation of purpose may require a 'zone of insulation' to shield managers from shareholder pressure.[45] Requiring shareholders to recognise the importance of sustainable long-term value creation may arguably have the effect of creating such a zone of insulation for corporate purposes. This will be further elaborated on in §5.05.

In short, Dutch law uses a stakeholder model in which companies are not required to be for-profit organisations. They can also opt for other goals and are therefore granted the autonomy to adopt purpose statements in which societal goals are addressed. These purpose statements can be viewed as part of the corporate strategy, meaning that the board of directors is empowered to draft such statements as long as they are not part of the articles of association. No shareholder approval is required since the law clearly states, at least for listed companies, that setting the company strategy is an autonomous task of the board.[46] As was mentioned in the previous section, purpose statements can also be given a basis in the articles of association by incorporating them into the object clause. In this case, shareholder approval is required as it would entail a change to the articles of association. However, as we will see below, object clauses only very rarely contain a wider societal purpose for the company.

42. Case 12/04969, *Invernostra S.L. v. Cancun Holdings* (Cancun), 4.04.2014, ECLI:NL:HR:2014:799. Case 21/03984, *Bab-Al Mustaqbal Real Estate Co. v. Intertrust (Curaçao) B.V.*, 10 February 2023, ECLI:NL:HR:2023:199.
43. Corporate Governance Code (NL) 2022 Principle 1.1.
44. Corporate Governance Code (NL) 2022 Principle 4.4.
45. Kershaw & Schuster, *supra* n. 5, at 4.
46. Civil Code (NL) Art. 2:129.

[B] The Use of Purpose in Dutch Corporate Practice

[1] Non-statutory Purpose Statements

To shed more light on the development of corporate purpose statements in the Netherlands, we examined the use of non-statutory purpose statements by Dutch listed companies over a period of nine years. We investigated these statements for companies listed on the AEX, AMX, and AScX indices of the Amsterdam Euronext stock exchange with a statutory seat in the Netherlands, a total of 60 companies. We collected the annual reports of these companies for 2013, 2017, and 2021 from their websites. The 2021 reports were available for all companies. The 2017 and 2013 reports were only available for 53 and 46 companies, respectively, since some were either only incorporated or listed after these years.

To identify purpose statements, we first searched for relevant key terms such as 'purpose', 'mission', and 'vision' and selected data which corresponded to strategic, high-level company statements about the ambitions and identity of the company. If these key terms were not found, we would read the annual report directly for these kinds of statements. Purpose-type statements were ignored if they were not strategic or did not seem applicable to the company as a whole. It was not, for example, enough for a sub-section in the sustainability report to say that 'Our company is dedicated to doing X' or for a business unit to make a similar claim. In general, it was not difficult to identify purpose statements, and most companies repeated the same phrases throughout their reports. If there were variations on the same purpose statement, then we selected the one that seemed to be the most comprehensive and provided the most information about the company's ambitions and identity.

We subsequently analysed the purpose statements in terms of the following questions:

(1) Does the company have a (sustainable) corporate purpose? (1) No. (2) Yes, does not include sustainability. (3) Yes, includes sustainability indirectly. (4) Yes, includes sustainability directly.
(2) Does the corporate purpose have an internal or external orientation? (0) N/A. (1) Internal. (2) External.
(3) Does the company formulate an explicit: (1) Mission. (2) Vision, (3) Purpose?[47]

We recruited the help of student assistants to collect the annual reports, identify purpose statements, and answer the above-mentioned questions for each company. All of their work was double-checked by one or both authors of this chapter.

In terms of findings, we can first note that there has been an increase in the number of companies with a purpose-type statement. For 2013, we found that 13 out of 46 companies (28%) did not have an identifiable purpose statement. By 2017, this

47. This refers to the terminology which a company uses to describe its aspirations, if they use a particular term at all. Some companies use several of these terms at the same time.

had decreased to 11 out of 53 (21%), and by 2021, it was only 3 out of 60 companies (5%). These findings show that companies find it more necessary than before to include purpose-type statements in their annual reports.

Second, we can identify that there has been a clear shift in terminology away from terms such as mission and vision and towards an explicit identification of purpose. More specifically, references to a mission declined from 52% to 30% between 2013 and 2021, and references to a vision declined from 35% to 15% over this same period. At the same time, references to purpose increased from 7% to 55% of companies. These findings are summarised in Table 5.1.

Table 5.1 Shift in the Terminology of Purpose-Related Statements

Year	*2013*	*2017*	*2021*
None / Other	39%	34%	23%
Mission	52%	40%	30%
Vision	35%	28%	15%
Purpose	7%	23%	55%

In terms of the different perspectives on the use of mission/vision/purpose terminology, the results broadly suggest that purpose is displacing, rather than supplementing, the use of these other kinds of statements.

Third, we found a substantial increase in the number of companies that refer, directly or indirectly,[48] to sustainability in their purpose statements (*see* Figure 5.1). In 2013, only 16 out of 46 companies (35%) referred to sustainability. By 2021, this amount had increased to 46 out of 60 (77%).

Figure 5.1 Purpose Statements and References to Sustainability

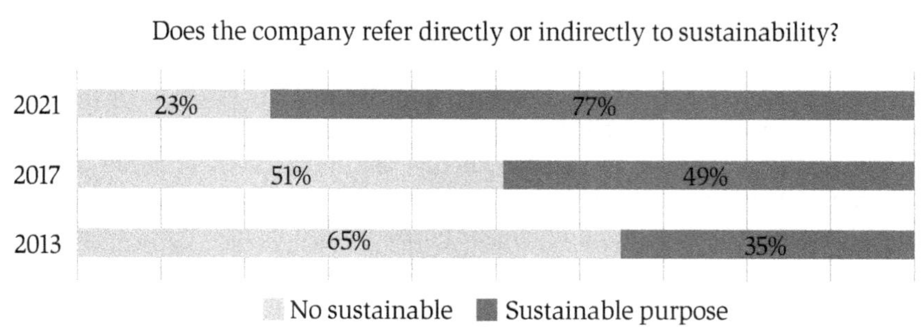

48. We counted a reference to sustainability as indirect when it did not feature directly in the purpose statement itself, but could be reasonably inferred from the nearby surrounding text and explanation.

Fourth, we identified that there has been a dramatic shift in the internal/external orientation of company purpose statements (*see* Table 5.2). To clarify, this question on orientation asks whether companies see their purpose as a means to improve the activities of the company itself (e.g., its efficiency or customer satisfaction) or as a means to improve something beyond the company (e.g., society or the environment). In 2013, there were more companies with an internal rather than an external orientation (19 against 14 companies). This had changed by 2021, so 50 companies (83 %) had an externally oriented purpose.

Table 5.2 The Internal/External Orientation of Purpose Statements

Year	*2013*	*2017*	*2021*
Internal orientation	41 %	36 %	12 %
External orientation	30 %	43 %	83 %
Not applicable	28 %	21 %	5 %

In general, these changes may imply that companies, next to focusing on their internal stakeholders such as shareholders and employees, also add external stakeholders such as society and the environment. Alternatively, it may signal a relative rebalancing of commercial activities for private gain towards taking into account external factors. However, our findings do not suggest that this is actually the case with regard to the corporate activity of the companies in our sample. It merely shows a rebalancing attempt for corporate purposes. More research is needed, but these findings are consistent with the idea that corporate purpose is part of a rhetorical shift that is more closely aligning the values, ideas, and language that companies use with the changing needs of society.[49]

Critically, however, it should be mentioned that non-statutory purpose statements are often very generically formulated. This has already been recognised in the literature on the topic[50] and is also confirmed by our previous research which reviewed corporate purposes in the 2020 annual reports of 35 Dutch listed companies.[51] It identified that 'almost none of these purpose statements are very specific when compared to what is expected of a corporate purpose in the contemporary corporate governance literature. The statements are often vague, generic slogans about ambition and positive intent'.[52] In our earlier research, we also examined whether the formulation of these company purposes was consistent with the ideas of Mayer and Edmans, two leading proponents from the literature on individual company purposes. According to Mayer:

> Purpose should be neither mundane nor aspirational. It is *not purely descriptive* of what a business does – a mission statement – nor unrealistic about what it seeks to do – an aspirational vision statement to save the world. It is *about solving*

49. Audebrand, *supra* n. 32.
50. Fleischer, *supra* n. 9, at 180. Fisch & Solomon, *supra* n. 22.
51. Bauer et al., *supra* n. 32.
52. Bauer et al., *supra* n. 32, at 103-104.

> *problems*, 'to produce profitable solutions to the problems of people and planet' and 'not to profit from producing problems for people or planet'... Purpose is, therefore, about finding ways of solving problems profitably where *profits are defined net of the costs of avoiding and remedying problems*.[53]

Edmans, for his part, argues that purpose statements should focus on activities where a company has a comparative advantage and should be dedicated towards the welfare of one or more clearly identified material groups of stakeholders.[54] We combined the suggestions of these authors and developed a two-fold 'Mayer-Edmans' test for corporate purposes which examined: (1) whether companies solve a problem in their purpose and (2) whether their purpose identifies a clear, material group of stakeholders. We found that less than half of our 35 companies satisfied the requirement of either author and that only 6% satisfied both. The results for this earlier 2020 data are summarised in Table 5.3.

Table 5.3 Mayer-Edmans Test for Corporate Purpose[55]

Requirement	*No. of Companies*	*Percentage of Companies*
1. Companies which solve a problem in their purpose [Mayer]	16	46
2. Companies which identify a material stakeholder group in their purpose [Edmans]	16	46
Companies which satisfy both requirements	2	6

In general, the vagueness of these corporate purpose statements suggested that there may be room for improvement in their formulation so that they are better able to support the company strategy and its social role in a concrete manner.

[2] Purpose Statements and Object Clauses in the Articles of Association

The research above shows that an increase in the use of non-statutory purpose statements is evident in the annual reports of Dutch-listed companies. We do not, however, see this same development reflected in statutory purposes, i.e., in the object clauses of the articles of association of Dutch listed companies. In their research, Kemp and Olaerts investigated the articles of association in force in 2021 of 132 Dutch incorporated companies with a national as well as a foreign listing.[56] They found that

53. Mayer, *supra* n. 4, at 889.
54. Edmans, *supra* n. 6, at 198.
55. Bauer et al., *supra* n. 32, at 55.
56. The research concerns companies incorporated in the Netherlands and listed at national as well as foreign stock exchanges. The research ended on 28 November 2021. Later changes were not

object clauses are mostly generically formulated. This means that for 51 companies out of 132, the object clause only contained a general description in the sense that it did not relate to the specific activities of the company. These generically formulated object clauses, for example, state that the goal of the company is to participate in other companies, finance other companies, provide loans and financial assistance, administer patents, etc. In addition to these generic descriptions, 81 out of 132 companies also have a more specific description of their activities next to the generic description. These more specific descriptions refer to the company's activities, such as the development of consumer goods related to mobility.[57] Furthermore, this research shows that sustainability, material stakeholders or principle values rarely appear in object clauses. On the rare occasions that it is mentioned, this is done in a very general manner and often refers only to the sustainability of the company's own products rather than the company's overall operations. The object clause of DSM, for example, referred[58] to the fact that the company wants to create value with regard to three basic values: economic performance, environmental quality, and social responsibility.[59] Other examples are Beter Bed Holding NV and Accell group NV which aimed to produce sustainable consumption goods and New Sources Energy NV which referred to the creation of sustainable energy products as one of its objectives.

This research shows that, as with non-statutory purpose clauses, the object clauses in the articles of association also remain very generic. Only a few companies refer to sustainability and this reference is often very broad. It follows that these clauses are unable to clearly steer the activities of the company or the behaviour of its agents. Moreover, the research shows that the increase in purpose statements is restricted to more general policy statements in the annual reports. These purpose statements are hardly ever reflected in the object clauses in the articles of association. Therefore, they are generally formulated by the board of directors without any shareholder involvement.

taken into account. *See* B. Kemp & M. Olaerts, 'Het vennootschappelijk doel', in Michael G. Faure (ed.) *Eindeloos getob. Liber Amicorum Kid Schwarz*, Instituut voor Ondernemingsrecht no. 125 (Wolters Kluwer 2022).

57. The authors refer to the articles of association of Accell Group NV as an example which contains the following: 'De vennootschap heeft ten doel het (doen) ontwikkelen en verkopen van duurzame consumentengoederen met betrekking tot mobiliteit voor de korte afstand, fitness en actieve recreatie, alsmede het deelnemen in, het besturen en financieren van en het verlenen van diensten aan vennootschappen en ondernemingen en het verrichten van al hetgeen daarmee verband houdt en daarvoor bevorderlijk kan zijn, een en ander in de ruimste zin' (Kemp & Olaerts, *supra* n. 55, at 398-399).
58. The company has now merged with Firmenich.
59. This relates to the object clause in DSMs articles of association before the merger with Firmenich. The company is now called DSM-Firmenich, a Swiss company and is therefore outside the ambit of our research into purpose statements of Dutch companies. However, also after the merger the object clause of the now Swiss AG also refers to the triple bottom line as it states in Art. 2 of its articles of association: 'Within the scope of its fields of activities the Company shall seek to create value along the triple bottom line of economic performance, environmental quality and social responsibility.'

§5.05 THE VALUE AND FUTURE OF PURPOSE STATEMENTS

It is not surprising that purpose statements are mainly formulated by the board of directors as part of general (strategy) statements, such as annual reports, rather than incorporated in the object clauses of the articles of association. This coincides with corporate practice in several other EU (and non-EU) countries, such as Germany, the UK, and France.[60] In general, there can be several reasons for using purpose statements as merely aspirational goals rather than incorporating them in the object clauses of the company.

First, this provides flexibility since it allows the board of directors to adjust the strategy and purpose as required. Second, one could argue that purpose clauses should be regarded as falling within the ambit of the power of the board as they are closely related to and interconnected with the strategy of the company. Third, leaving the purpose statement out of the articles of association arguably makes them more voluntary as they generally do not require the approval of the general meeting and can be easily changed if the board so desires.

Overall, whether incorporated in the articles of association or in the annual reports, it has to be admitted that most purpose statements are very broadly and vaguely formulated. For this reason, they have often been criticised in the literature and compared to not containing much more than a New Year's resolution.[61] Most likely, this is to avoid legal consequences attached to not following up on purpose statements. Nevertheless, this does not mean that purpose statements are devoid of any practical consequences.

First of all, it can be said that purpose statement can serve as a signalling tool for the company to show its employees, shareholders and other stakeholders the company's priorities in its strategy setting.[62] The effectiveness of this tool may, however, also require companies to formulate more precise purpose statements. These could then be used more concretely to guide decision-making throughout different levels of the company.[63] In the literature, it is also stated that a clearly defined, sustainable purpose can act as a reference point and anchor for sustainability-minded employees at different levels of the company. In this regard, it can support a formal and informal sustainability culture and send a signal to new generations of (potential) employees who are increasingly interested in sustainability.[64]

Purpose statements can also be used as a signalling tool towards shareholders. Prospective shareholders who disagree with the stakeholder priority setting by the company as reflected in its corporate purpose might be more likely to take their money elsewhere. While this could deprive the company of potential equity investors, it may

60. *See* about purpose statements in these countries Fleischer, *supra* n. 9.
61. Fleischer, *supra* n. 9, at 16, 20 with reference to Fisch & Solomon, *supra* n. 22.
62. Fleischer, *supra* n. 9, at 20.
63. Several authors argue that communication and coordination can be difficult in the absence of shared ideas and beliefs about what is important and valued in an organisation (Alvesson 2002; Linnenluecke & Griffiths 2010).
64. Luigi Guiso, Paola Sapienza & Luigi Zingales, 'The Value of Corporate Culture', 117 *Journal of Financial Economics* 1, 60-76 (2015).

also help it to tailor its shareholder population to something suited for obtaining its purpose. The most recent version of the DCGC also seems to help the board of directors in this respect. As mentioned earlier, it requires shareholders to 'recognise the importance of a strategy focused on sustainable long-term value creation for the company and its afliated [*sic*] enterprise'.[65] While ambiguous, this principle seems to reflect the idea that a shareholder should be sympathetic to the company's strategy aimed at sustainable long-term value creation and should not place the board under undue pressure. If the board does feel pressured in this way, it can trigger the 'response time'. This is a period of a maximum of 180 days during which the board of directors has an opportunity to respond to a shareholder request to place an item on the agenda of the general meeting which may result in a change in the company's strategy, for example, as a result of the dismissal of one or more board of directors or supervisory board members.[66] The power of shareholders is limited during these 180 days and they may not, for example, dismiss members of the board of directors. This may create a temporary zone of insulation for the board of directors against shareholder pressure, as advocated by Kershaw and Schuster (*see* §5.04[A] above).[67] While the principle of the DCGC was not written as a means to defend corporate purpose, it could be used to this effect, provided that the corporate purpose is also reflected in the corporate strategy that the shareholder action is seeking to change.

However, in order to have (practical) value, purpose statement has to be further integrated into the company's strategy and from there on into the various corporate policies.[68] This includes the adoption of consistent and coherent sustainability objectives and targets.[69] Another option is to include them in remuneration policies, so that they can work as a signalling tool for all stakeholders regarding the business aspects that the company wishes to emphasise or prioritise. Best practice 3.1.2 of the DCGC requires that, when setting the remuneration policy of the company, the objectives of the strategy for the implementation of sustainable long-term value creation are taken into consideration. Furthermore, it seems that Dutch-listed companies will have to adjust their remuneration policies to the corporate purpose if the latter is reflected in the strategy of the company. Purpose can also be used as a tool to reflect the outcomes of the dialogue between the company and its stakeholders. The DCGC requires companies to enter into a dialogue with their stakeholders. The outcomes of this dialogue can be used to inform the purpose statement and strategy more broadly.

65. Principle 4.4 of the DCGC.
66. Best practice 4.1.6 and 4.1.7 DCGC. Further protection is possible based on Art. 2:114b Dutch Civil Code which allows the board to invoke a reflection period of 250 days in case of, in short, shareholder activist campaigns involving dismissal of the board or a hostile takeover.
67. Kershaw & Schuster, *supra* n. 5, at 4. *See also* about limiting shareholder rights in the US and the UK: Davies, *supra* n. 10, at 21.
68. As explained by Younger et al., 'To deliver value for different stakeholders, purpose has to be more than a marketing slogan or a vague set of values. It has to become an organising principle, the reason why an organisation exists' (Rupert Younger, Colin Mayer & Robert G. Eccles, 'Enacting Purpose Within the Modern Corporation: A Framework for Boards of Directors', Enacting Purpose Initiative, 2 (2020)).
69. *See* for these and other recommendations on embedding sustainability by means of purpose statements: Bauer et al., *supra* n. 32.

Moreover, it could help companies identify their material stakeholder groups which, as noted above, is advised by Edmans when formulating a corporate purpose.

Secondly, as far as legal consequences are concerned, it should be mentioned that vague and broadly aspirational non-statutory purpose statements are unlikely to have any binding legal effect, whether they are taken up in the articles of association or merely formulated by the board of directors as part of company statements. One could argue that a purpose in the object clause of the articles of association is likely to have a stronger legally binding effect. An object clause can provide a further delineation of the powers of the board of directors and can serve as a means to give more direction to what the company interest entails, which is the applicable norm for judging decisions of the board. It has also been established in Dutch case law that violating a provision in the articles of association which is meant to protect the company raises the presumption that directors can be seriously blamed for their conduct.[70] Furthermore, a purpose statement in an object clause implies a further commitment by the parties involved, more specifically, the shareholders. After all, changing an object clause in the articles of association requires approval of the general meeting. However, in order for these purpose statements to have any meaningful legal effect, they again have to be more specific and integrated into the company's strategy and policies.

In some other jurisdictions, which do not have an explicit stakeholder model like the Netherlands, incorporating purpose into the articles of association may be necessary in order to move away from a shareholder orientation towards a more stakeholder-oriented corporate purpose. The incorporation of a more sustainable purpose in the object clause of the articles of association can have the effect of (voluntarily) broadening up the meaning of what the company interest entails and whose interests the board should serve. This can, for example, be the case in the UK. Section 172 of the UK Companies Act 2006 contains the 'enlightened shareholder model' that requires directors, in fulfilling their duties, to promote the success of the company for the benefit of its shareholders. In the process, they must take into account the long-term consequences of their decisions as well as a range of other interests, such as those of employees, the community, etc. Despite the fact that section 172 requires the board to take a whole range of other interests into account next to the shareholder interest, the default rule remains that the company has to be managed in the interest of the shareholders. It is, however, possible under section 172(2) for companies to opt out of this default rule, as it states: 'Where or to the extent that the purposes of the company consist of or include purposes other than the benefit of its members, subsection (1) has effect as if the reference to promoting the success of the company for the benefit of its members were to achieving those purposes.' Therefore, under the UK model, it seems possible to modify what the company's interests entail. Whether this requires approval of the general meeting and has to be taken up in the articles of association is a matter of UK law that we will not go into. However, it has been argued in the literature that a basis in the articles of association would indeed be needed and that a more general

70. Supreme Court 29 November 2002, ECLI:NL:HR:2002:AE7011, *JOR* 2003/2, m.nt. S.M. Bartman (Schwandt/Berghuizer Papierfabriek NV).

purpose statement in the annual accounts or on the company's website would not suffice.[71] Therefore, in order to achieve that, next to the default rule for interpreting what the company interest entails, a more stakeholder-inclusive company interest, approval of the general meeting and incorporation of the purpose in the articles of association can be required.

A question that can be raised is whether, in other jurisdictions such as the Netherlands, it is desirable to have a general meeting to vote on the purpose statement. We will not go deep into this discussion as the question itself merits a separate paper.[72] However, we will mention a few of the arguments discussed in the literature on this point. It has been argued, for example, that purpose statements in the articles of association or requiring the approval of shareholders would most likely lead to vague statements that are open for interpretation rather than have a direct binding effect. This would be partly due to the fact that shareholders may not be very willing to agree to very specific statements that allow the company and the board to move away from shareholder value[73] as well as due to the managerial freedom awarded to the board in many legal systems.[74] There may also be an accountability problem in the sense that stakeholders who may be affected if the board does not fulfil its corporate purpose generally do not have action rights.[75]

It should be emphasised that it does not follow from the above that non-statutory purpose statements cannot have legal consequences. On the contrary, if a company is serious about its purpose and has translated it into strategic targets and has adjusted its remuneration policy to fit its purpose and strategy, this can have a legal effect. This is not only the case in the Dutch context but is also likely from a European perspective. The reason for this is that the Corporate Sustainability Reporting Directive (CSRD)[76] requires companies in its scope to report on a range of issues related to sustainability, including, for example, a description of time-bound company targets related to sustainability matters and a description of progress with regard to these targets. Companies also have to disclose information on the existence of incentive schemes linked to sustainability matters which are offered to the board of directors and the supervisory board. They therefore have to report on a range of sustainability issues regardless of whether they have adopted a sustainable purpose. In this regard, the CSRD does not directly influence the adoption of purpose statements. However, if companies do adopt a specifically formulated, sustainable purpose and do not deliver on it or do not include its relevant aspects in their company strategy and policies, then this will become more visible as companies start to report in accordance with the new

71. Kershaw & Schuster, *supra* n. 5, at 10 and Davies *supra* n. 10, at 36.
72. *See* about the idea to give shareholders a say on purpose for example Edmans, *supra* n. 6, at 206; Fleischer, *supra* n. 9, at 22.
73. This would be the case, for example, in the 'Friedmanite' world that Davies describes (Davies, *supra* n. 10).
74. Fleisher, *supra* n. 9, at. 20, Davies, *supra* n. 10, at 10.
75. Fleisher, *supra* n. 9, at. 20.
76. Directive (EU) 2022/2464 of the European Parliament and the Council of 14 December 2022 amending Regulation (EU) No. 537/2014, Directive 2004/109/EC, Directive 2006/43/EC and Directive 2013/34/EU, as regards corporate sustainability reporting.

standards of the CSRD. This does not mean that it will automatically result in legal effects such as directors' liability. However, what the company has disclosed in terms of its purpose and related targets can be used to interpret what constitutes the interest of the company. This will apply regardless of whether the company has adopted an explicit sustainability-oriented purpose.

In summary, purpose statements are often broad and unspecific and generally belong in the realm of competences of the board of directors. This does not, however, mean that purpose statements are devoid of any legal and practical relevance. They can influence, with varying effects in different jurisdictions, how to interpret the company's interest, and we have seen that the CSRD requires companies to provide more specific information on the sustainability aspects of their strategy. Overall, it can be anticipated that the Directive will give stakeholders a clearer picture of whether a company delivers on its purpose in cases where the company has indeed adopted one and has tried to implement it throughout its organisation.

§5.06 CONCLUSION

We conclude that discussions on purpose have had an effect on corporate practice. Our research shows, at least for Dutch-listed companies, that there has been a notable increase in the use of purpose statements over the past decade. We have seen, moreover, that these statements have become increasingly oriented towards extrinsic rather than intrinsic aims. It cannot, however, be automatically inferred that these developments have had a standalone, positive effect on the sustainability of company operations. This is because, for example, purpose statements are often vaguely formulated, are seldom included in articles of association, and are typically formulated as a voluntary act by the board.

As noted, most company laws within the EU require the board of directors to fulfil their duties in the interests of the company. There is, however, no European approach as to what this entails. In countries with a shareholder-oriented view of the company's interest, a broader stakeholder-oriented purpose may help to voluntarily widen what the company's interest entails. Whether this is possible, of course, depends on national company law. The reporting requirements under the CSRD may make it easier for stakeholders to monitor whether the company is serious about its stated purpose.

Overall, it remains an open question whether and how purpose statements are able to make companies more sustainable. It seems, in any case, unlikely that purposes alone will lead to fundamental changes in company sustainability, given their typical vagueness and lack of legal effect. It is nonetheless relevant to consider their (potential) practical and legal consequences, as well as company relationships with other stakeholders and broader legal developments. In this regard, we saw, for example, that company purposes can serve as a signalling tool towards stakeholders, including shareholders. We also identified that, as companies take more steps to implement their purpose in concrete ways in their organisation, this may lead to an increase in legal effects over time, for example, due to the additional reporting requirements contained in the CSRD. Ultimately, this reaffirms that purposes are only as effective as their implementation by companies within the regulatory context that is provided by society.

CHAPTER 6

Hedge Fund Activism and ESG: Fit for Purpose?

Alexandros Seretakis

The rise of hedge fund activism promoting ESG concerns and the incorporation of ESG factors in investors' capital allocation decisions have created hopes that hedge fund activists will use their expertise in challenging the management of corporations in order to promote ESG goals. The present article will seek to analyse whether these hopes are justified and whether hedge fund activists have the incentives and competence to engage in ESG activism.

§6.01 INTRODUCTION

The last years have seen a noticeable shift in the investment strategy of hedge fund activists driven by the rise of investor activism promoting ESG concerns and the incorporation of ESG factors in investors' capital allocation decisions. In 2021, Engine 1, a little-known small hedge fund activist focused on climate change activism, shook the corporate establishment by placing three of its nominees on the board of directors of ExxonMobil, the largest private oil company and one of the world's largest corporations. With a tiny stake worth approximately USD 50 million in a multi-billion Dollar company, the fund, which criticized the company for its focus on fossil fuels and its reluctance to transition to cleaner energy, gathered the support of Exxon's biggest shareholders, namely BlackRock, Vanguard and State Street.[1] In early 2020, another notorious hedge fund activist, The Children's Investment Fund, which became famous

1. Derek Bower, *ExxonMobil Shareholders Hand Board Seats to Activist Nominees*, Financial Times, 26 May 2021 & Robert G. Eccles and Colin Mayer, *Can a Tiny Hedge Fund Push ExxonMobil Towards Sustainability*, Harvard Business Review, 20 January 2021.

for its acrimonious campaign against Deutsche Boerse,[2] launched its so-called Say on Climate Campaign, which seeks to encourage companies to establish net zero transition plans and put them to an annual advisory shareholder vote.[3] Even Carl Icahn, who earned a reputation as a corporate raider during the furious takeover battles of the 1980s,[4] attacked McDonald's, the fast food chain, over its treatment of pigs.[5]

These developments have created hopes that hedge fund activists will use their expertise in challenging the management of corporations in order to promote ESG goals. The present article will seek to analyse whether these hopes are justified and whether hedge fund activists have the incentives and competence to engage in ESG activism. Part I offers an introduction to the phenomenon of hedge fund activism and the tactics and demands of hedge fund activists. Part II discusses the rise of ESG activism and the crucial role of the Big Three in promoting ESG standards, while Part III examines whether the business model of hedge fund activists is compatible with ESG activism. As the present chapter will argue, hedge fund activists have neither the motivation nor the skills to engage in ESG-related activism.

§6.02 HEDGE FUND ACTIVISM

Modern hedge fund activism can trace its roots back to the 1970s and 1980s when individual investors such as Carl Icahn and Nelson Peltz began building controlling positions in U.S. corporations and aggressively agitating for actions that would grant

2. Deutsche Boerse's bid for the London Stock Exchange (LSE) provoked a shareholders' rebellion led by TCI, which resulted in the collapse of the bid and the resignation of Deutsche Boerse's Chief Executive Officer and Chairman of the Board of Directors. The revolt marked the advent of Anglo-Saxon aggressive shareholder activism in the traditionally closed and insider-dominated German corporate system. Following the outcry provoked by the shareholders' rebellion the former Chairman of the Social-Democratic Party of Germany Frank Muntefering described hedge funds as 'swarms of locusts'. For an excellent overview of this landmark revolt and its effects on German corporate governance, *see generally* Sudi Sudarsanam & Tim Broadhurst, *Corporate Governance Convergence in Germany Through Shareholder Activism: Impact of the Deutsche Boerse bid for London Stock Exchange,* 16 J. Mgmt. & Gov., 235 (2012).
3. Leslie Hook & Gillian Tett, *Hedge Fund TCI Vows to Punish Directors Over Climate Change,* Financial Times, 1 December 2019.
4. The U.S. takeover boom lasted from 1984 until 1989 and was characterized by a surge in hostile takeovers and leveraged buyouts. *See* Patrick Gaughan, *Mergers, Acquisitions, and Corporate Restructurings* 57-63 (5th ed. 2011). Hostile takeovers were viewed as the ultimate disciplinary mechanism against managerial incompetence and self-interest. *See* Henry G. Manne, *Mergers and the Market for Corporate Control,* 73 Journal of Political Economy 110, 113 (1965) DOI: 10.1086/259000. Multiple factors contributed to the end of the takeover boom, including the economic slowdown starting in 1989; the collapse of Drexel Burnham Lambert, an investment bank specialized in financing takeovers; the enactment of anti-takeover statutes by state legislatures; and the endorsement of takeover defenses by the courts of the state of Delaware, where the majority of public corporations have been incorporated following a series of landmark court decisions. *See* Steven M. Davidoff, *Takeover Theory and the Law and Economics Movement,* in *Research Handbook on the Economics of Corporation Law* 216 (Claire Hill & Brett McDonnell eds, 2012).
5. Patrick Temple-West, *Carl Icahn Loses Proxy Fight with McDonald's over Pig Welfare,* Financial Times, 26 May 2022. Icahn's campaign was influenced by his daughter which worked for the Humane Society, an animal welfare charity.

them short-term gains.[6] Faced with collective action problems, however, individual shareholders largely abstained from becoming involved in corporate governance.[7] The attention of policymakers and academics turned to the other powerful players in capital markets: institutional investors, such as mutual funds and pension funds.[8] However, the impact of institutional investors on corporate governance and performance has been negligible.[9] Institutional investor activism tends to be 'incidental' and 'ex-post.'[10] Regulatory requirements, such as diversification requirements for mutual and pension funds and liquidity requirements for open-ended mutual fund investors, conflicts of interest and their business model, which focuses on relative performance,[11] prevent institutional investors from becoming active owners.

In contrast to institutional investor activism, hedge fund activism is strategic and ex ante with hedge funds investing in order to engage in activism.[12] Activists typically amass large positions falling short of control blocks and typically below 10% of target stock[13] and engage in costly and time-consuming efforts to propose and aid in the implementation of changes in target companies. The activist lacking a controlling position in the target has to gather the support of other shareholders, mainly institutional investors, in order to implement its proposed changes.[14] The most common propositions of activists are a sale of the target, return of excess cash, sale or spinoffs

---

6. *See generally* John C. Coffee, Louis Lowenstein & Susan Rose-Ackerman, *Knights, Raiders, and Targets: The Impact of the Hostile Takeover* (Oxford University Press 1988).
7. *See* Daniel R. Fischel & Frank Easterbrook, *The Economic Structure of Corporate Law* 63-89 (Harvard University Press 1991); Bernard S Black, *Shareholder Passivity Reexamined*, 89 Michigan Law Review, 526-530 (1990) DOI: 10.2307/1289384.
8. Institutional investors and especially mutual funds and pension funds have come to dominate modern capital markets. In 2009, over 50% of US public equities were held by institutional investors. *See* Stephan Rabimov Matteo Tonello, *The 2010 Institutional Investment Report: Trends in Asset Allocation and Portfolio Composition* (Conference Bd., Research Report No. R-1468-10-RR, 2010), http://ssrn.com/abstract=1707512.
9. As Bernard Black stated '[t]he currently available evidence, taken as a whole, is consistent with the proposition that the institutions achieve the effects on firm performance that one might expect from this level of effort - namely not much'. Bernard S. Black, *Shareholder Activism and Corporate Governance in the United States, in The New Palgrave Dictionary of Economics and the Law* (John Eatwell et al. eds, 1998).
10. Traditional institutional investor activism seeks to safeguard the value of pre-existing investments. Thus, institutional investors will engage in activism only in case a company already part of the institution's portfolio is either underperforming or is in dire need of a shake-up in its corporate governance. Brian R. Cheffins & John Armour, *The Past, Present and Future of Shareholder Activism by Hedge Funds*, 37 Journal of Corporation Law, 56 no. 1 (2011).
11. The performance of mutual fund and pension fund managers is judged against the performance of their peers. Mutual fund and pension fund managers will typically hold shares in the same companies. As a result, a manager engaging in activism must bear all of the costs of the effort while sharing the gains with its competitors. Consequently, his performance relative to his competitors will decline.
12. *See generally*, Brian R. Cheffins & John Armour, *The Past, Present and Future of Shareholder Activism by Hedge Funds*, 37 Journal of Corporation Law, 51 no. 1 (2011).
13. Alon Brav et al., *Pre-disclosure Accumulations by Activist Investors: Evidence and Policy*, 39 Journal of Corporation Law, 12 no. 1 (2013). (examining all 13D filings by activist hedge funds in the United States from 1994 until 2007 and finding that activists acquire an average stake of 8.8% and median of 6.3%).
14. Ruth Sullivan, *Traditional Investors Adopt Activism*, The Financial Times, 5 May 2013. Institutional ownership in the top 1,000 US corporations has reached an average of 73%. *See* Stephan

of unrelated assets and refocusing corporate strategy,[15] improvements in firm governance, and changes in the target's long-term business plan.[16] Unconstrained by legal barriers and incentivized by high-powered compensation,[17] activists specialize in searching for undervalued[18] and poorly governed firms and are agitating for operational or governance improvements. Belonging to the group of value investors,[19] hedge fund activists spot targets that will benefit from intervention and identify the changes that will unlock shareholder value.[20]

Numerous studies have documented the positive effects of hedge fund activism on shareholders and target companies. In a study of activist interventions in the U.S. to date, Bebchuk, Brav, and Jiang find large average abnormal returns of approximately 6% in a 40-day window around the filing of a Schedule 13D announcing the presence of an activist hedge fund.[21] The study also documents subsequent improvements in operational performance following the activist's intervention. According to the authors, activists target companies whose operating performance at the time of intervention trails that of their industry peers or their own historical levels.[22] However, target companies outperform their peers during the five years following the intervention, with operating performance exceeding the intervention-year level in each year.[23] These studies point to the beneficial effects of activism for shareholders and the operational performance of target companies.

Nonetheless, the results of these studies and the concomitant positive view of hedge fund activism have been criticized by other studies. For instance, despite the substantial evidence that target firms earn *on average* positive abnormal returns around the disclosure date of the activist's stake, numerous studies find that a

Rabimov Matteo Tonello, *The 2010 Institutional Investment Report: Trends in Asset Allocation and Portfolio Composition* (Conference Bd., Research Report No. R-1468-10-RR, 2010), http://ssrn.com/abstract=1707512.

15. *See* William Bratton, *Hedge Funds and Governance Targets*, 95 Georgetown Law Journal, 1390-1397 no. 5 (2007) DOI: 10.2139/ssrn.928689.
16. *Ibid.*
17. While mutual funds are compensated on the basis of the assets under management, hedge fund compensation consists of both a management fee, ranging from one to two percent of the assets under management, and an incentive fee, usually set at twenty percent of the fund's profits and widely known as 'carried interest'. Carried interest creates a powerful incentive for hedge funds to seek absolute performance. *See* Ludwig Chincarini, *Hedge Funds – An Introduction, in Research Handbook on Hedge Funds, Private Equity and Alternative Investments* 13, 24 (Claire Hill & Brett McDonnell eds, 2012).
18. Brav, Jiang and Kim find that activists target firms with a low market relative to book value. Alon Brav, Wei Jiang & Hyunseob Kim, *Hedge Fund Activism: A Review, 4 Foundations and Trends (R) in Finance*, no. 3 (2010).
19. *See* William Bratton, *Hedge Funds and Governance Targets*, 95 Georgetown Law Journal, 1383 no. 5 (2007).
20. Ronald J. Gilson & Jeffrey N. Gordon, *The Agency Costs of Agency Capitalism: Activist Investors and the Reevaluation of Governance Rights*, 113 Columbia Law Review 863, 902 (2013).
21. Lucian Bebchuk, Alon Brav & Wei Jiang, *The Long-Term Effects of Hedge Fund Activism*, 115(5) Columbia Law Review 1085, 1120-1134 (2015) DOI: 10.3386/w21227. Large abnormal returns have been documented for activist interventions in Europe as well. *See* Marco Becht, Julian Franks & Jeremy Grant, *Hedge Fund Activism in Europe*, No. 283 ECGI-Finance Working Paper (2010).
22. *Ibid.*, 1101-1118.
23. *Ibid.*

significant proportion of firms actually earn negative abnormal returns.[24] What is more, Cremers et al. argue that the positive abnormal returns of target firms are explained by the superior stock picking and trading skills of activists.[25] In another study, the authors show that the results of the studies documenting the positive effects of activism on target company value suffer from self-selection bias as activist hedge funds tend to target firms that have been relatively poorly performing prior to the activists' interventions.[26] Moreover, companies targeted by activist hedge funds improve less in value subsequent to the start of an activist hedge fund campaign than *ex ante* similarly poorly performing control firms that are not subject to hedge fund activism.[27]

What is more, DesJardine and Durand examine 1,324 activist hedge fund campaigns between 2000 and 2016 and document that market value improves immediately after the intervention, but only temporarily, before turning negative, profitability increases only in years one and two after the intervention and cash flow decreases nearly immediately and for at least five subsequent years.[28] Finally, DesJardine et al. find that firms targeted by hedge fund activists significantly scale back and simplify their strategic actions, defined as long-run competitive actions requiring substantial investment.[29] In contrast, targeted firms pursue short-term-oriented actions that are not resource-intensive.

§6.03 THE RISE OF ESG ACTIVISM

The last decade has witnessed the fundamental transformation of the global economy and capital markets with the incorporation of environmental, social and governance concerns in corporate governance and finance. The rise of ESG investing can be traced back to 2006 and the adoption of the Principles for Responsible Investment by the UN in collaboration with a group of leading institutional investors.[30] As Bartlett and Bubb note, ESG is a term that captures ways that investors can improve their risk-adjusted returns by incorporating environmental, social, and governance considerations into

24. *See* Alon Brav et al., *Hedge Fund Activism, Corporate Governance and Firm Performance*, 63 Journal of Finance, 1729 (2008) DOI: 10.1111/j.1540-6261.2008.01373.x. (despite documenting average abnormal returns between 7% and 8%, the authors also find that 38% of target firms earned negative abnormal returns).
25. K.J. Martijn Cremers et al., *Hedge Fund Activists: Value Creators or Stock Pickers* (2021), https://papers.ssrn.com/sol3/papers.cfm?abstract_id = 3614029.
26. K.J. Martijn Cremers et al., *Hedge Fund Activism and Long-Term Firm Value* (2020), https://papers.ssrn.com/sol3/papers.cfm?abstract_id = 2693231.
27. *Ibid.*
28. Mark R. Desjardine & Rodolphe Durand, *Disentangling the Effects of Hedge Fund Activism on Firm Financial and Social Performance*, 41(6) Strategic Management Journal (2020) DOI: 10.1002/smj.3126.
29. Mark R. Desjardine et al., *Different Horizons: The Effects of Hedge Fund Activism Versus Corporate Shareholder Activism on Strategic Actions*, 48(7) Journal of Management, 1858-1887 (2022) DOI: 10.1177/01492063211022831.
30. *See* https://www.unpri.org/.

their investment process.[31] The most common justification for ESG is long-term value maximization.[32] Pursuant to the long-term value maximization rationale, the incorporation of ESG standards improves the financial performance of corporations and increases shareholder value.[33] For instance, companies which follow ESG standards are more likely to attract loyal customers and employees, capture business opportunities related to societal trends such as climate change, and avoid regulatory fines.[34] As a result, managers should focus on the creation of long-term shareholder value instead of prioritizing short-term profits. It should be noted that long-term value maximization justification accepts the view that corporations should be run solely for the benefit of shareholders and managers should focus exclusively on the maximization of shareholder value, also referred to as shareholder primacy.

Numerous studies have documented a positive association between ESG and financial performance. Research has found that investors in companies with good ESG performance are able to obtain higher returns than the average within their broader market.[35] Similarly, in their study, Dorfleitner et al. find that firms with CSR significantly outperform firms with weak CSR both in the medium and in the long term in certain areas. Moreover, an increase in ESG ratings leads to an increase in firm returns.[36] In their study, Berg et al., after correcting the noise in ESG ratings, documented a strong effect of ESG on stock returns.[37] Lopez De Silanes et al. find statistically significant evidence to support the view that ESG, and particularly the

31. Robert P. Bartlett & Ryan Bubb, *Corporate Social Responsibility Through Shareholder Governance* 11 (ECGI Law Working Paper No. 682/2023).
32. The other two justifications for ESG are stakeholder theory and shareholders' social preferences. According to the stakeholder theory, corporations should be run for the benefit of all stakeholders, including shareholders, employees, suppliers, communities, consumers and society at large. In contrast to the long-term value maximization justification, stakeholder theory argues that the pursuit of ESG goals should be prioritized even if it comes at the expense of financial performance of the company. Finally, the shareholder social preferences justification argues that apart from seeking to maximize their profits, shareholders also have ethical and moral concerns. As a result, managers should accept shareholders' preferences and seek to further ESG goals. *See* generally, Sharon Hannes et al., *The ESG Gap* (University of Pennsylvania Institute of Law and Economics Research Paper No. 23-22, 2022). For instance Baker et al. find that investors are willing, on average, to pay higher fees for ESG-oriented funds as compared to otherwise identical mutual funds without an ESG mandate, suggesting that investors expect higher returns, either financial or non-financial, from an ESG mandate. Malcolm Baker et al., *How Do Investors Value ESG?* (NBER Working Paper Series No. 30708, 2022).
33. *See generally*, Alex Edmans, *Grow the Pie: How Great Companies Deliver Both Purpose and Profit* (Cambridge University Press 2020).
34. Alex Edmans & Marcin T. Kacperczyk, *Sustainable Finance*, 69 Review of Finance, 1309 (2022) DOI: 10.1093/rof/rfac069.
35. Dan Byrne, *Companies with Good ESG Perform Better*, Corporate Governance Institute, https://www.thecorporategovernanceinstitute.com/insights/news-analysis/companies-with-good-esg-perform-better/.
36. Gregor Dorfleitner, Sebastian Utz, & Maximilian Wimmer, *Patience Pays Off – Corporate Social Responsibility and Longterm Stock Returns*, 8(2) Journal of Sustainable Finance & Investment, 132-157 (2018) DOI: 10.1080/20430795.2017.1403272.
37. Florian Berg et al., *ESG Confusion and Stock Returns: Tackling the Problem of Noise* (NBER Working Paper No. 30562, 2021), https://www.nber.org/system/files/working_papers/w30562/w30562.pdf.

governance dimension, is related to decreased risk.[38] In addition, Cheng et al. documented that firms with better corporate social responsibility performance have better access to finance, facing significantly less capital constraints.[39]

The promise of ESG has resulted in a massive influx of capital into so-called ESG funds, namely funds that claim to have some sort of a sustainable investing mandate. By the end of 2021, assets in ESG funds reached approximately USD 3 trillion, with European funds representing the lion's share of assets under management.[40] Both active, such as hedge funds, and passive funds, such as index funds, are increasingly adopting an activist stance with regard to promoting ESG standards. The most basic types of activism are negative and positive screening.[41] Negative screening refers to investors avoiding investing in companies that engage in ethically dubious activities, such as tobacco, weapons, pornography, etc. In contrast, positive screening refers to investors identifying and investing in companies that score high on ESG factors. However, increasingly investors are proactively seeking to change corporate policy with respect to ESG. Investors, such as hedge funds, screen companies and seek to identify the ones that could improve their ESG policies. The tools they use in order to influence companies' policies include the use of voting rights and direct engagement with management.

Moreover, the role of the Big Three (i.e., BlackRock, State Street and Vanguard) has been crucial in promoting ESG standards. The Big Three hold an exorbitant sway over modern capital markets. Bebchuk and Hirst estimate that, as of the end of 2021, the Big Three collectively held a median stake of 21.9% in S&P 500 companies, representing 24.9% of the votes cast at the annual meetings of those companies.[42] The Big Three are using their voting power to influence their portfolio companies' ESG policies.[43] The ESG revolution has led to significant changes to their proxy voting policies to incorporate ESG concerns.[44] For instance, starting with State Street's Fearless Girl campaign in 2017, the Big Three adopted policies of voting against

38. Florencio Lopez De Silanes et al., *Institutional Investors and ESG Preferences* (NBER Working Paper No. 631/2022), https://www.ecgi.global/sites/default/files/working_papers/documents/esgfinal_1.pdf.
39. Beiting Cheng et al., *Corporate Social Responsibility and Access to Finance*, 35 Strategic Management Journal, 1-23 (2011) DOI: 10.1002/smj.2131.
40. Harriet Agnew et al., *How ESG Investing Came to a Reckoning*, The Financial Times, 6 June 2022.
41. Tamas Barko et al. *Shareholder Engagement on Environmental, Social and Governance Performance* (5 ECGI Working Paper No. 509/2017, 2021).
42. Lucian Bebchuk & Scott Hirst, *Big Three Power, and Why It Matters*, 102 Boston University Law Review, 1552 (2022).
43. For instance, Webber et al. note that in contrast to their passive approach to conventional corporate governance issues, the Big Three index funds take a more aggressive and confrontational approach to ESG issues. The authors argue that the activist stance of index funds can be explained by their desire to win over the millennial generation, which places importance on social issues. David H. Webber et al., *Shareholder Value(s): Index Fund ESG Activism and the New Millennial Corporate Governance*, 93 Southern California Law Review, 1243 (2020) DOI: 10.2139/ssrn.3439516.
44. Weil, *The Big Three and ESG: A Guide to Blackrock, State Street and Vanguard Proxy Voting Policies and Guidance on Key ESG Issues*, https://www.weil.com/-/media/mailings/2023/q2/the-big-three--esg--a-guide-to-blackrock-state-street--vanguard-proxy-voting-policies--guidance-on-k.pdf.

directors' re-election at corporations whose boards were not making sufficient progress toward gender diversity.[45] Moreover, the Big Three are increasingly offering their support to hedge fund activists in their ESG campaigns. The Big Three's engagement seems to be making a difference. For example, Azar et al. find evidence that the Big Three engagements are more likely to target firms with high carbon emissions.[46] They also document that the Big Three engagements result in a reduction in carbon emissions. Finally, Gormley et al. argue that the Big Three's campaign for gender-diverse boards increased female directorships.[47] They estimate that one standard deviation greater ownership by the Big Three is associated with a 76% increase in the net flow of new female board members and an 11% increase in the overall proportion of female directors.

§6.04 HEDGE FUND ACTIVISTS AND ESG: FIT FOR PURPOSE?

Engine 1's spectacular victory over ExxonMobil has created hopes that hedge fund activists will assume a leading role, with the support of the Big Three, in promoting ESG standards.[48] According to this view, activists have the necessary expertise to identify companies which would benefit from the implementation of business changes and devise and execute alternative business plans for companies.[49] Moreover, they can use a wide array of tactics, including initiating litigation, public relations, social media and traditional media campaigns, negotiating settlements and launching proxy fights, to convince target management to fulfil their demands.[50] Nevertheless, the potential contribution of hedge fund activists in the ESG revolution is unlikely to be significant. Campaigns like the Engine 1 campaign against ExxonMobil are the exception rather than the norm. A survey of activist campaigns in Europe documents that from 2020 until 2022, only three campaigns included demands for environmental and social

45. Paula Loop & Paul DeNicola, *You've Committed to Increasing Gender Diversity on Your Board. Here's How to Make it Happen*, Harvard Business Review, 18 February 2019.
46. José Azar et al., *The Big Three and Corporate Carbon Emissions Around the World* (NBER Working Paper No. 715/2020), https://www.ecgi.global/sites/default/files/working_papers/documents/finalazardurokadachormazabal.pdf.
47. Todd A. Gormley et al., *The Big Three and Board Gender Diversity: The Effectiveness of Shareholder Voice*, 149 Journal of Financial Economics, 323-348 (2023) DOI: 10.1016/j.jfineco.2023.04.001.
48. For instance, according to Christie 'ESG hedge funds have the potential to initiate firm-specific ESG activism as "ESG arbitrageurs" in a manner that appeals to, and mobilizes, the sustainable capitalism of Big Three'. Anne Christie, *The Agency Costs of Sustainable Capitalism*, 55 UC Davis Law Review, 875 (2021) DOI: 10.2139/ssrn.3766478.
49. Sharon Hannes et al., *The ESG Gap* 24 (University of Pennsylvania Institute of Law and Economics Research Paper No. 23-22, 2022).
50. Martin Lipton, *Dealing with Activist Hedge Funds and Other Activist Investors*, Harvard Law School Forum on Corporate Governance, 6 October 2021, available at https://corpgov.law.harvard.edu/2021/10/06/dealing-with-activist-hedge-funds-and-other-activist-investors-4/. *See also* Lucian Bebchuk et al., *Dancing with Activists*, 137 Journal of Financial Economics, 1 (July 2020) DOI: 10.1016/j.jfineco.2020.01.001.

changes.[51] Hedge fund activists have neither the motivation nor the skills to engage in ESG activism.

The business model of activists is incompatible with ESG activism. Activists are looking to implement changes that will unlock value in the short to medium term. Indeed, Brav, Jiang, Partnoy, and Thomas find an average holding period of twenty-two months for activists targeting US companies,[52] while Becht, Franks, and Grant report an average holding period of 645 days (approximately twenty-one months) for their sample of activist interventions in Europe.[53] The changes that hedge funds demand from their targets focus mostly on operational changes and financial engineering that do not require lengthy execution, such as cost reductions, share buybacks, sale of the company and sales and spinoffs of assets. For instance, Greenwood and Schor find in their sample of activist interventions in the United States from 1993-2006 that the returns to activism are significant, mainly in instances where the target is acquired within eighteen months of the initial intervention.[54] As a result, they are driven by the activists' skills in effecting a takeover of the target. As Hannes et al. note, even in the case of Engine's 1 campaign against ExxonMobil, many of the plans proposed for ExxonMobil were classic activist hedge fund demands, which were only cloaked under an environmental dressing.[55] Hedge fund activists' focus on changes that will unlock value in the short term can be explained by their desire to offer their investors high returns on their investment which are independent of the overall performance of the market.[56]

Hedge fund activists are more skilled at facilitating efficient capital reallocation and promoting firm policies that will increase shareholder value, such as payouts, corporate governance changes, sale of the company, rather than devising and implementing a long-term plan and vision for the company. In contrast to activists' focus on the short to medium, the advancement of ESG goals requires the implementation of

51. Skadden, *The Informed Board* (Winter 2023), https://www.skadden.com/-/media/files/publications/2023/02/the-informed-board/european-activism-more-attacks-more-engagement-more-esg-coming-in-2023.pdf?rev=3bc4d02ff0654c23b379ae3f98544354.
52. Alon Brav et al., *Hedge Fund Activism, Corporate Governance and Firm Performance*, 63 Journal of Finance, 1729, 1741 (2008) DOI: 10.1111/j.1540-6261.2008.01373.x.
53. Marco Becht et al., *Hedge Fund Activism in Europe* (ECGI Working Paper No. 283/2010), http://www.ecgi.org/tcgd/2011/documents/Becht-Franks-Grant%20Hedge%20Fund%20Activism %20in%20Europe%202010.pdf.
54. Robin Greenwood & Michael Schor, *Investor Activism and Takeovers*, 92 Journal of Financial Economics, 362 (2009) DOI: 10.1016/j.jfineco.2008.05.005. The authors argue that the positive average abnormal returns reflect the market's expectation that the activist will put the firm in play and succeed in getting the target acquired at a premium to the current stock price.
55. For instance, Engine 1 focused its critique on ExxonMobil's poor share price performance, on inefficient capital expenditures on drillings and the disconnect between CEO pay and performance.
56. As Hannes et al. note 'corporate reforms that require longer period of time increase the exposure of investors to market fluctuations and to the "beta" of the market'. Hannes et al., p. 25. Hedge funds seek to offer their investors alpha defined as the excess return after adjusting for market-related volatility and random fluctuations. Alpha refers to the portion of the return that is attributable to manager's skills. In contrast, beta refers to the return correlation of a security with the market and the return volatility relative to the market. *See* Alexandros Seretakis, *Regulating Hedge Funds in the EU* 21 (Kluwer Law International 2022).

changes whose results will materialize over a long-term horizon. Any gains from ESG activism will accrue after years. Moreover, modern capital markets are also populated by myopic investors, which overvalue short-term profits while undervaluing long-term returns.[57] For instance, executives have acknowledged in different surveys that they are willing to decrease spending on 'discretionary' activities like marketing and R&D to meet short-term goals.[58] As a result, investors may in some cases actually penalize companies that seek to advance complex ESG goals.

Indeed, in a series of studies, Mark Desjardine and Rodolphe Durand show that hedge fund activists are actually detrimental to the advancement of ESG goals. In a study published in 2020, Desjardine and Durand found that companies targeted by activists significantly decreased labour force, operating expenses, R&D spending and capital expenditures.[59] Moreover, companies' social performance decreased by almost 25% in the five-year period following the activists' intervention. In another study of more than 500 companies between 2000 and 2016, the authors document that companies which spend more on CSR compared to their peers are more likely to be targeted by hedge fund activists.[60] The authors argue that activists consider CSR to be a signal that firms have wasteful intentions and capabilities and are willing to sacrifice short-term shareholder value.

§6.05 CONCLUSION

Overall, Engine 1's successful campaign should be seen as an isolated event rather than a harbinger of things to come. For example, celebrated activist Jeff Uben left ValueAct Capital, the hedge fund he founded, in order to focus on social and environmental investments, arguing that impact investing can no longer 'peacefully co-exist' with traditional hedge fund activism.[61] As the present article has demonstrated, hedge fund

57. Paul Docherty & Gareth Hurst, *Investor Myopia and the Momentum Premium Across International Equity Markets*, 53 Journal of Financial and Quantitative Analysis, 2465 (2018) DOI: 10.1017/s0022109018000431; Jeremy C. Stein, *Takeover Threats and Managerial Myopia*, 96 Journal of Political Economy, 61 (1988)DOI: 10.1086/261524; Alexandre Garel, *Myopic Market Pricing and Managerial Myopia*, 44 Journal of Business, Finance and Accounting (2017) DOI: 10.1111/jbfa.12262.
58. For example *see* Natalie Mizik & Robert Jacobson, *The Cost of Myopic Management*, Harvard Business Review, July-August, 2007.
59. *Ibid.*
60. Mark R. DesJardine et al., *Why Activist Hedge Funds Target Socially Responsible Firms: The Reaction Costs of Signaling Corporate Social Responsibility*, 64(3) Academy of Management Journal (2021) DOI: 10.5465/amj.2019.0238.
61. Svea Herbst-Bayliss, *Companies that Spend on Social-Causes Risk Hedge Fund Challenge*: Study, Reuters, 23 June 2020. ValueAct became famous when it amassed a mere 0.8% stake in Microsoft and forced longtime Microsoft CEO Steve Ballmer to resign and gained a board seat at the software giant. *See* Richard Waters, *Microsoft Cedes Board Seat to Value Act*, Financial Times, 30 August 2013. It should be noted following his exit from ValueAct and the set up of his new impact vehicle Inclusive Capital Partners, Ubben started becoming critical of ESG and returning to traditional shareholder activism by disclosing a stake in pharmaceutical giant Bayer and calling for the appointment of an outside chief executive. Patrick Temple-West and Ortenca Aliaj, *Investor Jeff Ubben Questions ESG Funds in Second Act as Activist*, Financial Times, 20 January 2023.

activists have neither the motivation nor the skills to engage in ESG activism. Hedge fund activists are more skilled at executing efficient capital reallocation and promoting firm policies that will increase shareholder value rather than devising and executing a long-term plan and vision for the company. In contrast, recent research shows that hedge fund activists can be a major obstacle to the efforts of regulators, politicians and investors worldwide to promote ESG goals.

CHAPTER 7

Corporate (Case) Law in the Age of Sustainability

Cees de Groot

§7.01 INTRODUCTION

Having been appointed as professor of company law at Leiden University, Steef Bartman took the initiative to set up a completely new law journal: *European Company Law* (ECL). The first issue was published in April 2004. Jaap Winter wrote an Editorial on this issue ('We all want to go to heaven but nobody wants to die') on the 13th company law directive on takeover bids, Steef Bartman wrote an article on this Directive ('Analysis and consequences of the EC Directive on takeover bids'), and Christel M. Grundmann-Van de Krol wrote an article ('New EC Prospectus Directive and the Lamfalussy Process'). The issue also held a number of country reports that highlighted recent developments in several European jurisdictions: a report from Belgium, a report from Denmark, a report from France, a report from Germany, a report from Italy, a report from the Netherlands, a report from Spain, and a report from the United Kingdom. Furthermore, the issue contained a survey of (recent) legislation and case law as well as a summarized selection of articles from other legal periodicals. This first issue was 40 pages long. With this issue, ECL got off to a flying start. ECL is now well established and in its twentieth year of publication.

Since 2004, company law has gone through many developments, including – more recently – the rising of sustainability-related issues. These issues have led to important legislation and case law. In the field of sustainability legislation, the European Union (EU) takes the lead with a large number of initiatives, including, e.g., the Taxonomy Regulation,[1] the Corporate Sustainability Reporting Directive (CSRD),[2] and the (proposed) Corporate Sustainability Due Diligence Directive (CSDD, CSDDD, CS-triple-D or CS-3D).[3] These three important initiatives are closely intertwined:

(1) the CSDD establishes obligations for affected companies 'regarding actual and potential human rights adverse impacts and environmental adverse impacts with respect to their own operations, the operations of their subsidiaries, and the value chain operations carried out by entities with whom the company has an established business relationship' (Article 1, section 1, under a);
(2) the CSRD obliges affected undertakings and parent undertakings to 'include in [the management report/the consolidated management report] information necessary to understand [the undertaking's/the group's] impacts on sustainability matters, and information necessary to understand how sustainability matters affect the undertaking's development, performance and position';[4] and
(3) the Taxonomy Regulation 'establishes the criteria for determining whether an economic activity qualifies as environmentally sustainable' and does so 'for the purposes of establishing the degree to which an investment is environmentally sustainable' (Article 1, section 1).

In the field of sustainability case law, climate change case law has especially gained importance.[5] Two examples of this kind of case law will be discussed below.

This contribution starts (in §7.02) by placing the development of corporate law (both legislation and case law) in a historical perspective. It does so by following the analysis of the time period of the so-called modern era, as that era is subdivided by the (Marxist) British historian Eric Hobsbawm (1917-2012). His narrative starts in 1789 and ends in 1991. Hobsbawm divides the modern era into four 'ages', which he calls the age of revolution, the age of capital, the age of empire, and the age of extremes. In §7.02, added to his analysis of these ages are a few notable examples of legislation and case law (chosen from both the United Kingdom and the Netherlands) that show how a particular age affects the legislation and case law of that period.

1. Regulation (EU) 2020/852 of the European Parliament and of the Council of 18 June 2020 on the establishment of a framework to facilitate sustainable investment, and amending Regulation (EU) 2019/2088 (text with EEA relevance), OJEU L 198/13-43.
2. Directive (EU) 2022/2464 of the European Parliament and of the Council of 14 December 2022 amending Regulation (EU) No. 537/2014, Directive 2004/109/EC, Directive 2006/43/EC and Directive 2013/34/EU, as regards corporate sustainability reporting (text with EEA relevance), OJEU 2022 L 322/15-80.
3. Proposal for a Directive of the European Parliament and of the Council on Corporate Sustainability Due Diligence and amending Directive (EU) 2019/1937 (text with EEA relevance), COM(2022) 71 final.
4. Implemented in Arts 19a and 29a of the Accounting Directive (Directive 2006/43/EC of the European Parliament and of the Council of 17 May 2006 on statutory audits of annual accounts and consolidated accounts, amending Council Directives 78/ 660/EEC and 83/349/EEC and repealing Council Directive 84/253/EEC (text with EEA relevance), OJEU 2006 L 157/87-107.
5. Cf. e.g. https://climatecasechart.com.

Section §7.03 gives a timeline for the years 1989-2022. This is the time period that (approximately) follows the four ages described by Hobsbawm. This timeline shows that climate change and sustainability are (also politically) high on the agenda from (at least) 2015. Building on this, §7.04 and §7.05 discuss recent case law from the Netherlands in the field of climate change: §7.04 goes into the judgment of the Supreme Court of the Netherlands in the case between *Stichting Urgenda* and *de Staat der Nederlanden*, and §7.05 gives a short discussion of some elements of the judgment of the district court of Den Haag (The Hague) in the case between *Vereniging Milieudefensie et al.* and *Royal Dutch Shell Plc*. In both judgments, the (European) Convention for the Protection of Human Rights and Fundamental Freedoms (ECHR) played a pivotal role. This is to be expected in a court case where a state is the defendant, but it is somewhat striking in a case where a corporation is the defendant, as the ECHR addresses states but not corporations. Building on these judgments, §7.06 ends with a short conclusion.

§7.02 THE MODERN ERA

[A] Introduction

The modern era is a phrase used to describe a historical epoch that started at the end of the eighteenth century and continues up until today. This implies that the modern era covers (parts of) four centuries: the eighteenth, nineteenth, twentieth and twenty-first centuries. This is a long time frame that itself could be subdivided into several parts. Hobsbawm does so for the period 1789-1991 in four books.

[B] The First Book

The first book in the series is *The Age of Revolution: 1789-1848*, originally published in 1962.[6] The book tells that in 1789, the world was largely rural (p. 11). In Europe, there were only a few cities that could be called large. These were London and Paris, maybe two more cities in France, two in Germany, four in Spain, five in Italy, two in Russia, and one in Portugal, Poland, Holland, Austria, Ireland, Scotland and the European part of Turkey. Against this background occurred the 'dual revolution' (p. 25). These revolutions are the Industrial Revolution in Britain (discussed in Chapter 2) and the French Revolution (discussed in Chapter 3). The Industrial Revolution produced 'the labouring poor' (Chapter 11). The French Revolution led to a focus on reason, science and progress (Chapter 12). Then came economic depression and the failure of harvests in the middle 1840s (p. 307).

As regards the development of company law in this period, in the Netherlands, the Commercial Code was enacted in 1838. This code regulated, *inter alia*, business partnerships and public limited companies. In a business partnership, the partners are liable for the debts of the partnership; in a public limited company, the shareholders are

6. Edition used: New York: Vintage Books 1996.

not liable for the debts of the company. The public limited company was (and still is) called the *naamloze vennootschap* (NV), from the French name *société anonyme* (SA). The words *vennootschap* and *société* mean 'company'. Both the word *naamloze* and the word *anonyme* can be translated as: not carrying a name, without a name. Article 23 of the Commercial Code described the *naamloze vennootschap* as follows: 'The naamloze vennootschap shall not carry a name, [in the sense that it] shall not carry the name of one or several of its partners, but derives its name solely from the object of its business enterprise.' This (now) somewhat obsolete provision meant that (whereas a business partnership that is engaged in the mining industry may, for instance, carry the name 'Jones and Smith'), a *naamloze vennootschap* that was engaged in the mining industry was not allowed to carry the name 'Jones and Smith NV'. It could be called, e.g., 'Mining Business of the Southern Netherlands NV'. This shows that the *naamloze vennootschap* at that time was a relatively new phenomenon and that the Commercial Code sought to avoid confusion. No one should be tempted to think that an enterprise was a partnership (where the partners are liable for the debts of the partnership), while, in fact, it was a *naamloze vennootschap* where the shareholders are not liable for the debts of the company.

The provisions in the Commercial Code fit neatly in *The Age of Revolution*: they reflect the beginning of the modern era, where the public limited company was recognized as an incorporated entity, but with some hesitation and reluctance.

[C] The Second Book

The second book, originally published in 1975, is *The Age of Capital: 1848-1875*.[7] This book discusses in Chapter 3 'the extraordinary economic transformation and expansion of years between 1848 and the early 1870s' (p. 43), and the way the world became more interconnected, *inter alia*, by railways and steamships, and telegraph systems, as a result of which an international economy came into existence. At the same time, the world remained a conglomerate of rivalling national economies in different nation-states. In Chapter 6, the book deals with the rise of representative democracies where liberal parties (supported by the entrepreneurial class) were mostly in power. The factory working class, however, remained largely poor (Chapter 12).

[D] The Third Book

The third book in the series, originally published in 1987, is *The Age of Empire: 1875-1914*.[8] This book deals with imperialism (i.e., colonialism: the partitioning of the world by the colonial powers, especially in Africa and the Pacific) and the globalization of the world economy. The latter was spurred, *inter alia*, by a technological revolution (the telephone, the phonograph, automobiles, planes) and the growing market for consumer goods (vacuum cleaners, gas cookers, but also bananas and tea) (Chapter 2).

7. Edition used: London: Abacus 2003.
8. Edition used: London: Abacus 2002.

The technical revolution and the growing market for consumer goods needed vast imports of products like oil, rubber, sugar and coffee (Chapter 3). This age also witnessed the coming into being of labour movements and social democratic parties (Chapters 4 and 5). In politics, nationalism was also on the rise (Chapter 6). In August 1914, a war broke out: World War I. As Hobsbawm puts it: 'the development of capitalism inevitably pushed the world in the direction of state rivalry, imperialist expansion, conflict and war' (p. 316).

As regards the development of corporate law in this period, the judgment of the (United Kingdom) House of Lords of 16 November 1896 in *Salomon v. Salomon* stands out.[9] In this case, following the bankruptcy of the company A. Salomon and Company, Limited (in the judgment also referred to as Salomon & Co Ltd), the liquidator (receiver) of the company, brought an action against the company's main shareholder, Mr A. Salomon. The liquidator held Mr Salomon liable for the unpaid debts of the company. The liquidator argued that the company was nothing more than an extension (an 'alias') of Mr Salomon. To advance this claim, the liquidator relied on the argument that the other shareholders of Salomon & Co Ltd played no real role in the affairs of the company. The House of Lords, however, decided that Mr Salomon could not be held personally liable for the debts of Salomon & Co Ltd.

Mr Salomon was in the business of producing shoes and boots in Whitechapel. He mainly sold to government agencies. Mr Salomon and his spouse had five children: four sons and one daughter. The sons, who also worked in the enterprise, argued that their position within the business should be put on a higher level. Mr Salomon, in order to accommodate that wish, decided in 1892 to convert his business into a company. The Companies Act (of 1862), as it then stood, required that a company should be established by at least seven founders who also became the company's shareholders. Mr Salomon, his spouse and their five children signed the memorandum of association of the company Salomon & Co Ltd. The memorandum of association designated Mr Salomon and his two eldest sons as the company's directors. At some point in time, the government agencies, which were Salomon & Co Ltd's major buyers, bought much fewer shoes and boots. Mr Salomon and his spouse, in an effort to rescue the company, lent money to Salomon & Co Ltd. This was of no avail. Salomon & Co Ltd went into bankruptcy. The company's liquidator found not enough assets to pay up the debts of the company to the full.

The judgment of the House of Lords centres around the question of whether Mr Salomon had simply continued his business in a company that he controlled, with the other shareholders being just mock shareholders. Both the trial judge and the Court of Appeal concluded that this was indeed the case. The trial judge 'was of opinion that the company was only an "alias" for Salomon; that, the intention being that he should take

9. *Salomon v. Salomon*, House of Lords, 16 November 1896, in the case between Aron Salomon (Pauper) (Appellant) and A. Salomon and Company, Limited (Respondents) (Lord Halsbury L.C., Lord Watson, Lord Herschell, Lord Macnaghten, Lord Morris, Lord Davey; leading speech by Lord Halsbury L.C.; Lord Watson, Lord Herschell, Lord Macnaghten, Lord Morris and Lord Davey concurring); www.bailii.org, databases, United Kingdom and Commonwealth, United Kingdom House of Lords Decisions, 1896, November, *Salomon v. Salomon & Co Ltd* [1896] UKHL 1 (16 November 1896).

the profits without running the risk of the debts, the company was merely an agent for him' (phrasing by Lord Herschell). The Court of Appeal also considered 'that the formation of the company was a mere scheme to enable Aron Salomon to carry on business in the name of the company' (phrasing by Lord Halsbury).

Mr Salomon appealed to the House of Lords. The House of Lords reversed the judgment of the Court of Appeal. In the words of Lord Macnaghten: 'In order to form a company limited by shares, the Act requires that a memorandum of association should be signed by seven persons, who are each to take one share at least. If those conditions are complied with, what can it matter whether the signatories are relations or strangers? There is nothing in the Act requiring that the subscribers to the memorandum should be independent or unconnected, or that they or any one of them should take a substantial interest in the undertaking, or that they should have a mind and will of their own [...] or that there should be anything like a balance of power in the constitution of the company. In almost every company that is formed the statutory number is eked out by clerks or friends, who sign their names at the request of the promoter or promoters without intending to take any further part or interest in the matter.'

The judgment of the House of Lords perfectly reflects *The Age of Empire*: a public limited company is a corporation that is an entity that is distinct and separate from its shareholder(s), and the shareholder(s) cannot be held liable for the debts of the company. Any opposite judgment would have been contrary to the needs of an expanding and modern economy. This judgment was groundbreaking in the development of company law as it recognized the company as an incorporated entity as opposed to a partnership. In the words of David Kershaw, the judgment was 'a case which foregrounded the legal entity in a way that was widely viewed as contrary to the prevailing understanding of the company as [...] a partnership'.[10]

[E] The Fourth Book

The fourth book, originally published in 1994, is *The Age of Extremes. A History of the World, 1914-1991*.[11] Eric Hobsbawm calls the years 1914-1991 the Short Twentieth Century (p. 3), that begins with World War I and ends with the collapse of the Soviet Union (p. 5). Within this period, (1) the years 1914 to the end of World War II are the Age of Catastrophe (p. 7), and (2) the years 1947-1973 are the Golden Age (p.8). The Golden Age was followed by the years 1974-1991: (3) the Crisis Decades (p. 8).

Within the Age of Catastrophe fell the economic decline of the years 1929-1933 (the Great Slump) (p. 87), which brings Eric Hobsbawm to the question: 'Why did the capitalist economy between the wars fail to work?' (p. 97). One of the reasons could be that during the preceding market boom in the 1920s, over-production occurred in the United States because demand for products could not keep pace with high production

10. David Kershaw, *The Foundations of Anglo-American Corporate Fiduciary Law*, Cambridge: Cambridge University Press 2018, p. 235.
11. Edition used: New York: Vintage Books 1996.

rates. As a result, car production in the United States in the following years 1929-1931 went down by half (p. 101). 'Would fascism have become very significant in world history but for the Great Slump? Probably not', Eric Hobsbawm argues (p. 130). World War II saw the mobilization of a broad antifascist coalition (p. 147), and a large number of countries stood up against fascism (p. 150). As Germany invaded the Soviet Union and declared war on the United States, the war became a (temporary) alliance between these latter countries (p. 164). World War II also demonstrated to the people living in the colonies of European countries that these countries were weak and could be defeated (p. 216).

During the Golden Age, the Cold War emerged (p. 226): 'while the U.S.A. was worried about the danger of a possible Soviet world supremacy some time in the future, Moscow was worried about the actual hegemony of the U.S.A.' (p. 234). The Cold War eventually ended in 1987. Apart from the Cold War, during the Golden Age, the world economy grew enormously, although at the cost of pollution and ecological deterioration (p. 261). Technological innovations boomed (pp. 265-267), and the welfare state came into being (p. 267). The economy became a transnational economy in which transnational firms played a major role (p. 277).

During the Crisis Decades, the world economy became less stable (p. 404). In this respect, Eric Hobsbawm writes: 'the central fact about the Crisis Decades is not that capitalism no longer worked as well as it had done in de Golden Age, but that its operations had become uncontrollable. Nobody knew what to do about the vagaries of the world economy or possessed instruments to manage them. The major instrument for doing so in the Golden Age, government politics, national or internationally coordinated, no longer worked. The crisis decades were the era when the national state lost its economic powers' (p. 408).

As regards the development of corporate law in this period, the judgment of the Supreme Court of the Netherlands of 21 January 1955 in the *Forum-Bank* case still stands out.[12] In the *Forum-Bank* case, two shareholders of NV Forum-Bank (Forum-Bank) had proposed that Forum-Bank would buy back shares these shareholders held in the company and that the price to be paid by Forum-Bank would mainly be used to reduce the amount of debt these shareholders owed to the company. When this proposal was discussed at the general meeting, both the management board and the supervisory board of Forum-Bank, as well as five of the eight shareholders who attended the general meeting, opposed the proposal. The management board and the supervisory board argued that accepting the proposal would not be in the interest of Forum-Bank itself and its shareholders, as it would undermine the liquidity of the bank, and that in accordance with the articles of association, this was a matter not to be decided by the general meeting but by the management board. When it came to a vote, the voting power of the two shareholders who had made the proposal (296 and 110 shares), combined with the votes of the one shareholder who supported the

12. Supreme Court of the Netherlands 21 January 1955, *NJ* 1959/43 (Forum-Bank). This paragraph is based on C. de Groot, 'The Duty of Directors to Be Guided by the Best Interests of the Company', in: C.G. Breedveld-de Voogd & A.G. Castermans et al. (eds), *Core Concepts in the Dutch Civil Code: Continuously in Motion*, Deventer: Wolters Kluwer 2016, pp. 187-209.

proposal (5 shares), was enough to have the proposal accepted by a majority of 411 votes in favour of the proposal to 117 votes against the proposal. This prompted two opposing shareholders to bring the matter before the district court, asking the district court to declare that the decision by the general meeting was null and void as it was outside the realm of the general meeting's powers. The district court ruled in favour of these claimants, and the court of appeal confirmed this judgment.

One of the two shareholders who had originally proposed that Forum-Bank would buy back the shares lodged an appeal to the Supreme Court of the Netherlands. In this appeal, the main argument was as follows: even if it were to be accepted that the competence to decide on buying back Forum-Bank's shares fell within the powers of the management board, the decision made by the general meeting could *not* be null and void because (in the phrasing by the Supreme Court):

> in spite of the fact that buying back the company's shares [...] falls within the competence of the management board, the general meeting has the power to instruct the management board to buy back shares of the company for a specified price from certain sellers because the managing directors are subordinate to the public limited company and the general meeting exercises the ultimate power in the public limited company.

The Supreme Court rebutted the appeal in a very short consideration:

> this argument, thus read, ignores that the general meeting too shall not transgress the powers given to it by statutory law or by the articles of association.

The judgment of the Supreme Court is an interesting outcome of *The Age of Extremes*: the board of directors of a public limited company is best in place to lead the corporation (as opposed to the shareholders). If decided otherwise, the Supreme Court would have halted economic development to occur in an efficient way. This is all the more so because *The Age of Extremes* was an age of confusion and uncertainty. The Supreme Court has since stuck to its view that the board of directors is at the heart of a public limited company rather than the shareholders.[13]

§7.03 THE AGE OF SUSTAINABILITY

The years shortly before and following 1991 show an era with an ongoing stream of events that seem to have no correlation with one another, but each has significant consequences. A number of these events are identified in two timelines: one timeline drawn up by the European Union (EU)[14] and another timeline drawn up by The Gilder Lehrman Institute of American History (GLI).[15] Combining these timelines, the following important events occurred (starting in 1989, all entries are citations):

13. Examples are Supreme Court 13 July 2007, ECLI:NL:HR:2007:BA7971, *JOR* 2017/178, *NJ* 2007/434 (ABN AMRO Bank) and Supreme Court 9 July 2010, ECLI:NL:HR:2010:BM0976, *JOR* 2010/228, *NJ* 2010/544 (ASMI).
14. https://european-union.europa.eu/principles-countries-history/history-eu.
15. https://www.gilderlehrman.org/history-resources/online-exhibitions/timeline-1945-present: 'The Gilder Lehrman Institute of American History was founded in 1994 by Richard Gilder and

(EU) 9 November 1989 – Fall of the Berlin Wall;
(GLI) After Iraq, led by Saddam Hussein, invaded Kuwait in August 1990, President Bush headed a coalition to set a deadline for Iraqi withdrawal;
(EU) 1991 – Break-up of Yugoslavia;
(GLI) The Soviet Union collapsed with Gorbachev's resignation in December 1991;
(EU) 7 February 1992 – Maastricht Treaty – The Treaty on European Union is signed in Maastricht in the Netherlands;
(EU) 1 January 1994 – The European Economic Area is created;
(GLI) 11 December 1997 – The Kyoto Protocol treaty was adopted by the United Nations Framework Convention on Climate Change;
(EU) 1 January 1999 – The euro is born;
(EU) 11 September 2001 – Terrorist attacks in the United States / (GLI) On Tuesday, 11 September 2001, terrorists executed a series of attacks masterminded by al-Qaeda leader Osama bin Laden;
(GLI) October 7 2001 – With British support, the United States launched 'Operation Enduring Freedom,' a combat effort in Afghanistan. The Taliban refused to cooperate with efforts to root out al-Qaeda in that country;
(EU) 1 January 2002 – Euro notes and coins launch in 12 countries;
(EU) 31 March 2003 – Peacekeeping operations in the Balkans;
(GLI) 20 March 2003 – President Bush ordered an attack on Baghdad with the intent of eliminating Saddam Hussein and his government;
(EU) September 2008 – Global economic crisis / (GLI) The 'Great Recession' in the United States lasted and the global recession that resulted from it lasted from December 2007 to June 2009;
(EU) 2010 – Europe tackles the financial crisis;
(EU) 12 December 2015 – Paris Agreement on climate change;
(EU) December 2019 – Towards a climate-neutral Europe [the European Green Deal];
(EU) January 2020 – Common EU response to COVID-19;
(EU) 31 January 2020 – United Kingdom leaves the EU;
(EU) February 2022 – Russia invades Ukraine.

In this timeline (at least) from 2015, climate change and sustainability are subjects that are high on the agenda. That is also reflected in the Taxonomy Regulation, the CSRD and the CSDD, which are discussed in the Introduction. The present era could, by all accounts, therefore, be called the Age of Sustainability. The growing importance of sustainability comes to the fore not only in legislation but also in case

Lewis E. Lehrman, visionaries and lifelong supporters of American history education. The Institute is the leading nonprofit organization dedicated to […] history education while also serving the general public. Its mission is to promote the knowledge and understanding of American history through educational programs and resources.'

law. The following sections discuss a judgment of the Supreme Court of the Netherlands on sustainability and (shortly) a judgment of the district court of Den Haag (The Hague) on sustainability that builds on the judgment of the Supreme Court.

§7.04 THE JUDGMENT OF THE SUPREME COURT OF THE NETHERLANDS IN THE CASE BETWEEN URGENDA AND THE NETHERLANDS

[A] Introduction

The Supreme Court of the Netherlands rendered a groundbreaking judgment on 20 December 2019 in the case between *Stichting Urgenda* and *de Staat der Nederlanden, ministerie van Economische Zaken en Klimaat*.[16] *Stichting Urgenda* translates into English as Foundation Urgenda (wherein Urgenda stands for Urgent Agenda), and *de Staat der Nederlanden, ministerie van Economische Zaken en Klimaat* translates into English as the State of the Netherlands, Department of Economic Affairs and Climate. The judgment of the Supreme Court was the apex of a lawsuit between *Stichting Urgenda* and *de Staat der Nederlanden* in which the former pleaded that *de Staat der Nederlanden* had not availed itself of its obligation to reduce the emission of greenhouse gases within the territory of the Netherlands.

[B] The Background of the Urgenda Case

The court case between *Stichting Urgenda* and *de Staat der Nederlanden* started in 2013 when *Stichting Urgenda* had brought proceedings against *de Staat der Nederlanden* before the district court of Den Haag (The Hague). *Stichting Urgenda* requested the district court to order *de Staat der Nederlanden* to take measures that would reduce the total emission of greenhouse gases in the Netherlands, preferably by 40% in 2020 (compared to 1990), or in the alternative by 25% in 2020 (compared to 1990), or as a fallback position by 40% in 2030 (compared to 1990). *Stichting Urgenda* substantiated its claim by arguing – basically – that:

(1) the global emission of greenhouse gases (especially carbon dioxide (CO2)) would lead to global warming, resulting in climate change;
(2) the emission of greenhouse gases in the Netherlands was above average in comparison to other countries;
(3) *de Staat der Nederlanden* was in a position to take measures to counter the emission of greenhouse gases in the Netherlands and had a duty of care to do so; and that
(4) *de Staat der Nederlanden* – by relying on an insufficient climate policy – breached its duty of care, resulting in a tort under Netherlands law.

16. ECLI:NL:HR:2019:2006, *AB* 2020/24, *NJ* 2020/41.

Stichting Urgenda based its claim that *de Staat der Nederlanden* committed a tort under Netherlands law, *inter alia*, in Articles 2 and 8 of the ECHR. Article 2 states that every person's right of life shall be protected by law; under Article 8, every person has the right to private life and family life (as well as every person's home and correspondence) are respected. The district court of Den Haag considered in respect of Articles 2 and 8 that these provisions can indeed serve as a source of inspiration to give substance to general standards of (private) law such as the prohibition to commit a tort (paragraph 4.46). The district court also referred to an authoritative 'Manual on human rights and the environment' (2012 edition) that had been compiled on the instructions of the Committee of Ministers of the Council of Europe. This manual mentioned in Article 2 of the convention that 'So far, the [European Court of Human Rights] has considered environmental issues in four cases brought under Article 2, two of which relate to dangerous activities and two which relate to natural disasters' (cited in paragraph 4.49). In Article 8 of the convention, the manual stated that 'The [European Court of Human Rights] highlighted [...] that neither article 8 nor any of the other articles of the Convention are specifically designed to provide general protection of the environment as such' (cited in paragraph 4.50). Nevertheless, the district court concluded on the meaning of Articles 2 and 8 for the court case between *Stichting Urgenda* and *de Staat der Nederlanden* that these provisions were relevant to establish the minimal measure of care that *de Staat der Nederlanden* should take into account to avoid committing a tort as pleaded by *Stichting Urgenda* (paragraph 4.52).

The district court granted the application made by *Stichting Urgenda* in its judgment of 24 June 2015, ordering *de Staat der Nederlanden* to take measures that would lead to a reduction of the emission of greenhouse gases in the Netherlands in 2020 by 25% as compared to 1990.[17]

De Staat der Nederlanden lodged an appeal to the Court of Appeal of Den Haag (The Hague). The court of appeal also discussed Articles 2 and 8 of the (European) Convention for the Protection of Human Rights and Fundamental Freedoms. A particularly important paragraph in the judgment of the court of appeal is:

> [...] the State has a positive obligation to protect the lives of citizens within its jurisdiction under Article 2 ECHR, while Article 8 ECHR creates the obligation to protect the right of home and private life. This obligation applies to all activities, public and non-public, which could endanger the rights protected in these articles, and certainly in the face of industrial activities which by their very nature are dangerous. If the government knows that there is a real and imminent threat, the State must take precautionary measures to prevent infringement as far as possible. [...] (paragraph 43)

The court of appeal affirmed the reasoning of the district court by considering that on the basis of Articles 2 and 8 of the ECHR, *de Staat der Nederlanden* would disregard its duty of care if it would not take measures that would lead to a reduction of the emission of greenhouse gases in the Netherlands in 2020 by 25%: 'A reduction of 25% should be considered a minimum' (paragraph 73). Thus, the appeal by *de Staat der*

17. ECLI:NL:RBDHA:2015:7145, *AB* 2015/336.

Nederlanden was without success, as the court of appeal in its judgment of 9 October 2018 confirmed the judgment of the district court.[18]

De Staat der Nederlanden lodged a final appeal to the Supreme Court of the Netherlands. This appeal was also to no avail, as it was dismissed by the Supreme Court.

[C] The Judgment of the Supreme Court of the Netherlands

The core of the judgment of the Supreme Court is Part 5. In this part ('Do articles 2 and 8 of the (European) Convention for the Protection of Human Rights and Fundamental Freedoms require the State to take measures?'), the Supreme Court analyses Articles 2 and 8 of the ECHR and the case law of the European Court of Human Rights on these provisions. The Supreme Court discusses the position adopted by *de Staat der Nederlanden* that the risk of climate change is a general concept that is not covered by Articles 2 and 8 because it is not specific enough to fall within the ambit of these provisions.

In Part 5, section (a) of the judgment, the Supreme Court considers – referring to the case law of the European Court of Human Rights – that the right of life that is enshrined in Article 2 of the ECHR also protects every person from the dangers caused by, *inter alia*, industrial activities and natural disasters, if these activities or disasters involve a real and immediate risk. This protection also extends to risks that occur in the long term (paragraph 5.2.2). Article 8 of the ECHR, although it does not protect the living environment of a person in general, likewise protects every person against serious environmental hazards. The Supreme Court goes on to consider that – in accordance with case law of the European Court of Human Rights – Article 8 obliges States to take reasonable and appropriate measures in the field of environmental matters, also concerning risks that do not materialize in the short term (paragraph 5.2.3). Also, it follows from the foregoing that Articles 2 and 8 of the ECHR have concurring scopes (paragraph 5.2.4).

The Supreme Court considers on a more general level that Articles 2 and 8 of the ECHR oblige States to take – in accordance with the so-called precautionary principle – (precautionary) measures, either to mitigate rising risks or to be able to adapt to risks that may occur (paragraph 5.3.2). These measures shall be consistent, timely, and taken with due diligence (paragraph 5.3.3). Although Articles 2 and 8 do not require that States take on impossible or disproportionate burdens, States do have the obligation to take measures that are both reasonable and appropriate (paragraph 5.3.4).

In Part 5, section (b) of the judgment, the Supreme Court considers that the ECHR shall be interpreted in accordance with the principle of effectiveness. This principle brings along that the provisions of the ECHR shall be interpreted in good faith, according to their common meaning, within the context in which they are being used

18. ECLI:NL:GHDHA:2018:2591, *AB* 2018/417 and (unofficial translation) ECLI:NL:GHDHA:2018:2610.

and according to their subject and purpose (paragraph 5.4.1). Furthermore, in interpreting the ECHR, regard must be given to other (similar) instruments of international law and the way these instruments are being interpreted as well as to the way the ECHR is being applied by its Member States: this is the so-called common ground method that also guides the interpretation of the ECHR (paragraph 5.4.2).

In addition to the precautionary principle and the common ground method, scientific knowledge and generally accepted standards may also play a role in the interpretation of the ECHR (paragraph 5.4.3).

The Supreme Court reiterates (in Part 5, sections (d) and (e) of the judgment) the stance taken by *de Staat der Nederlanden* that the European Court of Human Rights had never rendered a judgment in which it dealt with climate change as such. In this respect, the Supreme Court considers that the central question that it has to answer is whether Articles 2 and 8 of the ECHR can be used to impose an obligation on *de Staat der Nederlanden* to take measures to reduce the emission of greenhouse gases within the territory of the Netherlands (paragraph 5.6.3). This question is all the more difficult since the emission of greenhouse gases is not a national, but a worldwide issue. Had it been a purely national issue, the answer to the question could only have been positive (paragraph 5.6.2). Nonetheless, according to the Supreme Court, even taking into account that the emission of greenhouse gases is a worldwide issue, the answer to the question is 'sufficiently clear' (in Dutch: 'voldoende duidelijk') (paragraph 5.6.4). For that reason, *de Staat der Nederlanden* is obliged 'to do "its part"' (in Dutch: '"het zijne" te doen') (paragraph 5.7.1). The Supreme Court refers in particular to the United Nations Framework Convention on Climate Change to underline this conclusion (paragraphs 5.7.2-5.7.4).

Interlude: The United Nations Framework Convention on Climate Change of 1992 refers in the preamble to 'the valuable analytical work being conducted' by, *inter alia*, the World Meteorological Organization and the United Nations Environment Programme. The objective of the convention is the 'stabilization of greenhouse gas concentrations in the atmosphere' (Article 2). Under Article 3 section 1 of the convention, all parties to the convention 'should protect the climate system for the benefit of present and future generations of humankind, on the basis of equity and in accordance with their common but differentiated responsibilities and respective capabilities'. Added to that, under Article 4 section 2 of the convention, the developed country Parties and other Parties (as included in annex I) commit themselves specifically to the following: *inter alia*, to adopt policies and measures that 'will demonstrate that developed countries are taking the lead in modifying longer-term trends in anthropogenic emissions' (under a). Furthermore, under Article 4 section 3 of the convention, the developed country Parties and other developed Parties (as included in annex II) shall provide financial resources to the developing country Parties, and under Article 4 section 4, the Parties (as included in annex II) shall assist the developing country Parties that are particularly vulnerable to the adverse effects of climate change in meeting the costs of adaptation to those adverse effects.

Also, according to the Supreme Court, the obligations that states have under the United Nations Framework Convention on Climate Change are in line with the internationally recognized so-called no harm principle (paragraph 5.7.5). Under this principle, states shall not cause damage to each other. As concerns the emission of greenhouse gases, this principle entails that all states have a partial obligation to do what they can to reduce the emissions within their own territory.

§7.05 THE JUDGMENT OF THE DISTRICT COURT OF DEN HAAG (THE HAGUE) IN THE CASE BETWEEN VERENIGING MILIEUDEFENSIE *ET AL.* AND ROYAL DUTCH SHELL PLC.

The judgment of the Supreme Court of the Netherlands in the case between Urgenda and the State of the Netherlands is groundbreaking in the sense that the Supreme Court bases a legal obligation on the State of the Netherlands to reduce the total emission of greenhouse gases in the Netherlands in 2020 by (at least) 25% on Articles 2 and 8 of the ECHR that deal with the right of life and the right of private of life and family life respectively. This approach was followed by the district court of Den Haag (The Hague) in its judgment of 26 May 2021 in the case between (among others) Vereniging Milieudefensie (Friends of the Earth Netherlands) and Royal Dutch Shell Plc. (now: Shell Plc.).[19] Vereniging Milieudefensie *et al.* requested the district court to order Royal Dutch Shell Plc. to take measures that would reduce the total level of CO_2 emissions caused by the operations of the whole Shell group, preferably by 45% in 2030 (compared to 2019), or in the alternative by 35% in 2030 (compared to 2019), or as a fallback position by 25% in 2030 (compared to 2019). The request advanced by Vereniging Milieudefensie et al. related to three emission 'scopes':

- Scope 1: emissions that are the result of the operations of the companies within the Shell group of companies itself.
- Scope 2: emissions that are caused by the suppliers of the Shell group of companies. These emissions are 'indirect emissions' caused by parties from which the Shell group of companies purchases electricity, steam, or heating for its own operations. The Shell group of companies is in a position to influence the level of these emissions through its contractual relations with its suppliers.
- Scope 3: emissions that are caused by the customers of the Shell group of companies. These emissions are also 'indirect' emissions caused by customers of the Shell group of companies, including major customers that purchase crude oil and gas from the Shell group of companies. The Shell group of companies is in a position to influence the level of these emissions by deciding what products it sells or does not sell.

The district court granted the primary application made by Vereniging Milieudefensie et al., ordering Royal Dutch Shell Plc. to reduce (scope 1) or cause to be reduced (scopes 2 and 3) the total level of CO_2 emissions caused the operations of the Shell group of companies by 45% in 2030 (compared to 2019). In reaching this decision, the

19. ECLI:NL:RBDHA:2021:5337 and (unofficial translation) ECLI:NL:RBDHA:2021:5339, *JOR* 2021/208.

district court applied a wide variety of arguments. Among these were Articles 2 and 8 of the ECHR. The district court considered more specifically that '[f]rom the Urgenda ruling it can be deduced that Articles 2 and 8 of the ECHR offer protection against the consequences of dangerous climate change due to CO_2 emissions that lead to global warming' (paragraph 4.4.10). The district court acknowledged that the rights enshrined in these provisions in principle apply in the relationship between states and citizens, meaning that Vereniging Milieudefensie et al. 'cannot directly invoke these human rights with respect to [Royal Dutch Shell Plc.]' (paragraph 4.4.9). However, the district court also considered: 'Due to the fundamental interest of human rights and the value for society as a whole they embody, the human rights may play a role in the relationship between Milieudefensie et al. and [Royal Dutch Shell Plc.]. Therefore, the court will take into account the human rights and the values they embody in its interpretation of the unwritten standard of care.'

The latter considerations of the district court are remarkable. The district court acknowledges that Articles 2 and 8 of the ECHR in principle only have a 'vertical' scope of application: they govern the relationship between states and citizens. This means that these articles lack 'horizontal' application: they do not govern the relationship between citizens themselves. However, the district court takes a bold step in considering that, although these provisions do not have a 'horizontal' effect, they can play a role in the relationship between citizens themselves when applying the duty of care.[20]

§7.06 FINAL REMARKS: THE AGE OF SUSTAINABILITY

Section §7.01 discussed the rise of sustainability-related issues in legislation by referring to three (EU) legislative initiatives: the Taxonomy Regulation, the CSRD, and the (proposed) CSDD. Section §7.02 went into the history of the modern era and how that era is subdivided by Hobsbawm into four ages. This section also highlighted some elements of company law that show how company law developed in line with these ages. Section §7.03 concluded that the present era may be referred to as the Age of Sustainability. The judgment of the Supreme Court of the Netherlands in the case between *Stichting Urgenda* and *de Staat der Nederlanden*, discussed in §7.04, shows the importance of climate litigation and may be regarded as reflecting the Age of Sustainability. In this judgment, Articles 2 and 8 of the ECHR played a decisive role. The Supreme Court interprets these provisions in a broad way, including giving protection against the emission of greenhouse gases. In its judgment of 26 May 2021, discussed in §7.05, the district court of Den Haag (The Hague) in the case between (among others) Vereniging Milieudefensie and Royal Dutch Shell Plc., elaborated on the judgment of the Supreme Court by also applying Articles 2 and 8 of the ECHR. This is remarkable because these provisions are not written for 'horizontal' relationships between citizens themselves. This raises the interesting question of whether courts in

20. Cf. for a (critical) analysis of the judgment. B.M. Katan, 'Ieder het hare. Enkele opmerkingen bij het klimaatvonnis tegen Shell', *Ondernemingsrecht* 2021/106.

future cases relating to sustainability (including climate change) will find other novel ways to interpret the law in a way that reflects the challenges of the Age of Sustainability.

CHAPTER 8

Does Corporate Social Responsibility Account for Geopolitical Risks? French Law Approach

Mariia Domina

Corporate social responsibility has gained attention in recent years due to geopolitical risks, ranging from the pandemic COVID-19 and shortage of vaccines to the armed conflict in Ukraine. What role should a commercial company play in supporting global society in these uneasy times? We will strive to provide some answers by evaluating the French framework of corporate social responsibility in this context.

§8.01 INTRODUCTION

As a young 2nd year PhD researcher back in 2017, I was delighted when Professor Bartman accepted my paper on the Luxembourg investment funds for publication in the ECL. This was my first scholarly publication in a peer-reviewed European journal. Kind comments of Professor Bartman on my writing gave me a boost and motivation that were vital to the progression of my academic career.

According to the European Commission, corporate social responsibility (CSR) is 'a concept whereby companies integrate social and environmental concerns in their business operations and in their interactions with their stakeholders on a voluntary basis'.[1] The rethinking of CSR – a role that a company plays in our society – is a dominant theme of modern economy, which becomes even more prominent in the current geopolitical realities: pandemic COVID-19 and shortage of vaccines, climate

1. Green paper, *Promoting a European framework for corporate social responsibility*, COM/2001/0366 final.

change, war in Ukraine and in other countries, financial downturn and rising inflation, worsened hunger in developing countries and challenges to the protection of human rights. These factors will be referred to as geopolitical risks throughout this chapter.

The idea behind making a commercial company a socially responsible one is to ensure that it strives not only to make profits but also to contribute to the needs of society in a larger sense (environment, human rights, etc.). A commercial company is now perceived as an active player on the social scene that can help resolve societal issues (hunger, illnesses, global warming, etc.).

Historically, CSR was mainly employed via soft law. Examples include international standards, e.g., standards from the International Organization for Standardization (ISO), that incite companies to comply with the industry's best practices in the areas of employees' health and safety, as well as environmental protection. For example, ISO 26000 defines the scope of CSR by looking at seven central points: (1) organizational governance; (2) human rights; (3) working conditions in the company; (4) environment; (5) fair practices; (6) consumer treatment; and (7) communities and local development.

Yet, the weakness of soft law lies in its non-binding nature.[2] As a result, hard law rules were introduced to establish minimum standards of CSR. Since hard law rules are mandatory, companies may face heavy sanctions for non-compliance – this adds to the incentives for companies to comply with CSR.

The objective of this chapter is to reassess the role of CSR in the times of different geopolitical risks mentioned earlier. The choice to focus on the French law approach in this context is explained by the fact that France was one of the very first European countries to introduce the obligations of non-financial reporting and due diligence plan related to CSR, well before such measures became obligatory on the level of EU law.

This chapter is structured as follows. Section §8.01 will present the concept of CSR. Section §8.02 will discuss different legislative reforms of the French CSR, with a particular focus on the Law n° 2019-486 of 22 May 2019 relating to the growth and transformation of businesses (PACTE Law).[3] Section §8.03 will analyse the approach of French courts as to the CSR. The final section, by way of concluding remarks, will provide an answer as to whether French law allows companies to account for geopolitical risks in their CSR policies.

§8.02 CSR: SETTING THE SCENE

CSR can be described as the conduct of businesses that aim to resolve societal issues in a broader community.[4] A company is considered to be socially responsible if, during its business activities, it operates in ways that enhance our society. It is no longer enough

2. Andrew T. Guzman & Timothy Meyer, *International Soft Law*, 2 J. Legal Analysis 171, (2010).
3. JORF n° 0119 of 23 May 2019.
4. Oliver F. Williams, *Corporate Social Responsibility: The Role of Business in Sustainable Development* (2013), cited in: Mariam O. Asemah-Ibrahim, Emeke P. Nwaoboli & Ezekiel S. Asemah, *Corporate Social Responsibility in War Ridden-Zones of Russia-Ukraine from February to July 2022*, 5 CVU J. of Communication Studies 145, 146 (2022).

for a company to not harm the environment or discriminate against its employees to be considered socially responsible. What is needed is to make a positive impact, i.e., take active steps to improve the lives of people and contribute to the protection of the environment.

The awareness of current political, economic, and environmental issues made people more conscious of the impact of our generation on the planet and its population. Large campaigns on social media allow a large number of people to be informed about the issues our society and planet are facing. As a result, CSR has gained significant attention. Potential clients of the company want to feel that the company makes a positive impact on society. A socially responsible company is now emotionally attractive to people who believe that, by using the services of the company, they too can contribute to the greater good.[5] Some examples include 'green businesses', 'fair trade' and 'bio' products.

CSR holds businesses accountable for providing solutions to the problems in our society. One of the principles of CSR is that a company has a moral duty to allocate a portion of its profits to the community in order to enhance the quality of life. This accountability can be seen in the example of a surge in donations to charities, organization of free professional workshops, etc.

The business organizations do not operate in isolation; the actions they undertake will have an impact on their surroundings.[6] This relationship is reciprocal, i.e., the activities of companies will directly influence the environment and society, and therefore, the changes they bring will in turn affect the company. For example, if a business organization exhausts natural resources in the geographical area where it operates, there will be no future input for its commercial operations. Similarly, if its actions have a detrimental effect on society, the citizens will not be able to function effectively and there will be less qualified employees or prospective clients for the company. This connection between balancing profits, people, and the planet is the foundation of the triple bottom line (TBL) theory, as well as the stakeholder theory.

TBL theory was developed by Elkington.[7] In order to be sustainable, the companies should focus on three different bottom lines. The first is a classical one – the 'corporate account' bottom line, which is measured as a profit and loss account. The second is the 'people account', which defines how socially responsible a company is towards the people. The third is 'planet account', which looks at how responsible a company is towards the environment. TBL theory defines corporate sustainability as a sum of three main spheres – economic, social, and environmental – which includes three additional sub-spheres: social-environmental, environmental-economic and economic-social.[8] They include the following elements:

5. Mariam O. Asemah-Ibrahim, Emeke P. Nwaoboli & Ezekiel S. Asemah, *supra* n. 4.
6. *Ibid.*, *supra* n. 4, at 3-4.
7. John Elkington, *Towards the Sustainable Corporation: Win-Win-Win Business Strategies for Sustainable Development*, 36 California Management Review 90 (1994).
8. Agnieszka Zak, *Triple Bottom Line Concept in Theory and Practice*, 387 Societal Responsibility of Organizations. Directions of Changes 251, 253 (2015).

- economic: profit, cost saving, economic growth, research and development;
- social: standard of living, education, community, equal opportunity;
- environmental: natural resource use, environmental management, pollution prevention (air, water, land, waste);
- social-environmental: environmental justice, nature resources stewardship, locally and globally;
- environmental-economic: energy efficiency, subsidies and incentives for use of natural resources; and
- economic-social: business ethics, fair trade, workers' rights.

The stakeholder theory was developed by Freeman.[9] This theory argues that the company's stakeholders are people and entities that are affected by the business activities of the company. The stakeholders are the groups without whom a company cannot exist. These groups include customers, consumer advocates, owners, community organizations, governments, suppliers, environmentalists, special interest groups, employees, media and competitors. The stakeholder theory is thus based on the view that a company operates in an ecosystem of different participants whose interests are vital for the success of the company itself. As a result, the company should take into account the interests of its stakeholders if it wants to ensure its own long-term well-being.

Both theories acknowledge the importance of considering stakeholders' interests in the strategic decision-making process. By considering these two theories, companies can adopt a holistic approach to combining financial objectives, preserving the planet, and ensuring a positive impact on people.[10]

It thus becomes obvious that companies pursuing CSR should not remain silent during times of geopolitical risks that affect our society, such as a war in Ukraine and a constantly worsening financial downturn. This is because such geopolitical conditions affect the lives of ordinary people, as well as the environment (e.g., animals), and the companies with CSR policies need to step in to help these stakeholders survive and have a better quality of life. This will in turn improve the image of the company vis-à-vis its stakeholders.

Having discussed the theoretical underpinning of CSR, the next section of this paper will analyse several reforms in French law in this respect.

§8.03 FRENCH LEGISLATIVE FRAMEWORK OF CSR

Over the last two decades, France has progressively introduced numerous reforms to adapt its legal framework to the necessities of CSR.

9. Robert E. Freeman, *Strategic Management: A Stakeholder Approach*, 1984, Pitman Publishing Inc., 292 pp.; Robert E. Freeman, 'The Politics of Stakeholder Theory', *Management: A Stakeholder Approach* (1984); Robert E. Freeman, *The Politics of Stakeholder Theory*, 4 Business Ethics Quarterly 409 (1994).
10. Marina Mattera & Frederico Soto, *Dodging the Bullet: Overcoming the Financial Impact of Ukraine Armed Conflict with Sustainable Business Strategies and Environmental Approaches*, 24 The Journal of Risk Finance122, 123 (2023).

[A] Non-financial Reporting and Due Diligence Plan

Law of 15 May 2001 on new economic regulations was adopted with a view to mitigate the negative impacts of internal dysfunction and globalization. Based on the need to provide transparent information, this legal act required all French-listed companies to include social and environmental consequences of their activities in their annual management reports (non-financial reporting), in addition to the financial and accounting information. It should be noted that this reform took place more than 10 years before the introduction of the Directive 2014/95/EU on non-financial disclosure,[11] which highlights the aspiration of the French legislature to make its national legal framework environment-friendly.

On 21 September 2001, an explosion caused by ammonium nitrate at the AZF site in Toulouse resulted in the death of 31 people and injuries to around 2,500 people, as well as extensive material damage. This catastrophe became a catalyst for French policymakers to elaborate and adopt the Law of 30 July 2003 on the prevention of technological and natural risks and the repair of damage (Law Bachelot). This law imposed four key obligations: informing local residents, raising awareness amongst employees, controlling urban development by defining risk zones and recognizing a concept of technological risks. These obligations had to be addressed in the technological risk prevention plan, which implemented the 'urban development control' aspect of the industrial risk prevention policy for Seveso-high threshold sites. As a result, all French public limited companies operating one or more facilities classified as Seveso-high threshold must inform their shareholders about their environmental activities.

The directive on the control of major-accident hazards involving dangerous substances (directive SEVESO), initially adopted in 1982, was revised twice and the latest version (SEVESO3) was adopted on 4 July 2012.[12] The directive requires EU Member States to identify high-risk industrial sites to maintain a high level of prevention. Seveso sites produce or store substances that can be hazardous to humans and the environment. An establishment is classified as Seveso based on the maximum quantity of hazardous substances likely to be present. The directive lists hazardous substances, which have also been included in the nomenclature of installations classified for environmental protection at the national level.

Law of 3 August 2009 on the implementation of the Grenelle Environment Forum (Law Grenelle I) and Law of 12 July 2010 on the national commitment to the environment (Law Grenelle II) have introduced a plan of action to tackle ecological emergency and transition. To illustrate, a parent company can provide (and in some cases is obliged to) financial assistance to its subsidiary when the latter is held liable for environmental damage.

---

11. Directive 2014/95/EU of the European Parliament and of the council of 22 October 2014 amending directive 2013/34/EU as regards disclosure of non-financial and diversity information by certain large undertakings and groups OJ L330/1.
12. Directive 2012/18/EU, OJ L197/1.

Law of 27 March 2017 on the due diligence of parent companies and ordering companies (Due Diligence Law) requires French companies with more than 5,000 employees (in their own companies and in their subsidiaries in France) or 10,000 employees (in their own companies and in their subsidiaries in France and abroad) to publish a plan designed to prevent the risks of serious violations of human rights and fundamental freedoms, the health and safety of individuals and the environment, which may result from its activities and those of the companies it controls and its usual subcontractors or suppliers.

The provisions of the Due Diligence Law were codified in the French Commercial Code. To this effect, paragraph 1 of Article L225-102-4 of the French Commercial Code requires a company which employs at least 5,000 employees to implement a due diligence plan. This plan shall contain information about the due diligence measures that identify risks and prevent serious harm to human rights and fundamental freedoms, as well as the health and safety of individuals and the environment resulting from the activities of the company. Failure to comply with this obligation will lead to civil law liability (Article L 225-102-5 of the French Commercial Code).

[B] PACTE Law 2019

PACTE Law represents a major reform of the French CSR regime. Translated from French, PACTE stands for 'action plan for the growth and transformation of businesses'. One of the objectives of the PACTE Law of 22 May 2019 is to ensure that a company shares the corporate value created by business activities with its employees and that a company takes the social and environmental factors into account when formulating its corporate strategy.[13]

The PACTE Law brings important modifications to French corporate law.[14] Some examples include the duty of a corporate director to consider the interests of a wider group of stakeholders, the definition of the *raison d'être* of the company,[15]and the introduction of a company with a mission. These reforms reflect the evolution of the French corporate law doctrine, i.e., the commercial company is now seen as a collaborative entity in our society instead of just a legal form with purely financial ambitions.

The explanatory preamble to the PACTE Law states that the French Civil Code should be amended to include the concepts of corporate interest and purpose established in the case law.[16] The French Court of Cassation has historically relied on the

13. *La Loi PACTE: pour la croissance et la transformation des entreprises*, Ministère de L'Économie des Finances et de la Souveraineté Industrielle et Numerique (11 September 2019), https://www.economie.gouv.fr/loi-pacte-croissance-transformation-entreprises.
14. Mariia Domina-Repiquet, *Report from France. Law Pacte 2019: A Successful Modernization of Company Law?*, 30 European Company Law Journal 167, (2019).
15. Even before the introduction of the PACTE Law, the French government had already required a certain number of publicly owned companies to adopt their *raison d'être* to accelerate their contribution to sustainable development.
16. Antoine Tadros, *Regard critique sur l'intérêt social et la raison d'être de la société dans le projet de loi PACTE*, Recueil Dalloz 1765, (2018).

concept of corporate interest to determine the validity of the acts performed by corporate directors, e.g., controlling the abuse of voting rights[17] and assessing the grounds for dismissal[18] or liability of the director.[19] Therefore, the PACTE Law represents a codification of the principles established by the case law in this context.

We will focus on the following three reforms introduced by the PACTE Law: (a) management of the company in a sustainable way; (b) *raison d'être* of the company; and (c) a company with a mission.

[1] Management of the Company in the Sustainable Way

In 2017, French President Emmanuel Macron stated in his television interview that a company shall no longer be perceived as an aggregation of shareholders; instead, a new approach to the corporate philosophy should be defined.[20]

Undeniably, the view of a company that represents the (financial) interests of its shareholders is no longer sufficient; what is needed is to rethink the role that a commercial company plays in different social domains, such as protecting the well-being and personal fulfilment of employees and preserving natural resources of our planet. In other words, it is not enough to define a company as a nexus of contracts focused on maximizing financial benefits for the shareholders;[21] rather, a company should become an active player in achieving the wider interests of our modern society.

The PACTE Law added a second paragraph to Article 1833 of the French Civil Code, which now reads as follows: 'The company shall be managed according to its corporate objective, taking into consideration the social and environmental impacts of its activity' [translated by the author]. This obligation applies to all types of commercial companies under French law. Previously, only large-scale companies were subject to the declaration of non-financial performance under French law, which implies accounting for social and environmental impacts of corporate activity.[22]

The new legislation is silent on what a corporate objective is. French academics define 'corporate objective' as 'the set of activities determined by the articles of association that a company may carry out'.[23] It should be contrasted with 'corporate interest' which is the proper interest of the company as a legal person, distinct from the

17. Com. 18 avr. 1961, Bull. civ. III, n° 175; D. 1961. 661; JCP 1961. II. 12164, note Bastian D.; JCP S 1961. 257, note Dalsace A.
18. Com. 7 juin 1983, *Rev. sociétés* 1983. 796, note Le Cannu P.
19. Com. 7 oct. 1997, Bull. Joly 1997. 1074, § 385, note Daigre J.-J.
20. Lilian Alemagna, *'Et si on changeait la vocation de l'entreprise ?'*, 8 mars 2018, available at https://www.liberation.fr/france/2018/03/08/et-si-on-changeait-la-vocation-de-l-entreprise_1634802 (accessed on 10 August 2023) (8 March 2018), https://www.liberation.fr/france/2018/03/08/et-si-on-changeait-la-vocation-de-l-entreprise_1634802.
21. Report Notat-Senard(9 March 2018) discussed in Thibault de Ravel d'Esclapon, *Rapport Notat-Senard: l'entreprise, objet d'intérêt collectif*, Dalloz Actualité(13 March 2018), https://www.dalloz-actualite.fr/flash/rapport-notat-senard-l-entreprise-objet-d-interet-collectif.
22. Law No. 2017-399 of 27 March 2017 on the due diligence of parent companies and ordering companies, discussed earlier.
23. Isabelle Urbain-Parleani, *L'article 1835 et la raison d'être*, 3 Revue des sociétés 533, (2019).

interests of its directors and individual shareholders.[24] The exact scope of a corporate objective is to be interpreted by the judges on a case-by-case basis.

The duty of sustainable corporate management now applies to the directors of all commercial companies. For example, Article L.225-251, paragraph 1, of the Commercial Code provides that 'directors and the members of the managing body [of the public limited companies] shall be liable individually or jointly and severally, as the case may be, to the company or to third parties, for breaches of the legislative or regulatory provisions applicable to *sociétés anonymes* ...' [translated by the author].[25] Consequently, the breach of the duty of sustainable corporate management will give rise to different headings of liability of a corporate director.[26]

[2] **Raison d'être *of the Company***

Article 1835 of the Civil Code states that 'the articles of association may specify a *raison d'être* consisting of the principles with which the company equips itself and for the respect of which it intends to allocate means in carrying out its activity' [translated by the author]. *Raison d'être*, translated literally from French as 'the reason for existence', here refers to the purpose of the company.

Similar to the corporate objective, the corporate purpose is not defined on the legislative level. The corporate purpose can be described as the reason why the company is constituted, the principles that the company strives to follow and for which it intends to allocate resources in its business activity.[27]

Corporate purpose is a wider concept than the corporate objective. Whilst the latter outlines the activities that must be conducted by a company in the course of its business, the former defines the general principles of the business activities. *Raison d'être* has an impact on the way in which the company carries out the activities set forth in its corporate objective.[28]

Since the adoption of the PACTE Law, it is possible to include *raison d'être* in the articles of association of a company.[29] This is not mandatory, i.e., the company can decide whether it wishes to define its purpose in the constituting documents. One example of such inclusion is the French supermarket Carrefour. It has specified its *raison d'être* – 'quality food accessible to all' – in the articles of association on 14 June 2019.

---

24. For the definition of corporate interest in specific situations, *see*, Com. 16 oct. 2019, n° 18-19.373, Com. 23 sept. 2014, n° 13-17.347, CE 25 oct. 2010, req. n ° 309473, Crim. 16 déc. 2009, n° 08-88.305, CE 29 juill. 1998, req. n ° 108244.
25. *Société anonyme* is one of corporate legal forms available under French law. It is comparable to the English limited company plc.
26. *See*, Mariia Domina, *The Critical Analysis of the Sustainable Corporate Governance Obligation under French Law*, 8 Journal of Business Law 668 (2022).
27. Brigitte Clavagnier, *La 'raison d'être' en droit*, 3 Juris Associations (2019).
28. Urbain-Parleani, *supra* n. 23.
29. Article 1834 of the French Civil Code states as following: 'The provisions of this Chapter shall apply to all companies unless otherwise provided by law by reason of their form or object.' [translated by the author]. Shall we keep it or not? all translations are mine.

Consequently, a corporate director must manage the company in the company's interest,[30] which now includes *raison d'être* of the company if this is expressly mentioned in the articles of association.[31] A violation of these obligations will give rise to several headings of liability, both in civil and criminal law.[32]

[3] Company with a Mission

The PACTE Law establishes a company with a mission.[33] The objective is to create, in the future, a European company with a mission, something comparable to already existing *societas europaea*.[34] Similar legal structures already exist across the globe, for example, in Anglo-Saxon countries.[35]

As a result of the reform, French law now allows a company to decide whether it wants to set forth its mission.

The legal text does not define what a corporate mission is. Professor Couret suggests that a corporate mission is broader than a corporate purpose as it considers long-term value of the business activities of the company.[36] Therefore, the corporate director must always take into account the corporate interest whilst managing the company; taking into account corporate purpose and mission becomes obligatory only when they are stated in the constituting documents of the company. All these three concepts oblige a director to consider the social and environmental impact of the business activities.

Article L210-10 of the French Commercial Code states that in order to become a company with a mission, the articles of association must define the following elements: (1) the provisions as to the defined mission of the company according to Article 1835 of the French Civil Code; (2) the social and environmental objectives that a company will pursue; (3) the procedures for monitoring compliance with these objectives; (4) the creation of a mission committee that will control the compliance of the company with the above-mentioned procedures and present an annual report on the completion of the corporate missions; (5) how a third-party organization shall independently monitor the fulfilment of the social and environmental objectives; and (6) the registration of the status of the company as a company with a mission by the commercial court.

---

30. If this is not the case, the company director, whatever the form of the company, commits a management error which engages his responsibility and constitutes just cause for dismissal. *See*, Com. 26 avr. 2017, n° 15-14.627, *Rev. sociétés* 2017, 569, note Périn P.-L.; *Dr. sociétés* 2017. Comm. 142, note Heinich J.
31. Article L. 225-251 c. com.
32. Domina, *supra* n. 26.
33. Three new articles were introduced in the French Commercial Code to this effect: Articles L 210-10, L210-11 and L210-12.
34. Thibault De Ravel d'Esclapon, *supra* n. 21.
35. For a comparative overview of the company with a mission: Karsten E. Sorensen & Mette Neville, *Social Enterprises: How Should Company Law Balance Flexibility and Credibility?*, 15 EBOR 267 (2014).
36. Alain Couret, *Les sociétés à mission*, 7 Recueil Dalloz 432 (2020).

Professor Couret argues that a company with a mission may become a vehicle of choice in the French economy.[37] It is attractive for those shareholders that want to be 'socially and environmentally responsible'; this structure can be used to supervise work in the public interest[38] and resolve social and environmental problems. According to the survey conducted by Prophil, HEC Paris and Viavoice in February 2018, out of 623 leading French businesses, 68% wanted to have a special legal and fiscal framework for companies with a mission, whilst 48% believed that there is a significant potential for this legal form in France.[39] Furthermore, 73% alleged that the company with a mission will improve the corporate brand and 83% – the company's perception by the customers.[40]

We can conclude that adhering to the CSR principles, however general their content is in the national law, is now obligatory for all commercial companies under French law. Next section will look at the approach of French courts to CSR.

§8.04 A VIEW OF FRENCH COURTS ON THE CSR

The previous discussion evidenced numerous CSR obligations imposed by French legislators on commercial companies. Due to the general wording used to write down the actual content of these obligations, as well as the recent nature of these legislative initiatives, it is interesting to assess the position of French courts in this context.

We will discuss a very recent case, which also happens to be the first case on the obligation of the parent company to prepare a due diligence plan which respects the principles of CSR.

TotalEnergies SE, the head of the Total group which includes 1,140 companies operating in more than 130 countries on five continents, published its due diligence plan on 20 March 2019. It concerned a major oil project that TotalEnergies SE was developing with its subsidiary companies in Uganda and Tanzania. In June 2019, six non-governmental organizations (NGOs) served a formal notice to TotalEnergies SE, requiring it to modify its due diligence plan in order to comply with the legal requirements of the Due Diligence Law, whose provisions were codified in the French Commercial Code. They argued that this plan endangered human rights (e.g., forced eviction of the local population) and the environment (e.g., important greenhouse gas emissions, drilling of oil wells inside the national park, pumping large quantities of water from the lake, and the passage of an oil pipeline through protected areas). On 29 October 2019, following the end of the three-month period after submitting a formal notice, the NGO brought an application for interim measures before the Nanterre Court (civil) of the First of

37. Alain Couret, *supra* n. 36.
38. For example, revitalizing a region, safeguarding jobs.
39. Prophil, HEC Paris & Viavoice, *Les entreprises à mission, entreprises de demain?* (14 February 2018) cited in: Emmanuel Masset, *Vers la société à mission?*, 11 Revue des sociétés 635 (2018).
40. This may lead to the concerns of the company with a mission being used as a means of 'greenwashing' and 'fairwashing' of the potential clients. *See*, Corinne Lepage, *Le statut des entreprises à mission peut-il améliorer la prise en compte des défis environnementaux?*, Actu Environnement (26 March 2018), https://www.actu-environnement.com/blogs/corinne-lepage/77/corinne-lepage-statut-entreprise-mission-defis-environnementaux-114.html.

Instance.[41] They required TotalEnergies SE to comply with the legal requirements on the due diligence plan, i.e., prepare and publish a diligence plan that prevents serious violations of human rights and fundamental freedoms, the health and safety of individuals and the environment in connection with the aforementioned oil projects.

The idea behind bringing up a claim for interim measures is to allow an urgent response to the conduct of the alleged wrongdoer, since his actions may present an imminent danger. Interim measures preserve the rights of the parties until the dispute is assessed by the judge on the merits, which is different from the judge that imposed interim measures (Article 484 of the French Code of Civil Procedure). Article 488 of this code states that a judgement imposing interim measures does not have the authority of res judicata in the main proceedings, i.e., the proceedings that assess the case on the merits.

After more than three years of court proceedings, which included a question of the judicial competence – whether a civil or commercial court has competence in this matter – Paris Court (civil) of the First Instance has issued a court ruling on 28 February 2023[42] that denied the claims of the NGO for interim measures. Given the fact that this is the first legal case on the obligations of the parent company concerning its due diligence plan, three French university professors with expertise in the due diligence duty were consulted as *amici curiae*.

In its rulings, the Paris Court of First Instance highlighted the fact that the obligations related to the due diligence plan established by the Due Diligence Law and codified in Articles L. 255-102-4 and 5 of the French Commercial Code present several weaknesses. The actual content of the measures so introduced remains quite general, whilst the decree of the Conseil d'État to detail these measures is still not published. The Due Diligence Law does not provide for a classification of the due diligence duties and makes no reference to the guiding principles or pre-established international standards in this context. The 'positive law' does not indicate any specific rights concerned by this legal act, nor does it set forth any *modus operandi* or monitoring indicators for preparing and implementing the due diligence plan. The court also stressed the absence of an independent control body in this context. The judges concluded that the single concept that can be used here is that of 'reasonableness' of the measures, which is 'imprecise, vague and flexible' in the face of the 'monumental goals' assigned by the legal act and connected company law legislation.

The concept of 'reasonableness' is a common tool used by judges in the application of the law, which allows the legal rules to be adaptable to the changes in our society and thus respond efficiently to the facts of each case. It follows that the judges, even when presented with the legal rules of very general content, could nevertheless exercise control over the implementation of the duty of due diligence by analysing the reasonableness of the measures and, if required, referring to international principles of law (United Nations, Organization for Economic Co-operation and Development, etc.).

41. TJ Nanterre, ord., 11 févr. 2021, n° 20/00915 discussed in Philippe Métais & Elodie Valette, 'Devoir de vigilance: vers une option de compétence?', *Dalloz Actualité. Affaires-Civil* (17 January 2021), https://www.dalloz-actualite.fr/flash/devoir-de-vigilance-vers-une-option-de-competence.
42. TJ Paris, 28 févr. 2023, no. 22/53942; TJ Paris, 28 févr. 2023, no. 22/53943.

The court then, by applying the principle of reasonableness, deducted the *modus operandi* of drawing up a due diligence plan. Article L. 255-102-4 of the French Commercial Code states that the plan can be prepared 'where appropriate in the context of multi-stakeholder initiatives within sectors or at regional level' without precision as to who the stakeholders are. According to the judges, this implies that the plan must be drawn up 'in association with the stakeholders', since the legislator had 'expressly manifested its intention to see this due diligence plan drawn up as part of a joint construction and dialogue between the company's stakeholders and the company'. However, the only formal framework contained in the law is the requirement for formal notice to be given by 'any person with an interest therein' prior to referral to the court.

The court continued its reasoning by stating that this formal notice is a part of the 'collaborative process' of drawing up the plan, which includes an 'obligatory phase of dialogue and amicable exchange'. Considering that the amicable negotiation phase prior to referral to the court would be compulsory and that the effectiveness of this amicable negotiation would only be ensured by a 'firm and precise formal notice to identify the breaches attributed to the plan', it deduced that the absence of such a formal notice could only result in 'the inadmissibility of the request for an interim measure made to the court'.

The court ruled that the claims brought by the NGOs were inadmissible because of this lack of formal notice. Even though the NGOs had sent TotalEnergies SE a formal notice more than three months before the case was brought before the court in 2019, the court considered that this was not sufficient. What was required was a match between the allegations contained in the initial formal notice and those presented in support of the claims made on the day of the proceedings before the court (two 'events' that are separated by more than three years).

As a result, the court clarified the dismissal of the claim by NGO by stating that the 'present application is based on more than two hundred new documents compared with those annexed to the 2019 formal notice, so that there are grounds for considering that the objections that are the subject of the applications made by the plaintiffs in relation to the 2021 diligence plan [at the date of the court hearing at the end of 2022 it is the due diligence plan for the year 2021 that was the subject of the NGO's claim for interim measures] were not notified to TotalEnergiesSE in a formal notice prior to the referral to the court' [translated by the author].

This case raises several observations.

First, this judicial process, however long its duration was, gave an opportunity to TotalEnergies SE to rethink its approach to CSR within the corporate group in order to become more sustainable, as evidenced by the subsequent due diligence plan. An important motivation here is to improve the public image of the company, whereby stakeholders need to be reassured that a company respects the principles of CSR throughout its operations, be it in France or abroad.

Second, French courts are inclined to the idea that CSR should be based on a dialogue between a company and stakeholders, with limited legislative and judiciary involvement. This gives an opportunity to all associations and NGOs involved in the protection of human rights and environment to collaborate closely with commercial companies in order to redefine, if necessary, CSR of the latter.

Third, we argue that this case might have been decided differently if the imminent danger was to occur in France. In this context, a claim could have been brought on different grounds (imminent danger to the health and safety of people punished by the French Criminal Code, the right to withdraw from working in dangerous conditions guaranteed by the French Labor Code, as well as violation of legal rules contained in the French Code of Environment), not to mention the additional pressure that might have been exercised by French activist organizations on TotalEnergies SE. As regards the discussed case, we suggested that the courts of Uganda and Tanzania were better equipped to protect the health of its people and its environment by imposing interim measures on the actual local companies engaged in the projects.

Fourth, the court upheld the importance of reasonableness in deciding the actual content of the required actions. Let us recall that an approach of reasonableness allows the courts to adapt the legal rules to the actual situation and apply the legal rules more efficiently. This is particularly important in the context of CSR, which is based on general concepts such as 'considering the impact of the corporate operations on the environment and society as a whole'. By using the concept of reasonableness, the actual CSR obligations of the company can be redefined, *inter alia*, according to the geopolitical risks that it is facing.

§8.05 CONCLUDING REMARKS

This chapter highlighted the fact that the appreciation of French courts of the CSR obligations, which are established by the different legislative acts during the last two decades, is based on the notion of 'reasonableness'. This allows French companies to revise the corporate duties vis-à-vis particular geopolitical risks that they are facing.

As we have mentioned previously, the concept of CSR takes on an entirely different meaning in the current geopolitical realities: COVID-19 pandemic, shortage of vaccines, climate change, war in Ukraine and other parts of the world, pronounced food shortage in some developing countries and global financial downturn are just some very sad examples of the times that our society is experiencing. These geopolitical risks affect especially fragile groups of the population, such as people with modest resources, students, disabled and retired persons all over the world, adding to the social inequalities.

For example, researchers argue that the CSR policies of commercial companies are put to test during the war in Ukraine.[43] Due to the geopolitical risk related to the war in Ukraine, the majority of European companies, including French ones, have decided

43. Iryna Reshetnikova & Katarzyna Sanak-Kosmowska, *Corporate Social Responsibility in the Context of Russian Military Aggression in Ukraine*, 2 Marketing and Management of Innovations 138 (2023).

that it was unethical to continue doing business with Russian firms.[44] As a result, many of them have withdrawn from the Russian market, even before the international sanctions were imposed on the foreign companies that continued doing their business with the Russian Federation. It becomes obvious that a more dynamic approach to CSR is needed, e.g., by adding 'geopolitical responsibility' to *the raison d'être* of French companies.[45]

We argue that, from the perspective of French law, it would be possible to extend the CSR policies of French companies to account for new geopolitical risks, including climate change and rising inequalities around the globe.

This would be possible due to the three main reasons.

First, the discussed reforms of the French law impose different general CSR obligations on French commercial companies, allowing them, *inter alia*, to write down CSR commitments in the articles of association.

Second, the French approach to CSR is based on the dialogue between a company and different stakeholders. This dialogue allows rethinking and redefining, if necessary, CSR of a particular company in order to take into account the interests of specific groups of stakeholders, e.g. local population.

Third, French courts use a concept of 'reasonableness', which will allow them to decide whether the conduct of the company is reasonable vis-à-vis specific geopolitical risks it is facing.

To conclude, the French regime provides sufficient possibilities for companies to adapt their CSR policies to account for specific geopolitical risks. It would be interesting to follow closely the future French case law in this context to ascertain the extent of the 'reasonableness' applied to the CSR policies in times of geopolitical uncertainty.

44. Iryna Reshetnikova & Katarzyna Sanak-Kosmowska, *supra* n. 43; Marina Mattera & Frederico Soto, *supra* n. 10.
45. Amandine Lepoute, *Guerre en Ukraine: les entreprises ont une responsabilité géopolitique*, Challenges, l'actualité de l'économie (25 mars 2022), https://www.challenges.fr/green-economie/guerre-en-ukraine-les-entreprises-ont-une-responsabilite-geopolitique_806111.

CHAPTER 9

The Services Directive's Impact on Company Law and Company Structures

Karsten Engsig Sørensen

There are several provisions in the Services Directive that may impact national company law or the corporate structure used by service companies exercising free movement. Many aspects of the Directive seem to codify the jurisprudence of the CJEU, which applies to the freedom of establishment and the freedom to provide services. However, parts of Article 14 and Article 16 impact company law and company structure beyond the Treaty. Thus, the ban on discrimination of companies in Article 14, point 1 and the ban on certain restrictions on the freedom to choose the form of establishment are likely to make it easier to challenge such rules, as the CJEU has not allowed the Member States to try to justify such rules nor rely on the exception found in TFEU. Such an unconditional approach is likely to work for Article 14, point 1, but may be problematic for Article 14, point 3 which prohibits restrictions to choose between establishment in the form of a branch and a subsidiary. Also, the very broad range of requirements that may be caught by Article 16 resembles the broad ban on restrictions that can be challenged under Article 56 TFEU. If, however, the CJEU will only allow the Member States to rely on the four specific reasons mentioned in Article 16(1) and 16(3) for justification of national rules, its likely impact on national company law and structures seems to be dramatically increased.

§9.01 INTRODUCTION

During the last 20 years, the journal *European Company Law* and the accompanying books series have kept the focus on the development of European Union (EU) law and its impact on company law. Much of the credit for this important work belongs to Professor Steef Bartman.

To mark this anniversary, this contribution will focus on how the Services Directive may impact national company law or company structures. The Services Directive, Directive 2006/123/EC,[1] should have been implemented by the end of 2009 (not all Member States managed this), and thus, it emerged within the 20-year framework that is the focus of this book. After a slow start, the Services Directive has started to generate more and more preliminary rulings and infringement actions against Member States, and it has become clear that the Directive is likely to impact company law and company structure, as this contribution will document. Even though some questions have been settled by case law and the European Commission (the Commission),[2] there is still a range of issues left open, and thus, it is likely that this Directive will generate more scholarly debate in the coming 20 years.

What makes this development particularly interesting is the fact that the Services Directive to some extent offers a protection beyond that given by the freedom of establishment and the freedom to provide services under Articles 49 and 56 of the Treaty on the functioning of the European Union (TFEU).[3] The provisions which are most likely to affect company law and company structure are Articles 14, 15 and 16 of the Services Directive. Whereas the first two address the freedom of establishment for service providers with or without a cross-border element, the latter regulates the cross-border provision of services without an establishment. The fact that Articles 14 and 15 of the Services Directive can be used in a purely internal situation[4] clearly gives these a broader range than Article 49 TFEU, as it allows persons setting up a company in their home state to invoke the two provisions. Apart from this, the potential for deviating from the free movement rights in the Treaty seems to differ. Article 14 of the Services Directive provides for a list of prohibited requirements, and the requirements listed will not be allowed, even if they could pass the Gebhard test[5] or be excluded under Articles 51 and 52 TFEU. According to the Court of Justice of the European Union (CJEU), the prohibition is absolute, and there is no room for the Member States to argue for justification[6] and therefore it is more likely that such requirements will infringe on the Directive than that they will infringe Article 49 TFEU. However, Article 15 of the Services Directive is less likely to deviate from Article 49 TFEU (apart from the fact that

1. *Directive 2006/123/EC of the European Parliament and of the Council of 12 December 2006 on services in the internal market*, OJ EU 2006 L 376/36.
2. The Commission has in September 2022 issued the second edition of the publication: *Handbook on the Implementation of the Service Directive*, European Commission, https://op.europa.eu/en/publication-detail/-/publication/60e2d020-6c6f-11ed-9887-01aa75ed71a1. Even though the Commission cannot give authoritative interpretation of the Services Directive, the first edition of the Handbook has often been referred to by the Court of Justice of the European Union (CJEU), *see* for instance Case C-57/12, *Femarbel*, 11.7.2013, ECLI:EU:C:2013:517, paras 37, 43, 45 and 46 and Case C-294/14, *Hiebler*, 7.4.2016, ECLI:EU:C:2016:210, paras 32, 53 and 73.
3. The aim of going beyond the TFEU is also indicated in Recital 6 of the Services Directive.
4. That the provisions in Chapter III can be used in purely internal situations was confirmed in Joint Cases C-360/15 and C-31/16, 30.1.2018, ECLI:EU:C:2018:44, para. 110.
5. The Gebhard test being the four-point test developed in Case C-55/94, *Gebhard*, 30.11.1995, ECLI:EU:C:1995:411,
6. *See* Case C-593/13, *Rina Services*, 16.6.2015, ECLI:EU:C:2015:399, paras 28-35.

it applies to internal situations) as it lists a number of requirements potentially affecting the freedom of establishment that must be evaluated under a test that resembles the Gebhard test. The only difference between the Gebhard test and the test under Article 15 of the Services Directive is likely to be that the requirement in Article 15(2) of the Services Directive can be assumed to be a restriction and therefore in need of justification, without the need to evaluate whether market access is obstructed or whether the requirement only indirectly or hypothetically affects establishments.[7] Article 16 of the Services Directive concerns the freedom to provide services and only allows requirements regulating the access to or exercise of services to the extent that they are justified for reasons of public policy, public security, public health or the protection of the environment. Consequently, Member States will most likely not be allowed to rely on the broader range of justification that they can rely on when Article 56 TFEU is applied.[8] As such, Article 16 of the Services Directive also has the potential to deviate from the Treaty. Even though Article 16(1) of the Services Directive covers all requirements which affect the access to or exercise of service, Article 16(2) of the Services Directive lists several requirements that according to Article 16(3) of the Services Directive should also be tested against the four justifications mentioned in Article 16(1) of the Services Directive.[9] It is not quite clear what difference it makes whether a requirement is covered by Article 16(2) of the Services Directive or not, but likely, the list in Article 16(2) constitutes requirements that the Member States must be extra careful about examining for EU conformity.[10]

In §9.02, I discuss how the Services Directive is likely to impact either national company law or companies' structures, and in the following paragraphs, I then discuss the areas where such an effect most likely occurs.

§9.02 IMPACT ON COMPANY LAW OR COMPANY STRUCTURES

The Services Directive aims to facilitate the exercise of the freedom of establishment for service providers and their ability to provide services in other Member States without any establishment, *see* Article 1(1) of the Services Directive. A service provider is someone providing a service. In Article 4(1) of the Services Directive, 'service' is defined as 'any self-employed economic activity, normally provided for remuneration,

7. Thus, to be a restriction for the exercise of Art. 49 TFEU, the CJEU has insisted in multiple cases that market access is affected. *See also* Catherine Barnard, *The Substantive Law of the EU* 220-231 (Oxford University Press 7th ed. 2022).
8. So far, the CJEU has neither confirmed nor rejected this. It is, however, widely assumed that only the four reasons mentioned can be invoked by the Member States. *See* for instance: European Commission, *Handbook on the Implementation of the Services Directive* 61 (September 2022) and Panagiotis Delimatsis, *Yearbook of European Law* 188-150, at 218 (Oxford University Press, 2018).
9. Also, Art. 16(3) of the Services Directive allows Member States to apply for rules on employment conditions, which does not seem relevant here given the focus of this contribution.
10. According to the Commission, there is a strong presumption that the requirements in Art. 16(2) of the Services Directive cannot be justified according to Art. 16(3) of the Services Directive. *See* European Commission, *Handbook on the Implementation of the Services Directive* 61 (September 2022).

as referred to in Article 50 [now Article 57] of the Treaty'.[11] Service providers may be natural persons who are nationals of a Member State or legal persons as referred to in Article 54 TFEU who are established in a Member State, *see* Article 4(2) of the Services Directive. Article 54 TFEU includes a broad range of corporate forms, but it is limited to companies formed in the EU and excludes those which are non-profit-making. Articles 19-21 of the Services Directive also grant recipients of services some rights, and a company referred to in Article 54 TFEU will also benefit hereof.

Companies may use the Services Directive to challenge different national requirements that may hinder the activities protected by the Directive. These could include requirements found in national company law. Even though different types of rules are excluded from the Services Directive (*inter alia*, labour law, criminal law and tax law), company law is not. However, to the extent that there is a harmonisation of company law, the Services Directive will not apply, *see* Article 3(1) of the Services Directive. Thus, if an issue is governed by the Codified Company Law Directive[12] or any other secondary act, the Services Directive will not apply if there is a conflict between the harmonised rules and provisions in the Services Directive. The fact that an issue is partly regulated in secondary EU law does not mean that the topic in its entirety will be excluded. For instance, the fact that we have some harmonisation of the rules applicable to branches in other Member States does not mean that national regulation of branches that are not implementing harmonised rules is excluded. Also, even if there is a conflict between a provision in the Services Directive and the harmonised rules, the remaining provision in the Services Directive will still be applicable, given that there is no conflict there.[13]

Even though the Services Directive may be used to challenge national company law, it has not happened so far. But rules found in other types of national regulation may affect the company structure of a service provider. This could, for instance, be rules limiting the ability to choose the corporate form that the service provider prefers, rules affecting the ability to choose the management of preference, rules dictating the composition of shareholders, or rules that determine whether to use a branch or a subsidiary for an establishment. As it will become clear in the following, there are several cases in which the Services Directive is used by the CJEU to set aside this kind of national rule.

The Services Directive may also provide a company that is the recipient of services a greater freedom to choose its structure, for instance, where to incorporate (Article 20(1) of the Services Directive), where to be established (Article 19(b) of the Services Directive) or reside (Article 20(1) of the Services Directive). However, in the following, the focus will be on the rights of companies that are service providers.

11. The Services Directive does not cover all types of services, as several types of services are excluded from the Directive. *See* in particular Art. 2(2) of the Services Directive, but also the exception in Art. 17 of the Services Directive for the cross-border provision of services. This issue will not be discussed further in this contribution.
12. *Directive (EU) 2017/1132 of the European Parliament and of the Council of 14 June 2017 relating to certain aspects of company law*, O.J. EU 2017 L 169/46.
13. *See* European Commission, *Handbook on the Implementation of the Services Directive* 23 (September 2022).

§9.03 REQUIREMENTS RELATING TO THE CORPORATE FORM

A requirement to use a particular corporate form to be able to provide some types of services will affect the company structure of the service provider. Such requirements may take different forms, and they are addressed in different parts of the Services Directive.

According to Article 14, point 1, of the Services Directive, discriminatory requirements based on the nationality of the service provider or, in the case of companies, the location of the registered office are prohibited. To have a registered office in a particular Member State, a company will normally have to be incorporated in that Member State. Therefore, if a requirement dictates that a company is required to have a registered office in a Member State, if it provides services in that state, it will be equal to a requirement to use a local corporate form. This type of restriction is evidently a restriction on the freedom of establishment, as it makes it impossible for companies from other Member States to do so. Such a requirement would likely infringe Article 49 TFEU,[14] but under Article 14 of the Services Directive, it is even more straightforward to conclude that EU law is breached, as Article 14 of the Services Directive, as mentioned, does not allow the Member States to justify the rules nor to use Articles 51 and 52 TFEU.

The CJEU used Article 14, point 1, of the Services Directive in Case C-593/13, *Rina Services*, which concerned an Italian requirement stating that to operate as an SOA classified certification body, a company needed to have its registered office in Italy. The CJEU found this requirement to infringe Article 14, point 1, of the Services Directive, and it was in this case that the CJEU for the first time clarified that no justification can be given for the requirement listed in Article 14 of the Services Directive.[15] In a later judgment, the CJEU applied Article 14, point 1, of the Services Directive to requirements in Austria, stating that companies of civil engineers and companies of patent agents must have their seats in Austria. According to the CJEU, this was a requirement based directly on the location of the registered office.[16] The concept of 'seat' is not explained in the judgment. The concept could cover the actual place from where the company is governed, and therefore, it does not have to be the place where the company is registered, as is assumed by the CJEU. But even if that is not the case, a requirement dictating that a company must have an actual seat in a Member State is likely to be an indirect discrimination of foreign companies.

Such discriminatory requirements were also confronted by the CJEU in Case C-179/14, *Commission v. Hungary*, which addressed several requirements for being allowed to provide services in the form of issuing a so-called SZÈP card, a card that allowed employers to offer employees some leisure services with tax benefits. If the issuer was part of a group and only fulfilled the requirement to issue the card together with other companies in the group, the issuer would only qualify if the members of the group, including the patent company, were formed according to Hungarian law and

14. *See* Case C-101/94, *Commission v. Italian Republic*, 6.6.1996, ECLI:EU:C:1996:221.
15. *See* paras 25 and 28 respectively.
16. *See* Case C-209/18, *Commission v. Austria*, 29.7.2019, ECLI:EU:C:2019:632, para. 51.

were either public or private limited companies. The Commission had argued that these requirements infringed Article 15(2)(b) of the Services Directive, which covers an obligation for the provider to have a specific legal form. In his Opinion, Advocate General Bot disagreed, as he felt that the requirement of using Hungarian companies should be examined either under Article 14, point 1, or Article 16(2)(a) of the Services Directive, if the provider did not intend to make an establishment in Hungary.[17] The CJEU, however, examined both requirements (that it should be a Hungarian company and of a particular legal form) under Article 15(2)(b) of the Services Directive, as it argued that this provision must be understood in a broad sense.[18] Since Hungary had not put forward any justification for the rule, it was easy to establish that the Hungarian rules infringed Article 15(2)(b) of the Services Directive. So, in this case, it did not make any difference that both requirements were evaluated under Article 15 of the Services Directive and not Articles 14 and 15 of the Services Directive, respectively.

Article 14, point 1 of the Services Directive also prohibits indirect discrimination, and in Article 14, points 1(a)-(b) of the Services Directive, some examples hereof are mentioned. Of particular relevance for corporate service providers are requirements as to the nationality or residence of members of the management and/or shareholders.[19] Already, we have cases where the CJEU has established that such requirements may infringe Article 49 TFEU,[20] but again it is easier to apply Article 14 of the Services Directive, as it is unconditional.[21]

However, the examples mentioned in Article 14, points 1(a)-(b), of the Services Directive are not exhaustive, which is also indicated by the use of the words 'in particular'. In Case C-209/18, *Commission v. Austria*, the CJEU found that a requirement that companies of civil engineers must have at least one member or board member that has his practice as an engineer in Austria is in substance a requirement to be resident in Austria, and therefore infringes Article 14, point 1(b), of the Services Directive.

If there is a direct or indirect requirement for using a local company form to be able to provide services, such discriminating requirements are likely to infringe Article

17. Paragraph 114 of the Opinion of AG Bot in Case C-179/14, *Commission v. Hungary*, dated 17 September 2015.
18. *See* para. 62 of the judgment.
19. In Case C-206/19, *'KOB' SIA*, 11.6.2020, ECLI:EU:C:2020:463, Latvia required that companies where the controlling shareholder or shareholders and all persons entitled to represent the company are nationals of another Member State were only allowed to acquire agricultural land in order to farm if certain conditions were fulfilled. First, the shareholders and those able to represent the company must be residents in Latvia, and second, they must demonstrate that they have some knowledge of the Latvian language. Since these requirements were not imposed on shareholders and members of management that are Latvian nationals, the rules were infringing Art. 14, point 1, of the Services Directive. Thus, it was a case of direct discrimination of a physical person and not indirect discrimination of a company.
20. *See* for instance Case C-221/89, *Factortame*, 25.7.1991, ECLI:EU:C:1991:320.
21. When examining whether there is an indirect discrimination, it will normally be relevant to examine whether there is another objective reason for the requirements for nationality or residency that offers another explanation for the requirement than that of discrimination. However, given the explicit prohibition of such requirements in Art. 14, point 1(a)-(b), of the Services Directive it is not clear that there is a need for testing for such alternative explanations.

16 of the Services Directive in the situation where the provider does not aim to make an establishment. In his Opinion in Case C-179/14, *Commission v. Hungary*, Advocate General Bot argued that a requirement to use a Hungarian company to provide services in Hungary would infringe Article 16(2)(a) of the Services Directive as it would amount to a requirement of having an establishment in Hungary. It depends on national company law whether incorporation of a company requires a connection to the state that constitutes an establishment.[22] But even if an establishment is not required, a requirement to use a local corporate form to be able to provide services is likely to infringe Article 16(1)(a) of the Services Directive.

Instead of requiring the use of a local corporate form, a Member State may require that the provider uses a special type of corporate form. Such a requirement would be covered by Article 15(2)(b) of the Services Directive and, according to Article 15(3) of the Services Directive, must be examined according to a test that resembles the Gebhard test developed by the CJEU. So, in comparison to the requirements in Article 14 of the Services Directive, a close examination will often be needed to establish a breach of Article 15(2)(b) of the Services Directive, and it seems less likely that the latter will provide better protection of service providers than that offered by Article 49 TFEU.

According to Recital 73 of the Services Directive, Article 15(2)(b) of the Services Directive in particular covers a requirement to be a legal person (that is, a requirement to use a company for the activity), a requirement to be a company with individual ownership, to be a non-profit making organisation, or a company owned exclusively by natural persons. Some of these examples seem to address requirements that do not address the corporate form but the nature of the shareholders or members. The latter is addressed specifically in Article 15(2)(c) of the Services Directive; *see* below §9.06. But according to the CJEU, the recital indicates that the term 'specific legal form' should be understood in a broad sense.[23]

Thus, Article 15(2)(b) of the Services Directive would cover both a requirement not to be a company and a requirement to be a company of any kind or a particular type of company. The latter could take the form of either a requirement for a specific form or a prohibition of certain company forms for particular activities.[24]

So far, several cases have addressed such requirements under Article 15(2)(b) of the Services Directive. As already mentioned, Article 15(2)(b) of the Services Directive was applied by the CJEU in Case C-179/14, *Commission v. Hungary*, to set aside requirements whereby a provider operating a group must use particular commercial

22. For a comparative overview of the connection required to form companies *see*: Carsten Gerner-Beuerle et al., *Study on the Law Applicable to Companies* (2016), European Union, https://op.europa.eu/en/publication-detail/-/publication/259a1dae-1a8c-11e7-808e-01aa75ed71a1.
23. *See* Case C-179/14, *Commission v. Hungary*, 23.2.2016, ECLU:EU:C:2016:108, para. 62.
24. *See also* the European Commission, *Handbook on the Implementation of the Services Directive* 54 (September 2022). The Commission mentions an example from Case C-243/01, *Gambelli*, 6.11.2003, ECLI:EU:C:2003:597, where a listed company was denied the possibility to take up certain types of services.

corporate forms as well as using a Hungarian company. In Case C-729/17, *Commission v. Greece*, one of the requirements for mediator training providers was that they should be formed as a non-profit civil law partnership. This, the CJEU found to be caught by Article 15(2)(b) of the Services Directive.[25] Since the Greek government had not put forward any arguments to show that there was a justification for the requirement, the CJEU found that the conditions in Article 15(3) of the Services Directive were not fulfilled. In Case C-209/18, *Commission v. Austria*, the CJEU found both Article 15(2)(b) and Article 15(2)(c) of the Services Directive to be infringed, but it is not clear what part of the national legislation that breached the former, as the Austrian requirements focussed on the shareholders and therefore most likely infringed Article 15(2)(c) of the Services Directive.

The requirements to use a specific company form or abstaining from using certain forms may also be a requirement restricting the freedom to provide services under Article 16(1) of the Services Directive and will therefore only be allowed, if they are justified in one of the four justifications mentioned. So far, the CJEU has not used Article 16 of the Services Directive to evaluate such requirements.[26]

§9.04 AVOIDANCE OF LETTERBOX COMPANIES

One of the key principles established by the case law of the CJEU on the freedom of establishment is that a company that has been incorporated in one Member State has the right to transact business in a different Member State, even if it does not have any activities in the Member State it is incorporated in. This was established in Case C-212/97, *Centros*, and has been confirmed in many later cases – most recently in Case C-106/16, *Polbud*. There is also case law that establishes that a company that is incorporated in one Member State but only sells its services in other Member States (or maybe even just in one Member State) will be able to invoke the freedom to provide services according to Article 56 TFEU.[27]

25. *See* paras 60-61 of the judgment.
26. In Case C-10/22 *Jamendo*, Advocate General Szpunar in his Opinion, 25.5.2023, ECLI:EU:C:2023:437, concluded that a requirement that copyright management activities should be conducted by collective management organisations to the exclusion of independent management entities in other Member States infringed Art. 16(1) and Art. 16(2)(d) of the Services Directive. The CJEU however, decided that Art. 16 was not applicable since services for the management of copy rights and related rights was excepted from Art. 16 according to Art. 17(11).
27. *See* Case C-56/96, *VT4*, 5.6.1997, ECLI:EU:C:1997:284, paras 19-22. There are, however, older cases that indicate that where all service activities are directed at customers in one Member State (different from the one where the company is established) Member States may take steps to prevent abuse, *see* in particular Case C-23/93, *TV10*, 5.10.1994, ECLI:EU:C:1994:362, para. 21 and Case C-148/91, *Veronica*, 3.2.1993, ECLI:EU:C:1993:45, paras 12-13. For a discussion of these cases *see*, *inter alia*, Alexandre Saydé, *Abuse of EU Law and Regulation of the Internal Market* 122-137 (Oxford Hart Publishing, 2014), and Dimitrios Doukas, *Free Movement of Broadcasting Services and Abuse of Law in Prohibition of Abuse of Law: A New General Principle of EU Law* 63-91 (Rita de la Feria & Stefan Vogenaur eds, 2011).

Because of this case law, Articles 49 and 56 TFEU facilitate the use of letterbox companies.[28] In recent years, this protection has, however, been somewhat curbed by the application of the general principle prohibiting abuse.[29]

A reading of the Services Directive may indicate that such letterbox companies may not benefit from the Services Directive. Thus, it follows from Article 4(2) of the Services Directive that a service provider is a company which is 'established in a Member State'. In Article 4(5) of the Services Directive, an establishment is defined as 'the actual pursuit of an economic activity ... for an indefinite period and through a stable infrastructure from where the business of providing services is actually carried out'. According to Recital 37 of the preamble to the Services Directive, this definition intends to follow the definition laid down by the CJEU. Furthermore, it says: 'According to this definition, which requires the actual pursuit of an economic activity at the place of establishment of the provider, a mere letter box does not constitute an establishment.'

This statement indicates that some letterbox companies will not benefit from the Services Directive. One reading is that a company without any activities in any Member State will not benefit from the Services Directive. Such a reading would not be controversial as companies without any activities will not benefit from the free movement rights, since this requires that EU companies have an effective and continuous link with the economy of one of the Member States.[30] But what about a company that does not have any activities (or infrastructure) at this moment but plans to start such activities in the future? This would cover the Centros-like companies that are formed in Member State A to be used exclusively for activities in Member State B. As long as the company has not started the activities in Member State B, it will fail to have the economic activities required. As a consequence, such a Centros-like company may not be able to invoke the Services Directive to clear any barriers they encounter in Member State B when it either tries to establish there or tries to provide services there. The preparatory works for the Services Directive indicate that the reference to letterbox companies in Recital 37 was an attempt to avoid allowing Centros-like companies to benefit from the Services Directive.[31] Instead, Centros-like companies would have to rely on the free movement rights of the TFEU.[32]

It seems most likely that the CJEU will try to interpret the Services Directive so that Centros-like letterbox companies are also service providers benefitting from the

28. *See also* Karsten Engsig Sørensen, *The Fight Against Letterbox Companies in the Internal Market*, 52 Common Market Law Review 85, 85-118 (2015) DOI: 10.54648/cola2015004.
29. *See, inter alia*, Case C-359/16, *Altun*, 6.2.2018, ECLI:EU:C:2018:63, Joint Cases C-370/17 & C-37/18, *CRPNPAC*, 2.4.2020, ECLI:EU:C:2020:260 and C-356/15, *Commission v. Belgium*, 11.7.2018, ECLI:EU:C:2018:555.
30. The requirement has its origin in the General Programme for the abolition of restrictions on freedom of establishment, OJ 1962 C 36/62, Title I, which requires companies to have a 'real and continuous link with the economic activities of a Member State', in order to benefit from the freedom of establishment. Later, the requirement has been confirmed by the CJEU in C–208/00, *Überseering*, 5.11.2002, ECLI:EU:C:2002:632, para. 75.
31. *See* Paschalis Paschalidis, *Freedom of Establishment and Private International Law for Corporations* 96-107 (Oxford University Press, 2012).
32. *Ibid.*, at 105.

Services Directive. This is the interpretation that promotes the aim of enhancing free movement the most.[33] Also, a reading of Article 4(2) and Article 4(5) of the Services Directive may allow an inclusion of companies that are incorporated in one Member State and are about to start up activities and establish infrastructure in a different Member State. So, it is mainly the aforementioned Recital 37 that may indicate otherwise, and a recital is not binding in the same way as the provisions of the secondary act are.

This interpretation is also supported by Case C-66/18, *Commission v. Hungary*. The case concerned the Hungarian Law on higher education, which only allows a foreign higher education institution to carry out its activities in Hungary, if it genuinely offers higher education in the state in which it has its seat. This requirement was also applied to institutions in the EU and European Economic Area (EEA).

The Commission had argued that the legislation infringed both EU law and the General Agreement on Trade in Services (GATS). Regarding the first issue, it was argued that there were both an infringement of the freedom of establishment and an infringement of Article 16 of the Services Directive.

The CJEU reminded that it follows from previous case law that the freedom of establishment also protects a company that is formed in one Member State and is solely used for activities in another Member State, and here, the CJEU referred to the *Polbud* judgment. The requirement of activities in the state where the institution has its seat constitutes a restriction of the freedom of establishment, and the CJEU found that there was a restriction that could not be justified under the Gebhard test.

In addition to this, the CJEU found that the Hungarian law infringed the freedom to provide services under Article 16 of the Services Directive. Thus, those who provided services in the form of higher education could not deliver their services in Hungary (in this case, without being established), unless they fulfilled the requirement of having activities at the place of their seat. Therefore, Article 16(1) of the Services Directive was infringed, and the CJEU did not think that the legislation could be justified for reasons of public policy or public security according to Article 16(3) of the Services Directive.

In this case, the CJEU was clearly not minded to accept that a company should have activities in the Member State where it is formed. This indicates that the Services Directive also benefits such letterbox companies, just like Articles 49 and 56 TFEU do. It should be noted that Recital 37 of the Services Directive is not mentioned in the judgment nor in the Opinion given by the Advocate General in the case.

§9.05 REQUIREMENTS FOR THE FORMAT OF ESTABLISHMENT

Several provisions in Articles 14 and 15 of the Services Directive aim to ensure that a company that plans to establish itself in another Member State has a relatively free hand in deciding how to go about it.

---

33. Also, if Chapter III of the Services Directive should offer protection in a purely internal situation where persons set up a company in their home state, then the Services Directive should also protect the setting up of a company that plans business activities, but for good reasons does not have them already.

According to Article 14, point 2, of the Services Directive, Member States may not prohibit that a company has an establishment in more than one Member State. So far, this provision has not been applied by the CJEU, but there are several examples of the CJEU's use of this principle under Article 49 TFEU.[34]

More interesting, Article 14, point 3, of the Services Directive prohibits restrictions on the freedom to choose between a principal or secondary establishment. This provision prohibits a requirement that a provider must have its principal establishment in the territory of a Member State to be allowed to conduct a particular type of service there. In Case C-593/13, *Rina Services*, the CJEU seems to assume that the requirement that a company that operates as an SOA classified certification body needed to have its registered office in Italy could have the effect of restricting the provider's choice between principal and secondary establishment. The assumption seems to be that if the registered office has to be in Italy, then the principal establishment must also be placed there. However, not all Member States require that a company must have its main activity or even any activity in the Member State where the company is incorporated.[35]

Also, it will not be allowed for a Member State to require that a foreign company must have its principal place of business in the Member State of incorporation, as this would also restrict the freedom to choose to have the principal place of business elsewhere. In fact, as discussed in §9.04, Case C-66/18, *Commission v. Hungary*, indicates that the CJEU is unwilling to accept that a Member State requires that a company should have some activities in the Member State where it is incorporated.

Article 14, point 3, of the Services Directive is not limited to restrictions on the freedom to choose between a principal or secondary establishment, as it also (in the second part of the provision) prohibits restrictions on the right to choose between establishments in the form of an agency, branch or subsidiary. This part of the provision will prevent a Member State from prohibiting the use of one of the forms mentioned, which in practice is either a prohibition of the use of a branch or a subsidiary. This was confirmed by the CJEU in Case C-179/14, *Commission v. Hungary*, where branches of a company incorporated in another Member State than Hungary could not provide the service in question (the issuing of SZÈP card). The CJEU noted that this restricted the choice between the different forms of establishment, and as Article 14 of the Services Directive applies without exceptions, the Hungarian state could not give any justification, nor could they rely on Article 52 TFEU.[36]

It is possible that Article 14, point 3, of the Services Directive can also be used to set aside provisions that, even if they do not rule out one form of establishment, subject different types of establishments to different conditions. The wording of Article 14, point 3, of the Services Directive is not clear as it just prohibits restrictions on the freedom to choose between different forms of establishment. However, according to the Commission, Article 14, point 3, of the Services Directive prohibits requirements which grant certain forms of secondary establishment more favourable treatment than

34. *See* for instance Case 107/83, *Klopp*, 12.7.1984, ECLI:EU:C:1984:270, and Case 96/85, *Commission v. France*, 30.4.1986, ECLI:EU:C:1986:189.
35. *See* Gerner-Beuerle et al., *supra* n. 22.
36. *See* paras 44-47 of the judgment.

others.[37] But it is unclear how such a prohibition should be applied. Thus, setting up a branch and subsidiary is in many ways subject to different conditions, as the former 'just' requires a registration, whereas the latter requires the formation of a company with all that this entails. These differences seem very difficult if not impossible to remove in their entirety.

So far, the CJEU has not addressed the question of whether Article 14, point 3, of the Services Directive prohibits (some) types of differentiation between different forms of establishments. Often, the background for the prohibitions in Article 14 of the Services Directive can be found in the case law of Article 49 TFEU. The CJEU addressed the issue in Case C-253/03, *CLT-UFA SA*, paragraphs 13-15, where it stated:

> Under that provision, freedom of establishment for nationals of one Member State on the territory of another Member State includes the right to take up and pursue activities as self-employed persons and to set up and manage undertakings under the conditions laid down for its own nationals by the law of the country where such establishment is effected. The abolition of restrictions on freedom of establishment also applies to restrictions on the setting up of agencies, branches or subsidiaries by nationals of any Member State established in the territory of another Member State (Case 270/83 *Commission v. France* [1986] ECR 273, paragraph 13, and Case C-311/97 *Royal Bank of Scotland* [1999] ECR I-2651, paragraph 22).
>
> The second sentence of the first paragraph of Article 52 expressly leaves traders free to choose the appropriate legal form in which to pursue their activities in another Member State and that freedom of choice must not be limited by discriminatory tax provisions (*Commission v. France*, paragraph 22).
>
> Therefore, the freedom to choose the appropriate legal form in which to pursue activities in another Member State primarily serves to allow companies having their seat in a Member State to open a branch in another Member State in order to pursue their activities under the same conditions as those which apply to subsidiaries.

Thus, it is clear that the freedom to choose between different forms of establishments cannot be restricted through discriminating rules, and here, the CJEU refers back to its ruling in Case 270/83, *Commission v. France*. Thus, a Member State cannot defend a rule that discriminates against branches of foreign companies by pointing out that the foreign company could avoid being discriminated against by setting up a subsidiary instead. This, however, is not very surprising. But the CJEU apparently goes further, as in paragraph 15, it states that the freedom of establishment also ensures that companies may set up branches and subsidiaries 'under the same conditions'. In this case, the fact that income from branches was subject to a tax rate of 42%, whereas subsidiaries are taxed at either 33.5% or 30%, makes the setting up of branches less attractive. Therefore, it seems that any differences in taxation are likely to be restrictions, unless the differential treatment can be objectively justified.[38]

37. European Commission, *Handbook on the Implementation of the Service Directive* (September 2022), at 49. In a footnote the Commission refers to Case C-66/18, *Commission v. Hungary*, para. 44, but that paragraph does not say anything about rules favouring one form of establishment over others, but just recalls the wording of Art. 14, point 3, of the Services Directive.
38. *See* paras 16-18.

As Case C-253/03, *CLT-UFA SA* was a tax case, it may be questioned whether it can be transferred to company law matters. This, however, was what happened in a judgment handed down by the Court of the European Free Trade Association (EFTA Court) in Case E-9/20, *ESA v. Norway*. The case addressed Norwegian rules requiring EEA citizenship and residence in an EEA state for management and founders of certain Norwegian companies, and the key question in the case was whether these requirements infringed the freedom of establishment in Article 31 of the Agreement on the European Economic Area (EEA Agreement). It should be noted that the freedom of establishment under 31 of the EEA Agreement and 49 TFEU is identical.

The Norwegian government argued that the rules did not restrict the freedom of establishment, as there was no restriction if an EU/EEA company wanted to establish a branch in Norway. The Norwegian rules in question were only a potential restriction when a Norwegian company was formed. But a foreign company that is forming a Norwegian subsidiary must expect that there are a number of requirements that need to be complied with, and such a (parent) company cannot expect that the subsidiary is subject to the same rules on the composition of management as those applicable to the parent company itself.[39]

The EFTA Court found that the requirement of an EEA nationality for management and founders was a restriction of the freedom of establishment, and here, the EFTA Court referred to Case C-299/02, *Commission v. Netherlands*. Thus, if a company established in another EU/EEA state wants to form a subsidiary in Norway, its choice of management may be affected by the Norwegian requirements. The argument that such a company could instead form a branch (and be free to choose the management) was dismissed, as the EFTA Court found that the freedom of establishment includes the right to choose the appropriate legal form, including choosing a separate legal entity instead of a branch.[40] In a previous paragraph, the EFTA Court had already mentioned this freedom to choose the appropriate legal form of an establishment, and here they referred, *inter alia*, to Case C-253/03, *CLT-UFA SA*, paragraphs 13-15.[41] Having established that there was a restriction to the freedom of establishment, the EFTA Court then examined whether there was any justification for the requirement. As this was not the case, there was an infringement of Article 31 of the EEA Agreement.

First, the EFTA Court seems to establish that there is a restriction because the Norwegian rules may affect who to elect for the management of a subsidiary. Second, the EFTA Court also seems to argue that there is a restriction because the Norwegian requirements only apply to subsidiaries and not to branches. Since the latter argument is not really necessary – as it had already been established that there was a restriction – it may be questioned how much one should rely on the latter argument. However, the trust of the EFTA Court's arguments seems to be that the fact that different rules apply to subsidiaries and branches was enough to establish a restriction.

Based on these cases, it may be argued that Article 14, point 3, of the Services Directive includes restrictions in the form of different conditions for setting up

39. *See* para. 68 of the judgment.
40. *See* para. 86.
41. *See* para. 75.

branches and subsidiaries. In both Case C-253/03, *CLT-UFA SA* and E-9/20, *ESA v. Norway*, the courts went on to examine whether there was a justification for the differences, and potentially, this may justify most of the differences applicable to branches and subsidiaries. However, under Article 14, point 3, of the Services Directive, there is no room for looking into such justification, and therefore, the consequences of making such differences into restrictions will be more far-reaching and probably unsustainable. This calls for a different interpretation of Article 14, point 3, of the Services Directive.

In the end, the CJEU will have to decide on how to handle this, but a possibility could be to interpret the last part of Article 14, point 3, of the Services Directive as a prohibition of conditions that discriminate between setting up branches and subsidiaries.[42] A discrimination test would allow a test of whether the different conditions between branches and subsidiaries can be explained by the nature of the particular form or not. Thus, requiring a minimum capital for forming a subsidiary may be explained by the fact that setting up a company requires capital, whereas setting up a branch does not require the contribution of capital. However, other requirements that cannot be explained by such fundamental differences between a branch and a subsidiary will be prohibited. This likely includes a requirement for EEA nationality for the management of a subsidiary when there is no such requirement for a branch manager. Even though such an interpretation would limit the impact of Article 14, point 3, of the Services Directive in the area of company law, the provision will still have a large potential for challenging national company law.

According to Article 15(2)(e) of the Services Directive, Member States need to examine any ban on having more than one establishment in the territory of one Member State. In principle, such a ban can be justified under the test in Article 15(3) of the Services Directive, but attempts to do so in previous cases (decided under Article 49 TFEU) prove that this is very difficult.[43] So far, there are no cases in which the CJEU uses Article 15(2)(e) of the Services Directive, but it seems unlikely that the provision will add much to the already existing case law.

If a company wants to provide services in another Member State without having an establishment, that right is protected by Article 16 of the Directive. According to Article 16(2)(a) of the Services Directive, the requirement to have an establishment in the territory as a prerequisite for being allowed to provide services, there is a restriction to the provisions of services. In principle, Member States could try to justify the requirement in one of the four reasons mentioned in Article 16(3) of the Services Directive, but it is likely very difficult to have such requirements accepted. The CJEU used Article 16(2)(a) of the Services Directive in Case C-179/14, *Commission v. Hungary*, where one of several requirements for being allowed to issue SZÈP cards was

42. The wording of Art. 14, point 3, of the Services Directive refers to restrictions and not discrimination, and this may make the suggested interpretation less likely. But in tax cases the CJEU has often managed to couple discrimination and restrictions as normally only tax rules that discriminate cross-border activities are termed 'restrictions'. So, there is a precedence for interpreting restrictions as discriminatory requirements.

43. *See* Case C-140/03, *Commission v. Greece*, 21.4.2005, ECLI:EU:C:2005:242 and Case C-117/05, *Seidl*, 2.12.2005, ECLI:EU:C:2005:739.

that a provider has offices open to the public in every municipality in Hungary with more than 35,000 inhabitants. This clearly was a requirement for having a (substantial) establishment and therefore a violation of Article 16(2)(a) of the Services Directive.[44] Hungary tries to justify the restriction on grounds relating to consumer and creditor protection. The CJEU found that the requirement could not be justified according to Article 16(3) of the Services Directive. The CJEU made it clear that it found that the requirement was not proportional, and therefore, the CJEU (intentionally) avoided ruling on whether reasons, such as consumer and creditor protection that are not covered by the four reasons mentioned in Article 16(3) of the Services Directive could be invoked by a Member State.[45] Thus, the CJEU avoided having to decide on this thorny issue.

§9.06 REQUIREMENTS FOR SHAREHOLDERS

According to Article 15(2)(c) of the Services Directive, Member States should be careful to check requirements which relate to the shareholding of the company. Such requirements are only valid if they can pass the test in Article 15(3) of the Services Directive. This regulation supplements the prohibition of nationality or residency requirements for shareholders in Article 14, points 1(a)-(b) of the Services Directive, *see* above §9.03.

Article 15(2)(c) of the Services Directive has been used in several judgments, and these cases indicate that it will not be easy for the Member States to pass the test in Article 15(3) of the Services Directive. Often, the Member States require that all or some of the shareholders perform the profession that the company itself is engaged in or at least are family to persons exercising such a profession.[46] It could also be different requirements as to the nature of shareholders. Thus, in Case C-729/17, *Commission v. Greece*, it was a requirement that a mediator training institution must have at least one bar association and one business chamber as a member.

Often, the Member States argue that these requirements are justified by the need to protect the independence of the service provider and to protect the provider's customers. The CJEU often points out that this aim may be achieved without requiring that all or most of the shares be owned by professionals, and sometimes, it may be achieved by alternative regulations such as rules on professional conduct. So far, the Member States have not been able to convince the CJEU that the requirements in Article 15(3) of the Services Directive are fulfilled in any of the cases mentioned.

44. Paragraph 107 of the judgment.
45. *See* para. 116.
46. *See* Case C-297/16, *CMVRO* (retailor of veterinary medicinal products must be owned by mainly veterinary practitioners), 1.3.2018, ECLI:EU:C:2018:141, and Case C-209/18, *Commission v. Austria*, 29.7.2019, ECLI:EU:C:2019:632 (addressing requirements for members of companies engaged in civil engineering, as patent agents or veterinary surgeons). *See also* the pending case C-295/23, *Halmer Rechtsanwaltsgesellschaf UG*, about practicing lawyers.

The judgment mentioned seems to follow in the footsteps of earlier cases determined under Articles 49 and 56 TFEU and therefore does not necessarily add much to these rules.

§9.07 CONCLUSIONS

This short contribution indicates that there are several provisions in the Services Directive that may impact national company law or the corporate structure used by service companies exercising free movement. Many aspects of the Services Directive seem to codify the case law of the CJEU. This is clearly the case for the different parts of Article 15(2) of the Services Directive, which are subjected to a test in Article 15(3) of the Services Directive that resembles the Gebhard test developed by the CJEU under Article 49 TFEU. The main impact of Article 15 of the Services Directive thereby seems to be that the fact that some rules are highlighted as restrictive requirements in Article 15(2) of the Services Directive may make it more likely that such rules will be challenged – either by the Commission or by businesses. Also, contrary to Article 49 TFEU, it applies to purely internal situations.

However, it seems more likely that the parts of Article 14 of the Services Directive addressed above and Article 16 of the Services Directive impact company law and company structure beyond the TFEU. Thus, the ban on discrimination of companies in Article 14, point 1, of the Services Directive and the ban on certain restrictions on the freedom to choose the form of establishment are likely to make it easier to challenge such rules, as the CJEU has not allowed the Member States to try to justify such rules nor rely on the exception found in TFEU. Such an unconditional approach is likely to work for Article 14, point 1 of the Services Directive but may be problematic for Article 14, point 3 of the Services Directive. This is shown to be the case in particular in any attempt to give a broad interpretation of the concept of restrictions on the freedom to choose between establishment in the form of a branch and a subsidiary. It will be up to the CJEU to handle this thorny issue, but a possible solution is pointed out. Also Article 14, like Article 15, applies to purely internal situations.

Also, the very broad range of requirements that may be caught by Article 16 of the Services Directive resembles the broad ban on restrictions that can be challenged under Article 56 TFEU. If, however, the CJEU will only allow the Member States to rely on the four specific reasons mentioned in Article 16(1) and 16(3) of the Services Directive for justification of national rules, its likely impact on national company law and structures seems to be dramatically increased.

Finally, the half-hearted attempt to prevent letterbox companies from benefitting from the Service Directive seems unlikely to materialise.

CHAPTER 10

Digital Incorporation: The Case for a Trustworthy Commercial Register

Christoph Teichmann

In 2019, the European Union introduced an online formation procedure for limited liability companies. While some Member States had already introduced such procedures many years before, others found it difficult to accept a purely digital procedure for incorporating a company. This debate revealed a fundamental dissent: The incorporation procedure of many continental jurisdictions is based on the concept of preventive judicial control ('vorsorgende Rechtspflege') administered by notaries; other Member States understand incorporation primarily as a service offered to the founders which should be as unbureaucratic and flexible as possible. This paper argues, however, that preventive judicial control, in the context of commercial and company law, is not just a burden to businesses but rather a contribution to reducing transaction costs as it increases the trustworthiness of the commercial register. EU secondary law nowadays helps to reconcile the two objectives. On the one hand, Member States with notarial systems accepted the idea to offer an electronic formation procedure; on the other hand, secondary law now emphasizes the need for effective preventive control in a way that had not been articulated so clearly at the European level before.

§10.01 INTRODUCTION

A few years ago, the European Proposal to introduce an electronic procedure for the incorporation of companies put a finger in an open wound in European company law. It revealed that Member States had a completely different understanding of the procedure that should precede the registration of a company. In some continental states, such as Germany, Spain or Austria, notaries have always been involved in checking the identity of applicants and the legality of the documents submitted. Other states prefer a quick registration and attach less importance to effective control of the submitted data and documents. The former group expressed fears that an electronic procedure might increase the risk of errors and abuses. As in many other areas of company law, this discussion was always accompanied in a highly competent manner in *European Company Law*, founded by *Steef Bartman* 25 years ago.[1]

It is the aim of this paper to show that in retrospect the debate on electronic formation has actually led to an overall improvement in preventive control standards.[2] This assumption will be traced in four steps: First, the contrast of views on preventive control will be worked out, which clearly emerged on the European level with the proposal regarding online incorporation (*infra* §10.02). Second, the added value of preventive judicial control for the area of company law will be elaborated on (*infra* §10.03). Third, it shall become apparent how the discussion on online formation has finally led to a strengthening of the preventive control elements in EU law (*infra* §10.04). The European Commission's recent proposal for further reform of the Company Law Directive points in the same direction (*infra* §10.05). The basic findings of the paper will be summarized with some conclusions (*infra* §10.06).

§10.02 THE EUROPEAN DEBATE ON PREVENTIVE CONTROL

[A] Introducing Digital Incorporation: The Moment of Truth

In 2019, the EU Directive regarding the use of digital tools in company law (hereinafter 'Directive 2019') introduced an online formation procedure for limited liability companies.[3] For some Member States, such as Estonia and Denmark, online formation was already well-established, whereas countries like Germany, Austria or Spain initially found it difficult to accept a purely digital procedure. In these states, the incorporation of companies traditionally takes place with the assistance of notaries. Their function is to check whether the company has been founded in accordance with the rules and procedures of the applicable companies act; for that end, notaries have personal contact with the founders and the future directors of the company, offer legal advice and check the validity of the incorporation documents. Online formation, in the wording of the Directive 2019, means that the founders do not have to appear in person before any national authority. From a German perspective, it was argued that such a

1. *See*, among others, a paper on the proposed reform of the single-member company directive, which already addressed the issue of online formation, by Iris Wuismann, *The Societas Unius Personae (SUP)*, ECL 12, 34-44 (2015), as well as Florian Möslein's Editorial, *Back to the Digital Future? On the EU Company Law Package's Approach to Digitalization*, ECL 16, 4-5 (2019).
2. Some of the following observations are based on earlier publications: Christoph Teichmann, *Die digitale GmbH-Gründung: Ein Entwicklungssprung für die vorsorgende Rechtspflege*, 112 GmbH-Rundschau, 1237-1248 (2021); Christoph Teichmann, *Das Informationsmodell des Europäischen Gesellschaftsrechts im digitalen Zeitalter*, 3 Recht Digital, 357-364 (2023).
3. Directive (EU) 2019/1151 of the European Parliament and of the Council of 20 June 2019 amending Directive (EU) 2017/1132 as regards the use of digital tools and processes in company law, Official Journal of the European Union, OJ L 186/80, 11.7.2019.

procedure might result in a considerable loss of quality and lead to incorrect entries in the commercial register.[4]

The debate about online formation revealed a dissent that had rarely been talked about before at the European level: Many continental jurisdictions are based on the concept of preventive judicial control (*'vorsorgende Rechtspflege'*).[5] In their view, the procedure for incorporating a company should ensure the legality of the formation and avoid erroneous registrations. Many other Member States, however, understand incorporation primarily as a service offered to the founders. They need a legal entity to start their business; registration therefore should be as unbureaucratic and flexible as possible and should enable founders to take off immediately. The need to arrange an appointment for physically meeting a notary is not really compatible with such a regulatory intention. While Estonia in one case was able to incorporate a company within 18 minutes, German authorities may well need several days or even weeks to register a company.[6]

It seems, however, that the European Commission, when proposing online formation of companies, underestimated how deeply the opposing views were rooted in the national legal traditions. Replacing notaries with electronic instruments is not just a technical matter – it raises the fundamental question of what registration is all about: Shall information which is to be recorded in the commercial register be verified *ex ante* by a public authority? Or shall it simply be copied and pasted from the data submitted by the applicants and be registered without further ado?

[B] Preventive Control in European and National Law

As a matter of fact, preventive control has been part of European company law ever since the adoption of the first company law directive in 1968[7]: Member States may either draw up and certify the instruments of the constitution *'in due legal form'* or *'provide for preventive administrative of judicial control'* (nowadays Article 10 of the

4. *See*, for instance, the analysis by the president of the German Notaries Chamber Jens Bormann, *Die digitalisierte GmbH*, 46 Zeitschrift für Unternehmens- und Gesellschaftsrecht, 621, 633-635 (2017), as well as (on an earlier EU proposal) Peter Kindler, *Die Einpersonen-Kapitalgesellschaft als Konzernbaustein – Bemerkungen zum Kompromissvorschlag der italienischen Ratspräsidentschaft für eine Societas Unius Personae (SUP)*, 179 Zeitschrift für das gesamte Handelsrecht und Wirtschaftsrecht, 330, 393-346 (2015).
5. For a comparative analysis *see*, among others: Christoph Teichmann, *Die elektronische Gründung von Kapitalgesellschaften*, 109 GmbH-Rundschau, 1-15 (2018), as well as Jens Bormann & Peter Stelmaszczyk, *Das kontinentaleuropäische Gesellschaftsrecht im Wettbewerb der Rechtsordnungen*, 39 Zeitschrift für Wirtschaftsrecht, 746-774 (2018).
6. The Impact Assessment preceding the proposal for the above-mentioned directive correctly stated on p. 16: 'when procedures require the physical presence in front of a competent authority the time for completing the registration is longer than when procedures are done fully online.' (European Commission, SWD(2018) 141 final, 25.4.2018). The Impact Assessment compares Estonia and Germany on pp. 124-125.
7. First Council Directive of 9 March 1968 (68/151/EEC), Official Journal of the European Communities, OJ L 65/8, 14.3.1968.

consolidated Company Law Directive (CLD)[8]). For the German reader, this seems to solve the dispute. Preventive control, as applied by notaries, is mandatorily regulated in EU law; in one way or another, it should be applied everywhere, not only in states with a notarial system. But this view was challenged by a PhD study on the origins of the first company law directive. It found that a simple statement of compliance, signed by the founders, could be assumed to be a sufficient instrument of preventive control.[9]

Such a statement, obviously, does not prevent incorrect data from being entered into the register, as could (and still can) be observed in the UK. According to sec. 13 of the UK Companies Act, 'a statement that the requirements of this Act as to registration have been complied with' may be accepted by the registrar 'as sufficient evidence of compliance'. Accordingly, the UK Companies House explains on its website that it does not verify the accuracy of the information that companies send to it;[10] it is therefore not surprising that the same website shares the following information with us: Companies House deals with around 50 to 100 cases of corporate identity theft every month[11]. Comparable cases of identity theft are almost unknown in Germany; the last case of identity theft that has been reported in case law dates back to the year 2012.[12] It is obviously more difficult to cheat a notary in physical presence than to send a false statement to an authority that expressly declares that it will not verify it.

Further discussion on the European level, however, made clear that a lack of scrutiny is not necessarily associated with a digital procedure. Preventive judicial control and the use of digital instruments are not contradictory as such.[13] In fact, the use of digital tools can even contribute to improving the quality of the formation process as they offer new ways to verify the information which is to be recorded in the register. Estonia and Denmark, for instance, have been quite successful in this respect, applying checks and verifications that are not possible in a paper-and-pencil procedure.[14] Certainly, there are security gaps here as well. But Germany does not necessarily fare better in the overall comparison:[15] While Estonia checks the criminal records of potential directors highly effectively by background checks of the relevant databases, Germany still relies on a declaration of compliance. The person to be nominated

8. Directive (EU) 2017/1132 of the European Parliament and the Council of 14 June 2017 relating to certain aspects of company law (codification), Official Journal of the European Union, OJ L 169/46, 30.6.2017 (hereinafter 'Company Law Directive' or 'CLD').
9. Lenard Bock, *Der Harmonisierungserfolg der Publizitätsrichtlinie*, Nomos, 33-35 (2016).
10. The Companies House frankly admits: 'we do not have the statutory power or capability to verify the accuracy of the information that companies send to us'. (Service information (companieshouse.gov.uk) (last visited 18 October 2023). The same statement could be found on the website when the UK was a member of the European Union (cf. Bormann/Stelmaszczyk, *supra* n. 5, 769).
11. Protect your company from corporate identity theft - GOV.UK (www.gov.uk) (last visited 18 October 2023).
12. Oberlandesgericht Brandenburg, 5 U 66/11, 33 Zeitschrift für Wirtschaftsrecht, 2103-2106 (2012); the case is also interesting for its ignorance of the European implications of the issue (for a critical analysis Christoph Teichmann, *Der Schutz des Rechtsverkehrs nach § 15 Abs. 3 HGB*, Festschrift für Karsten Schmidt, 471-484 (C.H. Beck 2019)).
13. This has also been acknowledged by representatives of notaries, *see* Bormann, *supra* n. 4, 642-646.
14. *See* Teichmann, *supra* n. 5, 7-10.
15. *Ibid.*, 9.

as director is asked to confirm that he or she has not committed any crime that would disqualify him or her from being nominated as a director (§ 8 (3) GmbH-Gesetz).[16] It is precisely such a declaration of compliance that continental authors have always been considered completely unsuitable with regard to the UK.

§10.03 PREVENTIVE JUDICIAL CONTROL AND ITS RELEVANCE FOR COMPANY LAW

[A] Avoiding Legal Conflicts *Ex Ante*

Preventive judicial control is a trademark of civil law in Germany and other continental countries that is closely linked to the activity of notaries.[17] As opposed to courts, which deal with legal conflicts as they come to the surface, the function of notaries is to solve conflicts before they actually occur. A court usually only becomes active when a legal conflict arises and must be decided. By then, however, the child had already fallen into the well, the dispute had broken out and must be dealt with – consuming a great deal of human and time resources. The activity of notaries, on the other hand, is intended to avoid disputes from the outset. Every legal adviser knows that a good contract helps to prevent conflicts from arising. If, for example, the by-laws of a company[18] contain a clear provision as to the exclusion of a shareholder and the calculation of the compensation due, these questions do not have to be clarified in Court later.

The need for advice is particularly high in the case of a company's by-laws because the company is typically set up for a long time and the founders often lack the foresight and experience to anticipate future conflicts. Limitation of foresight is a well-known problem in the economic analysis of contracting.[19] It has been correctly

---

16. Neither the German notary nor the registrar at the commercial register have direct access to the database which lists offences leading to disqualification. The registrar could send an enquiry to the competent authority, but the number of such enquiries tends towards zero, according to practitioners. If there is no particular indication to doubt the correctness of the director's declaration, the company will be registered without further verification.
17. For Germany, *see* Teichmann, *supra* n. 5, 1-3; for Italy and Spain *see* Rolandino Guidotti & Alessio Bartolacelli, *Societas Unius Personae (SUP) from the Italian Perspective, in Private Companies in Europe: The Societas Unius Personae (SUP) and the Recent Developments in the EU Member States* 89, 102 (Thomson Reuters 2016) and Antonion Roncero Sánchez, *'Societas Unius Personae': Analysis from the Perspective of Spanish Law, in Private Companies in Europe: The Societas Unius Personae (SUP) and the Recent Developments in the EU Member States* 199, 209-212 (Thomson Reuters 2016).
18. The term 'bylaw' refers to the document containing all the specific rules applicable to the company. Some jurisdictions distinguish the bylaws from the 'articles of incorporation' i.e., the contract expressing the will of the parties to create a company (*cf.* Marco Ventoruzzo et al., *Comparative Corporate Law* 133-134 (West Academic Publishing 2015). In Germany, both aspects are covered by one document, called '*Gesellschaftsvertrag*' and subject to notarial deed (§ 2 (1) *GmbH-Gesetz*).
19. *See* Richard A. Posner, *Economic Analysis of Law* 95 (Wolters Kluwer 2007). Cf. *also* Gregor Bachmann et al., *Regulating the Closed Corporation* 10 (De Gruyter 2014): 'Future conflicts are frequently not anticipated at the time of formation … .'

stated:[20] 'A well-drafted corporate charter and by-laws, as any contract, can be a work of art. A bad one can be a receipt for disaster.'

Having this in mind, German law stipulates that the by-laws of a company must be established by notarial deed.[21] With this requirement, the notaries come on the scene, whose duty is to ensure a legally effective drafting that meets the interests of the parties. The relevant provision reads like a textbook for diligent contract drafting (with the only particularity that the law enforces the drafting and advice of notaries, even if the parties themselves should be of the opinion that they do not need such legal advice and that the notary is not acting in the interest of one of the parties):[22] The notary shall ascertain the will of the parties, clarify the facts at hand, inform the parties of the legal implications of the transaction and reproduce their declarations clearly and unambiguously in the deed. In doing so, he or she shall ensure that errors and doubts are avoided and that inexperienced and unsophisticated parties are protected.

[B] Reduction of Transaction Costs in Day-to-Day Business

[1] Evidence for Existence of a Company

This procedure, which precedes the formation of a company, has another function in addition to avoiding disputes: It can be assumed to be a general feature of all the company law systems within the European Union that a limited liability company acquires legal personality at the moment of registration in the commercial register.[23] Hence, the quality of the entry (existence of a company) depends on the quality of the procedure (preventive control).[24] It is not an accident that the provision on preventive control (Article 10) in the Company Law Directive is to be found in the section on 'nullity of the limited liability company and validity of its obligations'.

The systematic link between preventive control and nullity of companies is highlighted in the recitals of the Directive. They refer to the necessity 'in order to ensure certainty in the law as regards relations between companies and third parties, and also between members, to limit the cases in which nullity can arise and the retroactive effect of a declaration of nullity, and to fix a short time limit within which third parties may enter an objection to any such declaration'.[25] The coordination of national provisions concerning the nullity of companies 'is of special importance, particularly for the purpose of protecting the interests of third parties'.[26]

---

20. Marco Ventoruzzo et al., *supra* n. 18, 142.
21. § 2 (1) *GmbH-Gesetz* for the private company, § 23 (1) *Aktiengesetz* for the public company.
22. § 17 of the Act on notarial deeds (*Beurkundungsgesetz*).
23. Stefan Grundmann, *European Company Law* 137, no. 235 (Intersentia 2007). Legal personality of the company in formation ('Vorgesellschaft') is acknowledged in some Member States, but arguably not a principle of European company law (Grundmann, *supra*, 136, no. 234).
24. Segismundo Álvarez Royo-Villanova, *Proposal Regarding the Use of Digital Tools and Processes in Company Law: The Practitioner's Perspective,* 16 European Company and Financial Law Review, 149, 156 (2019).
25. Recital 6 CLD.
26. Recital 7 CLD.

Consequently, the preventive control mechanism serves as a justification for the following provisions in the Directive: Once registered, a company exists beyond any doubt. Even if the registration suffers certain defects, the company continues to exist until being deleted from the register. Nullity has to be pronounced by a court of law (Article 12(1) CLD) and it will not for itself affect the validity of any commitments entered into by the company (Article 12(3) CLD). The company continues to exist until the procedure of winding up has been completed by deleting the company from the register.[27] This results in a strong protection of third parties who rely on the content of the register.

[2] Evidence for Power of Representation

European law also protects the interests of those who wish to conclude contracts with the company and obtain reliable knowledge of the power of representation of the company's organs: Once the formalities of disclosure have been fulfilled, the company cannot hold any defects in the appointment of organs against a third party (Article 8 CLD). An exception applies only if the third party was aware of the defect in appointment, for which, however, the company bears the burden of proof. Furthermore, Article 9 CLD provides for the unlimited and unrestricted power of representation of the representative bodies.[28] In other words, third parties can fully rely on the content of the register – as long as the person they are contracting with is registered as a person with authority to represent the company, the contract will be valid.

This legislative intention, too, is reflected in the recitals: The protection of third parties shall be ensured by provisions which restrict to the greatest possible extent the grounds on which obligations entered into in the name of a company are not valid.[29] Third parties must have the possibility to inform themselves about the essential documents of the company as well as some information concerning them, in particular, the personal data of those who can represent the company.[30] These recitals clearly explain the need for a reliable commercial register. It shall facilitate doing business with a company by offering information that third parties can rely on.

[3] No Need for Expensive Legal Opinions

The importance of such a reliable source of information becomes clear when looking at legal systems that do not cater for an official commercial register. In the USA, for example, there is no general commercial register from which reliable information on the legal status of a company can be retrieved. In practice, this means that legal

27. Alexander Schall & David Günter, *art 12 n.2, in European Corporate Law* (Peter Kindler & Jan Lieder eds, Bloomsbury Publishing 2021).
28. Cf. Schall/Günter, *supra*, Art. 9 nn. 14 et seq.
29. Recital 5 CLD.
30. Recital 8 CLD.

opinions must be obtained before important business transactions are concluded. First of all, lawyers have to check whether the contracting party exists as a legal entity at all, and second, whether the persons acting on its behalf are authorized to represent it. As a textbook on legal opinions explains, 'an opinion on the power of a corporation to enter into and perform its obligations under the agreement appears in most closing opinions whatever the nature of the transaction'.[31]

According to the same textbook, an opinion that the company has been '*duly incorporated*' means the following: The opinion maker has to verify whether the incorporators at the time of incorporation complied with all requirements in effect at that time under the applicable corporation statute and whether government officials took the steps required by that statute to bring the company into existence as a corporation.[32] As a next step, the '*duly authorized*' opinion requires that the proper body or bodies within the company approve the agreement in a manner required by the corporation law of the state in which the company was incorporated and the company's charters and by-laws and that the approval remains in effect on the closing date.[33]

Back in Europe, the existence of the company as well as the power of representation by its organs can be clarified beyond doubt and with legal certainty simply by checking the commercial register, at no expense at all.[34] Unlike in the USA, it does not have to be examined whether the representative body acting externally is authorized to conclude the contract internally.[35] The comparison with the United States illustrates the clear link between preventive control and the protection of third parties once the company has been registered. If preventive control helps to ensure that the information in the commercial register is trustworthy and legally correct, a reduction in transaction costs can be achieved, since business partners will obtain reliable information at no cost from the commercial register.

As a fun fact, it is worth mentioning that U.S. clients nevertheless pay incredibly high fees to their German lawyers asking for legal opinions on the existence of a German company and on the power of representation of its organs, even if German lawyers try to explain the system of commercial registers, their U.S. clients simply cannot believe that Europe has such an efficient and comparably cheap system which is unknown to U.S. corporate law.

31. Donald W. Glazer, Scott FitzGibbon & Steven O. Weise, *Glazer and Fitzgibbon on Legal Opinions* 233 (Wolters Kluwer 2008).
32. *Ibid.*, 193-194.
33. *Ibid.*, 266-267.
34. Article 19(2) CLD, as modified by the Directive 2019, states that Member States must offer basic documents and information free of charge – such as the registered office of the company, the status of the company, the object of the company, particulars of any person who as an organ or a member of an organ is authorized to represent the company.
35. This is also due to the fact that US corporate law has no doctrine of corporative representative power. The organ of a company has no authority as such to act on behalf of the corporation. Instead, general concepts of the law of agency, such as 'actual' or 'apparent authority' apply (for an introduction to the problem, *see* J. Mark Ramseyer, *Business Organizations*, 1-17 (Wolters Kluwer 2d ed. 2018)).

[C] Relevance for Freedom of Establishment

Finally, it should be borne in mind that the possibility of retrieving reliable information from the register plays a pivotal role in European case law regarding freedom of establishment. The well-known liberal interpretation of the freedom of establishment by the European Court of Justice is systematically linked to the availability of trustworthy information in the national commercial registers. In its groundbreaking *Inspire Art decision*, the Court approved the cross-border operation of letterbox companies with a reference to the EU rules on corporate information.[36] The Court rejected the host state's argument that it had to protect domestic creditors from the risks of a foreign letterbox company with the following argument: On the basis of harmonized European company law, creditors may obtain the necessary information from the register that enables them to protect themselves against such risks. In the commercial register of the foreign company, they can find out about its legal form and about its capital; they can also inspect the company's balance sheet there. Consequently, they do not need to be protected by minimum capital rules or other national restrictions.[37] At that time, the case concerned a British private company that wanted to operate in the Netherlands. This consideration, after Brexit, does no longer apply to British companies. But it remains valid for any other company incorporated in an EU Member State and doing business in other Member States.

§10.04 HOW ONLINE INCORPORATION STRENGTHENS PREVENTIVE CONTROL

[A] From the SUP Proposal (2014) to the Digitization Directive (2019)

In 2014, the European Commission proposed a Directive on a single-member private limited liability company, the so-called Societas Unius Personae (SUP).[38] Its provision for online registration proved to be one of the major stumbling stones.[39] Article 14(3) of the SUP Proposal read: 'Member States shall ensure that the registration procedure for newly incorporated SUPs may be completed electronically in its entirety without it

36. Case C-167/01, *Inspire Art*, 30.9.2003, ECLI:EU:C:2003:512.
37. *Ibid.*, no. 135.
38. Proposal for a Directive of the European Parliament and of the Council on single-member private limited liability companies, Brussels, 9.4.2014, COM(2014) 212 final (hereinafter the 'SUP Proposal').
39. *See*, among others, Peter Kindler, *Die Einpersonen-Kapitalgesellschaft als Konzernbaustein – Bemerkungen zum Kompromissvorschlag der italienischen Ratspräsidentschaft für eine Societas Unius Personae (SUP)*, 179 Zeitschrift für das gesamte Handelsrecht und Wirtschaftsrecht, 330, 393-346 (2015). How negotiations in the Council watered down the Commission's approach is elaborated by Christoph Teichmann & Andrea Götz, *How to Make a Molehill out of a Mountain: The Single-Member Company (SUP) Proposal after Negotiations in the Counci*, in *Private Companies in Europe: The Societas Unius Personae (SUP) and the Recent Developments in the EU Member States*, 29-54 (A. Jorge Viera González & Christoph Teichmann eds, Thomson Reuters 2016).

being necessary for the founders to appear before any authority in the Member State of registration (online registration).'

In the states that take preventive control seriously, it met with little understanding that the Commission did not want to make a preliminary check mandatory, as Article 14(5) of the SUP Proposal pointed out: 'Member States *may* lay down rules for verifying the identity of the founding member ... and the acceptability of the documents and other information submitted to the registration body.'[40] At that time, the British Limited was one of the most popular legal forms in many EU Member States and it was feared that the cases of 'identity fraud', as mentioned above, would spread to other countries if European law allowed to lower the standards of registration.[41]

In this respect, the Directive 2019 shows a remarkable learning progress of the relevant players:[42] On the one hand, representatives of the notaries made friends with the idea of offering an electronic formation procedure.[43] On the other hand, the European Commission no longer left preventive control at the discretion of the Member States. Instead, Article 13g(2) of the Directive 2019 stipulates: 'Member States *shall* lay down detailed rules for the online formation of companies.'[44] This is followed by a list of those rules that must be adopted 'at least' (Article 13g(3)), including the verification of the legal capacity and identity of the applicants as well as the procedures for verifying the appointment of directors.

[B] Cross-Border Online Incorporation by Notaries: A Competitive Advantage?

Germany and other Member States, which were first concerned about notarial participation, have been calmed down by a provision which allows Member States to entrust notaries with handling the online incorporation (*see* Article 13g paragraph 4 lit. b Directive 2019). The involvement of notaries as 'gatekeepers', which has sometimes been perceived as a stumbling block in international comparison, could even prove to be a competitive advantage in the further course of development. This is because, in contrast to domestic incorporations, which are already quite efficient in some Member States, cross-border procedures may require a legally competent intermediary.

When presenting its proposals on online incorporation, the European Commission always pointed out that there were already numerous Member States that

40. Emphasis added by the author.
41. Peter Ries, *Socieats Unius Personae – cui bono?*, 17 Neue Zeitschrift für Gesellschaftsrecht, 569 (2014).
42. The full development from a first attempt to regulate online registration (SPE Proposal in 2008) to the Digitization Directive 2019 is analysed by Christoph Teichmann & Andrea Götz, *Metamorphosen des Europäischen Gesellschaftsrechts: SUP, Company Law Package und SPE 2.0*, 27 Zeitschrift für Europäisches Privatrecht, 260-286 (2019).
43. *See* as a representative of German notaries Bormann, *supra* n. 4, for Spain Royo-Villanova, *supra* n. 24.
44. Emphasis added by the author.

successfully practised online incorporation. However, this comparison did not address the challenges of cross-border incorporation, for it was precisely the progressive states that had tailored electronic incorporation entirely to their national infrastructure. Denmark and Estonia, for instance, offered online incorporation only for their own citizens[45] and the necessary background checks could only be done using the relevant national databases.[46] In a cross-border situation, the procedure reaches a higher level of complexity. It will be difficult to develop a fully automated system in the same way as was previously possible for domestic incorporations.

If we look at online incorporation in Estonia and Denmark from the point of view of the identification of the participants, the link to the national infrastructure becomes clear:[47] In Estonia, the founders identify themselves with their electronic ID card, which is equipped with a chip card and requires the entry of a PIN. After the process is completed, an automated confirmation email is sent to the personal email box of the person whose ID card was used. In Denmark, a confirmation email is also sent after each electronic registration so that unauthorized registrations can be immediately detected and corrected by the presumed applicant. This only works efficiently because all citizens have an electronic address at which they can be reached by state authorities and which they consult regularly. In both states, the system also carries out a background check of relevant data. In this way, it is possible, for example, to prevent the appointment of a person as a director who is subject to disqualification. This automated query also presupposes that the person in question is a national citizen whose offences are recorded in a national database.

In the cross-border context, electronic incorporation by foreign legal entities poses additional difficulties. This case is likely to have considerable practical relevance, as the electronic procedure, saving time and cost, could be attractive for companies that want to establish a subsidiary abroad. However, since a legal entity as such has no identity document and cannot act on its own behalf, a two-stage examination is indicated here. First, it must be clarified whether the legal entity exists at all. Subsequently, it must be checked for the person who acts on behalf of the legal entity whether he or she is authorized to represent the legal person. Insofar as the legal entity is registered in another EU Member State, the registrar or notary can inspect the commercial register. Access to the registers of other EU states is possible via the Business Registers Interconnection System (BRIS). However, BRIS is only a portal to which the national registers are connected; it cannot be searched electronically in an automated form. The search has to be done manually. Consequently, procedures which are managed by notaries may be more efficient than procedures which used to work fully electronically.

45. It is true, Estonia also offers a so-called 'e-citizenship' for foreign nationals. But in order to obtain this option, nationals from other Member States have first to appear in person at an Estonian embassy or consulate.
46. Cf. the comparative study by Teichmann, *supra* n. 5.
47. Cf. Teichmann, *supra* n. 5, 7-10.

[C] Digital Incorporation as a Benchmark for Non-digital Incorporations

[1] Systematic Interpretation of the Company Law Directive as Modified in 2019

After the introduction of digital incorporation, the question arises whether the verification steps explicitly required in Directive 2019 should actually only apply in the case of digital incorporation. The obligation to ensure the legal capacity and identity of the applicants is located in the section on 'online procedures'. The general provision on preventive control in Article 10 CLD, instead, remained unchanged. Does that mean that a lower standard of preventive control may be applied in case of a non-electronic procedure?

In the *author*'s opinion, the Company Law Directive as modified in 2019 should be interpreted systematically in such a way that the standard of review for online procedures reflects the general understanding of a sophisticated preventive control and, as a consequence, must also apply to other forms of formation, too.[48] As a confirmation, recital 20 of the Directive 2019 may be evoked which provides the following justification for regulating safeguards for online incorporation: 'Furthermore, in order to tackle fraud and company hijacking and to provide safeguards for the reliability and trustworthiness of documents and information contained within national registers, provisions concerning online procedures provided for in this Directive should also include controls on the identity and legal capacity of persons seeking to form a company ...' Obviously, reliability and trustworthiness of the registered information is a regulatory objective that applies not just to online formations but to all sorts of formations. It is expressly mentioned for online incorporations simply because in this case the danger of fraud seemed to be more imminent than in traditional procedures.[49] As this reading of the Directive, elaborated by academics, may not prevail throughout Europe unless it is explicitly reflected in the wording of the Directive, it is to be welcomed that the European Commission now wants to explicitly regulate the general standard of preventive control for any type of incorporation procedure.

[2] The Commission's Proposal for Reform (2023)

In March 2023, the European Commission presented a proposal for a Directive paying special attention to the quality of the data that can be retrieved from the commercial register.[50] In addition, the proposal aims to include partnerships in the scope of the Directive as well as increase the transparency of corporate group structures; these

48. Teichmann, *supra* n. 2, 1243.
49. *See* the critical voices mentioned *supra* n. 4.
50. Proposal for a Directive of the European Parliament and of the Council amending Directives 2009/102/EC and (EU) 2017/1132 as regards further expanding and upgrading the use of digital tools and processes in company law, Brussels, 29.3.2023, COM(2023) 177 final.

issues, however, will not be further treated in this paper.[51] The proposal has been preceded by work of the Informal Company Law Expert Group (ICLEG).[52]

According to the Commission's Proposal, Article 10 CLD shall regulate the same preventive checks that were already adopted in 2019 for online incorporations: 'Member States shall ensure that their laws for the formation of companies ... lay down a procedure for the legality check of a company's instrument of constitution, and for its statutes if they are contained in a separate instrument' (proposed Article 10 (2) CLD). Through the legality check, it shall be ascertained at least that the formal requirements for the instrument of the constitution (and for the statutes) are fulfilled; the mandatory minimum content is included; there are no evident substantive legal irregularities; the contribution has been paid in accordance with national law. Moreover, the majority of rules as laid down currently in Article 13 (4) and Article 13g(3) CLD (for online incorporation) shall apply *mutatis mutandis* to other forms of formation of companies (proposed Article 10(4) CLD). Hence, the standard already applicable to online formation shall explicitly be extended to other forms of formation.

In addition, a newly introduced 'EU Company Certificate' is intended to make it easier for companies to prove their existence and essential company data to authorities abroad (Article 16b of the Proposal). The certificate shall be issued by the competent authority where the company is registered. It shall be accepted in all Member States as conclusive evidence of the incorporation of the company and of the information listed in Article 16b(2) CLD (among others: name, registered office and status of the company, as well as particulars of any persons who represent the company as a body or a member of such body and whether those persons may do so alone or are required to act jointly). Particularly welcome is the provision according to which the Commission is to provide a multilingual template for the Certificate (Article 16b(8) of the Proposal). This could solve the language problem that has been insurmountable until now, as hardly any Member State is currently willing to make its register data available in a language other than its own official language.

As a further measure to facilitate cross-border business, the EU Commission proposes the introduction of a 'Digital EU power of attorney' (Article 16 c of the Proposal). For this purpose, a multilingual standard model will be provided by the Commission. The issuing national authority must check whether a valid power of attorney exists under the law of the state in which the company is registered. The power of attorney, which only exists in digital form, is not accessible to everyone but should only be accessible to persons with a legitimate interest, such as notaries, lawyers or financial institutions. These documents shall be exempt from legalisation (apostille) or any similar formality (proposed Article 16d(2) CLD). Up to now, this has

51. For an overview of the proposal, *see* Jessica Schmidt, *Upgrading Digital Company Law*, 26 Neue Zeitschrift für Gesellschaftsrecht, 593-602 (2023), and Christoph Teichmann, *Das Informationsmodell des Europäischen Gesellschaftsrechts im digitalen Zeitalter*, Recht Digital, 357-364 (2023).
52. The ICLEG reports on transparency of company data and on cross-border use of company information are retrievable at company law and corporate governance (europa.eu), last visited 18 October 2023).

been a considerable obstacle for digital procedures in cases where the applicant does not apply in person but is represented by a third party with power of attorney.[53]

§10.05 CONCLUSIONS

The traditional system of preventive administration of justice does not only serve to prevent disputes. In the context of commercial and company law, it also reduces transaction costs because legal transactions find trustworthy information in the commercial register. A potential contracting party can always rely on the existence of a registered company and can also use the register to determine the persons who have the power to represent a company. In legal systems that do not have a trustworthy commercial register, these questions have to be clarified by costly legal opinions, which are not necessary in the European legal system.

The system of preventive control is also rooted in European secondary law, although not all Member States apply the same standards. The Company Law Directive provides that once a company has been registered, its nullity can only be established under narrow conditions and by court decision. In this respect, there is legal certainty throughout Europe that once a company has been registered, it will continue to exist as long as a court ruling to the contrary has not been entered in the register. Furthermore, secondary law protects the trust in the unlimited and unrestricted power of representation of organs. Any defects in the appointment can only be asserted by the company if they were known to a third party.

These achievements seemed to be at stake when the European Commission proposed the introduction of an electronic incorporation. In Germany, in particular, there were fears that this would lead to a considerable reduction in the quality standard of preventive control administered by notaries. Over the years, however, it has been possible to work out solutions for Directive 2019 that ultimately enable functionally adequate online formation procedures to be administered with or without notaries. It is worth noting that the secondary law now emphasizes the need for effective preventive control in a way that always seemed self-evident for Germany and other continental systems but had not yet been articulated so clearly at European level.

In this way, the project of online incorporation by notaries may even develop into a competitive advantage in the medium term. This is because the systems of electronic formation known so far from other Member States, which all manage without the involvement of notaries, owe their efficiency to their embedding in a national digital infrastructure. They will probably not be able to cope with the increased complexity of cross-border incorporation with the same efficiency. Instead, the cross-border context requires qualified intermediaries who are able to deal with the particular hurdles of transnational transactions.

The recent European Commission's Proposal for further harmonization promises a considerable increase in efficiency in the cross-border digital use of commercial

53. Cf. Jan Lieder, *Digitalisierung des Europäischen Unternehmensrechts*, 21 Neue Zeitschrift für Gesellschaftsrecht, 1081, 1085 (2018).

register data. A positive aspect is the clear statement that a legal check must always take place when setting up a company. This strengthens the value of the register. Standardization measures such as the EU certificate for companies and the digital EU power of attorney are also to be welcomed. The Commission will provide a template for both documents. Anyone who has ever tried to find clear and comprehensible information in a foreign register via BRIS will appreciate how much this may increase the accessibility of corporate information.

CHAPTER 11

Cash Payments to Shareholders in Cross-Border and Domestic Mergers

Andrea Vicari

The process of completing the Capital Market Union requires overcoming obstacles that delay it. The recent Directive on cross-border mergers (2019/2121/EU) has introduced or enhanced the possibility of reducing the veto rights of minority shareholders with respect to these transactions, allowing companies under certain conditions to allocate cash or other financial instruments instead of shares and permitting them to withdraw. The article examines the process of gradual evolution of the EU merger regulation from issues of shareholder "protection" versus issues of "efficiency" of the company and the market, analyzing the most relevant provisions of the Directive, both with respect to cross-border mergers and to their influence on domestic legislations.

§11.01 INTRODUCTION

With a certain degree of approximation, we can say that in recent decades, the interest of legislation, case law and scholars in Europe has often been oriented—particularly in the case of extraordinary transactions—more toward issues of: "shareholder protection" than toward issues of "efficiency" (of the firm and the market).

For what it may be worth, by conducting a quick search on a standard company law database, entering the headings "shareholder protection" and the headings "enterprise efficiency/market efficiency," the contributions (articles, comments) devoted to the former topic are far more numerous than those devoted to the latter.

At the level of legislation, the most important Directive for company law (1132/2017/EU) reports the words "protection/protect" more than 50 times. The word "efficiency" is never found.

Even in Directive 2004/25/EC on takeovers, the words "protect/protection" are found 12 times, and the word "efficiency" never.

Evidently, the efficiency of the company and the markets can hardly be reconciled with the right of the shareholders "to remain as such," which in many cases entails a kind of veto right of the minorities (and a lengthening of time) with respect to extraordinary transactions.

Consider the case of a merger: in most of the Member States (with a few exceptions), the resolution must be passed by the extraordinary shareholders' meeting, and all minority shareholders must be guaranteed a stake in the post-merger company, with a minimal possibility of allocation of cash or other securities.

From the point of view of economic analysis of law, as is well known, efficiency means not ensuring the right of the party participant (in our case, the shareholder) to keep the same "slice of the pie" (i.e., the same "number of shares"), but to have even a smaller slice but in a larger pie (i.e., is it better to have 10% of a company worth 100, or 5% of the same company, but worth 1.000)?

Another issue is whether that smaller slice should also be secured to the "same taste" (i.e., always shares of a certain class) or it can be secured to a different taste (i.e., other securities, money).

A third point concerns the information that should be made about the cake and how its "baking process" can be attended to (these are the issues of "information" and the procedural guarantees that should be given to shareholders).

I think that currently, one of the most topical issues in EU company law is precisely this. Is it always right to protect shareholders "as such" (i.e., to allow them the right to keep the "same slice of the pie" and "with the same taste") or is it appropriate to consider whether—in order to foster issues of efficiency—they should be protected in different forms.

Where do we stand today?

What is new is that European company law is beginning to move toward a system where it is important for the pie to increase, even at the expense of the size of slices (and, perhaps, their flavor and information and procedural aspects).

Important indications showing that company law is moving in this direction, even at the expense of "classic" forms of shareholders' protection, come from the Commission's 2020 Action Plan, which established that it is time to complete the Capital Markets Union and it is necessary to converge national markets into a true single one (the document notes that "deepening the CMU is complex and no single measure will complete it. Therefore, the only way to progress is to move steadily in all areas where barriers to the free movement of capital still exist. A lot still remains to be done and it is now time to step up the level of ambition").

Shareholders' rights "as such" cannot be an obstacle to the fulfilment of this market, which presupposes the ease of access of firms to it.

An efficient market also presupposes the facilitation of the "submarket," that is the market for corporate control (and, therefore, extraordinary transactions).

The next sections will therefore first examine the most recent developments in the merger regulation, which have accentuated its "managerial" character and already restricted shareholders' rights to some extent (§11.02, §11.03 and §11.04).

Then, I will deal with the most recent regulatory innovations introduced or developed by Directive 2019/2121/EU: the possibility of awarding cash payments to shareholders in lieu of shares in the event of a merger (§11.05); the possibility for shareholders to claim only cash payments in case of unfair exchange ratio and incorrect information (§11.06), also with reference to shareholders belonging to special classes (§11.07). The possibility for shareholders to obtain cash payments by exercising their right of withdrawal and in all these cases to obtain, instead of cash, other financial instruments will also be examined (§11.08 and §11.09). A short conclusion will follow.

§11.02 THE EVOLUTION OF THE LAW OF MERGERS

The law of mergers has essentially experienced four eras.

The first, prior to 1978, was when legislation was composed in each Member State of a few rules dedicated to the merger proposal, the balance sheet, the shareholders' resolution and the deed. A merger, from a theoretical point of view, was considered a case of extinction of the company.

The second, initiated with the third directive (78/855/EEC, later recast into Directive 2017/1132/EU), which regulated, on the one hand, the enhancement of the information to be given to shareholders and, on the other hand, the regime of the stability of the transaction. Since then, the literature has begun to reconstruct the transaction essentially in terms of statutory modification.

The third era began with Directive 2009/109/EC which made seemingly minor but in fact major changes, particularly with reference to the procedure.

The fourth phase is on the horizon, and we are definitely getting into it with the new regulation of cross-border transactions: Directive 2019/2121/EU (which completes the path started by Directive 2005/56/EC).

In my opinion, the regulation of mergers (and, more generally, of extraordinary transactions) is of great interest to company law, given that many legislative innovations introduced by the legislature with regard to such transactions are then found over time extended to other areas of "ordinary" company law.

And the interest is all the greater at the historical moment when—for various reasons—the push forward of the law on extraordinary transactions is induced by various competing reasons, forcing for acceleration and legislative change.

Currently, the transition to the new phase is stimulated on several fronts: on the one hand, the essential framework of the legislation on domestic mergers is more than 40 years old; on the other hand, the new law of cross-border transactions is pushing with much more vigor toward the creation of the single European market and convergence.

From the latter point of view, in particular, the change of pace is significant: while the previous Directive of 2005 dealt essentially with the "formalities" for carrying out transactions domestically (preparatory acts, certificate, etc.), Directive 2019/2121/EU (as was already, albeit in much less relevant terms, Directive 2017/1132/EU) reiterates that the rules on such transactions "represent a significant milestone in improving the functioning of the internal market for companies and firms and their exercise of the freedom of establishment" and places this discipline in broader functional context (recital 1).[1] The pressure toward convergence is strong, and, therefore, the changes to be incorporated within national companies act prove to be very incisive.

Within the framework of this development, it is important to examine how the forms of protection granted by the legislation to shareholders are evolving and to highlight the aspects being appreciated positively and the critical ones.

It must, however, be borne in mind that, while it is true that the rules on cross-border transactions apply only to (very peculiar) mergers in which—in addition to the domestic one—at least one company from at least one other Member State participates, it is, however, clear that, at the moment when a series of innovative rules (different from those provided for purely national mergers) are applied to such a transaction, they are inevitably destined to reverberate—initially even only at the level of interpretation—on the rules dictated for domestic mergers. The rules on cross-border mergers are, therefore, also highly relevant to domestic transactions.

§11.03 DIRECTIVE 78/855/EEC: MERGERS AND THE "PROTECTION" OF SHAREHOLDERS' RIGHTS

It is appropriate to begin with an examination of the principles of Directive 1978/855/EEC (the "Third Directive") and to analyze the intervention made on the same by Directive 2009/109/EC.

The Third Directive aimed essentially at three objectives: (i) to ensure that shareholders receive "adequate information" in a manner "as objective as possible" (*see* recital no. 4); (ii) to protect the rights of shareholders "suitably," in order to avoid transactions that prejudiced their interests (see recital no. 4); and (iii) to ensure "certainty in the law" by limiting the cases of invalidity of acts and the time limit within which a suit for invalidity could be initiated (*see* recital 9).

Thus, at the heart of the Third Directive were placed the "rights" of shareholders and their "protection" against potentially "detrimental" transactions.

Shareholders were recognized a very significant information set and they were given, at least "formally," the right to vote and to contest the shareholders' meeting resolution.

Shareholders were also granted the right to "remain as such": Articles 3 and 30 of the Third Directive (inspired by the principle of equal treatment) established that normally a cash payment in excess of 10% of the value of the shares issued could not

1. The Directive of 2005 contained only one reference to the single market in its first recital, while the Directive of 2019 dedicates seven (the first ones) to the need to complete such market. For further details on the transition from the "first" to the "second" directive on cross-border transactions, *see* Thomas Papadopoulos, *Reviewing the Implementation of the Cross-Border Mergers Directive*, in *Cross Border Mergers: EU Perspectives and National Experiences* 3 (Thomas Papadopoulos ed., Springer, 2019).

be allotted; this cash "adjustment" below that limit has always been understood by the doctrine as a monetary portion that must be recognized to all shareholders and not to some shareholders only, and this exclusively to deal with the problem of share fractions.

This approach—which placed the "rights" of shareholders strongly at the center of the system—has proven itself, however, only partially successful. Many provisions have been found to be dysfunctional and costly.

The extensive information that was designed—essentially—for shareholders should have provided them with a protection that has, however, never really existed in the merger system, at least as conceived in the majority of the Member States.

This is a consequence, on the one hand, of the short time limit introduced by the various company acts to challenge the flaws of the resolution and, on the other hand, of the fact that the interpretation (in particular) of the case law has severely restricted the space for shareholders to question it. Very rare have been—as is well known—in over 40 years the cases of challenge of the merger resolution followed by the suspension of the effects of the latter: almost always the courts—in making the comparative assessment between the corporate interest in carrying out the merger and the interest of the challenging shareholder in invalidating the resolution—have made the former prevail over the latter.

§11.04 DIRECTIVE 2009/109/EC: TOWARD THE QUALIFICATION OF THE MERGER AS A "MANAGERIAL" DECISION AND THE RETHINKING OF SHAREHOLDER PROTECTION

The Directive 2009/109/EC took note of the risk of disclosure "in excess" and took corrective action.

It has been recognized that disclosure can become costly, both in terms of production and in terms of lengthening the time of the procedure, and it has been provided that the balance sheet, directors' report and expert report are not necessary if the shareholders unanimously waive them.

The directive, however, in addition to initiating steps to shorten the timeframe of the transaction, has also aimed to achieve another important objective, probably less perceived.

It has, in fact, begun to conceive the merger no longer as a (tendentially detrimental) transaction that must necessarily "protect" the interests of shareholders and has opened up the possibility of understanding it as a managerial initiative, functional to make the company evolve—more rapidly—also in the interest of the same shareholders, to be protected possibly in different ways.

This new vision has been accompanied by the implementation in many Member States—in the meanwhile—of other provisions going along these more managerial lines.

Some legislations have implemented the opportunity granted by Article 8 of the Third Directive (later transposed into Article 94 of Directive 2017/1132/EU), which allows avoiding the general meeting of the incorporating company (where such a company holds at least—but also only—51% of the share capital of the incorporated company) if the shareholders of the incorporating company have obtained the right to examine the relevant documents (project, annual accounts, reports, etc.) at the registered office of the company (following appropriate notice).[2]

Other Member States have regulated so-called simplified mergers: these transactions are performed under the sole responsibility of the board of directors (and no longer of the shareholders); moreover, if the controlling company holds at least 90% of the capital of the merged company, it can avoid delivery to the minority shareholders of the merged company of the merger documents, if the acquiring company agrees to buy out (or have third parties buy out) these shareholders in money.

These various provisions—and the others that line up in the same direction—are significant from a regulatory point of view: they break with the traditional framework espoused by various domestic legislations (which are historically inspired by the principle of "equal treatment" and privilege for shareholders the right to vote over the exit remedy).

§11.05 DIRECTIVE 2121/2019/EU AND THE NEW REGULATORY PARADIGM

Over the recent years, therefore, the regulatory paradigm has shifted, allowing the merger (and interpretation of the law) to be set up in a more modern key.

This set-up still finds resistance in many Member States, but the line seems to have been drawn. And it is all the more defined where one considers the new European law of cross-border mergers.

I point out below the rules of main interest contained in Directive 2019/2121/EU, amending Directive 2017/1132/EU:

(i) Article 126a(4) (in combination with Article 116) does not set forth the 10% limit for the cash payment. This implies that the 10% limit can be exceeded for cross-border mergers, and now we must seek a better understanding of the purpose of such payment.

(ii) The new Article 126(4) stipulates that the merger resolution cannot be contested if the share exchange ratio has been inadequately set or the information given with regard to the share exchange ratio did not comply with the legal requirements. The possibility of challenging the merger resolution due to unfairness of the exchange ratio and violation of the

2. Cf. Art. 2:331 of the Dutch Civil Code. As a further point of flexibility, the vote of the shareholders of the incorporating company on the merger can be avoided by implementing a so-called triangular merger arrangement, by merging a subsidiary of the incorporating company (potentially established specifically for this purpose and into which the relevant assets have been merged by decision of the administrative body) with the company being merged into, rather than with the incorporating company itself. Moreover, the Dutch legal system allows even more easily that the shareholders of the merged company be directly allocated shares in a group company: *see* Art. 2:333(a)(1) of the Dutch Civil Code (for all these aspects, refer to Maarten A. Verbrugh, *Implementation of the cross-Border Merger Directive in the Netherlands*, in *Cross-Border Mergers*, 413 ff. (T. Papadopoulos ed., 2019)).

related information is thus excluded, and shareholders are left with only the right to a cash payment (borne by the company).

(iii) Article 126a(7) stipulates that Member States may also provide that the company resulting from the cross-border merger can provide shares or other compensation instead of a cash payment.

(iv) Finally, it is stipulated that shareholders who do not intend to accept the cross-border merger must be granted the right of withdrawal: Article 126a allows Member States to regulate the right for shareholders to sell their shares in exchange for adequate cash payment if they do not agree to the cross-border merger.

§11.06 THE CASH PAYMENT BELOW 10% AND ABOVE 10%

I will now proceed to examine in detail the mentioned provisions which express some "new" methods of carrying out the transaction and the "new" forms of protection for the shareholders which all Member States adjust their legislations to.

Pursuant to Article 90(1) of Directive 2017/1132/EU, Member States must allow only additional cash payments of up to a maximum of 10% of the nominal amount or notional value of the allocated shares; according to the European legislator, such "minor payments" do not alter the "nature of the merger" and additional cash payments must only serve to offset the fractions of shares originated by the exchange ratio and cannot be improperly used to "buy" a shareholder.

On the contrary, Article 116 of Directive 2017/1132/EU (to be read in the context of cross-border mergers) stipulates now that domestic laws must permit a cash payment exceeding 10%, at least if the law applicable to one of the participating companies in the merger allows for a cash payment to such greater extent.[3]

The provision raises the question of whether such a cash payment should be considered compensation to be allocated on an equal basis to all shareholders or if it should instead be understood as a form of payment reserved for only certain shareholders. This is, in effect, consideration for a partial or total liquidation (provided that the shareholder can dispose of the entire shareholding).

The second view must be preferred. This interpretation is shared by scholars interpreting Article 116, who recognize that the Directive opens the possibility of a sort of "cash-merger." This is supported not only by the genesis of the provision—

3. Thomas Papadopoulos, *Reviewing the Implementation of the Cross-Border Mergers Directive, in Cross-Border Mergers*, 9 (T. Papadopoulos ed., 2019),—quoting the study conducted by the EU Commission (*Study on the application of the cross-border mergers directive* (Bech-Bruun and Lexidale eds., 2013)—reports that there are eight Member States that have not adopted a limit on cash payment and have transposed Art. 30 (now 116) of the directive (the study dates back to 2013, and the Author writes in 2019); the States are listed on page 111 of the Study. The provision is positively assessed by the EMCA: *see* the commentary on §11.05.

apparently based on the Danish model referring to Article 285 of the Companies Act—but above all by the absence of any maximum limit.[4]

This interpretive result is also induced by the new Article 125(3) of the Directive, which requires experts to make an additional assessment expressly referring to the adequacy of the cash settlement and the correctness of the methods used for it, and places this task at the center of their activity (along with the verification of the fairness of the exchange ratio).[5]

In conclusion, even when national laws do not waive the 10% limit provided for by Article 90 of Directive 2017/1132/EU in the case of domestic mergers and maintain the percentage of the cash payment below 10% (serving as a corrective measure with respect to the determination of an exchange ratio that results in share fractions), the same national laws must necessarily admit that if the applicable law of at least one of the participating companies in the merger allows for a cash payment exceeding 10%, cash can be allocated above this threshold to some shareholders only (but still to all shareholders who wish to avail themselves of it) and that even in cases where the registered office of the post-merger company is in a Member State which does not allow such a payment exceeding 10% according to national law.

To be precise, this transaction does not constitute a true "cash merger" (which, on the contrary, involves a model where the company has the "right" to obligate minority shareholders to accept cash instead of shares). It can, however, either happen that shareholders of company "A" from a Member State which does not provide for such a possibility (of cash compensation exceeding 10%) must accept the liquidation of the shareholders of the other company "B" who have required to be cashed out (shareholders "A" thus actually undergo a cash merger), or that the same shareholders "A" are allotted fewer shares than they should receive (as a consequence of the fixation of an unfair exchange ratio) and at this point they themselves can choose to be entirely liquidated (possibly agreeing to a modification of the merger proposal or in the event that the proposal includes alternatives).

§11.07 THE CASH PAYMENT IN CASE OF UNFAIR EXCHANGE RATIO AND IN THE ABSENCE OF CORRECT INFORMATION

The second norm to be analyzed is Article 126(4) of the Directive, which stipulates that the merger resolution cannot be contested if the share exchange ratio has been inadequately set or the information given with regard to the share exchange ratio did not comply with the legal requirements.

4. Cf. Tobias de Raet, *sub* § 116, in *European Corporate Law: Article-by-Article Commentary* 574s (Peter Kindler & Jan Lieder eds., 2021). It is frequently noted that it would be absurd to insist on granting a minimum number of shares to be allocated, as this would ultimately only be a requirement that could be easily bypassed through ingenious contracts.
5. *See* along these lines also e.g., T. Papadoupolos, *Legislation Commentary: Amendments on the EU Harmonization of Cross-Border Mergers after the Adoption of Directive 2019/2121*, EBLR 910 (2023).

The possibility of challenging the merger resolution due to the unfairness of the ratio and the violation of information is therefore excluded, and shareholders are left with only the right to cash payment (borne by the company).

The provision reproduces the rules of certain Member States (Germany, Denmark, etc.), whereby, although shareholders are always entitled to challenge the merger resolution based on general rules, they cannot invoke the remedy if they assert the incongruity of the exchange ratio or the lack of correct information relating to it.

The traditional explanation of the legislative rationale is that the merger should be understood as a transaction benefiting all shareholders and should not be delayed by disputes that can be resolved simply by paying more money to some. As noted by various parties, however, this logic is controversial because it can lead to an unfair transaction and heated discussions about valuations (as it becomes easier to argue over this specific aspect). Nevertheless, it has been unequivocally adopted by the legislator.

As for the information, the reasoning is that "in the case of an inadequate share exchange ratio, very often the information given to the shareholders on that ratio, especially in the management report according to Article 124, will be incorrect as well. ... If the aim is to exclude a challenge in cases of incorrect valuation, it probably is preferable to cover cases of misinformation on these issues as well."[6]

The provision in this regard is indeed quite clear, but it is also true that a minimal amount of information must be provided in order to allow the shareholder to make the necessary assessments: in fact, the provision does not refer to the hypothesis of a total lack of information, but rather to the "noncompliance" with the law of the information, which can also be equated with the case where the information is not only flawed but also "substantially absent."

However, the possibility of challenging the merger resolution and requesting a suspension of its effects still remains for those resolutions that affect the rights of shareholders other than the right to receive a fair exchange ratio and/or accurate information regarding the same and for resolutions that are manifestly abusive.

The first hypothesis primarily concerns procedural flaws (consider, for example, the case of a resolution adopted in violation of publication deadlines for the merger proposal or the call of the shareholders' meeting) and, above all, cases of incorrect information that do not relate to the exchange ratio.

In the case of domestic mergers, it is generally believed that the company is only required to explain the legal and economic aspects of the exchange ratio and not the industrial reasons for the transaction (the so-called business purpose of the merger), even in light of the clear provision of Article 95 of Directive 2017/1132/EU; for these reasons, the scope for challenging domestic merger resolutions due to informational flaws is considered to be very limited.

However, the new Article 124(1) of the Directive now provides otherwise: the provision stipulates that the managers' report must also justify "the legal and economic

6. Cf. Paul L. Davies et al., *The Commission's 2018 Proposal on Cross-Border Mobility: An Assessment*, ECFR 213 (2019).

aspects of the cross-border merger" and "the implications of the cross-border merger for the company's future activity."

Furthermore, under Article 94 of Directive 2017/1132/EU, information must also be provided by the directors in the presentation of the merger proposal.

Therefore, there is a potential to challenge the merger resolution in these respects. Nevertheless, it is evident that the trend is towards significantly reducing the possibility of challenging merger resolutions.

As for "abusive" mergers, it is believed that the resolution may be contested when the unfairness of the exchange ratio is disputed within the framework of a transaction that can be more broadly qualified as collusive between the management bodies of the participating companies, with the aim of abusing the minority.[7]

Some authors argue that so-called value-destroying mergers are also excluded from the scope of application of Article 126(4) of the Directive. However, the exact concept is not clearly identifiable, as economically irrational and detrimental mergers proposed by the directors and approved by the majority shareholders primarily concern the responsibility of the former for proposing and executing the resolution (and possibly of the latter according to applicable rules on a case-by-case basis), rather than the invalidity of the resolution itself.[8]

§11.08 THE CASH PAYMENT FOR SHARES OF A SPECIAL CLASS IN CASE OF AN UNFAIR EXCHANGE RATIO AND THE VOTE OF THE SPECIAL SHAREHOLDER'S MEETING IN THE EVENT OF PREJUDICE

It must now be inquired whether Article 126(4) of the Directive—which excludes the possibility of contesting the merger resolution with reference to the exchange ratio—also applies to the case of an unfair determination of that "particular" exchange ratio that regards "special" shares.

The presence of multiple categories of shares requires, as is known, the determination of a "double" exchange ratio (or multiple double ratios, as there are categories): once the economic capital of the company is reconstructed, it must be determined first the so-called internal parity, i.e., the exchange ratio between shares belonging to different categories and ordinary shares for each company (in order to establish the proportion of the aforementioned economic capital attributable to special shares and ordinary shares), and then the so-called external parity, i.e. the exchange ratio between shares of each category of the company and the shares of the company with which they are intended to be converted.

7. Cf. Thomas Papadopoulos, *Legislation Commentary: Amendments on the EU Harmonization of Cross-Border Mergers after the Adoption of Directive 2019/2121*, EBLR 915 (2023).

8. Cf. Thomas Papadopoulos, *Protection of Shareholders in Cross-Border Mergers: The New Harmonized Rules*, ECFR 989 (2021) and Martin Winner, *Protection of Creditors and Minority Shareholders in Cross-Border Rransactions*, ECFR 72 (2019).

I believe it is correct to apply Article 126(4) of the Directive only to cases of incongruous determination of the exchange ratio depending on an erroneous determination of the economic capital value of the company; on the contrary, I think that there is "prejudice" for the special rights in the case of unfairness at the level of internal or external parity.

If one agrees with such a conclusion, it must be acknowledged that a relatively broad possibility remains for special shareholders to challenge the merger resolution (outside the scope of Article 126(4) of the Directive) in cases where the special shareholders' meeting was not convened or did not vote positively, that is, in all cases where an uncompensated prejudice is at issue.

Therefore, it is a factual observation that such an interpretation grants significant protection to special shareholders; this, however, seems consistent with the approach of Directive 2017/1132/EU on domestic mergers and the particularly broad interpretation that tends to be given to Article 93 of the same.[9]

However, it is also true that while on the one hand, the European legislator appears to provide strong protection to special shareholders, on the other hand, it is undeniable that this results in inevitable implications for the feasibility of the merger, which can be obstructed by the veto power of a special class (or classes) of shareholders.

This outcome, upon closer examination, does not seem entirely coherent with the (much lesser) protection granted to ordinary shareholders by Directive 2019/2021/EU, which is now relegated to a purely "indemnification" level, precisely with the declared purpose of ensuring the greater feasibility of the transaction. This fundamental inconsistency should probably be further reflected upon.[10]

§11.09 THE RIGHT OF WITHDRAWAL IN RELATION TO A CHANGE IN APPLICABLE LAW AND IN CASE OF MODIFICATION OF SHAREHOLDERS' RIGHTS

The right of withdrawal is granted by the Directive to shareholders in two main cases. The first results from a change in the company's nationality; the second occurs when the company remains domestic, but the shareholders' main rights are impacted.

On the one hand, Article 126a of the Directive allows Member States to regulate the right for shareholders to sell their shares in exchange for adequate cash compensation in case of cross-border mergers; on the other hand, the second part of Recital 18 of Directive 2019/2021/EU states that "Member States should be free to decide to

9. Cf. also *EMCA*, ss. 5.06 ff.

10. Cf. specifically Gökçe Kurtulan, *Minority Shareholder Protection in Cross-Border Mergers: A Must for or an Impediment to the European Single Market?*, EBOR 101 (2017). It must be highlighted—for comparison with U.S. law—that while section 11.04(f) of the MBCA requires a separate vote for each class or series of shares that are to be converted into shares, other securities, etc. in the case of a merger (unless otherwise provided by the bylaws), conversely, § 8, § 251(c) of the Delaware Code only requires approval of the merger by a majority of the voting shares at the general meeting: *see*, for all, in this regard, Franklin A. Gevurtz & Christina M. Sautter, *Mergers and Acquisition Law*, 86 (St. Paul MN 2019).

extend that right also to other members, for example ... to members for whom there would be no change of applicable law but for whom certain rights would change due to the operation."

This option granted to national legislators to allow withdrawal even to shareholders of the company (typically the acquiring entity) that does not change the applicable law has been criticized. It has been noted that "although the applicable law does not change for the shareholders of the resulting (acquiring) company, the cross-border merger constitutes a major change for such shareholders, could modify some of their rights and could affect negatively their financial interests. Nevertheless, Recital 18 of the Preamble focusing on a specific category of shareholders of the resulting (acquiring) company with modified rights is a special provision and does not support an extension of the exit right to all shareholders of the resulting (acquiring) company; despite the minimum harmonization character of Art. 126a, an extension of exit right to all shareholders of the resulting (acquiring) company would be against the spirit of the general provision of Art. 126a, demanding a change of law."[11]

This observation is correct. The right to withdraw pursuant to Recital 18, second part, could be invoked very frequently in cross-border mergers where the post-merger company remains domestic, as the entry of new shareholders from original states may easily result in various modifications to the bylaws concerning voting rights or participation.[12]

According to some scholars, following this approach, one could consider "cross-border mergers as one among many other circumstances where there is so much impact on the rights of minority shareholders, that they should have a right of sell-out. This approach is to a certain extent comparable with the approach taken in the Takeover Bid Directive"; in other words, there is a risk that the right of withdrawal might stem from the transaction "itself," similar to public takeover offers.[13]

11. Cf. Thomas Papadopoulos, *Protection of Shareholders in Cross-Border Mergers: The New Harmonized Rules*, ECFR 989 (2022); *see also* Gökçe Kurtulan, *Minority Shareholder Protection in Cross-Border Mergers: A Must for or an Impediment to the European Single Market*, EBOR 101, 105, 118 (2017). On the other hand, the reason for granting the right of withdrawal in the event of a change in legislation has also itself been called into question: *see* Marieke Wyckaert and Koen Geens, *Cross-Border Mergers and Minority Protection: An Open-Ended Harmonization*, ECL 294 (2008): "national legislators may be concerned about the fact that shareholders of a company governed by such law will, following the merger, become shareholders of a company governed by the national law of another Member state"; if that view is shared, and "the European legislator itself admits that forty years of European harmonization in company law has not led to at least sufficiently comparable corporate forms to induce a minimum of confidence for their 'users' throughout Europe, it may be a better idea to continue to work on that harmonization"; less critical is, i.e., Jessica Schmidt, *Cross-Border Mergers, Divisions and Conversions: Accomplishments and Deficits of the Company Law Package*, ECFR 255, 2019.

12. Marco Ventoruzzo, *Cross-Border Mergers, Change of Applicable Corporate Laws and Protection of Dissenting Shareholders: Withdrawal Rights under Italian Law*, ECFR 47 (2007), provides the example of changing the cases of withdrawal or the criteria envisaged for the valuation of shares also in the case of withdrawal: a merger with a foreign company, which involves the application of the laws of a different state, will likely also entail a (somehow) different regulation of withdrawal rights and applicable valuation criteria.

13. Cf. Marieke Wyckaert & Koen Geens, *Cross-Border Mergers and Minority Protection: An Open-Ended Harmonization*, ECL 295 (2008). With reference to the relationship between merger transactions and the right of withdrawal, Alexandros Seretakis, *Appraisal Rights in the US and*

As a result, to avoid this effect, the domestic provisions on the right of withdrawal should be interpreted in a generally restrictive sense in the context of cross-border mergers, under the risk of classifying national regulations as a form of gold-plating (strictly speaking, Article 126a of the Directive grants withdrawal rights only to shareholders who, as a result of the merger, acquire shares in the company resulting from the merger which is governed by the law of a Member State other than that of the respective company, despite the wording of the second part of Recital 18) or of an assessment of the compatibility of national withdrawal provisions under Article 273 TFEU with the provisions of Article 126(a) of the Directive.

§11.10 COMPENSATION IN FORMS OTHER THAN CASH

Finally, one last point has to be considered: according to Article 126a(7) of the Directive, the compensation to be awarded in case of an unfair exchange ratio (and incorrect information concerning the ratio) and in case of withdrawal can be granted in the form of "shares or other compensation instead of a cash payment." This specifically refers to the allocation—besides shares of the post-merger company itself—of financial instruments (shares of other companies, bonds, etc.).[14]

Many domestic provisions may still refer only to "cash payment" or "indemnification" without further clarification. In such a case, it should be understood that, unless it is deemed that the national legislator's intention was clearly to interpret this payment as "indemnification 'only' in cash," the allocation of financial instruments—at least provided they are liquid—should be allowed; at the very least, such allocation should always be acceptable in the case of cross-border mergers where the Member State of the other participating company in the merger permits it.

---

the EU, in *Cross-Border*, 71 et seq.—drawing on the U.S. experience—points out that while in the early 2000s, merger transactions allowing for withdrawal saw the exercise of the right by shareholders in only 2%-3% of cases, a decade later, withdrawal requests were made in about 20% of transactions: withdrawal was triggered, therefore, in one out of every five transactions. The author notes that, in order to overcome the "withdrawal risk," acquiring (incorporating) companies demand the inclusion of a clause in the merger documents that grants them the right to withdraw from the transaction if a certain number of shareholders, typically 10/15%, exercise the right of withdrawal. The purpose of this clause is to protect the acquirer from a substantial increase in the cost of the transaction in the event that a large number of shareholders exercise the right. For a particularly critical interpretation regarding the possibility of broadly recognizing the right of withdrawal in the case of a merger, *see*, for example, Franklin A. Gevurtz & Christina M. Sautter, *Mergers and Acquisition Law*, 108 ff. (St. Paul MN 2019), according to whom it should not be permitted for a minority, unable to block the merger by vote, to do so with the threat of withdrawal.

14. Cf. Jessica Schmidt, *The Mobility Aspects of the EU Commission's Company Law Package: Or—"the Good, the Bad and the Ugly,"* ECL 16 (2019) who notes that "since a mandatory cash compensation entails significant liquidity risks for companies, it indeed seems sensible to allow them to instead provide additional shares" (i.e., the company's first option should be to compensate with own shares); Tobias de Raet, *sub* § 126a, in *European Corporate Law: Article-by-Article Commentary*, 653 (Peter Kindler & Jan Lieder eds., 2021): compensation can consist of "any other consideration" ("this gives the respective company the flexibility and eliminates the risk of having to make—unforeseen—cash pay outs which may lead to liquidity problems)."

The Directive's provision is objectively very general, and it also leads to a broader consideration of whether all cash payments could be made in different financial instruments other than money, including cash payments below 10%.[15]

§11.11 CONCLUSION

The need to complete the UCM, the Directive on cross-border mergers, and the attention of scholars will push in the coming years more and more toward solutions that will allow—in order to promote the firm's and market efficiency—cash payments to be awarded to shareholders in the event of a merger.

Much more problematic (or at any rate to be better investigated), however, appears to be the legislative choice to grant shareholders in broad terms the right of withdrawal, given that this remedy may prove to be a formidable tool for hindering extraordinary transactions.

Likewise, the current state of the legislation does not allow a good understanding of the kind of protection acknowledged to "special" shareholders (who enjoy the more complex regime recognized by domestic legislations to the "categories" or "classes" of shares).

Finally, even if a favorable attitude is taken toward the possibility of allocating shareholders cash instead of shares in mergers (both transnational and domestic), it remains in many respects uncertain in what cases and under what conditions they may be assigned other financial instruments instead of cash.

15. According to Tobias de Raet, *sub* § 126a, in *European Corporate Law. Article-by-Article Commentary*, 652s (Peter Kindler & Jan Lieder eds., 2021). "Article 126a(7) can only apply to the right to challenge the cash compensation or the share exchange ratio pursuant to Article 126(4) and (6)."

CHAPTER 12

The Disclosure of Inside Information under the Market Abuse Regulation and the Proposed Listing Act

Tom Vos & Victor Burki

The European Commission's Listing Act package, proposed in December 2022, aims to enhance the attractiveness of European public capital markets by reducing the regulatory burdens for listed companies. This chapter analyses the proposed amendments to the rules on the disclosure of inside information in the Market Abuse Regulation (MAR) and compares the proposed amendments with the current legal framework for the disclosure of inside information. Under the Proposed Listing Act, intermediate steps in protracted processes would no longer need to be disclosed immediately, even if they already amount to inside information. Issuers would only need to disclose the final step in the protracted process. In addition, the Proposed Listing Act would amend the conditions for the possibility for the issuer to delay the disclosure of inside information by replacing the general condition that the delay of disclosure is not likely to mislead the public with three more specific conditions, which were already contained in the European Securities and Markets Authority (ESMA) Guidelines. The proposed amendments could bring a welcome change to the MAR by lowering the compliance burden of listed companies with regard to the disclosure of inside information relating to protracted processes.

§12.01 INTRODUCTION

In a taxi ride after a company law workshop at the annual Ius Commune conference, Steef Bartman once invited one of the authors of this chapter to submit an article for the

European Company Law journal, warning that the article should be 'short, interesting and practical'. With this chapter, we have aimed to write something that matches these criteria in the hope that Prof. Bartman will appreciate it.

In December 2022, the European Commission proposed several measures to make European public capital markets more attractive for companies, especially for small and medium-sized enterprises (SMEs), which together are called the 'Listing Act package'. The idea behind the Listing Act package is to reduce the regulatory burden for companies in the phase before an initial public offering (pre-IPO phase) (with a proposal for a new directive on multiple voting rights,[1] for example), the IPO phase (with amendments to the Prospectus Regulation,[2] for example), and the post-IPO phase (with amendments to the Market Abuse Regulation,[3] (MAR)).[4]

In this chapter, we focus on the amendments to the MAR and in particular on the proposed amendments to the rules regarding disclosure of inside information. These proposed amendments are contained in the proposal of the European Commission for a new regulation.[5] In this chapter, we refer to that proposal for regulation as the 'Listing Act'[6] and we refer to the MAR as it would be amended by the Listing Act as the 'Amended MAR'.

It should be noted that this chapter was finalized and submitted when the Listing Act was just a proposal from the European Commission. Since then, the Council and the European Parliament have reached a political compromise on amendments to the Listing Act, including some changes to the provisions on the disclosure of inside information.[7] Because the final text of the Listing Act was not yet available when this chapter was finalized, we focused our discussion on the text of the proposal from the European Commission.

Section 12.03[A] of this chapter discusses the elimination by the Listing Act of the requirement in MAR to immediately disclose intermediate steps in a protracted process, even if those intermediate steps amount to inside information. Next, §12.03[B] discusses the conditions for the possibility for issuers to delay the disclosure of inside information under the Listing Act, and especially the new, more specific conditions that

---

1. *Proposal for a directive of the European Parliament and of the Council on multiple-vote share structures in companies that seek the admission to trading of their shares on an SME growth market*, COM/2022/761 final.
2. *Regulation (EU) 2017/1129 of the European Parliament and of the Council of 14 June 2017 on the prospectus to be published when securities are offered to the public or admitted to trading on a regulated market, and repealing Directive 2003/71/EC*, O.J. EU L 168, 30.6.2017.
3. *Regulation (EU) No. 596/2014 of the European Parliament and of the Council of 16 April 2014 on market abuse* (MAR), OJ EU L 173, 12.6.2014.
4. *Proposal for a Regulation of the European Parliament and of the Council amending Regulations (EU) 2017/1129, (EU) No. 596/2014 and (EU) No. 600/2014 to make public capital markets in the Union more attractive for companies and to facilitate access to capital for small and medium-sized enterprises* (Listing Act), COM(2022) 762 final, at 2-3.
5. *Supra* n. 4.
6. *Supra* n. 4. Although the Listing Act package also contains other proposals, such as a proposal for a new directive.
7. Council, *Listings on European stock exchanges: Council and Parliament agree on new act*, 1 February 2024, https://www.consilium.europa.eu/en/press/press-releases/2024/02/01/listings-on-european-stock-exchanges-council-and-parliament-agree-new-act/#: ~ :text = The%20Council%20and%20the%20Parliament,list%20on%20European%20stock%20exchanges.

replace the general condition that the delay of the disclosure of inside information should not mislead the public. The idea behind these amendments is to avoid forcing issuers to disclose information too early when the information has not yet reached a high degree of certainty, as this could mislead investors.[8] In addition, the proposed amendments aim to reduce compliance costs and provide more legal certainty about the (delayed) disclosure of inside information.[9]

To properly contextualize those amendments, we first start with a discussion of the rules on disclosure of inside information under the current version of MAR (§12.02). In §12.02[A], we discuss the definition of inside information, with a particular focus on the requirement that the information is sufficiently precise and how this relates to the disclosure of intermediate steps in a protracted process. Section §12.02[B] discusses when issuers can delay the disclosure of inside information under the current version of the MAR. For both topics, we will also give some examples of how the current version of the MAR has been applied by the Financial Supervision and Markets Authority (FSMA), the financial supervisor in Belgium. We focus on Belgium because it is our home jurisdiction, but other EU Member States face similar questions as to how these legal concepts should be interpreted so that our analysis is relevant to a broader audience. To keep it simple, we focus on the disclosure of inside information relating to shares issued by an EU company listed on a regulated market or relating to shares of which the issuer has approved the trading on a multilateral trading facility.

§12.02 DISCLOSURE OF INSIDE INFORMATION UNDER THE CURRENT MAR

[A] The Definition of 'Inside Information' under the MAR

[1] Definition Containing Four Cumulative Conditions

Article 7(1) of the MAR defines 'inside information' in relation to financial instruments as: 'information of a precise nature, which has not been made public, relating, directly or indirectly, to one or more issuers or to one or more financial instruments, and which, if it were made public, would be likely to have a significant effect on the prices of those financial instruments or on the price of related derivative financial instruments'.

From this follows that four cumulative conditions need to be fulfilled for information to qualify as 'inside information':

(1) The information must not be public.
(2) The information must relate to an issuer or to a financial instrument.
(3) The information must be material.
(4) The information must be precise.

8. Listing Act, *supra* note 4, at 5 and at recital 58.
9. *Ibid.*, at 5 and 7.

We discuss each of these conditions below, but we will expand most on the condition that the information must be precise. It is mainly that condition which is impacted by the amendments of the Listing Act.

[2] Condition One: The Information Is Not Public

The information may not be publicly available.[10] Information that is available against payment of a fee, for example, information in a specialized journal or database, qualifies as public information if it is available to a sufficient number of investors for the information to be incorporated in the market price.[11] However, information that is only disclosed to a few financial analysts[12] or to the shareholders[13] of the company (for example, in a general meeting) is not public.

It is irrelevant whether the information is actually accessed as long as it can be accessed.[14] Even information that has been disclosed in a way other than that mandated by the MAR can be considered public.[15] The market must also have had the possibility to absorb the information,[16] which traditionally meant a period of at least 30 minutes after publication in Belgium, although recent technology may suggest that this period could become shorter[17] (30 minutes is also the normal duration during which the FSMA will suspend trading in the shares if inside information is published during trading hours[18]).

10. Stefan Mees & Michiel Stuyts, *Insider trading anno 2017*, 5 Tijdschrift voor Rechtspersoon en Vennootschap - Revue pratique des sociétés 523, 527 (2017).
11. Marco Ventoruzzo & Chiara Picciau, *Commentary on Article 7: Inside Information in Market Abuse Regulation – Commentary and Annoted Guide* 282 (Marco Ventoruzzo & Sebastian Mock eds, Oxford University Press 2022).
12. Rüdiger Veil, *European Capital Markets Law* 203 (Hart 2017).
13. Benoît Feron & Adrien Fink, *Market Abuse – The Belgian General Legal Framework in Market Abuse – Les abus de marché* 12 (Inez de Meuleneere, Anne Sophie Pijcke & Merel Rosiers eds, Anthemis 2016); Deborah Janssens & Jan-Willem Geeroms, *Revised Rules in Belgium on (Delaying) Disclosure of Inside Information, Insider Lists and PDMR/PCA Dealings in Market Abuse – The Belgian General Legal Framework* in *Market Abuse – Les abus de marché* 65 (Inez de Meuleneere, Anne Sophie Pijcke & Merel Rosiers eds, Anthemis 2016).
14. Benoît Feron & Adrien Fink, *Market Abuse – The Belgian General Legal Framework in Market Abuse – Les abus de marché* 12 (Inez de Meuleneere, Anne Sophie Pijcke & Merel Rosiers eds, Anthemis 2016).
15. Marco Ventoruzzo & Chiara Picciau, *Commentary on Article 7: Inside Information in Market Abuse Regulation – Commentary and Annoted Guide* 280-281 (Marco Ventoruzzo & Sebastian Mock eds, Oxford University Press 2022).
16. *Ibid.*
17. Stefan Mees & Michiel Stuyts, *Insider trading anno 2017*, 5 Tijdschrift voor Rechtspersoon en Vennootschap - Revue pratique des sociétés 523, 530 (2017); Benoît Feron & Adrien Fink, *Market Abuse – The Belgian General Legal Framework in Market Abuse – Les abus de marché* 12 (Inez de Meuleneere, Anne Sophie Pijcke & Merel Rosiers eds, Anthemis 2016).
18. Benoît Feron & Adrien Fink, *Market Abuse – The Belgian General Legal Framework in Market Abuse – Les abus de marché* 13 (Inez de Meuleneere, Anne Sophie Pijcke & Merel Rosiers eds, Anthemis 2016).

[3] *Condition Two: The Information Relates (Directly or Indirectly) to an Issuer or to a Financial Instrument*

For the definition of 'financial instrument', the MAR refers to MiFID II,[19] which contains in its Annex 1, Section C a list of financial instruments. This includes, among others, all securities that are negotiable on the capital market.

The Committee of European Securities Regulators (CESR) has issued guidance with non-exhaustive lists of examples of which information could constitute inside information concerning an issuer, provided the information is sufficiently material. The CESR guidance contains two separate lists: one with examples of information that directly relates to an issuer and another list with examples of information that indirectly concerns an issuer.[20]

The distinction between information that directly versus indirectly concerns an issuer can be explained as a distinction between issuer-specific information versus market information (such as information on upcoming regulations, interest rates, etc.).[21] The distinguishing factor is whether the information falls within the issuer's field of activity or affects the decision-making procedure in the company specifically.[22] The distinction is important because the only information that directly concerns the issuer must be immediately disclosed by the issuer (*see* further in §12.02[B]).

[4] *Condition Three: The Information Must Be Material*

The information is material if it is likely to have a significant effect on the price of the financial instrument (or of a related derivative financial instrument).

Article 7(4) MAR clarifies that this means 'information a reasonable investor would be likely to use as part of the basis of his or her investment decisions'. Some legal doctrine has argued that the concept of a 'reasonable investor' should be interpreted as a rational investor who pays attention to the fundamental value of the issuer.[23] A

---

19. *Directive 2014/65/EU of the European Parliament and of the Council of 15 May 2014 on markets in financial instruments* (MiFID II), OJ EU L 173, 15.5.2014.
20. CESR, *Second set of CESR Guidance and information on the common operation of the directive to the market, July 2007*, CESR/06.562B, Nos 1.15 and 1.16.
21. Marco Ventoruzzo & Chiara Picciau, *Commentary on Article 7: Inside Information in Market Abuse Regulation – Commentary and Annoted Guide* 282-283 (Marco Ventoruzzo & Sebastian Mock eds, Oxford University Press 2022).
22. Rüdiger Veil, *European Capital Markets Law* 357 (Hart 2017).
23. Marco Ventoruzzo & Chiara Picciau, *Commentary on Article 7: Inside Information in Market Abuse Regulation – Commentary and Annoted Guide* 270 and 284-285 (Marco Ventoruzzo & Sebastian Mock eds, Oxford University Press 2022); Deborah Janssens & Jan-Willem Geeroms, *Revised rules in Belgium on (delaying) disclosure of inside information, insider lists and PDMR/PCA dealings in Market Abuse – the Belgian general legal framework* in *Market abuse – Les abus de marché* 63 (Inez de Meuleneere, Anne Sophie Pijcke & Merel Rosiers eds., Anthemis 2016); *See also* Rüdiger Veil, Marc Wiesner & Moritz Reichert, *Disclosure and Enforcement under the EU Listing Act*, 19 European Company and Financial Law Review 445, 496-499 (2022) (arguing that the text of MAR should be amended to clarify that the test should be which information would be considered relevant by a *rational* investor concerned about the *fundamental value* of the company).

reasonable investor will base his or her investment decisions on the information that is *ex ante* available to him or her.[24] The preamble of MAR considered that '[e]x post information can be used to check the presumption that the ex ante information was price sensitive, but should not be used to take action against persons who drew reasonable conclusions from ex ante information available to them'.[25]

The words 'likely to have a significant effect' mean that a potential impact on the share price suffices. This was also confirmed by the Court of Justice of the European Union (CJEU) in the *Spector* case, which held that the capacity to have a significant effect on prices must be assessed, a priori, in the light of the content of the information at issue and the context in which it occurs. It is not necessary to examine whether the disclosure actually had a significant effect on the price.[26]

The following are some recent examples of information which was considered sufficiently material by the FSMA to constitute inside information:

- the fact that the Netherlands Food and Consumer Safety Authority (NVWA) informed an issuer active in processing and packaging of meat products that it may be the source of an outbreak of the listeria bacteria and ordered a recall and a production halt of certain products (the company had not adequately disclosed this information);[27]
- the fact that, in a non-binding offer for a sale/purchase transaction between shareholders, the shares in a company are valued significantly higher than the valuation by analysts (a director of the company who possessed that information had executed trades of the shares in that company);[28]
- the fact that an issuer is contemplating a capital increase through an accelerated book building procedure (a participant to the market sounding prior to the transaction had, several minutes after having received the information through the market sounding, placed a sell order on the relevant shares);[29]

24. MAR, *supra* n. 3, at recital 14 ('Reasonable investors base their investment decisions on information already available to them, that is to say, on ex ante available information. Therefore, the question whether, in making an investment decision, a reasonable investor would be likely to take into account a particular piece of information should be appraised on the basis of the ex ante available information. Such an assessment has to take into consideration the anticipated impact of the information in light of the totality of the related issuer's activity, the reliability of the source of information and any other market variables likely to affect the financial instruments, the related spot commodity contracts, or the auctioned products based on the emission allowances in the given circumstances.').
25. MAR, *supra* n. 3, recital 15.
26. CJEU, Case C-45/08, *Spector Photo Group NV and Chris Van Raemdonck v. CBFA*, 23.12.2009.
27. *Settlement agreed between the FSMA and What's Cooking Group NV*, FSMA (18 July 2023), https://www.fsma.be/sites/default/files/media/files/2023-07/2023-07-18_minnelijkeschikkin g-1.pdf; For a similar case, *see also Settlement agreed between the FSMA and Greenyard NV*, FSMA (1 December 2020), https://www.fsma.be/sites/default/files/legacy/content/NL/Sanc ties/2020-12-01_minnelijkeschikking.pdf.
28. *Settlement agreed between the FSMA and Mr. X*, FSMA (3 January 2023), https://www.fsma.be/ sites/default/files/media/files/2023-01/2023-01-03_reglementtransactionnel.pdf.
29. *Settlement agreed between the FSMA and Mr. X*, FSMA (26 April 2022), https://www.fsma.be/ sites/default/files/media/files/2022-04/2022-04-26_reglementtransactionnel.pdf.

- the decision by the board of directors of a biotech company to halt studies for the development of a certain product as well as the failure by the same company to accelerate its patient recruitment (which acceleration had been announced in the company's IPO prospectus) (the company had not adequately disclosed this information);[30] and
- the fact that the chief executive officer (CEO) of an issuer is in advanced negotiations with another company to become CEO of that other company which will result in the termination of her position as CEO with the issuer (the CEO sold shares in the company where she was currently the CEO).[31]

[5] Condition Four: The Information Must Be Precise

[a] General

Article 7(2) MAR clarifies that information is precise if 'it indicates a set of circumstances which exists or which may reasonably be expected to come into existence, or an event which has occurred or which may reasonably be expected to occur, where it is specific enough to enable a conclusion to be drawn as to the possible effect of that set of circumstances or event on the prices of the financial instruments or the related derivative financial instrument'.

This implies two cumulative sub-criteria. First, the information must lead to a reasonable expectation of an event or a set of circumstances (the 'reasonable expectations test'). Some legal scholars argue that this implies that the future event must be more likely to happen than not, i.e., the probability of the event happening should be higher than 50%.[32] However, other authors have, in our view correctly, rejected that the reasonable expectation test means 'more likely than not'.[33] In any case, in the *Geltl* case, the CJEU explicitly rejected the argument that the magnitude of the impact of the information must be taken into account to determine the required probability, the

30. *Settlement agreed between the FSMA and Bone Therapeutics SA*, FSMA (27 July 2021), https://www.fsma.be/sites/default/files/media/files/2021-07/2021-07-27_reglementtransactionnel.pdf.
31. *Settlement agreed between the FSMA and Mme. A*, FSMA (29 June 2020), https://www.fsma.be/sites/default/files/legacy/content/FR/Sanctions/2020-06-29_reglementtransactionnel.pdf.
32. Rüdiger Veil, *European Capital Markets Law* 198-199 (Hart 2017); Marco Ventoruzzo & Chiara Picciau, *Commentary on Article 7: Inside Information in Market Abuse Regulation – Commentary and Annoted Guide* 276 (Marco Ventoruzzo & Sebastian Mock eds, Oxford University Press 2022).
33. Deborah Janssens & Jan-Willem Geeroms, *Revised Rules in Belgium on (Delaying) Disclosure of Inside Information, Insider Lists and PDMR/PCA Dealings in Market Abuse – The Belgian General Legal Framework* in *Market Abuse – Les abus de marché* 292 (Inez de Meuleneere, Anne Sophie Pijcke & Merel Rosiers eds, Anthemis 2016) 61; Laurent Legein, *Application du règlement abus de marché aux operations de fusion-acquisition et OPA in Financiële regulering: een dwarsdoorsnede* (Intersentia 2019).

so-called probability/magnitude formula.[34] The CJEU also stated that it suffices that the event should have a realistic prospect of occurring[35] and recognized that 'it cannot be ruled out that information relating to an event which is unlikely to occur may have a significant effect on the price'.[36]

Second, the information must be specific enough to conclude that it can possibly have an impact on the price of the financial instrument (the 'specificity test'). The CJEU held in the *Lafonta* case that the direction of the impact on the share price (positive or negative) does not need to be clear for the information to be considered sufficiently precise as long as a change in price can be reasonably anticipated.[37] This has led to a broad conception of 'inside information' in the EU.[38] Some authors find the *Lafonta* case law hard to reconcile with the guidance of the CESR that inside information should allow investors to invest with no or a low amount of risk[39] – which would not be the case if the direction of the share price impact is not clear.[40] However, in our view, the conclusion that inside information should also cover information that is not clear on the direction of the expected share price movement is correct. Indeed, the knowledge that a price change (in either direction) will occur could be sufficient for investors to make certain investment decisions (e.g., through a so-called straddle position of call and put options, allowing profits to be generated in case of significant price volatility, regardless of the direction of the share price movement).

Whether information is sufficiently precise sometimes proves difficult to assess in practice. This is particularly the case for information which does not arise at once but rather matures and becomes more precise over time. In this respect, the FSMA has taken the position that the non-renewal of the CEO's mandate may already constitute inside information before it has formally been resolved if the negotiations by that person to become CEO of another company have sufficiently advanced.[41] Similarly, in respect of merger and acquisition (M&A) transactions, the question often arises when the information on the transaction has become sufficiently precise to constitute inside information. Often, this will already be the case well before the execution of the final

34. CJEU, Case C-19/11, *Markus Geltl v. Daimler AG*, 28.6.2012, para. 50. *See* for a discussion: Rüdiger Veil, *European Capital Markets Law* (Hart 2017) 199-201. The probability/magnitude-approach is the one taken in the US to define inside information.
35. CJEU, Case C-19/11, *Markus Geltl v. Daimler AG*, 28.6.2012, para. 56.
36. *Ibid.*, para. 54.
37. CJEU, Case C-628/13, *Jean-Bernard Lafonta v. AMF*, 11.3.2015; *see also* Marco Ventoruzzo & Chiara Picciau, *Commentary on Article 7: Inside Information* in *Market Abuse Regulation – Commentary and Annoted Guide* 278 (Marco Ventoruzzo & Sebastian Mock eds, Oxford University Press 2022).
38. *See* for this conclusion: Stefan Mees & Michiel Stuyts, *Insider trading anno 2017*, Tijdschrift voor Rechtspersoon en Vennootschap – Revue pratique des sociétés 523, 530 (2017).
39. CESR, *Second set of CESR Guidance and information on the common operation of the directive to the market, July 2007*, CESR/06.562B, No 1.8.
40. *See* for a similar conclusion: Stefan Mees & Michiel Stuyts, *Insider trading anno 2017*, 5 Tijdschrift voor Rechtspersoon en Vennootschap – Revue pratique des sociétés 523, 530 (2017); Rüdiger Veil, *European Capital Markets Law* 205 (Hart 2017).
41. *Settlement agreed between the FSMA and Mme A*, FSMA (29 June 2020), https://www.fsma.be/sites/default/files/legacy/content/FR/Sanctions/2020-06-29_reglementtransactionnel.pdf.

transaction documents.[42] All will depend on the facts of the case. For example, if it appears from non-binding offers received from potential investors that their valuation of the company is much higher than the valuation by analysts, this may already constitute inside information at that early stage of the transaction process.[43]

[b] Intermediate Steps in a Protracted Process

Importantly, for the purpose of this chapter, MAR specifically provides that intermediate steps in a protracted process can also amount to inside information. Article 7(2) MAR stipulates that 'in the case of a protracted process that is intended to bring about, or that results in, particular circumstances or a particular event, those future circumstances or that future event, and also the intermediate steps of that process which are connected with bringing about or resulting in those future circumstances or that future event, may be deemed to be precise information'. If an intermediate step in a protracted process satisfies all of the criteria for inside information, it will constitute, by itself, inside information.[44] These provisions codify the *Geltl* case of the Court of Justice.[45]

The following examples of intermediate steps in a protracted process are given in the recitals of the MAR: 'the state of contract negotiations, terms provisionally agreed in contract negotiations, the possibility of the placement of financial instruments, conditions under which financial instruments will be marketed, provisional terms for the placement of financial instruments, or the consideration of the inclusion of a financial instrument in a major index or the deletion of a financial instrument from such an index'.[46] The *Geltl* case law held that it suffices that there is a realistic prospect that the event will occur.[47] As set out above, this has led to a broad conception of inside information.[48] The preamble of MAR furthermore states that the notion of an intermediate step in a protracted process 'should not be interpreted as meaning that the magnitude of the effect of that set of circumstances or that event on the prices of the financial instruments concerned must be taken into consideration'.[49]

42. Laurent Legein, *Application du règlement abus de marché aux operations de fusion-acquisition et OPA in Financiële regulering: een dwarsdoorsnede* 301 (Intersentia 2019).
43. *Settlement agreed between the FSMA and Mr. X*, FSMA (3 January 2023), https://www.fsma.be/sites/default/files/media/files/2023-01/2023-01-03_reglementtransactionnel.pdf.
44. Article 7(3) MAR.
45. Stefan Mees & Michiel Stuyts, *Insider trading anno 2017*, 5 Tijdschrift voor Rechtspersoon en Vennootschap – Revue pratique des sociétés 523, 529 (2017).
46. MAR, *supra* n. 3, at recital 17.
47. CJEU, Case C-19/11, *Markus Geltl v. Daimler AG*, 28.6.2012. This has been incorporated in recital 16 of the MAR, which states that '[a]n intermediate step in a protracted process may in itself constitute a set of circumstances or an event which exists or where there is a realistic prospect that they will come into existence or occur, on the basis of an overall assessment of the factors existing at the relevant time'.
48. *See* for this conclusion: Stefan Mees & Michiel Stuyts, *Insider trading anno 2017*, 5 Tijdschrift voor Rechtspersoon en Vennootschap – Revue pratique des sociétés 523, 529 (2017); Jean-Pierre Blumberg, *Voorkennis in het kader van het vrijwillig openbaar bod anno 2017 in In het vennootschapsbelang* 3 (Eric Dirix, Robby Houben & Eddy Wymeersch eds, Intersentia 2017).
49. MAR, *supra* note 3, at recital 16.

The conditions to determine whether an intermediate step of a protracted process constitutes inside information are the same conditions as set out above for any other information that relates to an issuer or to financial instruments.[50] Accordingly, the assessment of whether intermediate steps constitute inside information applies irrespective of the question of whether the final transaction eventually materializes.[51] In practice, the most relevant condition will be the condition that the information must be sufficiently precise. Indeed, in a protracted process, it will not always be clear whether the event may reasonably be expected to occur or whether a conclusion can be drawn as to a possible price effect of the information.

By way of example, the following intermediate steps in protracted processes have been considered by the FSMA to constitute inside information:

- Receipt of a letter in which the counterparty to a strategic partnership agreement voices its intention to terminate that partnership agreement, notwithstanding the fact that the letter invites the parties to the partnership to further discuss that termination and that the partnership agreement does not foresee the right to unilaterally terminate the partnership.[52]
- The decision by an issuer, on the basis of the non-binding offers of three bidders, to admit those three bidders to the second stage of an auction sale process for the sale of a business line that represents 90% of the issuer's activities.[53]
- The decision by the top management of a bidder to prepare a public takeover bid on a target.[54]

[B] (Delayed) Disclosure of Inside Information under the MAR

According to Article 17(1) of the MAR, an issuer must inform the public as soon as possible of inside information which directly concerns that issuer. Inside information that indirectly concerns the issuer must not be disclosed by the issuer, as the issuer is not necessarily aware of this information before it becomes public.[55]

50. *See also* the last sentence of Recital (16) to MAR: 'An intermediate step should be deemed to be inside information if it, by itself, meets the criteria laid down in this Regulation for inside information'.
51. *See* in that sense also: *Inside information under point (a) of Article 7(1) of the MAR*, BaFin (German Financial Supervisory Authority) (consulted on 17 September 2023), https://www.bafin.de/dok/14247444.
52. *Settlement agreed between the FSMA and Biocartis Group NV*, FSMA (6 July 2023), https://www.fsma.be/sites/default/files/media/files/2023-07/2023-07-18_minnelijkeschikking.pdf.
53. *Decision of the sanctions committee of the FSMA v-à-v W.*, FSMA (27 December 2021), https://www.fsma.be/sites/default/files/media/files/2022-01/2021-12-27_decision.pdf.
54. *Anonymised extract of the decision of the sanctions committee of the FSMA v-à-v A.*, FSMA (12 March 2013), sanctions committee of the FSMA v-à-v W., 27 December 2021, https://www.fsma.be/sites/default/files/legacy/sitecore/media%20library/Files/sanc/nl/2013-03-12_voorkennis.pdf.
55. Alain Pietrancosta, *Commentary on Article 17: Public Disclosure of Inside Information in Market Abuse Regulation – Commentary and Annoted Guide* 464 (Marco Ventoruzzo & Sebastian Mock eds, Oxford University Press 2022).

Immediate public disclosure of inside information is sometimes harmful to the company. Therefore, the issuer can decide, on its own responsibility, to delay the public disclosure of inside information, if three conditions are fulfilled:[56]

(a) 'immediate disclosure is likely to prejudice the legitimate interests of the issuer;
(b) delay of disclosure is not likely to mislead the public;
(c) the issuer is able to ensure the confidentiality of that information'.

The disclosure of inside information relating to intermediate steps in a protracted process may also be delayed under the same conditions.[57]

The European Securities and Markets Authority (ESMA) guidelines for competent authorities further clarify the condition of 'legitimate interests of the issuer'. Those guidelines provide a non-exhaustive and indicative list of legitimate interests of the issuers that are likely to be prejudiced by immediate disclosure of inside information and situations in which delay of disclosure is likely to mislead the public.[58] The guidelines are non-binding for competent authorities, but if competent authorities intend to deviate, they have to explain why to ESMA within two months of the publication of the guidelines. The competent authorities of all Member States have notified that they intend to comply with the guidelines.[59]

The ESMA guidelines give a list of examples of legitimate interests,[60] which expand on the examples already mentioned in recital 50 of the MAR:[61]

(a) the issuer is conducting negotiations where the outcome of such negotiations would likely be jeopardized by immediate public disclosure. Examples of such negotiations may be those related to mergers, acquisitions, splits and spin-offs,

56. Article 17(4) MAR.
57. Article 17(4), second subparagraph MAR.
58. *MAR Guidelines. Delay in the disclosure of inside information and interactions with prudential supervision*, ESMA (13 April 2022), https://www.esma.europa.eu/sites/default/files/library/esma70-156-4966_mar_gls-delay_in_the_disclosure_of_inside_information.pdf.
59. *Guidelines compliance table*, ESMA (3 April 2023), https://www.esma.europa.eu/sites/default/files/2023-02/esma70-449-741_compliance_table_mar_gls_srep.pdf.
60. *MAR Guidelines. Delay in the disclosure of inside information and interactions with prudential supervision*, ESMA (13 April 2022), https://www.esma.europa.eu/sites/default/files/library/esma70-156-4966_mar_gls-delay_in_the_disclosure_of_inside_information.pdf, 5-6.
61. Recital 50 of the MAR gives the following examples: '(a) ongoing negotiations, or related elements, where the outcome or normal pattern of those negotiations would be likely to be affected by public disclosure. In particular, in the event that the financial viability of the issuer is in grave and imminent danger, although not within the scope of the applicable insolvency law, public disclosure of information may be delayed for a limited period where such a public disclosure would seriously jeopardize the interest of existing and potential shareholders by undermining the conclusion of specific negotiations designed to ensure the long-term financial recovery of the issuer; (b) decisions taken or contracts made by the management body of an issuer which need the approval of another body of the issuer in order to become effective, where the organization of such an issuer requires the separation between those bodies, provided that public disclosure of the information before such approval, together with the simultaneous announcement that the approval remains pending, would jeopardize the correct assessment of the information by the public.'

purchases or disposals of major assets or branches of corporate activity, restructurings and reorganizations.

(b) the financial viability of the issuer is in grave and imminent danger, although not within the scope of the applicable insolvency law, and immediate public disclosure of the inside information would seriously prejudice the interests of existing and potential shareholders by jeopardizing the conclusion of the negotiations designed to ensure the financial recovery of the issuer;

(c) the inside information relates to decisions taken or contracts entered into by the management body of an issuer which need, pursuant to national law or the issuer's bylaws, the approval of another body of the issuer, other than the shareholders' general assembly, in order to become effective, provided that:

  (i) immediate public disclosure of that information before such a definitive decision would jeopardize the correct assessment of the information by the public; and

  (ii) the issuer arranged for the definitive decision to be taken as soon as possible.

(d) the issuer has developed a product or an invention and the immediate public disclosure of that information is likely to jeopardize the intellectual property rights of the issuer;

(e) the issuer is planning to buy or sell a major holding in another entity and the disclosure of such an information would likely jeopardize the implementation of such plan;

(f) a transaction previously announced is subject to a public authority's approval, and such approval is conditional upon additional requirements, where the immediate disclosure of those requirements will likely affect the ability for the issuer to meet them and therefore prevent the final success of the deal or transaction;

(g) the issuer is an institution subject to the CRR [Capital Requirements Regulation] and a decision to carry out a redemption, reduction, repurchase, repayment or call of own funds instruments or a reduction, distribution or reclassification as another own funds item of the share premium accounts related to own funds instruments has been taken but not yet authorized by the competent authority as defined under Article 4(1)(40) of CRR, pursuant to Article 77 of CRR;

(h) the issuer is an institution subject to prudential supervision under the CRD [Capital Requirements Directive] and has received a draft SREP [Supervisory Review and Evaluation Process] decision or preliminary information related thereto which will become final at a later stage upon completion of the decision-making process of the Prudential Competent Authority. In such case, a premature announcement of any inside information constituting the draft SREP decision or preliminary information related thereto would be in contrast with the SREP procedure and in particular with the institution's right to be heard, potentially unduly prejudicing the institution's interest for a fair appreciation of the impact of that information by the market.

It has been argued that the ESMA Guidelines are too restrictive with regards to the possibility of delaying the disclosure because the decision still has to be approved by the supervisory board in a two-tier board structure: the ESMA Guidelines only allow such a delay if disclosure *would 'jeopardize the correct assessment of the information by the public'*, whereas it could be argued that the delay of disclosure is also important to protect the supervisory board's ability to come to an independent decision.[62] It is also noteworthy that ESMA refused to include the following situations as a legitimate interest in its guidelines: the delay of disclosure of the resignation of a CEO until the appointment of a successor and the delay of disclosure by a parent company because it still needs to check the accounting information received from its subsidiaries.[63] In general, the interest of the issuer in retaining its reputation or avoiding a negative share price reaction is as such not considered legitimate either.[64]

The ESMA Guidelines also clarify when the delay of the disclosure of inside information is likely to mislead the public, providing three concrete situations:[65]

(a) the inside information whose disclosure the issuer intends to delay is materially different from the previous public announcement of the issuer on the matter to which the inside information refers to; or
(b) the inside information whose disclosure the issuer intends to delay regards the fact that the issuer's financial objectives are not likely to be met, where such objectives were previously publicly announced; or
(c) the inside information whose disclosure the issuer intends to delay is in contrast with the market's expectations, where such expectations are based on signals that the issuer has previously sent to the market, such as interviews, roadshows or any other type of communication organized by the issuer or with its approval.

These three situations are based on two principles: first, the inside information differs from market expectations; and second, such market expectations are based on the issuer's previous communications.[66]

To be able to fulfil the third condition, the confidentiality of insider information, the issuer must establish appropriate internal procedures. If confidentiality is no longer ensured, the issuer must disclose the inside information as soon as possible.[67] Even a rumour gives rise to this disclosure obligation, provided that it is 'explicitly related to inside information' and 'sufficiently accurate to indicate that the confidentiality of that information is no longer ensured'.[68] The issuer can therefore no longer adopt a 'no comment' policy, even if the source of the rumour lies outside the issuer.[69] In practice,

62. Rüdiger Veil, *European Capital Markets Law* 374 (Hart 2017).
63. *See* for a discussion: Alain Pietrancosta, *Commentary on Article 17: Public Disclosure of Inside Information in Market Abuse Regulation. Commentary and Annoted Guide* 480 (Marco Ventoruzzo & Sebastian Mock eds, Oxford University Press 2022).
64. Rüdiger Veil, *European Capital Markets Law* 370 (Hart 2017).
65. ESMA, *MAR Guidelines. Delay in the disclosure of inside information and interactions with prudential supervision*, 13 April 2022, https://www.esma.europa.eu/sites/default/files/library/esma70-156-4966_mar_gls-delay_in_the_disclosure_of_inside_information.pdf, 6.
66. Alain Pietrancosta, *Commentary on Article 17: Public Disclosure of Inside Information in Market Abuse Regulation – Commentary and Annoted Guide* 482 (Marco Ventoruzzo & Sebastian Mock eds, Oxford University Press 2022).
67. Article 17(7), first subparagraph MAR.
68. Article 17(7), second subparagraph MAR.
69. Rüdiger Veil, *European Capital Markets Law* 377 (Hart 2017).

issuers who have delayed the disclosure of inside information often monitor the press and other public media outlets and have emergency press releases ready to be published in case of a leak of the information.

If an issuer had delayed the disclosure of inside information using the exception described above, the issuer must inform the competent authority of this immediately after the public disclosure of the inside information and provide a written explanation of how the conditions discussed above were met.[70] If the inside information no longer exists (becomes 'stale'), because the final event never occurs, nothing needs to be disclosed to the public or to the competent authority.[71] Complying with this rule is often experienced as a high burden by issuers and carries the potential of legal liability. This explains the preference for listed companies to reach the conclusion that the information does not qualify as inside information rather than qualifying the information as inside information and then delaying its disclosure. Member States may provide that the explanation is to be provided only upon the request of the competent authority.[72]

§12.03 DISCLOSURE OF INSIDE INFORMATION UNDER THE LISTING ACT

[A] No Separate Definitions of Inside Information

As explained above, the MAR contains a single definition of 'inside information', which applies both to the requirement for issuers to immediately disclose inside information as well as to the prohibition on insider dealing. As also explained above, the definition has gotten extensive applications from the CJEU in the cases of *Geltl*,[73] *Spector*,[74] and *Lafonta*.[75]

It has been argued in legal doctrine that this one-step approach must be abandoned in favour of a two-step approach where a general definition of inside information is used for the prohibition of insider dealing, while the obligation to disclose is limited to a defined list of information items (similarly to the regime in the United States of America (USA)). An alternative approach proposed by legal doctrine is to keep a general definition of inside information for the disclosure rule but to exempt

70. Article 17(4), third subparagraph MAR.
71. *Questions and Answers on the Market Abuse Regulation*, ESMA (25 November 2022), https://www.esma.europa.eu/sites/default/files/library/esma70-145-111_qa_on_mar.pdf, Q5.2, 14.
72. Article 17(4), *in fine*, MAR. Belgium has not opted for this mechanism and Belgian issuers are hence required to proactively inform the competent authority (the FSMA) of the delayed disclosure after the inside information has been made public.
73. CJEU, Case C-19/11, *Markus Geltl v. Daimler AG*, 28.6.2012 (intermediate steps of a protracted process can also constitute inside information).
74. CJEU, Case C-45/08, *Spector Photo Group NV and Chris Van Raemdonck v. CBFA*, 23.12.2009 (to determine whether information was price sensitive, it is not relevant whether the information eventually did actually impact the price of the financial instrument).
75. CJEU, Case C-628/13, *Jean-Bernard Lafonta v. AMF*, 11.3 (information can also be sufficiently precise to constitute inside information even if the direction of the expected price evolution is not clear).

intermediate steps in a protracted process. In those cases, only the final event would need to be disclosed.[76]

In its consultation paper, the European Commission queried: (i) whether MAR should distinguish between a definition of inside information for the purposes of market abuse prohibition and a notion of inside information triggering the disclosure obligation and (ii) whether it should be clarified that inside information relating to a multi-stage process need only be made public once the end stage is reached, unless a leakage has occurred.[77]

In the current text proposals of the Listing Act, a single definition of inside information would remain, but the requirement to immediately disclose such inside information would indeed not apply to intermediate steps in a protracted process.

[B] No Disclosure of Intermediate Steps in a Protracted Process

The Listing Act proposes to amend the disclosure requirement of Article 17(1) of the MAR by stipulating that the disclosure requirement 'shall not apply to intermediate steps in a protracted process as referred to in Article 7(2) and (3) where those steps are connected with bringing about a set of circumstances or an event'. Recital 58 of the Listing Act adds: 'the issuer should only disclose the information related to the event that this protracted process intends to bring about, at the moment when such information is sufficiently precise, such as when the management board has taken the relevant decision to bring about that event'.[78] In other words, issuers only need to disclose the final step in the protracted process, even if the intermediate steps also independently constitute inside information. This makes it significantly easier for listed companies to manage the disclosure requirements relating to protracted processes. Nevertheless, if the information about the intermediate steps of the protracted process qualifies as inside information, the confidentiality of the inside information needs to be ensured. If the inside information leaks anyway, the issuer must disclose the inside information to the public as soon as possible.[79]

The European Commission is also empowered to adopt a delegated act with a non-exhaustive list of relevant information and the moment when the issuer can be reasonably expected to disclose each piece of information.[80] Such guidance will likely help to provide more legal certainty to issuers with regard to their disclosure obligations, for example, with regard to what can be considered the final step at which moment the inside information needs to be disclosed.

---

76. For more background on these various proposals, *see*: Rüdiger Veil, Marc Wiesner & Moritz Reichert, *Disclosure and Enforcement under the EU Listing Act*, 19 European Company and Financial Law Review 445, 488 et seq. (2022).
77. *Targeted Consultation Listing Act*, European Commission (19 November 2021), https://finance.ec.europa.eu/regulation-and-supervision/consultations/finance-2021-listing-act-targeted_en.
78. Recital 58 of the Listing Act also states: 'In the case of non-protracted processes related to one-off events, notably when the occurrence of those events does not depend on the issuer, the disclosure should take place as soon as the issuer becomes aware of that event.'
79. Article 17(1b) Amended MAR.
80. Article 17(1a) Amended MAR.

To be clear, the definition of inside information in Article 7 MAR is not amended so that information relating to intermediate steps in a protracted process can still qualify as inside information by itself and therefore trigger the prohibition on insider dealing in Article 14 MAR.[81] The Listing Act therefore creates a different concept of inside information for the prohibition on insider dealing and for the disclosure of inside information. This could address the criticism in the legal doctrine on the unified concept of inside information for the prohibition of insider dealing and the disclosure of inside information.[82] It is also in line with recommendations of the High-Level Forum on the Capital Markets Union.[83]

[C] Revised Conditions for Delaying the Disclosure of Inside Information

The Listing Act also proposes to amend the conditions for the possibility of the issuer delaying the disclosure of inside information on its own responsibility.[84] The conditions that immediate disclosure is likely to prejudice the legitimate interests of the issuer and that the issuer is able to ensure the confidentiality of the inside information are retained. However, the general condition that the delay of disclosure is not likely to mislead the public is replaced by three more specific conditions for the inside information:

(i) it is not materially different from the previous public announcement of the issuer on the matter to which the inside information refers;
(ii) it does not regard the fact that the issuer's financial objectives are not likely to be met, where such objectives were previously publicly announced;
(iii) it is not in contrast with the market's expectations, where such expectations are based on signals that the issuer has previously sent to the market, including interviews, roadshows or any other type of communication organized by the issuer or with its approval.

In practice, this amendment will not constitute a big change, as these conditions are taken almost word for word from the ESMA Guidelines (*see* above in 12.02[B]). However, a key difference is that the EMSA Guidelines only provided non-exhaustive examples of situations where the delay of disclosure would be likely to mislead the public, whereas the amendment in the Listing Act limits the analysis to the three

81. Listing Act, *supra* n. 4, at 23.
82. *See*, e.g., Marco Ventoruzzo & Chiara Picciau, *Commentary on Article 7: Inside Information in Market Abuse Regulation – Commentary and Annoted Guide* 265-266 (Marco Ventoruzzo & Sebastian Mock eds, Oxford University Press 2022); Alain Pietrancosta, *Public Disclosure of Inside Information and Market Abuse in Market Abuse Regulation – Commentary and Annoted Guide* 47 (Marco Ventoruzzo & Sebastian Mock eds, Oxford University Press 2022); Rüdiger Veil, Marc Wiesner & Moritz Reichert, *Disclosure and Enforcement under the EU Listing Act*, 19 European Company and Financial Law Review 445, 490-492 (2022).
83. *A new vision for Europe's Capital Markets*, High Level Forum on the Capital Markets Union (June 2020), https://finance.ec.europa.eu/system/files/2020-06/200610-cmu-high-level-forum-final-report_en.pdf, p. 67.
84. These conditions were discussed above in §12.02[B].

conditions above. This means that it is no longer necessary to assess whether the delay of disclosure misleads the public in any other way than the three situations mentioned.

What is also new in the Listing Act is that the issuer will need to inform the competent authority immediately after its decision of its intention to delay the disclosure of inside information, and not simply at the moment when the inside information is finally disclosed, as is currently the case (*see* above in 12.02[B]). The written explanation of how the conditions for delaying the disclosure are met also needs to be given at that moment. However, the delay must not be authorized by the competent authority, although the competent authority can decide to bring enforcement actions against the issuer if it believes the conditions for the delay are not met.

§12.04 CONCLUSION

In conclusion, the European Commission's proposal for the Listing Act package would have significant implications for the regulation of the disclosure of inside information in European capital markets, particularly with regard to the treatment of intermediate steps within protracted processes. Under the proposed amendments to MAR, issuers would only be required to disclose the final step in such processes. These amendments address the long-standing criticism in legal doctrine on the unitary definition of inside information for purposes of both disclosure and insider trading. The amendments may provide greater flexibility and legal certainty for listed companies. Moreover, the proposed amendments would introduce more specific conditions for delaying the disclosure of inside information. While the new conditions would not represent a significant departure from the existing ESMA Guidelines, they would further strengthen legal certainty. The Listing Act will therefore likely be welcomed by listed companies, provided that the proposed amendments survive the EU legislative process.

CHAPTER 13

The Development of the European Remuneration Framework and Its Effect on Executive Remuneration in Dutch Banks

Tom Dijkhuizen[*]

In this contribution, the author describes the development of the European Remuneration Framework after both Enron and the financial crisis of 2007-2008 and its (subsequent) effect on Executive Remuneration in Dutch Banks. Two interesting trends in addressing the remuneration issue at European and national level are apparent. On the one hand, formal laws and regulations have replaced forms of self-regulation. Also, the focus of the legislative reforms shifted from strengthening pay governance to regulating pay design. The question is, however, if the pendulum will stay put or swing back.

§13.01 INTRODUCTION

Executive remuneration has undoubtedly been a key topic on the European and domestic regulatory agenda for over two decades now. Originally, executive remuneration was thought of as the solution to the principal-agent problem between the shareholders of a (dispersed) publicly owned company and this company's executive

* This contribution draws and elaborates on different previous publications of the author on the subject of executive remuneration such as, among others: Tom C.A. Dijkhuizen, *The EU's Approach to Banks' Executive Remuneration, in Executive Directors' Remuneration in Comparative Corporate Perspective* 49-68 (Christoph van der Elst ed., 2015); Tom C.A. Dijkhuizen, *Een eerste stap in de implementatie van de herziene Aandeelhoudersrichtlijn*, 29 Maandblad voor Vermogensrecht 129, 129-137 (2018); Tom C.A. Dijkhuizen, *De implementatie van de herziene Aandeelhoudersrichtlijn – de eindsprint is ingezet*, 28 Maandblad voor Vermogensrecht 163, 163-170 (2019).

directors. The idea was that a well-designed remuneration policy would give these directors incentives to decide on and pursue those actions that would maximize shareholder wealth.[1] The corporate scandals that shook the financial markets at the turn of the century, such as *Enron* in the United States and *Parmalat* in Europe,[2] gave, however, rise to popular unease with high levels of executive remuneration[3] and led to regulatory responses on the European level and across many jurisdictions.[4] While the original objective of the European regulatory regime on executive remuneration was focused on enhancing *pay governance*,[5] the focus shifted to *pay design* in the wake of the financial crisis as legislative responses to this financial crisis aimed to change the executive remuneration structures and models in the financial sector. The objective of this chapter is twofold: this chapter will analyse the (development of the) European executive remuneration framework, in particular with regard to banks, while it will also address the impact of this European framework on the executive remuneration regime in the Netherlands, in particular in Dutch banks.

This chapter is structured as follows. After the introduction, the chapter will first address the legislative initiatives taken in response to the aforementioned corporate scandals on the European level (§13.02) as well as in the Netherlands (§13.03). In §13.04, this chapter will provide an overview of the post-crisis financial sector reforms on the European level, whereafter §13.05 will provide an overview of the legislative reforms in the Netherlands. In §13.06, I will elaborate on the 'hard' remuneration rules for banks that were introduced in Europe by the Third Capital Requirements Directive (CRD III) and the implementation of this Directive in the Netherlands. In §13.07, I will discuss the Fourth Capital Requirements Directive (CRD IV) and its implementation in the Netherlands through the Act on the Remuneration Policies of Undertakings (*Wet beloningsbeleid financiële ondernemingen*). Thereafter, I will briefly elaborate on the more recent introduction of the revised Shareholders' Rights Directive (SRD II) and its implementation (§13.08).[6] In the final section, I will draw some concluding remarks

1. Michael C. Jensen & Kenneth J. Murphy, *Performance Pay and Top-Management Incentives*, 98 J. of Pol. Econ. 225, 225-226 (1990). *Cf.* Alexandra Laurell, *Failures in Remuneration Policies: The Rise of Shareholder Responsibility?*, 10 Eur. Co. L. 116, 118-119 (2013).
2. Christoph van de Elst & Marinka van Falier, *The European Remuneration Framework: Recent Policy Changes and Their Implications on Executive Remuneration Contracts, in Executive Directors' Remuneration in Comparative Corporate Perspective* 15 (Christoph van der Elst ed., 2015).
3. Guido Ferrarini, Niamh Moloney & Cristina Vespro, *Executive Pay: Convergence in Law and Practice across the EU Corporate Governance Faultline*, 4 J. Corp. L. Stud. 243, 243-244 (2004).
4. Jennifer G. Hill, *Regulating Executive Remuneration: International Developments in the Post-Scandal Era*, 3 Eur. Co. L. 64, 64 (2006). Hill refers in note 7 to Jennifer G. Hill, *Regulatory Responses to Global Corporate Scandals*, 23 Wis. Intl. L. J. 367 (2005).
5. 'Pay governance' refers to 'the different but interlinked governance mechanisms which can support the adoption of effective incentive contracts, in particular board monitoring (particularly by independent directors), disclosure and shareholder voice', Guido Ferrarini, Niamh Moloney & Maria C. Ungureanu, *Executive Remuneration in Crisis: A Critical Assessment of Reforms in Europe*, 10 J. Corp. L. Stud. 73, 85 (2010).
6. The section does not discuss all (relevant) legislative developments, such as the entry into force of the Fifth Capital Requirements Directive and its implementation on the Dutch national level in the (amended) Sound Remuneration Policies 2017 or the entry into force of the Dutch Act on Further Remuneration Measures for Financial Undertakings as well as other developments, such

about the European executive remuneration framework and its effect on (the development of) executive remuneration in Dutch banks.

§13.02 LEGISLATIVE REFORMS ON THE EUROPEAN LEVEL AFTER *ENRON*

The above-mentioned corporate scandals made a serious dent in the premise that a well-designed remuneration policy could align the interests of the executives and shareholders and therefore could also enhance corporate performance. The first initiative that the European Union (EU) took as a direct reaction to the Enron case was to extend the mandate of the High Level Group of Company Law Experts, also named the Winter Group after its chairman, to address a number of issues related to best practices in corporate governance and auditing, *inter alia*, the role of non-executive and supervisory directors and the remuneration of management.[7]

On the first topic, the Winter Group advocated strengthening the role of the independent members of the non-executive and supervisory boards. These independent members should, from the view of the Winter Group, play a decisive role with regard to the appointment and remuneration of directors and the audit of the financial statements.[8] Regarding remuneration, the Winter Group stated, on the one hand, that the form and level of remuneration should remain a matter for the companies and their shareholders, but, on the other hand, that remuneration systems should be subject to adequate board control, which in turn should be based on sufficient information rights,[9] so that shareholders could provide sufficient countervailing power.[10] Against that background, the Winter Group advised the European Commission (EC) to issue rules in the form of (non-binding) recommendations that are addressed to the Member States, covering, among other things, the disclosure of the individual remuneration of both (non-)executive and supervisory board directors. The recommendation also had to include provisions on shareholders' approval of share and option schemes for executive directors. Schemes granting shares and share options and other forms of remuneration of directors linked to the share price should require the prior approval of the shareholders' meeting on the basis of a proper explanation by the remuneration committee of the applicable rules and of their likely costs.[11] The Winter Group's

---

as the publication of the revised Dutch Corporate Governance Code 2022 that also encompasses remuneration provisions, as such discussion would be (far) beyond the scope of this contribution.

7. This High Level Group already existed. In the beginning the group was set up to make recommendations on a modern regulatory framework in the EU for company law and already dealt with issues related to the Takeover Bids Directive. Their mandate was further extended by the Commission following the ECOFIN Council Meeting in Oviedo, The High Level Group of Company Law Experts, *Report of the High Level Group of Company Law Experts on a Modern Regulatory Framework for Company Law in Europe*, 43 (2002), https://www.ecgi.global/sites/default/files/report_en.pdf.
8. The High Level Group of Company Law Experts, *supra* n. 7, at 60.
9. The High Level Group of Company Law Experts, *supra* n. 7, at 64-65.
10. Geert T.M.J. Raaijmakers & Frans G.K. Overkleeft, *Bestuurdersbeloning, de nieuwe Code en de kredietcrisis*, Tijdschrift voor Financieel Recht 87, 87 (2009).
11. The High Level Group of Company Law Experts, *supra* n. 7, at 76.

recommendations were welcomed by the EC as its 2003 Company Law Action Plan was largely in line with these recommendations.[12] The recommendation regarding the role of non-executive and supervisory directors would be followed up in the medium term, while the recommendation concerning executive directors' remuneration would be adopted in the short term, as this action was in the EC's opinion key to the restoration of confidence in the financial markets after *Enron*.

First, on 14 December 2004, the EC adopted Recommendation 2004/913/EC, fostering an appropriate regime for the remuneration of directors of listed companies.[13] The EC did not aim to change the design of the remuneration policies with this recommendation, but as remuneration 'is one the key areas where executive directors may have a conflict of interest and where due account should be taken of the interests of the shareholders', remuneration systems should be subjected to appropriate governance controls, 'based on adequate information rights'.[14] The recommendation also encompassed provisions concerning: (i) the disclosure of a company's statement on the remuneration policy, which should be submitted to the annual general meeting for approval;[15] (ii) disclosure of individual directors' remuneration;[16] and (iii) the required prior approval of share-based schemes.[17]

In the following year, the Commission adopted Recommendation 2005/162/EC on the role of non-executive or supervisory directors of listed companies and on the committees of the (supervisory) board.[18] This recommendation was also in line with the recommendations of the Winter Group as the recommendation required that the (supervisory) boards of listed companies 'should comprise a sufficient number of committed non-executive or supervisory directors, who play no role in the management of the company or its group and who are independent in that they are free of any material conflict interests'[19] and also requires that the composition of these boards ensure that the independent non-executive or supervisory directors play an effective supervisory role regarding the directors' nomination and remuneration and audit, as the potential for conflict of interest in these areas is particularly high.[20]

12. European Commission, *Communication from the Commission to the Council and the European Parliament. Modernising Company Law and Enhancing Corporate Governance in the European Union – A Plan to Move Forward*, COM(2003) 284 final, at 12.
13. European Commission, *Commission Recommendation 2004/913/EC of 14 December 2004 fostering an appropriate regime for the remuneration of directors of listed companies*, OJ EU L 385/55 (2004) (hereinafter also: 2004 Recommendation).
14. European Commission, *supra* n. 13, at 55.
15. Articles 3(1), 3(3), 3(5), 4(1) and 4(2) of the 2004 Recommendation respectively.
16. Articles 5(1), 5(3) and 5(4) of the 2004 Recommendation.
17. Articles 6(1) and 6(2) of the 2004 Recommendation.
18. European Commission, *Commission Recommendation 2005/162/EC of 15 February 2005 on the role of non-executive or supervisory directors of listed companies and on the committees of the (supervisory) board*, OJ EU L 52/51 (2005) (hereinafter also: 2005 Recommendation).
19. European Commission, *supra* n. 18, at 52. The requirement is implemented in Article 4 of the 2005 Recommendation.
20. European Commission, *supra* n. 18, at 52. The requirement is implemented in Art. 5 and Annex I of the 2005 Recommendation.

§13.03 THE INTRODUCTION OF (FURTHER) EXECUTIVE REMUNERATION REGULATIONS IN THE NETHERLANDS

[A] Executive Remuneration Regulations in the Dutch Civil Code

These recommendations had, however, little to no effect in the Netherlands. The Dutch legislator had already introduced further regulations on executive remuneration by introducing two types of rules on remuneration, namely: (i) rules on the disclosure of remuneration and (ii) rules on the power to set remuneration in its Act on the disclosure of executive and supervisory directors' remuneration and shareholdings,[21] that came into force on 1 September 2002.[22] This act introduced Articles 2:383c-2:383e of the Dutch Civil Code (DCC), which provide, among other things, that a listed company must disclose the executive directors' individual remuneration.[23]

In September 2003, the Dutch legislator proposed a new Article 2:135 DCC in the second memorandum of amendment (*nota van wijziging*) to the Act, adapting the statutory two-tier rules[24] aimed to strengthen the position of the general meeting in the determination of executive directors' remuneration. In this proposal, the legislator noted that although the general meeting could determine the executive directors' remuneration, this task was often delegated to the supervisory board under the Articles of Association. It was, however, the question if these supervisory board members could be seen as (sufficiently) independent and would be guided by the interests of the company and its affiliated enterprise when performing their duties with regard to the remuneration policy,[25] as the supervisory board directors and executive board directors were, in the view of the legislator, mostly acquaintances of each other with the result that the independence of these supervisory directors was at stake.[26] The legislator also doubted whether shareholders were able to check and (counter)balance the 'get-together'[27] of executive and supervisory board directors, who both had a large information advantage over these shareholders. These doubts were reinforced by 'excessive income developments'[28] and 'excesses'.[29] In short, the proposed Act was aimed at restoring the balance of power within the listed company with regard to executive directors' remuneration.

21. *Act of 18 April 2002 amending Book 2 of the Civil Code and some other laws in connection with the disclosure of the remuneration and shareholdings of executive and supervisory directors*, Bulletin of Acts and Decrees 225 (2002).
22. Bulletin of Acts and Decrees 422 (2002).
23. Article 2:383c DCC.
24. *Parliamentary Papers II* 2002/03, 28 179, no. 31, at 2.
25. *Parliamentary Papers II* 2002/03, 28 179, no. 31, at 6.
26. *Parliamentary Papers II* 2002/03, 28 179, no. 31, at 6.
27. Emmanuel C.H.J. Lokin, *Variabele beloning in perspectief*, in: *Onderneming en beloning* 141 (Corjo J.H Jansen & Leonard G. Verburg eds, 2014)at 176.
28. *Parliamentary Papers II* 2002/03, 28 179, no. 31, at 4.
29. *Parliamentary Papers II* 2002/03, 28 179, no. 31, at 6.

The act that was adopted on 6 July 2004[30] and entered into force on 1 October 2004,[31] provided that the general meeting of a public company (*naamloze vennootschap*) is authorized, pursuant to Article 2:135(1) DCC, to adopt the remuneration policy. The remuneration of individual executive directors is determined in line with (within the boundaries of) the adopted remuneration policy. Pursuant to Article 2:135(4) DCC, the general meeting is also authorized to determine the remuneration of the individual, unless another competent body of the company is designated by the articles of association. This competent body must, however, always submit a proposal to the general meeting for approval with regard to remuneration schemes that include remuneration in the form of shares or options.[32]

[B] The (Introduction of the) Tabaksblat Code

The growing attention to corporate governance and the aforementioned accounting scandals also prompted the establishment of a new Corporate Governance Committee.[33] This committee, often referred to as the Tabaksblat Committee in reference to its chairman, published the Dutch Corporate Governance Code, also known as the Tabaksblat Code. This Code consisted of both principles and best practice provisions. Listed companies were required to state in the annual report how they had applied the principles. In addition, the 'comply or explain'-principle was applied in respect of the best practice provisions. Companies had to either include in their annual report the way they applied these provisions or explain why they did not or did not fully apply certain provisions.[34]

The Tabaksblat Code addressed both *pay governance* and *pay design*.[35] The Code, for instance, entailed a strong focus on disclosure requirements, which were, however, in line with the aforementioned legislation.[36] An important innovation was the

30. *The Act of 9 July 2004 amending Book 2 of the Civil Code in connection with amending the statutory two-tier regime*, Bulletin of Acts and Decrees 370 (2004).
31. Bulletin of Acts and Decrees 405 (2004).
32. Article 2:135(2) and (3) DCC. Following the entry into force of the 'Act of 30 June 2010 amending Book 2 of the Civil Code in connection with the introduction of a right for the works council of public companies to express an opinion on important management decisions and decisions to appoint, suspend and dismiss executive and supervisory directors as well as on the remuneration policy on 1 July 2010', Bulletin of Acts and Decrees 250 (2010), the concerned paragraphs are renumbered to paras 4 and 5.
33. The establishment of this new Corporate Governance Committee also responded to the lack of compliance with the 40 recommendations of the first Corporate Governance Committee in 1997 and the publication of the Winter Group report. Cf. The Corporate Governance Committee, *The Dutch corporate governance code. Principles of corporate governance and best practice provisions*, 66 (2003); *see also*, Asser/Maeijer/Van Solinge & Nieuwe Weme 2-II* 2009, no. 30, at 37.
34. To this end, on 31 December 2004 the Corporate Governance Code was designated by order in council with retroactive effect to 1 January 2004 as a code of conduct as referred to in Art. 2:391(5) DCC, thus giving the code a statutory basis. Decree of 23 December 2004 establishing further regulations regarding the content of the annual report, Law Gazette (747) 2004.
35. Raaijmakers & Overkleeft, *supra* n. 10, at 88.
36. It followed, from instance, from the second part of principle II.2 that schemes that reward executive board directors in shares or rights to take shares, and major changes to these schemes,

introduction of a remuneration report for listed companies.[37] This report, in which a listed company would represent its remuneration policy to be pursued in the coming financial year and subsequent years, as well as the manner in which the remuneration policy had been put into practice in the past year,[38] mainly had an accountability function, as it had to be placed on the company's website and the main points of the report were to be included in the supervisory board's report,[39] that was part of the annual accounts of the public company.[40]

In addition, the Code also addressed the role of the supervisory board with regard to remuneration policy. If the supervisory board consisted of more than four members, the supervisory board appointed a remuneration committee from among its members.[41] Besides preparing the aforementioned remuneration report, this remuneration committee was also assigned the task of making proposals for both the remuneration policy and individual remuneration for executive board members.[42] To fulfil this task properly, independence had to be guaranteed as much as possible. The Tabaksblat Code therefore contained some provisions in this respect.[43]

Lastly, the Code also included provisions on the level and structure of directors' remuneration. When determining the level and structure of remuneration, matters such as the development of results and share price, as well as other developments relevant to the company, had to play a role. If the remuneration consisted of both a fixed and a variable component, the latter had to be linked to predetermined, measurable and influenceable targets to be achieved partly in the short term and partly in the long term. The variable component also had to have the aim of binding directors to the company and its objective.[44] This is reflected, among other things, in the fact that options became available to the executive board member only after three years, provided the performance criteria were met.[45]

§13.04 THE LEGISLATIVE REFORMS ON THE EUROPEAN LEVEL IN RESPONSE TO THE FINANCIAL CRISIS

[A] Immediate Responses to the Emergence of the Financial Crisis at the European Level

The attention to executive remuneration sharply increased after the emergence of the financial crisis of 2007-2008'. Two themes were central to the subsequent public

had to be submitted to the general meeting for approval. Here, the committee was perhaps already anticipating the impending amendment to Art. 2:135 DCC.

37. Cf. Cornelis de Groot, *Bezoldiging van bestuurders van naamloze vennootschappen*, 14 Ondernemingsrecht, 466 (2005).
38. Best practice provision II.2.9.
39. Best practice provision II.2.13 and Principle II.2 respectively.
40. Best practice provision III.1.2.
41. Principle III.5.
42. Best practice provision II.5.10.
43. Best practice provision III.5.11.
44. Principle II.2, first part. Cf. Raaijmakers & Overkleeft *supra* n. 10, at 88.
45. Best practice provision II.2.1.

debate, namely: (i) the level of remuneration and (ii) the structure of remuneration policies in the financial sector.[46] Although the public debate did not show a sharp boundary between the two themes,[47] the High Level Group on Financial Supervision in the EU, also referred to as the Larosière Group after its chairman, argued in its report that policy-makers in Europe should focus primarily on the structure of remuneration policies, as the remuneration structures and the resulting perverse incentives were seen as a cause of the financial crisis.[48]

Although the financial crisis increased public attention to the regulation of remuneration structures in the financial sector, there were (more urgent) problems to solve at that time. The financial crisis threatened the survival of (in some cases, even fundamentally sound) banks, and Member States had to resort to state aid measures to ensure their continuity. These measures, however, should not unnecessarily distort competition between banks.[49] The EC therefore deemed it necessary to provide guidance with regard to these state aid measures through communications, in which it also addressed the remuneration policy of state-supported banks. The EC suggested, among other measures, that Member States should be empowered to intervene in the remuneration policies of these state-aided banks to prevent (executive) management from receiving undue benefits.[50] The EC further proposed a limitation of executive remuneration or bonus payments as long as the state aid would not be repaid.[51] Although these provisions were aimed at restoring the stability and functioning of financial markets without distorting competition, they also regulated the design of remuneration policies of state-supported financial institutions. Moreover, the entire financial sector seemed to embrace these provisions and consider them applicable.

---

46. The High Level Group on Financial Supervision in the EU, *Report*, Brussels, 25 February 2009, https://ec.europa.eu/economy_finance/publications/pages/publication14527_en.pdf, p. 30; *Cf.* Guido Ferrarini & Maria C. Ungureanu, *Executive Pay at Ailing Banks and Beyond: A European Perspective*, 5 Cap. Mkts. L. J. 197, 198 (2010).
47. Raaijmakers & Overkleeft, *supra* n. 10, at 87.
48. The High Level Group on Financial Supervision in the EU, *supra* n. 46, p. 30; *Commission Recommendation 2009/384/EC of 30 April 2009 on remuneration policies in the financial services sector*, preamble point 2, OJ EU L 120/22 (2009).
49. European Commission, *Communication from the Commission – The application of State aid rules to measures taken in relation to financial institutions in the context of the current global financial crisis*, preamble point 5, OJ EU C 270/8 (2008); *see also*, Guido Ferrarini & Maria C. Ungureanu, *Economics, Politics, and the International Principles for Sound Compensation Practices: An Analysis of Executive Pay at European Banks*, 64 Vand. L. Rev. 431, 456 (2011).
50. European Commission, *supra* n. 49, at 8.
51. European Commission, *Communication from the Commission – The recapitalisation of financial institutions in the current financial crisis: limitation of aid to the minimum necessary and safeguards against undue distortions of competition*, 9, OJ EU C 10/2 (2009); European Commission, *Communication from the Commission on the treatment of impaired assets in the Community banking sector*, OJ EU C 72/1 (2009); *see also*, Ferrarini & Ungureanu, *supra* n. 49, at 456-457.

[B] The Introduction of (International) Principles and Guidelines

At the same time, a global debate on reforming remuneration policies in the financial sector emerged. Although the EU was considered the major initiator,[52] the G20 became the appropriate forum[53] to reach a global political consensus on proposals to drastically change the global financial landscape.[54] A global political consensus on the necessity for global standards for remuneration structures led to the FSF Principles for Sound Compensation Practices[55] (FSF Principles), which were drafted by the Financial Stability Forum (FSF). These six principles were broadly formulated and addressed, among other things, the governance of remuneration policies and the relationship between remuneration policies and risk management. On 25 September 2009, the Financial Stability Board (FSB)[56] published the FSB Principles for Sound Compensation Practices - Implementation Standards.[57] These standards contained specific proposals on both pay governance and pay design.

Although the aforementioned principles and standards were the result of an international regulatory response, they reflected 'regulatory thinking that already commanded significant support' of a broadly united Europe[58] and a European response to the problems associated with the design of executive remuneration followed suit with the issuing of two non-binding Recommendations on 30 April 2009, namely Recommendation 2009/384/EC on remuneration policies in the financial sector (hereinafter 'the 2009 Financial Sector Recommendation')[59] and Recommendation 2009/385/EC on the regime for the remuneration of directors of listed companies (hereinafter 'the 2009 Listing Companies Recommendation').[60] Both recommendations were, in line with the FSF Principles, a deliberate break with the past, as the 2009 Financial Sector Recommendation held provisions on the structure of variable compensation,[61] the deferral of variable remuneration[62] and the performance assessment[63]

52. European Commission, *Communication to the Spring European Council. Towards European recovery. Part 1*, at 19.
53. Eilís Ferran, *New Regulation of Remuneration in the Financial Sector in the EU*, 9 Eur. Co. & Fin. L. Rev. 1, 9 (2012).
54. Emmanuel C.H.J. Lokin, *Voorop lopen in de internationale discussie: de Code Banken na Pittsburgh*, 4 Ondernemingsrecht, 186 (2010).
55. Financial Stability Forum, *FSF Principles for Sound Compensation Practices*, 2 April 2009, http://www.financialstabilityboard.org/publications/r_0904b.pdf.
56. The Financial Stability Board is the successor to the Financial Stability Forum and created following the G20 meeting in London. Lokin, *supra* n. 54, at 186.
57. Financial Stability Board, *FSB Principles for Sound Compensation Practices: Implementation Standards*, 25 September 2009, http://www.financialstabilityboard.org/publications/r_090925c.pdf.
58. Ferran 2012, *supra* n. 53, p. 12.
59. European Commission, *Commission Recommendation 2009/384/EC of 30 April 2009 on remuneration policies in the financial services sector*, OJ EU L 120/22 (2009).
60. European Commission, *Commission Recommendation 2009/385/EC of 30 April 2009 complementing Recommendations 2004/913/EC and 2005/162/EC as regards the regime for the remuneration of directors of listed companies*, OJ L 120/28 (2009).
61. Article 4(1) of the 2009 Financial Sector Recommendation.
62. Articles 4(3) and 4(4) of the 2009 Financial Sector Recommendation.
63. Articles 5(1) to 5(4) of the 2009 Financial Sector Recommendation.

and the 2009 Listing Companies Recommendation entailed, among others, provisions on the structure of variable compensation[64] and on the vesting of share-based remuneration.[65]

The European regulatory approach became thus predominantly focused on pay design, next to pay governance. However, as these recommendations were not binding, Member States could opt to implement them either through company law reforms or through corporate governance codes. Consequently, most Member States opted to incorporate the recommendations in forms of self-regulation over strict legislative measures.

§13.05 LEGISLATIVE RESPONSES TO THE FINANCIAL CRISIS IN THE NETHERLANDS

[A] A Revised Dutch Corporate Governance Code

The financial crisis also led to increased attention to the remuneration policies in the Dutch financial sector. The first response came in the form of an updated Corporate Governance Code (which was also named the Frijns Code after the chairman of the committee that published the Code) in which executive remuneration took a more prominent position.[66] Although the Corporate Governance Code Monitoring Committee (hereinafter 'the Frijns Committee') had already presented a draft revised corporate governance code, the Frijns Committee amended this presented draft to incorporate new principles and best practice provisions in order to reflect the developments following the financial crisis.

In the Code Frijns, the focus was shifted from pay governance to pay design, as remuneration structures that were inconsistent with sound risk management might have contributed to the financial crisis.[67] The Frijns Committee previously considered that this structure should also be subject to 'objective ceilings'[68] but eventually came up with a number of concrete benchmarks against which both the structure and the level of remuneration should be determined. For instance, the first part of Principle II.2 stipulated that the variable component of the remuneration should be appropriate in relation to the fixed component of the remuneration. This was intended to ensure that a supervisory board would critically scrutinize the total remuneration and this, in turn, would have a dampening effect on the granting of remuneration that would consist predominantly of variable components.[69] Furthermore, following the same principle, variable remuneration should be linked to targets that were predominantly long-term

64. Articles 3(1) to 3(5) of the 2009 Listing Companies Recommendation.
65. Articles 4(1) to 4(4) of the 2009 Listing Companies Recommendation.
66. Raaijmakers & Overkleeft *supra* n. 10, at 89.
67. Corporate Governance Code Monitoring Committee, *Dutch corporate governance code. Principles of good corporate governance and best practice provisions*, 10 December 2008, https://www.mccg.nl/publicaties/codes/2008/12/1/corporate-governance-code-2008-en, pp. 50, 53; Raaijmakers & Overkleeft *supra* n. 10, at 89.
68. Raaijmakers & Overkleeft *supra* n. 10, at 89.
69. Cf. Raaijmakers & Overkleeft *supra* n. 10, at 90.

in nature. It was also added that the remuneration structure should not encourage risk-taking that does not fit within the adopted strategy.[70] In addition, the Code Frijns introduced some requirements and powers for the supervisory board. Among other things, the Code introduced a *clawback* mechanism that would enable the supervisory board to *clawback* variable remuneration that had been granted to an executive director on the basis of incorrect financial information.

[B] The Introduction of the Dutch Banking Code

The financial sector itself also took action after the onset of the financial crisis. The starting signal for this was the so-called gentlemen's agreement, concluded on 30 March between the Dutch Minister of Finance and the financial sector. In this agreement, the sector committed itself to a 'sustainable and moderate' remuneration policy that would not encourage irresponsible risk-taking and a disproportionate focus on short-term gains and shareholder value.[71]

Following (the onset of) the financial crisis and the share leasing and usurious policy scandals (*woekerpolis-affaires*), (consumer) confidence in banks had suffered a formidable blow with the result that it took more than the concluded gentlemen's agreement to regain this confidence. For this reason, the sector itself came up with some initiatives, including the establishment of an advisory committee on the future of banks in November 2008 by the Dutch Banking Association (NVB).[72] The advisory committee, which was also named the Maas Committee after its chairman, was tasked with making recommendations to improve the functioning of Dutch banks in order to restore the trust in these banks.[73] In its report[74] that was released on 7 April 2009, the Maas Committee also made some recommendations regarding remuneration policy. Among other things, the Maas Committee advocated that the total income of bank executives should be in reasonable proportion to the remuneration structure within the bank.[75] The Maas Committee also made the noteworthy recommendation to cap the total variable remuneration at a maximum of 100% of the fixed remuneration.[76]

These recommendations were incorporated in the – so-called – Banking Code that was drafted by the NVB.[77] This Code, after its entry into force on 1 January 2010, applied to all banks holding a banking licence granted under the Dutch Financial Supervision Act (DFSA)[78] and contained principles with respect to which banks are

70. Principle II.2, first part. Cf. Raaijmakers & Overkleeft *supra* n. 10, at 90.
71. *Parliamentary Papers II* 2008/09, 31 371, no. 154, at 2.
72. This committee is also known as the Maas Committee, named after its chairman.
73. Adviescommissie Toekomst Banken, *Naar herstel van vertrouwen*, 7 April 2009, at 7, https://www.nvb.nl/media/1668/000603_000593-rapport-adviescommissie-toekomst-banken-def.pdf.
74. Adviescommissie Toekomst Banken, *supra* n. 73.
75. Recommendation 2.1; *see also*, Adviescommissie Toekomst Banken, *supra* n. 73, at 22.
76. Recommendation 2.11; *see also*, Adviescommissie Toekomst Banken, *supra* n. 73, at 24. The 100% cap was to apply only to larger banks with a sizeable international business, as well as smaller banks with relatively low fixed income.
77. NVB, *Banking Code*, 9 September 2010, at recital 1, https://www.nvb.nl/media/1656/000596_code-banken-2010.pdf.
78. NVB, *supra* n. 77, at recital 2.

subject to the 'comply or explain'-principle. Banks to which the Code applied had to either include in their annual report how they apply the principles or explain why they have not fully applied certain principles.[79]

With regard to remuneration policy, the Code stated that the remuneration policy to be pursued shall be prudent, sound and sustainable in line with its strategy and risk appetite, objectives and values. It should also take into account the long-term interests of the bank, the relevant international context and public support. The aforementioned principle therefore served as a guideline for the supervisory board and the executive board when performing their tasks in relation to remuneration policy.[80] In addition to some principles regarding the governance of the remuneration policy, the Code also contained a number of pay design principles, such as the principle that each bank should set a maximum ratio of variable component of the remuneration to the fixed component as the bank deemed appropriate. However, the variable component should not exceed 100% of fixed component of the remuneration.

[C] The introduction of Principles for a Sound Remuneration Policy

The Dutch financial regulators, the Dutch Central Bank (DNB) and the Netherlands Authority for the Financial Markets (AFM), also got involved in the public debate on remuneration policies within the financial sector and published their Principles for Sound Remuneration Policies in the Financial Sector on 6 May 2009.[81] These principles, which follow the FSF Principles,[82] provided guidance as to how regulators would approach the subject of executive remuneration in anticipation of a codification of the principles in law and regulations.[83] The principles could also provide guidance to financial undertakings for a critical assessment of their (current) remuneration policies.[84] It was expected that financial undertaking would act not by the letter but by the spirit of the principles.[85] The principles addressed three issues, namely: (i) the principles to be used for the remuneration policy, (ii) the governance of remuneration policy, and (iii) the design of the variable remuneration structure.

79. NVB, *supra* n. 77, preamble point 5. To this end, on 1 June 2010, the Banking Code was designated by Order in Council with retroactive effect to 1 January 2010 as a code of conduct as referred to in Art. 2:391(5) DCC, thus giving the code a statutory basis. *See, Decree of 1 June 2010 establishing further regulations regarding the content of the annual report of banks*, Bulletin of Acts and Decrees 215 (2010). Please note that the decree requiring Dutch banks to report on their compliance with the (old) Banking Code in their annual reports has been repealed as from 1 January 2016. As from that date, only the reporting requirements set out in the new Banking Code, which replaced the old Banking Code on 1 January 2015, will apply.
80. NVB, *supra* n. 77, Principle 6.1.1; cf. Dave H. Cross, *Beloningen in de financiële wereld; effecten van de financiële crisis, in En na de crisis? – Nederlands Genootschap van Bedrijfsjuristen 1930-2010* 115 (Theo J.G.C. Raaijmakers et al. eds, 2010).
81. AFM & DNB, *Principes voor beheerst beloningsbeleid*, May 2009; *see also, Parliamentary Papers II* 2008/09, 31 371, no 215.
82. E.L.M. van Kranenburg, *Ontwikkelingen in het beheerst beloningsbeleid*, 11-12 Tijdschrift voor Financieel recht 407, 412 (2009); Cross, *supra* n. 80, at 118.
83. AFM & DNB, *supra* n. 81, at 3.
84. Van Kranenburg, *supra* n. 82, at 412.
85. AFM & DNB, *supra* n. 81, at 4.

The principles on the latter two topics were further elaborated by DNB in so-called best practice provisions.[86] In the first topic, DNB stated that companies with remuneration structures where the variable component constituted the largest part of the remuneration should have a strong governance structure.[87] This should entail, according to DNB, that, among others, the supervisory board understands and is involved in those aspects of the remuneration policy that have an impact on risk management.[88] Regarding the design of the variable remuneration structure, DNB stipulated, among other things, that the allocation of variable remuneration should take into account financial risks and that there should be an appropriate ratio between fixed salary and variable remuneration. This had the effect of setting a prudent cap on variable remuneration to be awarded within each company.[89] DNB, however, stated that these best practice provisions only provide guidance for the implementation of a remuneration policy in line with the principles, but adherence to these best practice provisions does not automatically lead to remuneration policies that meet the requirements of the principles.[90] Ultimately, the DNB itself would test whether a sound remuneration policy was in place.

§13.06 THE INTRODUCTION OF HARD RULES ON EXECUTIVE REMUNERATION ON THE EUROPEAN LEVEL: CRD III

The 2009 Recommendations were, as previously mentioned, considered the first regulatory European response to the financial crisis, but after EC reports[91] showed that the application of recommendations by the Member States was neither uniform nor satisfactory,[92] the EC decided that the time was right to issue rules on executive remuneration in the financial sector through a directive. The Commission issued these rules by including them in the revised Capital Requirements Directive (CRD III) that was published on 24 November 2010.[93] CRD III also required the Committee of European Banking Supervisors (CEBS) to issue guidelines on sound remuneration

86. DNB, *Naar een beheerst beloningsbeleid. Rapportage van het onderzoek naar de beloningsituatie bij Nederlandse financiële ondernemingen*, September 2009; *see also*, *Parliamentary Papers II* 2008/09, 31 371, no. 254.
87. DNB, *supra* n. 86, at 5; cf. Van Kranenburg, *supra* n. 82, at 414.
88. DNB, *supra* n. 86, at 5; cf. Van Kranenburg, *supra* n. 82, at 414.
89. DNB, *supra* n. 86, at 5.
90. DNB, *supra* n. 86, at 12; cf. Van Kranenburg, *supra* n. 82, at 414.
91. European Commission, *Report from the Commission to the European Parliament, the Council, the European Economic and Social Committee, and the Committee of the Regions on the Application by the Member States of the EU of the Commission 2009/384/EC Recommendation on Remuneration Policies in the Financial Sector*, COM(2010) 286 final; European Commission, *Report from the Commission to the European Parliament, the Council, the European Economic and Social Committee, and the Committee of the Regions on the Application by the Member States of the EU of the Commission 2009/384/EC Recommendation*, COM(2010) 285 final.
92. Cf. Ferrarini & Ungureanu, *supra* n. 49, at 477.
93. *Directive 2010/76/EU of the European Parliament and of the Council of 24 November 2010 amending Directives 2006/48/EC and 2006/49/EC as regards capital requirements for the trading book and for re-securitisations, and the supervisory review of remuneration policies*, OJ EU L 329/3 (2010).

policies in order to 'promote supervisory convergences in the assessment of remuneration policies and practices'.[94] On 10 December 2010, CEBS issued its Guidelines on Remuneration Policies and Practices, which were aimed at providing convergence with regard to the implementation of the remuneration principles in national legislation. Although CRD III is applicable to credit institutions and certain investment firms, I will refer to these institutions as banks hereinafter.

CRD III is in particular focused on pay design, as the third recital already stated that 'in order to address the potentially detrimental effect of poorly designed remuneration structures on the sound management of risk and control of risk-taking behaviour by individuals, ... [risk management arrangements, strategies, processes and mechanisms; TCAD] should be supplemented by an express obligation for credit institutions and investment firms to establish and maintain, for categories of staff whose professional activities have a material impact on their risk profile, remuneration policies and practices that are consistent with effective risk management'.[95] The provisions of CRD III, therefore, did not only apply to the (non-)executive directors but also to so-called *identified staff*. This identified staff entails senior management, risk takers, staff engaged in control functions and any employee receiving an amount of total remuneration that takes them into the same remuneration bracket as senior management and risk takers, whose professional activities have a material impact on the risk profile of the bank.[96]

CRD III entailed, among others, specific rules on the structure of remuneration packages that follow the previously mentioned FSF Principles and the FSB Implementation Standards. In order to align the incentives of individual staff members with the long-term interests of the financial institution, a substantial portion of at least 50% of the variable remuneration should consist of shares or share-linked instruments or equivalent non-cash instruments, in case the bank is not listed. It should also be possible to include contingent capital, i.e., a capital instrument that is converted into equity or otherwise written down when the institution is subject to severe financial problems.[97] Banks are also required to set appropriate ratios between the fixed and the variable components of the total remuneration.[98] Moreover, a substantial portion of at least 40% to 60% of this variable remuneration should be deferred over an appropriate period of time of at least three to five years.[99] CRD III, however, also contained

94. Committee of European Banking Supervisors, *Guidelines on Remuneration Policies and Practices*, 10 December 2010, at 7.
95. CRD III, recital 3; CRD Annex I, s. 11, para. 23 (a).
96. Jaap Winter, *The Financial Crisis: Does Good Corporate Governance Matter and How to Achieve It, in Financial Regulation and Supervision: A Post-crisis Analysis* 383 (Eddy Wymeersch, Klaus J. Hopt & Guido Ferrarini eds, 2012). The term 'identified staff' has been codified in Art. 92(2) of *Directive 2013/36/EU of the European Parliament and of the Council of 26 June 2013 on access to the activity of credit institutions and the prudential supervision of credit institutions and investment firms, amending Directive 2002/87/EC and repealing Directives 2006/48/EC and 2006/49/EC*, O.J. EU L 176/338 (2013) (hereinafter: CRD IV).
97. CRD III, recital 7; CRD Annex I, s. 11, para. 23 (o) (ii).
98. CRD Annex I, s. 11, para. 23 (l).
99. The portion to be deferred should increase with the level of seniority or responsibility of the person remunerated: CRD III, recital 9; CRD Annex I, s. 11, para. 23 (p).

provisions on (the strengthening of pay governance) as it, for instance, required significant banks to establish a remuneration committee.[100]

As follows from the above, the CRD III signalled a deliberate break with the past regulatory approach on the European level. Although CRD III encompasses provisions concerning pay governance, the measures provided for by the directive are primarily focused on pay design structures, in particular in relation to the variable part of remuneration. Furthermore, the directive did apply to a wider range of employees of banks than only the (non-)executive directors. Most important, however, is that with the introduction of CRD III, the European regulatory approach regarding banks' executive remuneration consisted of hard rules instead of soft law. Member states were, therefore, obliged to implement the measures through company law reforms.

[A] The Implementation of CRD III in Dutch Laws and Regulations

CRD III was implemented in the Dutch regulatory framework less than a week after the CEBS Guidelines were published.[101] First of all, the Minister of Finance published the Decree on Restrained Remuneration Policy in the Financial Supervision Act on 14 December 2010 in order to implement the CRD III provisions.[102] This decree enabled DNB to draft regulations on remuneration policy in the financial sector. After the introduction of the decree, DNB issued the Regulation for a Sound Remuneration Policy in the Financial Supervision Act 2011 (Rbb 2011) on 16 December 2010.[103] The decree and the regulation both entered into force on 1 January 2011. It was notable that the scope of Rbb 2011 was wider than CRD III as insurers, premium pension institutions and clearing institutions were also covered by it.[104]

The aforementioned provisions from CRD III were implemented in the Rbb 2011. For instance, Article 18 Rbb 2011 stipulated that a substantial part, and in any event at least 50% of any variable remuneration, had to consist of a balanced mix of shares or related instruments (contingent capital) that properly reflect a bank's credit quality. Furthermore, Article 19 Rbb 2011 provided that a substantial part, and in any case, at least 40% of variable remuneration, shall be deferred over a period of three to five years appropriate to the nature of the business, its risks and the activities of the employee concerned. If the variable remuneration awarded is a particularly high amount,[105] this percentage was increased to 60%.

---

100. CRD Annex I, s. 11, para. 24.
101. Floris C.A. van de Bult, *Beloningen in de financiële Sector: Never Waste a Good Crisis*, in: *Onderneming en beloning* 235 (Corjo J.H Jansen & Leonard G. Verburg eds, 2014), at 238.
102. *Decree of 19 November 2010, amending the Decree on Prudential Rules DFSA and the Decree on Conduct of Business Supervision of Financial Undertakings DFSA* (Decree on Restrained Remuneration Policy DFSA), Bulletin of Acts and Decrees 806 (2010).
103. *DNB Regulation of 16 December 2010, containing rules on the sound remuneration policy of financial undertakings (Regulation on controlled remuneration policy DFSA 2011)*, Government Gazette 20931 (2010). This regulation should be read in conjunction with the CEBS Guidelines.
104. Article 1 Rbb 2011; *see also*, Astrid M. Helstone, *Financieel toezicht op beloningen*, 2 Tijdschrift voor Arbeid & Onderneming 63, 66 (2012); van de Bult, *supra* n. 101, at 240.
105. Both the Rbb 2011 and the CEBS Guidelines do not specify the term 'particularly high amount'.

The introduction of CRD III can be characterized as an important turning point in the approach to remuneration issues, as the legislator on the European level moved from an approach through recommendations and self-regulatory instruments to a strict regulatory framework.[106] This is particularly true for variable remuneration. The directive and the corresponding regulation impose strict requirements on the design of (variable) remuneration by, among other things, setting requirements on the form and retention periods. As a result thereof, the national legislators also had to introduce a new regulatory regime based on hard rules instead of soft law.

§13.07 CRD IV AND THE DUTCH ACT ON THE REMUNERATION OF FINANCIAL UNDERTAKINGS

After the introduction of CRD III, the EC and the European Council were of the opinion that the European executive remuneration framework was robust enough to cope with the remuneration issues in the financial sector. The European Parliament took, however, a different view, as it considered the introduction of a bonus cap as the only measure that would be able to curb excessive risky behaviour in the banking sector.[107] This bonus cap was eventually included in CRD IV,[108] but only after tough negotiations.

As said, CRD IV predominantly introduced, among some other provisions on remuneration, a bonus cap that would cap the ratio of variable to fixed remuneration for identified staff in Article 94 CRD IV. This article provides, under paragraph 1(g)(i) CRD IV, that the variable component of remuneration shall not exceed 100% of the fixed component of total remuneration. Under paragraph 1(g)(ii) CRD IV, shareholders, owners or partners of the financial institution are allowed to grant variable remuneration exceeding 100% but not exceeding 200%. Moreover, in the case of increasing the bonus ceiling to 200% of fixed remuneration, some special requirements must be met. These requirements, which are set out in Article 94(1)(g)(ii) CRD IV, imply, among others, that the shareholders, owners or associates must act on the basis of a detailed recommendation from the bank in which the latter explains the rationale for and scope of the requested approval. This provision also stipulates that the shareholders, owners or associates of the financial undertaking may agree to such an increase only if they decide by a majority of at least 66%, provided that at least 55% of

106. Cf. Helstone, *supra* n. 104, at 65; Hein W.P. Van den Hout, *Handhavingskader beheerst beloningsbeleid en de positie van bestuurders en commissarissen bij financiële ondernemingen*, 2 Tijdschrift voor Arbeid & Onderneming 50, 50-51 (2013); Van de Bult, *supra* note 101, at 239.

107. European Parliament, 'MEPs cap bankers' bonuses and step up bank capital requirements', https://www.europarl.europa.eu/news/en/press-room/20130225IPR06048/meps-cap-bankers-bonuses-and-step-up-bank-capital-requirements.

108. *Directive 2013/36/EU of the European Parliament and of the Council of 26 June 2013 on the access to the activity of credit institutions and the prudential supervision of credit institutions and investment firms, amending Directive 2002/87/EC and repealing Directives 2006/48/EC and 2006/49/EC*, OJ EU L 176/338 (2013).

the ownership rights are represented. If this percentage is less than 55%, consent must be given by a majority of 75% of the property rights represented.[109]

Both provisions, Article 94(1)(g)(i) and (ii) CRD IV, allow Member States to reduce the bonus cap. Incidentally, Article 94(1)(g)(iii) CRD IV provides another option for increasing variable remuneration. This provision allows up to 25% of variable remuneration to be disregarded when calculating the bonus cap if this specific remuneration is paid entirely in the form of instruments whose payment is deferred for at least five years.[110] Again, Member States have the option to reduce this maximum percentage.

[A] The Implementation of CRD IV in the Netherlands

The bonus cap and the other provisions from CRD IV have been implemented in the Netherlands in the Capital Requirements Directive and Regulation (Implementation) Act,[111] which entered into force on 1 August 2014.[112] The bonus cap was implemented in section 317a DFSA, while the other provisions were included in a (renewed) regulation on sound remuneration policies, namely the Regulation on Sound Remuneration Policies DFSA 2014 (Rbb 2014), that also entered into force on 1 August 2014.[113] The bonus cap provision in the Capital Requirements Directive and Regulation (Implementation) Act would, however, have been short-lived, as it soon became clear that the Dutch government opted for a reduced bonus cap,[114] as it was already announced in its so-called coalition agreement.[115] This reduced bonus cap was eventually introduced in the Act on the Remuneration of Financial Undertakings,[116] that entered into force on 1 January 2016.[117]

Following Article 1:121(1) DFSA, the variable remuneration awarded by a Dutch financial undertaking to a natural person working under its responsibility shall not

109. Cf. Van de Bult, *supra* note 101, at 248.
110. *See also*, Van de Bult, *supra* note 101, at 249.
111. *Act of 25 June 2014 amending the Financial Supervision Act and some other laws to implement Directive 2013/36/EU of the European Parliament and of the Council of 26 June 2013 on the access to the activity of credit institutions and the prudential supervision of credit institutions and investment firms, amending Directive 2002/87/EC and repealing Directives 2006/48/EC and 2006/49/EC*, OJ EU L 176 (2013) and to implement *Regulation (EU) no. 575/2013 of the European Parliament and of the Council of 26 June 2013 on prudential requirements for credit institutions and investment firms and amending Regulation (EU) No 648/2012*, OJ EU L 176 (2013), Bulletin of Acts and Decrees 253 (2014).
112. With the exception of Art. VIII, which would enter into force on 1 January 2015. *See*, *Decree of 15 July 2014 determining the time of entry into force of the Capital Requirements Directive and Regulation Implementation Act and the Capital Requirements Directive and Regulation Implementation Decree*, Bulletin of Acts and Decrees 304 (2014).
113. *Regulation of the Nederlandsche Bank N.V. of 21 July 2014 on rules regarding the controlled remuneration policy of financial enterprises*, Government Gazette 21933 (2014).
114. *See*, Minister Dijsselbloem's parliamentary letter dated 22 April (reference FM/2013/774 M), at 7.
115. *Parliamentary Papers II* 2012/13, 33 410, no. 15, at 14.
116. *Act of 28 January 2015 amending the Financial Supervision Act containing rules regarding the remuneration policy of financial undertakings*, Bulletin of Acts and Decrees 45 (2015).
117. Bulletin of Acts and Decrees 46 (2015).

exceed 20% of the fixed remuneration of that person on an annual basis. Consequently, the bonus cap is not only limited to the employees of the financial undertaking, but it also includes natural persons that perform any activity for the financial undertaking on the basis of a services agreement or secondment.[118] Article 1:121(2) DFSA, however, provides for some exceptions to this provision. For instance, an exception is made in respect of persons working within the Netherlands who have agreed to remuneration arrangements that partly or completely deviate from an applicable collective labour agreement. A bonus cap of 20% on average applies to this entire category. This exception provides the financial undertaking some room for manoeuvre if it would want to reward persons within the aforementioned category more generously as long as the average over the entire group does not exceed 20%. A distinction is also made with regard to where individuals perform their work. For example, if a person mainly works in a Member State within the European Economic Area (EEA), the financial undertaking can grant a higher maximum variable remuneration of 100% of the fixed remuneration in line with CRD IV.[119]

Another legislative development on the subject of variable remuneration was the entry into force of the Act amending Book 2 DCC and the DFSA in connection with the power to adjust and clawback bonuses and profit-sharing of directors and day-to-day policymakers[120] on 1 January 2014.[121] Following the introduction of this act, a public company (or the corporate body that has determined the variable remuneration) has the ability to adjust and *clawback* variable remuneration under Articles 2:135(6) and (8) DCC, whose powers also apply to all day-to-day policymakers.[122] These measures were further extended in relation to financial undertakings in the Dutch Act on the Remuneration of Financial Undertakings, as the *clawback mechanism* applies to all natural persons working under the responsibility of the financial undertaking.[123] Also, in line with CRD IV, Article 1:127, DFSA[124] stipulates when the power of adjustment and recovery should be used in any case. This is the case when: (i) the person has failed to meet appropriate standards of competence and proper conduct,[125] or (ii) the person was responsible for conduct that led to the position of the company being significantly worsened.

Moreover, the act introduced additional requirements for financial undertakings. For example, if the financial undertaking is required to prepare an annual report, it must present its remuneration policy in its annual report. In addition, the company

118. Cf. Charlotte Koolstra & Willemijn Pieters, *More Stringent Remuneration Rules for Financial Entities in the Netherlands*, Butterworths Journal of International Banking and Financial Law, 203 (2023).
119. Article 1:121(3) DFSA.
120. *Parliamentary Papers I* 2012/13, 32 512, A; *Stb.* 2013, 563.
121. *Stb.* 2013, 589.
122. Articles 1:111(1) and (2) DFSA.
123. Article 1:126(2) DFSA.
124. Article 94(1)(n) CRD IV.
125. The standards referred to are fundamental principles that any person working under the responsibility of a financial undertaking can reasonably be expected to observe, such as the principles contained in the statutory moral and ethical declaration, internal codes of conduct and relevant laws and regulations, *Parliamentary Papers II* 2013/14, 33 964, no. 3, at 43.

must, among other things, be transparent as to the number of persons who may be entitled to variable remuneration and as to the number of persons earning in total more than one million euros annually.

§13.08 MORE RECENT REGULATORY DEVELOPMENTS: SRD II AND THE DUTCH ACT ON FURTHER REMUNERATION MEASURES FOR FINANCIAL UNDERTAKINGS

[A] The Revised Shareholders' Rights Directive (SRD II)

Following the introduction of CRD IV, it could be said that the shareholders' influence on the executive remuneration policy of financial undertakings seems to be waning due to the introduction of binding regulations regarding the design and level of remuneration. At the same time, however, there was a growing attention to the shareholders' position in the determination and implementation of remuneration policy on the European level. This attention stemmed mainly from the European Commission's ambition to increase shareholder involvement in listed companies. The lack of this involvement, in addition to a lack of adequate transparency within these listed companies, was seen by the EC as a cause of shortcomings in the corporate governance of European listed companies.[126]

The EC already recognized the importance of sufficient shareholder engagement within this framework in 2010, in the Communication 'Europe 2020'.[127] This was therefore followed in 2012 by an action plan[128] to, among other things, increase this engagement in order to strengthen the corporate governance of European listed companies. In this action plan, the EC announced that it would revise the directive on the exercise of certain rights of shareholders (the Shareholders' Directive)[129] to increase shareholder engagement. Through this revision, the Commission also hoped to contribute 'to the long-term sustainability of EU companies, create an attractive environment for shareholders ..., thus contributing to growth, jobs and greater EU competitiveness'.[130] This led to the publication of a proposal to revise the Shareholders' Rights Directive on 9 April 2014, which was initially submitted to Member States for

126. European Commission, *Proposal for a Directive of the European Parliament and of the Council amending Directive 2007/36/EC as regards the promotion of long-term shareholder engagement and Directive 2014 2013/34/EU as regards certain elements of the corporate governance statement*, COM(2014) 213 final, at 2.
127. The European Commission, *Communication from the Commission – Europe 2020. A strategy for smart, sustainable and inclusive growth*, COM(2010) 2020 final.
128. The European Commission, *Communication from the Commission to the European Parliament, the Council, the European Economic and Social Committee and the Committee of the Regions. Action Plan: European company law and corporate governance - a modern legal framework for more engaged shareholders and more sustainable businesses*, COM(2012) 740 final.
129. *Directive 2007/36/EC of the European Parliament and of the Council of 11 July 2007 on the exercise of certain rights of shareholders in listed companies*, OJ EU L 184/17 (2007).
130. European Commission, *supra* n. 126, at 2.

consultation until 18 May 2014. Finally, the Revised Shareholders' Rights Directive (SRD II) was published on 17 May 2017.[131]

SRD II entails specific pay governance provisions, as remuneration is considered 'one of the key instruments for companies to align their interests and those of their directors'. Therefore, and 'in view of the crucial role of executive directors in such companies', it is considered important that: (i) the remuneration policies of companies are determined in an appropriate manner by competent bodies within the company, and (ii) shareholders have the possibility to express their views regarding the remuneration policy of the company.[132] In order to ensure that shareholders have an effective '*say on pay*', shareholders should, among others, not only be granted the right to hold a binding or advisory vote on the remuneration policy,[133] but companies should enclose the individual remuneration of executive directors in their remuneration reports in order to enhance transparency and accountability.[134]

In order to obtain these objectives, SRD II provides for a binding (or advisory) vote for the general meeting on the company's remuneration policy.[135] In addition, the directive also requires that listed companies have a clear and understandable remuneration policy that is in line with the 'company's business strategy, long-term interests and sustainability. Moreover, this remuneration policy should be clear and understandable, describe the different components of fixed and variable remuneration, including all bonuses and other benefits in whatever form which can be awarded to directors and indicate their relative proportion. The remuneration policy must also explain how the pay and employment conditions of employees of the company were taken into account when establishing the remuneration policy.[136] Companies are required to submit their remuneration policy to a vote by the general meeting at every material change and in any case at least every four years.[137] If the general meeting does not approve the proposed new policy, the company shall continue to pay remuneration to its directors in accordance with the existing approved policy and shall submit a revised policy for approval at the following general meeting.[138]

Furthermore, SRD II requires listed companies to draw up a clear and understandable remuneration report, providing a comprehensive overview of the remuneration, including all benefits in whatever form, awarded or due during the most recent financial year to individual directors, including to newly recruited and to former

131. *Directive (EU) 2017/828 of the European Parliament and of the Council of 17 May 2017 amending Directive 2007/36/EC as regards the encouragement of long-term shareholder engagement*, OJ EU L 132/1 (2017).
132. SRD II, recital 28.
133. SRD II, recital 28.
134. SRD II, recital 33.
135. Articles 9a(1), 9a(2) and 9a(3) SRD II respectively.
136. Article 9a(6) SRD II.
137. Article 9a(5) SRD II. SRD II also requires, following Art. 9a(2) that if a company does not have a remuneration and the general meeting does not approve the proposed policy, the company may continue to pay remuneration to its directors in accordance with its existing practices and shall submit a revised policy for approval at the following general meeting.
138. Article 9a(2) SRD II.

directors, in accordance with the (approved) remuneration policy.[139] In this way, the disclosed information should become clear, comprehensive and comparable, allowing shareholders to better understand the relationship between remuneration and performance. Companies are required to submit their remuneration report to a vote by the general meeting every year. The company shall explain in the following remuneration report how the vote by the general meeting has been taken into account.[140]

[B] Implementation of SRD II on the National Level

SRD II has been implemented in the Netherlands in the revised Dutch Shareholders' Directive II Implementation Act,[141] that entered into force on 1 December 2019.[142] Under Dutch law, as discussed in §13.03, the general meeting is authorized to adopt the remuneration policy. The remuneration of individual executive directors is determined in line with the adopted remuneration policy. Pursuant to Article 2:135(4) DCC, the general meeting is also authorized to determine the remuneration of the individual, unless another competent body of the company is designated by the articles of association.[143] Following the above, the effect of SRD II on the pay governance of Dutch-listed companies is, therefore, somewhat limited.

An important difference is, however, that the remuneration policy of a Dutch-listed company must be approved at least every four years by the general meeting for which at least 75% of the votes need to be cast in favour of the policy, unless the articles of association of the company provide for a lower percentage.[144] If the proposed policy is not approved, the remuneration of the (non-)executive directors[145] must be in line with the existing remuneration policy (or practice). The company is then also required to submit a revised remuneration policy to a vote during the next general meeting.

Furthermore, Articles 2:135a and 2:135(b) DCC contain a list of subjects that must be reflected in the remuneration policy and remuneration report, respectively, both for the executive directors as well as the non-executive directors.[146] The remuneration policy should, for instance, reflect the way that the remuneration policy contributes to the company strategy, the long-term interests and the sustainability of the company, and this policy takes into account the identity, mission and values of the company, pay ratios within the company and the societal support (*maatschappelijk*

139. Article 9b(1) SRD II.
140. Article 9b(4) SRD II.
141. *Act of 6 November 2019 amending Book 2 of the Civil Code, the Financial Supervision Act and the Securities Giro Act to implement Directive 2017/828/EU of the European Parliament and the Council of 17 May 2017 amending Directive 2007/36/EC as regards the promotion of the long-term engagement of shareholders*, OJ EU L 132 (2017), Bulletin of Acts and Decrees 423 (2019).
142. Bulletin of Acts and Decrees 436 (2019).
143. Cf. Thomas W.J. Hoeben & Floris C.A. van de Bult, *De Aandeelhoudersrichtlijn en beloningen van bestuurders, grote wijzigingen?*, 15 Bedrijfsjuridische berichten 194 (2018).
144. Article 2:135a(2) DCC.
145. Article 2:145(2) DCC read in conjunction with Art. 2:135a DCC.
146. Article 2:145(2) DCC read in conjunction with Art. 2:135a DCC and Art. 2:135b DCC.

draagvlak).[147] The remuneration report should, among others, entail, for every individual director: (i) the total amount of remuneration, split per category, (ii) the ratio between the variable component and the fixed component of the remuneration, and (iii) the way the awarded remuneration is in line with the remuneration policy and contributes to the long-term performance of the company.[148] These disclosure requirements aim to enable the shareholders to assess the relationship between performance and remuneration and, therefore, have an effective say on pay.

§13.09 CONCLUSION

Over most of the past two decades, remuneration policy has been at the centre of the corporate governance debate. There was a growing attention to executive remuneration in response to accounting scandals, which was subsequently reinforced by the onset of the financial crisis and the popular consensus that the structure of remuneration policies in the financial sector (and the perverse incentives as a result thereof) were seen as a cause of that crisis. Two interesting trends in addressing the remuneration issue at the European and national levels are apparent. On the one hand, formal laws and regulations have replaced forms of self-regulation. Also, the focus of the legislative reforms shifted from strengthening pay governance to regulating pay design. The effect of the European executive remuneration framework on executive remuneration in Dutch banks has been the most apparent with the introduction of formal remuneration rules following CRD III, as CRD IV and SRD II predominantly introduced further rules with regard to pay design and pay governance, respectively. The question is, however, if the pendulum will stay put or swing back. Interestingly, the United Kingdom abolished the bonus cap with effect from 31 October 2023.

Following this abolishment, it was Goldman Sachs that, only recently, announced that it had removed the bonus cap for its material risk takers as this would provide Goldman Sachs 'greater flexibility to manage fixed costs through the cycle and pay for performance.'[149]

On the other hand, (public) attention for the (direct) relationship between executive remuneration and sustainability and/or ESG performance has increased significantly over the last years. This concerns listed companies in general, but also – listed and non-listed – banks in the particular. For instance, the proposal for the Corporate Sustainability Due Diligence Directive (CS3D)[150], that was published on 23 February 2022, provided for a provision that linked the variable component of executive remuneration to the directors' contribution to the company's business and

147. Article 2:135a(6) DCC.
148. Article 2:135b(3) DCC.
149. Reuters, *Goldman Sachs scraps EU-era bonus cap for top bankers in UK, source says,* 3 May 2024, https://www.reuters.com/business/finance/goldman-sachs-scraps-eu-era-bonus-cap-top-bankers-uk-source-says-2024-05-02/.
150. European Commission, Proposal for a Directive of the European Parliament and of the Council on Corporate Sustainability Due Diligence and amending Directive (EU) 2019/1937, COM(2022) 71 final.

long-term interest and sustainability.[151] This provision was, however, deleted in the Council's general approach to the proposal, due to strong concerns of the Member States regarding this provision.[152] In its general approach, the Council stated that the form and structure of executive remuneration 'are matters primarily falling within the competence of the company and its relevant bodies or shareholders'.[153] Subsequently, this provision was not included in (the consolidated version of) the CS3D that was adopted by the European Parliament on 24 April 2024.[154] Although this legislative proposal to link the variable component of executive remuneration to sustainability and/or ESG performance of a (listed) company was rejected, it is expected, at least in the Netherlands, that executive remuneration will be scrutinized from an ESG perspective. For instance, Eumedion, the corporate governance and sustainability platform for institutional investors holding shares in Dutch listed companies, announced in its spearhead letter (speerpuntenbrief) for the 2024 Annual General Meeting (AGM) season that it considered a remuneration policy that supports sustainable long-term value creation as the important focus point for the 2024 AGM season.[155] We will have to await whether this growing public attention will (eventually) result in either self-regulation or in formal laws and regulations regarding the ESG performance of banks, either listed or non-listed.

151. Article 15(3) of the Proposal for a Directive of the European Parliament and of the Council on Corporate Sustainability Due Diligence and amending Directive (EU) 2019/1937.
152. Council of the EU, Proposal for a Directive of the European Parliament and of the Council on Corporate Sustainability Due Diligence and amending Directive (EU) 2019/1937 – General Approach, 30 Nov. 2022, 2022/0051(COD), https://data.consilium.europa.eu/doc/document/ST-15024-2022-REV-1/en/pdf.
153. Council of the EU, *supra* n. 152, p. 9.
154. European Parliament, European Parliament legislative resolution of 24 Apr. 2024 on the proposal for a directive of the European Parliament and of the Council on Corporate Sustainability Due Diligence and amending Directive (EU) 2019/1937 (COM(2022)0071 – C9-0050/2022 – 2022/0051(COD)), P9_TA(2024)0329, https://www.europarl.europa.eu/doceo/document/TA-9-2024-0329_EN.pdf.
155. Eumedion, *Eumedion Focus Letter 2024*, 11 Oct. 2023, https://www.eumedion.nl/clientdata/215/media/clientimages/Focus-Letter-2024-DEF.pdf?v=231012081230.

CHAPTER 14

Shareholder Inspection Rights and the Valuing of Shares: A Comparative Perspective Between Delaware and the Netherlands

Philippe Hezer

This chapter explores the potential use of shareholder inspection rights in exit processes to value shares in closely held companies, comparing Delaware and Dutch law. Shareholders' ability to access private information of a company to value their shares differs significantly between these jurisdictions due to differences in legal traditions. In Delaware, shareholder inspection rights are derived from shareholders' underlying property rights as owners of the company, resulting in a significantly lower threshold. Sincere valuation purposes will generally justify inspection of books and records. Under Dutch law, such access to private information may be granted to protect shareholders against information asymmetries, imposing a relatively high threshold. This concerns situations in which an exiting shareholder deals with an insider who is privy to private information of the company. Based on recent case law, this chapter provides guidance as to when shareholder protection is triggered under Dutch law.

§14.01 INTRODUCTION

Any person has a vested interest in understanding the value of their assets, which may include shares held in the capital of companies. Shareholders are typically able to determine the value of listed shares based on the market prices available on the exchange or platform on which those shares are listed and traded. Moreover, in such cases, applicable regulatory disclosure regimes serve to ensure that information relevant to the share price is shared with the market through ad hoc and periodic disclosures. However, typically, there will be no such marketplace for shares in privately held companies, nor will such extensive disclosure regimes apply.[1] Shareholders of privately held companies will therefore depend on access to private information to value their shares.[2] At the same time, however, companies have a vested interest in protecting the confidentiality of their private information, which is a valuable asset in itself.[3] This holds especially true given the sensitive nature of the information typically sought to ascertain the value of shares, which includes forward-looking commercial and financial information, among others. Access to such information can be a highly contentious topic, also given the risk of that information being misused or leaked.

Doctrine on shareholder information rights seeks to regulate such conflicts of interest between shareholders and the company concerning access to private information. In the Netherlands, this doctrine has seen notable development over recent years; however, limited guidance is available to shareholders seeking private information to value their shares. This marks a stark contrast when compared to Delaware, where it is generally accepted that shareholders may invoke inspection rights to obtain private information required to value their shares.

This chapter explores how the doctrine developed in Delaware relates to Dutch law. In doing so, I have focused on the position of minority shareholders in closely held private companies that are exploring an exit.[4] First, in §14.02, I provide an overview of shareholder inspection rights in Delaware and their use by shareholders seeking to

---

1. For instance, in the Netherlands, companies will generally only be required to publish annual accounts within 12 months after the end of the relevant financial year, meaning that public financial information will generally be historic in nature. Moreover, private companies may be able to apply certain exemptions that limit the scope of the information so disclosed.
2. For the purpose of this chapter, 'private' information is understood to refer to information that is not disclosed or made generally available to the public.
3. *See* for various perspectives, *e.g.*, G.S. Geis, 'Information litigation in corporate law', *Alabama Law Review*, vol. 71, no. 2 (2019), p. 451; J.N. Druey, 'Die Pflicht zur Halbwahrheit: Über die Aporien organisationsrechtlicher Informationsansprüche anhand des Aktionärs-Auskunftsrechts', in: F. Bitter et al. (eds), *Festschrift für Karsten Schmidt: zum 70. Geburtstag*, Köln: Verlag Dr. Otto Schmidt 2009, p. 261; L. Timmerman, 'Het aan ondernemingen toekomende recht op geheimhouding', in: J.H. Christiaanse et al. (eds), *Tot vermaak van Slagter: Feestbundel aangeboden aan prof. mr. W.J. Slagter ter gelegenheid van zijn 65e verjaardag*, Deventer: Kluwer 1988, pp. 318-319; and W.C.L. van der Grinten, 'Openheid en openbaarheid in de particuliere sector', *De NV* 1976, p. 222.
4. The reasons for this limitation of scope are as follows. First, larger (or even controlling) shareholders will often have a level of (de facto) control or leverage allowing them to obtain private information sought. The same applies to shareholders that can obtain information through board representative(s). In such cases, the shareholder would not be reliant on their shareholder information rights. Secondly, shareholders of listed companies typically will not require access to private information to value their shares as they can typically rely on market data. Moreover, under Dutch law, the inspection rights discussed in this chapter will not be available to shareholders of listed companies (Supreme Court 9 Jul. 2010, *NJ* 2010/544 annot. P. van Schilfgaarde (*ASMI*), para. 4.6; and Enterprise Chamber 22 Jun. 2022, *JOR* 2023/64 annot. W. Lazar (*ICTS*), para. 3.8). Finally, I have only considered shareholders seeking information to value their shares with a view on a potential exit from the company. While there may also be

value their shares. I then set out the Dutch legal framework for shareholder information rights and inspection rights, more specifically, in §14.03. In §14.04, I present an analysis of recent Dutch case law on shareholders seeking access to private information to value their shares. Based on the foregoing, the Delaware and Dutch doctrines are compared in §14.05. Finally, this chapter is concluded with closing remarks in §14.06.

§14.02 SHAREHOLDER INSPECTION RIGHTS IN DELAWARE

[A] Common Law Inspection Right

Courts in common law jurisdictions have historically held that shareholders have a right to inspect books and records of the companies in which they hold shares. An early ruling on such shareholder inspection rights was rendered in *Dominus Rex v. The Fraternity of Hostmen in Newcastle-Upon-Tyne*, a 1745 case in which the English court found that 'every member of the corporation had, as such, a right to look into the books for any matter that concerned himself' and that 'such books (...) are the common property of aggregate bodies acknowledged as such by our law, in which every member has an interest as being the evidence of some property or franchise being vested in him, or of his having conducted himself in the exercise of that franchise correctly'.[5] This doctrine has developed into a general rule granting shareholders a common law right to inspect books and records of the companies in which they hold shares, provided that such inspection takes place at a reasonable time and place and a proper purpose exists for the inspection.[6]

Two overlapping theories underly such shareholder inspection rights, i.e., ownership theory and agency theory.[7] Ownership theory is of particular relevance to this study. Under that theory, shareholders are considered to be the owners of the company and hence also the beneficial owners of the books and records of the company. While the company is a separate legal entity from its shareholders and holds legal title to the company's assets (including its books and records), the shareholders are thus viewed as having underlying ownership of those assets derived from their ownership of the company. According to ownership theory, inspection rights empower shareholders to inspect that which is effectively already theirs.[8]

---

other grounds that could arguably require that shareholders ascertain the value of their shares (*e.g.*, for accounting purposes), these fall outside of the scope of this chapter for practical purposes.

5. *See Rex v. Fraternity of Hostmen*, 93 Eng. Rep. 1144 (1745).
6. *See* B. Jeffries, 'Shareholder Access to Corporate Books and Records: The Abrogation Debate', *Drake Law Review*, vol. 59, no. 4 (2011), p. 1100.
7. *See, e.g.*, B. Jeffries, 'Shareholder Access to Corporate Books and Records: The Abrogation Debate', *Drake Law Review*, vol. 59, no. 4 (2011), pp. 1099-1100; and R.S. Thomas, 'Improving Shareholder Monitoring of Corporate Management by Expanding Statutory Access to Information', *Arizona Law Review*, vol. 38, no. 1 (1996), pp. 335-336.
8. Cf. the North Caroline Supreme Court in *Parsons v. Jefferson-Pilot Corp.*, 426 S.E.2d 685 (N.C. 1993), ruling that 'the rationale behind the common law right of inspection is that those in charge of the corporation are merely agents of the shareholders, and a shareholder's right to inspect a corporation's books and records is only the right to inspect and examine that which is his own'.

The common law inspection right has been codified by all US states, with some notable differences among them.[9] In Delaware, shareholder inspection rights have been codified in section 220 of the Delaware General Corporation Law (DGCL), which provides the following:

> Any stockholder (...) shall, upon written demand under oath stating the purpose thereof, have the right during the usual hours for business to inspect for any proper purpose, and to make copies and extracts from:
> (1) The corporation's stock ledger, a list of its stockholders, and its other books and records; and
> (2) A subsidiary's books and records, (...).

The common law inspection right and its many codifications are primarily qualified by the requirement of a proper purpose. This is an open-ended standard that, in summary, requires 'a purpose relating to the interest that the shareholder sought to protect by seeking inspection' that is 'germane to the petitioner's interest or status as a stockholder'.[10] Section 220(b) DGCL defines a proper purpose as 'a purpose reasonably related to such person's interest as a stockholder'.[11] The proper purpose not only qualifies shareholders' ability to invoke their inspection right but also limits the scope of that right: shareholders are only entitled to inspect those books and records that are 'essential and sufficient' for the articulated purpose of the inspection.[12]

Delaware courts have accepted a duty to police proceedings on books and records requests to protect the company's legitimate interests and to prevent possible abuse of shareholder inspection rights.[13] The requirement of a proper purpose helps to protect the company from books and records requests that may be disproportionately disruptive or harmful or that are otherwise made in bad faith.[14] Inspection rights, for instance, may not be invoked to satisfy mere idle curiosity or constitute a fishing expedition.[15] If

9. *See* B. Jeffries, 'Shareholder Access to Corporate Books and Records: The Abrogation Debate', *Drake Law Review*, vol. 59, no. 4 (2011), p. 1110. A large number of states follow the Model Business Corporation Act (MBCA), which includes provisions on shareholder inspection rights in §16.02 up to and including §16.04 MBCA.
10. *See Shaw v. Agri-Mark, Inc.*, 663 A.2d 464 (Del. 1995).
11. Section 220(b) DGCL.
12. *See, e.g., Thomas & Betts Corp. v. Leviton Mfg. Co.*, 681 A.2d 1026, 1035 (Del. 1996); and *Helmsman Mgmt. Serv., Inc. v. A&S Consultants, Inc.*, 525 A.2d 160 (Del. Ch. 1987).
13. *See, e.g., Highland Select Equity Fund, L.P. v. Motient Corporation*, 906 A.2d 156 (Del. Ch. 2006): 'The finding in the Opinion that Highland's conduct amounted to an abuse of the legitimate rights afforded to it under Section 220 was specifically based on the circumstances existing during the course of the litigation, on Highland's failure to fashion a demand in a good faith effort to comply with controlling precedent, and on the court's duty to police such proceedings "to prevent possible abuse of the shareholder's right of inspection."', referring to *CM & M Group, Inc. v. Carroll*, 453 A.2d 788 (1982).
14. Cf. §16.02(b)(1) of the MBCA, explicitly requiring that the books and record request is not only for a proper purpose, but also made in good faith. Note that, while the DGCL is not based on the MBCA, the same requirement applies in Delaware as this principle is derived from the common law.
15. *See* G.S. Geis, 'Information Litigation in Corporate Law', *Alabama Law Review*, vol. 71, no. 2 (2019), p. 417; and B. Jeffries, 'Shareholder Access to Corporate Books and Records: The Abrogation Debate', *Drake Law Review*, vol. 59, no. 4 (2011), p. 1101, with references to case law.

a purported proper purpose is found to be pretextual, this may justify the books and records request being denied.[16]

[B] Valuing Shares as a 'Proper Purpose' for Inspecting Books and Records

Delaware courts have held that it is of paramount importance for the proper purpose test to be met, although typically, this open standard is applied broadly, and so many 'proper purposes' have been accepted in case law.[17] Importantly, three types of justifications have traditionally been accepted as proper purposes to invoke inspection rights,[18] i.e.:

(i) communications with other shareholders for a governance event, for instance, to gain access to a list of shareholders to contact in relation to a proxy contest;
(ii) investigations into suspected corporate mismanagement, for instance, to obtain information required to explore grounds for a potential derivative suit; and
(iii) determining the value of the shares held by that shareholder.

Accordingly, as a starting point, shareholders of Delaware companies can invoke their section 220 DGCL inspection right to demand inspection of books and records to obtain information required to value their shares. It is generally understood that a low threshold applies to such requests. In fact, it has been argued that shareholders will only need to assert that they seek access to certain information to ascertain the value of their shares to justify inspection of books and records.[19]

Shareholders are in principle not required to establish an end use for the resulting valuation.[20],[21] As part of its defences against the books and records request, the

16. *See, e.g., Pershing Square, L.P. v. Ceridian Corp.*, 923 A.2d 810 (Del. Ch. 2007): 'A corporate defendant may resist demand where it shows that the stockholder's stated proper purpose is not the actual purpose for the demand. This showing is not made where a secondary improper purpose exists. Instead, in order to succeed, the defendant must prove that the plaintiff pursued its claim under false pretenses, and its primary purpose is indeed improper.'
17. *See, e.g., Melzer v. CNET Networks, Inc.*, 934 A.2d 912 (Del. Ch. 2007), noting that '[t]here is no shortage of proper purposes under Delaware law', citing 14 different justifications for books and records requests that have been accepted as proper purposes in case law.
18. *See, e.g.*, G.S. Geis, 'Information Litigation in Corporate Law', *Alabama Law Review*, vol. 71, no. 2 (2019), p. 423; and B. Jeffries, 'Shareholder Access to Corporate Books and Records: The Abrogation Debate', *Drake Law Review*, vol. 59, no. 4 (2011), p. 1102.
19. Cf. G.S. Geis, 'Information Litigation in Corporate Law', *Alabama Law Review*, vol. 71, no. 2 (2019), p. 445, noting that a 'low hurdle' applies: 'If a shareholder wants to value her shares, then what more does she really need to show? Nothing – the plain request should suffice. Unless some evidence emerges that the purported valuation justification is a pretext, the shareholder information entitlement seems almost automatic. Who doesn't want to know what their property is worth?'
20. *See Woods v. Sahara Enters.*, 238 A.3d 879 (Del. Ch. 2020): 'The Company's position [that the shareholder needs to demonstrate a reason for valuing their shares] is contrary to Delaware law. It would require that a stockholder establish both a proper purpose (valuing shares) and an end use for the resulting valuation. Delaware law does not require that a stockholder establish both

company may argue that such request should be denied by demonstrating that the shareholders' purported purpose is not their actual purpose and that their actual (primary[22]) purpose for conducting the inspection is indeed improper.[23] Shareholders may reply by explaining the need for the inspection sought.[24] The defendant company's burden of proof as to the purported purpose being improper typically serves as a significant hurdle to a successful defence.[25]

As follows from the above, a low threshold applies to books and records requests seeking information to value shares under section 220 DGCL. Sincere valuation purposes will generally justify inspection of books and records. There is no requirement for shareholders to have taken concrete steps to market their shares or even that such shareholders have decided to sell any shares.[26] Delaware courts have also

---

a purpose for seeking an inspection and an end to which the fruits of the inspection will be put. Cf. Lebanon Cty. Emps.' Ret. Fund v. AmerisourceBergen Corp., 2020 WL 132752, at *11-14 (Del. Ch. 2020). It is sufficient under Delaware law that a stockholder has a proper purpose reasonable related to its interests as a stockholder, such as valuing its shares. See 8 Del. C. § 220(b).'

21. While Delaware courts have long recognised that the valuation of shares, particularly in closely held private companies, as a proper purpose for inspection, not every case may be equally clear-cut. *See, e.g., Mehta v. Kaazing Corporation*, C.A. No. 2017-0087-JRS (Del. Ch. 2017), in which the Delaware Chancery Court required the shareholder to identify a particular need or reason to value their shares: 'It is settled in Delaware law that the valuation of one's stock can be a proper purpose for the inspection of books and records if there is a particular need or reason for the valuation. In this case, however, Mehta has not demonstrated that valuing his membership interests justifies inspection since he has failed to identify any reason why he needs to value his membership interests at this time.' The Delaware Chancery Court thus appeared to rule that merely reciting a proper purpose for inspection would not suffice, shifting the burden of proof of establishing a present further need for the inspection to the shareholder.
22. Once a proper purpose has been established, any secondary purpose or ulterior motive is irrelevant. *See Skouras v. Admirality Enterprises, Inc.*, 386 A.2d 674 (Del. Ch. 1978).
23. *See Woods v. Sahara Enters.*, 238 A.3d 879 (Del. Ch. 2020), referring to *Pershing Square, L.P. v. Ceridian Corp.*, 923 A.2d 810 (Del. Ch. 2007).
24. *See, e.g., Woods v. Sahara Enters.*, 238 A.3d 879 (Del. Ch. 2020), also confirming that if no such credible use for the inspection can be provided, the court may use this to infer that the shareholder's stated purpose is not its actual purpose.
25. *See, e.g., Woods v. Sahara Enters.*, 238 A.3d 879 (Del. Ch. 2020); *Pershing Square, L.P. v. Ceridian Corp.*, 923 A.2d 810, 817 (Del. Ch. 2007), in which it is noted that '[s]uch a showing is fact intensive and difficult to establish'. *See also Marathon Partners v. MF Worldwide Corporation*, Civil Action No. 018-N, (Del. Ch. 2004): 'It is the corporation's burden to demonstrate that a plaintiff does not have a proper purpose for seeking inspection of stocklists. In contrast, it is the stockholder's burden to establish that she has a proper purpose for seeking to inspect books and records other than stocklists.' A different view appears to be taken in L. Bai and S. Meyer, 'No Peeking: Addressing Pretextual Inspection Demands by Competitor-Affiliated Shareholders', *Virginia Law & Business Review* vol. 18, no. 2 (2024), in which is reference is made to *Woods v. Sahara Enters.*, 238 A.3d 879 (Del. Ch. 2020), noting that 'in 2020, the Delaware Court of. Chancery inexplicably shifted the initial burden of proof from the shareholder to the target company for the inspection.' (p. 233).
26. *See, e.g., Kortüm v. Webasto Sunroofs, Inc.*, 769 A.2d 113 (Del. Ch. 2000): 'But the facts that no specific offer to purchase or sell is pending at this moment, or that WAG has not yet decided whether (or not) to purchase or sell, do not – alone and without more – defeat the factual bona fides of its valuation purpose.'; and *Radwick Pty. Ltd. v. Medical Incorporated*, Civil Action No. 7610, (Del. Ch. 1984), in which the valuation purpose was accepted as proper while it was noted that 'Radwick acknowledges that it has not yet determined whether it will attempt to buy or sell Medical stock and that, depending on the prices offered, it may decide to do nothing. However, the fact that Radwick is holding open these options is only a reflection of the business realities

accepted more generally that there may be situations in which shareholders need to value their shares to enable them to decide whether to sell their shares and, if so, on what terms.[27]

§14.03 SHAREHOLDER INSPECTION RIGHTS IN THE NETHERLANDS

[A] The Dutch Approach to Shareholder Information Rights

The Netherlands is a civil law jurisdiction and takes a different approach to the position and rights of shareholders when compared to common law jurisdictions. This also has an impact on the theories underlying shareholder access to private information. Under Dutch law, shareholders are considered to be members of the company that are granted certain control and/or profit rights in exchange for the provision of risk-bearing capital. This means that shareholders are not deemed to be the 'owners' of the company and do not have an underlying (beneficial) ownership of the company's assets. Among other things, this means that ownership theory cannot be applied to justify information rights. The Dutch Supreme Court has confirmed that there is no hierarchical relation between the shareholders and the directors(s) and so shareholders cannot be considered the highest power within the company.[28] As such, the absence of a hierarchical order between shareholders and the board also means that shareholders do not have a special position within the company's governance that would justify general access to private information. The latter is also reflected in the stakeholder-oriented governance model employed in the Netherlands. [29] Moreover, this governance model is not well-suited for a strict application of agency theory.

of any possible transaction where the party is not forced to accept the deal regardless of its terms. Lepley testified that Radwick intends to "sit with" its Medical stock only if it is unable to buy or sell at what it determines to be a reasonable price.'

27. *See, e.g.*, *Helmsman Mgmt. Serv., Inc. v. A&S Consultants, Inc.*, 525 A.2d 160 (Del. Ch. 1987): 'It is clearly inferable from the evidence that this is such a case [i.e., a situation where a shareholder in a closely held company needs to value his shares to enable him to decide whether or not to sell, and, if so, on what terms]. There is a very limited market for Helmsman's A & S stock; indeed, given the corporation's right of first refusal, the only potential buyer may be A & S. For that reason, Helmsman must necessarily resort to A & S's books and records to establish a value as a predicate for deciding whether its stockholdings are marketable and, if so, on what terms. Those considerations, plus Helmsman's interest in extricating itself from a minority stockholder position in a corporation with which it is no longer in a friendly relationship, persuade me that Helmsman's valuation purpose is valid in fact as well as in law.'
28. Supreme Court 21 Jan. 1955, *NJ* 1959/43 annot. L.J. Hijmans van den Bergh (*Forumbank*).
29. In summary, directors of a Dutch company owe their fiduciary duties not to shareholders as a class but rather to the company and its business, focusing on long-term value creation. In doing so, directors must weigh all relevant stakeholder interests, including those of employees, shareholders, creditors and customers, among others. *See also* Supreme Court 4 Apr. 2014, *JOR* 2014/290 annot. R.G.J. de Haan (*Cancun*), paras 4.2.1 and 4.2.2; and Supreme Court 10 Feb. 2023, *JOR* 2023/119 annot. B. Kemp (*Cordial*), paras 3.4.2 and 3.4.3.

As a starting point, only the board, having been delegated the task of managing the company,[30] disposes of the company's assets, including its private information. Shareholder information rights therefore require a legal basis in law, the company's constitutional documents or contract. Statutory shareholder information rights are ultimately based on a weighing of interests.[31] A shareholder's interest in access to certain private information of the company is weighed against the company's interest in maintaining the confidentiality of that information. It is generally understood that companies have an inherent interest in maintaining the confidentiality of private information, and so, as a starting point, companies will *not* be held to divulge private information to their shareholders, even if the company would not suffer any immediate or foreseeable harm from that disclosure.[32] Only if the relevant shareholder interest is reasonable and of sufficient weight can there be an obligation to divulge private information to that shareholder.

[B] The Case for a Shareholder Inspection Right under Dutch Law

Dutch law does not provide for a general shareholder inspection right like section 220 DGCL.[33] At first glance, Dutch statutory company law appears to only grant limited information rights to shareholders. Individual shareholders have a statutory right to ask questions during shareholders' meetings[34] and a limited right to inspect certain

30. *See* R. Kraakman et al., *The Anatomy of Corporate Law: A Comparative and Functional Approach*, Oxford (UK): Oxford University Press 2017, pp. 11-13 on delegated management with a board structure as one of the core structural characteristics of the business corporation.
31. *See, e.g.*, P.J. van der Korst, *Bedrijfsgeheimen en transparantieplichten. Vertrouwelijke bedrijfsgegevens in het vermogensrecht, burgerlijk procesrecht, vennootschapsrecht en effectenrecht* (diss. Nijmegen), Serie vanwege het Van der Heijden Instituut deel 92, Deventer: Kluwer 2007, p. 162: 'The shareholders' right to information is the result of balancing the shareholders' financial and control interests with the company's interest in confidentiality. The company has an independent interest which is not necessarily outweighed by the interests of the shareholders.' (informal translation by author). *See* for a broader perspective G.J.W. Arendsen de Wolff, *De informatieplicht van de onderneming. Informatieverstrekking en geheimhouding in de betrekking tussen de onderneming en de werknemersvertegenwoordigers* (diss. Utrecht), Sociaal- en Arbeidsrechtelijke Reeks 3, Deventer: Kluwer 1976, pp. 33 et seq.
32. Cf. L. Timmerman, 'Het aan ondernemingen toekomende recht op geheimhouding', in: J.H. Christiaanse et al. (eds), *Tot vermaak van Slagter: Feestbundel aangeboden aan prof. mr. W.J. Slagter ter gelegenheid van zijn 65e verjaardag*, Deventer: Kluwer 1988, pp. 318-319, confirming that disclosure can also be harmful to the company if there are no immediate concrete damages: 'In my view, the term "harmfulness" should be interpreted broadly. It does not have to concern material damage directly measurable after disclosure. It may relate to difficulties experienced by a company in its functioning, for example if it has to take into account that it could be forced to disclose internal deliberations in preparation of a decision to outsiders.' (informal translation by author).
33. I note that there is some debate in Dutch literature as to whether Art. 3:15j of the Dutch Civil Code (DCC), pursuant to which certain interested parties have a right to inspect books and records insofar as they have a direct and sufficient interest in doing so, can also be invoked by shareholders. This discussion falls outside of the scope of this chapter.
34. *See* Art. 2:107/217(2) DCC. While this right is strictly allocated to the general meeting, it is effectively exercised by individual shareholders. *See*, in the context of a listed company,

documents.[35] These information rights are not well-suited to obtain private information required to value shares. For instance, the right to ask questions during a general meeting is generally not well-suited for complex, technical or detailed matters. Hence, despite its broad scope, this right is not well-suited to facilitate the valuation of shares.

In closely held private companies, however, the company's duty of care vis-à-vis its shareholders may require that certain private information is disclosed to such shareholders.[36] That duty of care is derived from the Dutch law principle of reasonableness and fairness.[37] In summary, each of the company, its directors and its shareholders are required to act in accordance with the principles of reasonableness and fairness vis-à-vis each other. In determining what is considered reasonable and fair in a given situation, generally accepted principles of law, current juridical views in the Netherlands and the relevant societal and private interests involved in the case must be taken into account, among other such factors.[38] This allows for a flexible, open norm that can be tailored to fit a wide range of situations.

Such disclosure obligations generally arise in situations where this is required to protect or otherwise further shareholder interests.[39] In such cases, the company is required to make an ad hoc disclosure on a given event or matter to (potentially) affected shareholders. Moreover, case law suggests that in certain especially closely held companies (*e.g.*, quasi-partnerships), a more general right to ask questions outside of a general meeting may be recognised even if it is not tied to a given

---

Supreme Court 9 Jul. 2010, *NJ* 2010/544 annot. P. van Schilfgaarde (*ASMI*), para. 4.6; and, in the context of a closely held private company, Enterprise Chamber 24 May 2017, *ARO* 2017/131 (*CL International*), para. 3.13.

35. There are certain limited inspection rights, such as the right to inspect the shareholders' register (Art. 2:85(4), and Art. 2:194(5) DCC), the right to inspect a list of resolutions adopted by the general meeting (Art. 2:120/230(4) DCC) and the right to inspect documents that are deposited for inspection at the company's offices, such as annual accounts that have been approved by the board but not yet adopted by the general meeting (Art. 2:101/219(1) DCC).
36. *See* Enterprise Chamber 8 Jun. 2022, *ARO* 2022/118 (*Cloud Solutions*), para. 3.7; Enterprise Chamber 6 Apr. 2023, *JOR* 2023/182 annot. A.F.J.A. Leijten (*i3*), para. 4.58; and Enterprise Chamber 6 Apr. 2023, *JOR* 2023/183 annot. A.F.J.A. Leijten (*Ergo Buildings*), para. 3.10. Cf. Enterprise Chamber 22 Jun. 2022, *JOR* 2023/64 annot. W. Lazar (*ICTS*), para. 3.8: 'Depending on the circumstances of the case, the provisions of Article 2:8 of the DCC in closely held companies may mean that the management board is obliged, either on its own initiative or at the shareholder's request, to exercise transparency even outside the context of the general meeting and to provide generous information to the shareholder. Such a situation does not arise in this case where it concerns a public limited company with a few hundred shareholders and a listing on the OTCQB' (informal translation by author).
37. Article 2:8(1) DCC. *See* Supreme Court 1 Mar. 2002, *NJ* 2002/296 annot. J.M.M. Maeijer (*Zwagerman*).
38. Article 3:12 DCC.
39. Most case law on this topic concerns a duty of care that arises in relation to conflict of interests. In such cases, enhanced standards of care require, among other things, that appropriate transparency is observed towards shareholders. Reference is made to the landmark rulings of Enterprise Chamber 26 May 1983, *NJ* 1984/481 annot. J.M.M. Maeijer (*Linders/Hofstee*) and Supreme Court 1 Mar. 2002, *NJ* 2002/296 annot. J.M.M. Maeijer (*Zwagerman*). *See also* my annotation to Enterprise Chamber 27 Feb. 2020, *JOR* 2020/203 (*Fuelplants*) on more recent developments.

circumstance requiring shareholder protection.[40] In such cases, there is no (or only limited) actual delegation of management, which in turn justifies a lower threshold for shareholder access to private information.

If the company is under a duty of care requiring disclosure of private information to a shareholder, that information must be provided on the company's own initiative and – notably – at the shareholder's request, as applicable.[41] In appropriate cases, the latter may effectively allow for a shareholder inspection right under Dutch law. The scope of that inspection right is determined by the extent to which the shareholder has a reasonable (and sufficient) interest in obtaining certain information, except insofar as an overriding interest of the company would prohibit such disclosure.[42]

[C] Enforcement of Inspection Rights

The requirement of the company and its shareholders to act vis-à-vis one another in accordance with reasonableness and fairness is a duty that can be legally enforced. This means that shareholders can invoke Article 2:8 DCC directly, allowing them to enforce the aforementioned inspection right. While Dutch courts have traditionally been reluctant to award these types of claims,[43] recent case law shows early signs that suggest courts may be more willing to award such claims going forward.[44]

To invoke or enforce their inspection right, shareholders will generally need to demonstrate that:

(i) they have a reasonable interest in obtaining the information sought;
(ii) in the present circumstances, the company is under a duty of care vis-à-vis the shareholders, requiring the disclosure of certain information; and
(iii) the information sought falls within the scope of that disclosure obligation.

40. *See* my annotation to Enterprise Chamber 24 Aug. 2021, *JOR* 2021/296 (*Allure*); and M.L. Lennarts, 'Het recht op informatie van kapitaalverschaffers in besloten verhoudingen – de open norm rules', in: L. Timmerman et al. (eds), *De rol van open normen in het ondernemingsrecht*, Uitgave vanwege het Instituut voor Ondernemingsrecht deel 130, Deventer: Wolters Kluwer 2023, pp. 119-121. A notable example in case law is Enterprise Chamber 13 Mar. 2020, *ARO* 2020/87 (*Brouwer Bloembollen*), para. 3.9.
41. *See, e.g.*, Enterprise Chamber 31 Oct. 2019, *ARO* 2019/193 (*Bosal*), para. 3.18; Enterprise Chamber 27 Feb. 2020, *JOR* 2020/203 annot. P.L. Hezer (*Fuelplants*), para. 3.15; and Enterprise Chamber 13 Mar. 2020, *ARO* 2020/87 (*Brouwer Bloembollen*), para. 3.9.
42. *See* Enterprise Chamber 3 Feb. 2022, *JOR* 2022/172 annot. P.L. Hezer (*Steenfabriek*), para. 3.12: 'That obligation to provide the requested information in more detail or in more substance finds its limit where there is no reasonable interest for [the shareholder] to obtain the information, or where an overriding interest of the company precludes it, for example because providing the requested factual substantiation is disproportionately burdensome for the company' (informal translation by author).
43. Reference is made to my annotation to Arnhem-Leeuwarden Court of Appeal, 3 May 2022, *JOR* 2023/2 annot. P.L. Hezer (*Intercont*), paras 10 et seq.
44. *See, e.g.*, Amsterdam District Court (summary judge) 15 Dec. 2021, ECLI:NL:RBAMS:2021:7409; and The Hague District Court 6 Apr. 2022, *RO* 2022/37; and The Hague District Court 15 Nov. 2023, ECLI:NL:RBDHA:2023:17634.

The company may defend against such claim by disputing that these cumulative criteria are met and, as an affirmative defence, argue that the provision of the relevant private information would be contrary to an overriding interest of the company.

The concept of a 'reasonable interest' is newly introduced in case law and has not been further defined. I believe that this is a status-related test, much like the proper purpose test in Delaware. This means that the relevant interest must be derived from the capacity as shareholder. I note that Article 2:8 DCC applies to shareholders in their capacity as shareholders only. Moreover, information rights follow from the membership relationship between the shareholder and the company[45] and, much like, for example, voting rights,[46] (only) serve the shareholder's interest in the company. Such application is also consistent with the ancillary nature of information rights: obtaining information is not a purpose as such but rather serves to enable shareholders to fulfil their role and position within the company.[47]

§14.04 DUTCH GUIDANCE ON ACCESS TO PRIVATE INFORMATION IN EXIT PROCESSES

[A] Introduction

There has been limited 'US-style' information litigation in the Netherlands. Of the published case law, only a small subset of cases concern shareholders seeking information to value their shares. In addition to legal hurdles, there is generally limited practical incentive for shareholders to invest in litigation to value their shares. Limited (if any) market appetite for unlisted minority shares combined with the strong transfer restrictions commonly adopted by Dutch privately held companies mean that, in practice, there is often no viable option for minority shareholders to sell their shares to third parties without consent or cooperation from their fellow shareholders. Dutch corporate governance in private companies emphasises shareholder protection through regulation of appropriate conduct over exit rights.[48]

45. *See* Asser/Kroeze 2-I 2021, no. 215; and, for a broader perspective, B. Kemp, *Aandeelhoudersverantwoordelijkheid: de positie en rol van de aandeelhouder en aandeelhoudersvergadering* (diss. Maastricht), Serie vanwege het Van der Heijden Instituut deel 129, Deventer: Wolters Kluwer 2015, pp. 139 et seq.
46. Cf. Supreme Court 30 Jun. 1944, *NJ* 1944/465 (*Wennex*), in which the Dutch Supreme Court qualified a shareholder's voting right as a right granted to shareholders to serve their interests within the company.
47. *See* J. Valesco, 'The Fundamental Rights of the Shareholder', *U.C. Davis Law Review* vol. 40, no. 2 (2006), pp. 426-427.
48. *See also* L. Timmerman, 'Mensenrechten van minderheidsaandeelhouders: voice, exit of gelijke behandeling', in: H. Beckman et al. (eds), *De nieuwe macht van de kapitaalverschaffer*, Uitgave vanwege het Instituut voor Ondernemingsrecht deel 57, Deventer: Kluwer 2007, pp. 39-40: 'As the share ownership protection in the law becomes weaker, the need for a well-regulated exit, a right of exit, will increase. However, the opposite is also true: the better the ownership protection of the share is regulated, the less need there is for a very flexible exit arrangement for the minority shareholder. (...) Traditionally, Dutch company law has quite a few provisions by which a shareholder can be forced to demonstrate decent behaviour (I refer to Article 2:8 DCC, Article 2:15(1)(b) DCC and the right of inquiry). (...) An exit right for a minority shareholder

Still, situations may arise in which shareholders - voluntarily or otherwise -face an exit from the company. In such a case, exiting shareholders have a clear interest in knowing the value of their shares. It has been argued that, in private companies, shareholders of Dutch companies will simply need to rely on (limited) public information for such purposes.[49] Recent case law suggests, however, that certain circumstances may justify that shareholders in closely held companies are entitled to access private information of the company to value their shares. This case law can be divided into three categories: (i) negotiations between shareholders seeking to explore a consensual deal on an exit of one or more such shareholders; (ii) compulsory share transfers through court proceedings; and (iii) compulsory share transfers triggered by contractually agreed-upon mechanics. I will elaborate on each of these categories below.

[B] Guidance in Case Law

[1] Negotiations for a Consensual Deal

In the *Holwerda* case, it was implicitly recognised that a shareholder may in certain cases be entitled to certain private information required to value their shares. This case concerned a closely held family business that was run by three brothers. One such brother, who was not on the board, sought to exit the family business and offered his shares to his two brothers, who were on the board of the family business. As part of negotiations on that consensual sale, information was shared, allowing the exiting shareholder to value his shares; however, no deal was ultimately reached. The exiting brother subsequently brought litigation, arguing, among other things, that he did not receive sufficient information to value the shares.

In its December 2021 ruling, the Enterprise Chamber held that the company was under a duty of care requiring it to provide certain information to the exiting brother.[50] The Enterprise Chamber ruled that sufficient information had indeed been provided for

subject to a very low hurdle fits only in a system in which the majority shareholder is not obliged to behave reasonably or at least this behaviour can only be very difficult to enforce from him. In Dutch company law, in my opinion, this is not the case' (informal translation by author).

49. Cf. the annotation of Raaijmakers under Supreme Court 13 Dec. 1991, *AA* 1993/0054 annot. M.J.G.C. Raaijmakers (*UVO-Lopik*), p. 59: 'Finally, the valuation of the shares in "AvdB bv" will be apparent or easily determined on the basis of the annual accounts (audited by an external auditor) or an interim report drawn up on the same basis' (informal translation by author).
50. *See* Enterprise Chamber 21 Dec. 2021, *ARO* 2022/27 (*Holwerda*), in particular para. 3.3, in which the closely held nature of the company was specified: 'In the case of HS situation, where it is a family company of which two of the three shareholders are also directors, the provisions of Article 2:8 of the DCC additionally imply that the company's board must provide [the exiting shareholder], as a shareholder who is not a member of the board, with generous disclosure regarding the company's affairs even outside the context of the general meeting. To a similar extent, this applies in respect of HHLS' (informal translation by author). HS and HHLS are abbreviations used to refer to two group companies in which the exiting shareholder held shares.

the purpose of valuing shares but did not further specify the scope of the disclosure obligation. While the exact extent of information provided is not entirely clear from the judgment, the Enterprise Chamber notes that the exiting brother was allowed to inspect certain information that he had requested and that his questions as to the information shared were answered.[51] It appears that comprehensive information was ultimately provided, although a portion of it was only shared after the litigation had been brought:

> [A]t the hearing, the company provided an overview of the actions taken in response to [the exiting shareholder]'s requests for information. It was not clear to them what information was still missing, and in the ensuing discussion at the hearing, it was acknowledged on behalf of [the exiting shareholder] that much information had been provided in the run-up to the hearing. The company agreed at the hearing that they would continue to respect [the shareholder]'s information rights.[52]

Taking the above into account, the Enterprise Chamber concluded that 'the provision of information from the board of the companies to [the exiting shareholder] – although late in starting in certain respects – does not provide any well-founded reason to doubt the correct policy and course of events'.[53] Hence, the exiting shareholder's claim was denied.

The *Holwerda* case suggests that a broad right to information for the purpose of valuing shares may be recognised in case of consensual negotiations on an exit when there is an information asymmetry between the shareholders involved. A duty of care requiring the disclosure of such information helps ensure, within reasonable boundaries, a level playing field between shareholders that are on the board and those that are not. This allows the shareholders involved to make an informed decision as to the sale of the relevant shares and prevents misuse of such information asymmetry (*e.g.*, by only selectively presenting information favourable to the position of such shareholders or otherwise seeking to misrepresent the real value of the shares).

[2] Compulsory Share Transfers Pursuant to Statute

[a] Statutory Squeeze-Out Proceedings

The Enterprise Chamber appears to have taken a more conservative approach in so-called squeeze-out proceedings, allowing for the compulsory sale of shares held by the minority shareholder(s) to a ≥95% majority shareholder.[54] In *Boonstra Beheer* and *Fuikebrug*, two recent squeeze-out proceedings concerning closely held companies, the

51. *See* Enterprise Chamber 21 Dec. 2021, *ARO* 2022/27 (*Holwerda*), para. 3.5, for a list of information shared.
52. Enterprise Chamber 21 Dec. 2021, *ARO* 2022/27 (*Holwerda*), para. 3.5, final bullet (informal translation by author).
53. Enterprise Chamber 21 Dec. 2021, *ARO* 2022/27 (*Holwerda*), para. 3.6 (informal translation by author).
54. Article 2:92a/2:201a DCC. *See also* Art. 2:359c DCC, which may apply to squeeze-out proceedings brought after completion of a public bid on a Dutch company that is or was listed on a regulated market.

Enterprise Chamber denied interim claims by shareholders seeking disclosure of information to value their shares and to assess the valuation by the court-appointed independent valuation expert, respectively.[55] In dismissing these interim disclosure claims, the Enterprise Chamber emphasised t'he special authorities of such independent court-appointed valuation experts to inspect the company's books and records.[56] In light thereof, the Enterprise Chamber ruled that shareholders had not duly substantiated what interest they would have in (also) gaining access to such information, also in view of the risk of such disclosure claims being used as fishing expeditions.[57]

In 2018, the Enterprise Chamber had already come to a similar conclusion in the *Xeikon* case, which concerned squeeze-out proceedings brought by a bidder following the completion of a public bid to obtain the remaining minority shares.[58] In that case, an opposing minority shareholder also brought an interim disclosure claim seeking certain information required to value their shares and assess the valuation experts' findings. The Enterprise Chamber denied claim on similar grounds as in *Fuikebrug* and *Boonstra Beheer*.[59]

In each of the *Fuikebrug*, *Boonstra Beheer* and *Xeikon* cases, a valuation expert was appointed by the Enterprise Chamber, which appeared to play a key role in the Enterprise Chamber's reasoning for denying the interim disclosure claim. The involvement of an independent court-appointed expert, in addition to statutory safeguards ensuring that they are able to come to a duly informed valuation, provided appropriate protection to the minority shareholders involved. However, the Enterprise Chamber has significant discretion in deciding whether to appoint one or more valuation experts to establish the value of the shares.[60] Given the costs and delays typically associated with the expert valuation process, majority shareholders will generally submit financial

55. *See* Enterprise Chamber 14 Jun. 2022, *ARO* 2022/141 (*Boonstra Beheer*); and Enterprise Chamber 1 Nov. 2022, *ARO* 2022/217 (*Fuikebrug*). Each of these claims was brought under Art. 843a of the Dutch Code of Civil Procedure, which allows a basis to bring a claim seeking access to certain documents in relation to (pending or potential) proceedings or otherwise. For such a claim to be granted, the plaintiff will need to demonstrate, among other things, that they have a 'legitimate interest' in obtaining certain specified documents concerning a legal relationship to which the plaintiff is a party.
56. *See* Enterprise Chamber 1 Nov. 2022, *ARO* 2022/217 (*Fuikebrug*), para. 3.6; and Enterprise Chamber 14 Jun. 2022, *ARO* 2022/141 (*Boonstra Beheer*), para. 3.18: 'Pursuant to Article 2:201a(5), in conjunction with Article 2:351(1) and (2), of the DCC, the expert to be appointed by the Enterprise Chamber is authorised to inspect the books, records and other data carriers of Boonstra Beheer and, on request, may be authorised to consult the aforementioned information of companies closely associated with Boonstra Beheer, such as 3B Horeca. Against that background, it would have been for Turkovic to substantiate in a sufficiently concrete manner what interest she has in the documents sought if an expert is appointed. Since she failed to do so and also failed to put forward sufficiently concrete arguments as to what interest she has in the documents claimed, the incidental claim will be dismissed' (informal translation by author).
57. *See* Enterprise Chamber 1 Nov. 2022, *ARO* 2022/217 (*Fuikebrug*), paras 3.4 and 3.6.
58. Enterprise Chamber 18 Dec. 2018, *JOR* 2019/104 annot. D-J.F.F.M. Duynstee (*Xeikon*).
59. *See* Enterprise Chamber 18 Dec. 2018, *JOR* 2019/104 annot. D-J.F.F.M. Duynstee (*Xeikon*), para. 2.32.
60. *See* Art. 2:92a/201a(5) DCC, granting the Enterprise Chamber the possibility, at its discretion, to appoint one or three independent valuation experts to report on the value of the shares.

information, including financial reports and fairness opinions, to substantiate the price offered,[61] to duly substantiate the price offered.

If minority shareholders dispute the value of the shares as presented by the majority shareholder, the Enterprise Chamber will typically appoint an expert unless it is able to determine the value independently.[62] I would expect the Enterprise Chamber to come to a similar conclusion if minority shareholders seek the disclosure of additional information to reach an independent valuation of their shares. The appointment of a valuation expert helps ensure that the price ultimately paid for the minority shares is duly and independently established, without requiring that sensitive information be disclosed to such minority shareholders that will presumably exit the company in the near future. This helps safeguard both the interests of the company and the shareholder.

It is ultimately up to the Enterprise Chamber to ascertain the value of the shares. In making that assessment, the Enterprise Chamber has significant discretion and is not bound by the findings of any (court-appointed) valuation expert(s). While it will generally attach significant importance to the valuation report, in making its assessment, the Enterprise Chamber will also address any duly substantiated objections against the findings of the valuation expert raised by the minority shareholder(s).[63] In *Boonstra Beheer*, the exiting shareholder was ultimately able to successfully raise such objections without access to private information of the company, leading to a notable increase in the consideration paid for the shares.[64]

[b] Statutory Exit Proceedings

The same reasoning has been used in so-called statutory exit proceedings.[65] These are proceedings brought by a shareholder seeking an order compelling one or more of their fellow shareholders and/or the company to acquire their shares. Such a claim can be brought if, in summary, it cannot reasonably be expected from the claimant to remain

---

61. *See* on the information typically required by the Enterprise Chamber in privately held companies, e.g., T. Salemink, *GS Rechtspersonen, artikel 2:201a BW, aant. 5.3* (2023) and P.M. Storm, *Corporate litigation bij de Ondernemingskamer*, The Hague: Boom Juridisch 2018, p. 574.
62. *See* Enterprise Chamber 16 May 2017, *ARO* 2017/122 (*Aspria*), para. 3.12, in which the Enterprise Chamber ruled that '[a]s a starting point in statutory squeeze-out proceedings, if the purported value is disputed by the defendant, the Enterprise Chamber will appoint an expert to establish that value, unless the Enterprise Chamber finds that it is able to independently determine the price' (informal translation by author). *See* for a recent example Enterprise Chamber 23 Jan. 2024, ECLI:NL:GHAMS:2024:198 (*SnowWorld*), para. 3.9, in which the Enterprise Chamber appointed a valuation expert in response to defences filed by minority shareholders against the valuation report submitted by the claimant. Note that it is relatively uncommon for minority shareholders to appear in the proceedings and so typically the valuation will not be disputed. In squeeze-out proceedings concerning closely held companies in which the minority shareholder(s) do not appear in the proceedings to bring defences, the Enterprise Chamber may be more inclined to rely on valuation reports submitted by the claimant (*see, e.g.*, Enterprise Chamber 28 Jul. 2015, *ARO* 2015/261 (*NAGRON*)).
63. *See, e.g.*, Enterprise Chamber 30 Jan. 2024, ECLI:NL:GHAMS:2024:259 (*Boonstra Beheer*), para. 2.12.
64. *See* Enterprise Chamber 30 Jan. 2024, ECLI:NL:GHAMS:2024:259 (*Boonstra Beheer*), para. 2.31.
65. Article 2:343 DCC.

a shareholder in the company in view of actions by their fellow shareholders and/or the company that have significantly prejudiced the claimant's interests. If that claim is awarded, the court will typically need to appoint one or more valuation experts to determine the value of the shares.[66]

Although exit proceedings are rarely brought, there is some precedent of shareholders bringing interim disclosure claims seeking disclosure of information required to value their shares in the context of such proceedings. I refer to *Mecus v. Helisa et al.*, in which Mecus sought to exit a joint venture with Helisa. As part of its exit claim, Mecus sought the appointment of a valuation expert while also seeking disclosure of certain information that it allegedly required so that 'the value of the shares (or the decrease thereof) can be determined in full'.[67] The Gelderland District Court granted the exit claim but denied the interim disclosure claim, ruling that:

> However, since the expert to be appointed by the court – who is to determine the value (decrease) of the shares – is presumably granted unrestricted access to the records required by him in his investigation, Mecus has no interest in its claim for disclosure of those records.[68]

In the appellate proceedings of *Bakker Beheer v. Haasnoot Beheer*, the Enterprise Chamber denied a similar interim disclosure claim on similar grounds:

> It follows from the foregoing [on the appointment of a valuation expert] that Bakker Beheer now has no remaining interest in granting the interim disclosure claim. In the context of the expert opinion to be issued, Haasnoot Beheer will have to provide all information to the expert that the expert deems necessary.[69]

These rulings mirror the reasoning applied by the Enterprise Chamber in squeeze-out proceedings, as evidenced by the *Fuikebrug*, *Boonstra Beheer* and *Xeikon* cases.

[3] Compulsory Share Transfers Pursuant to Contract

Interestingly, the same may not apply when a contractual obligation to transfer shares is triggered.[70] In September 2023, the Rotterdam District Court ruled in summary

66. *See* Art. 2:343(2), in conjunction with Art. 2:339 DCC. The court is required to appoint a valuation expert unless (a) parties agree on the price of the shares; or (b) clear valuation mechanics have been set out in the company's articles of association or an agreement (Art. 2:339(3) DCC).
67. *See* Gelderland District Court 14 Sep. 2022, ECLI:NL:RBGEL:2022:5344 (*Mecus v. Helisa et al.*), para. 4.17.
68. Gelderland District Court 14 Sep. 2022, ECLI:NL:RBGEL:2022:5344 (*Mecus/Helisa et al.*), para. 4.17 (informal translation by author).
69. Enterprise Chamber 19 May 2020, *ARO* 2020/138 (*Bakker Beheer/Haasnoot Beheer*), para. 3.46 (informal translation by author).
70. It is not uncommon for Dutch shareholders' agreements to include mechanics on a compulsory transfer of shares, for instance in the context of so-called leaver provisions. These mechanics typically provide for mutual good faith negotiations on the transfer price and, if no agreement is reached, so-called binding advice proceedings in which the value of the shares is determined by one or more valuation experts. Such valuation experts are often deemed to be independent and

proceedings on a claim by a shareholder that had triggered a compulsory transfer of their shares under a shareholders' agreement.[71] This shareholder was not represented on the board and so they did not have access to private information from the company's books and records. The court ruled that the exiting shareholder had 'an interest in accessing the information to which it is entitled under the Shareholders' Agreement. After all, [the exiting shareholder] will need to be able to be reasonably informed of [the company]'s financial situation in order to assess the correctness of what is submitted to the binding adviser in the context of the valuation of the shares'.[72] In this specific case, however, the shareholders' agreement provided a contractual basis for such information right and so this outcome was in line with the parties' agreement.

Would the outcome have been the same without this contractual right to information? In such case, the exiting shareholder would arguably have had a similar interest in being able to verify the information shared with the valuation expert that will determine the value of their shares. The argument could be made that this justifies a level playing field in terms of access to information as seen in the *Holwerda* case. A recent ruling by the summary judge of The Hague District Court appears to confirm such approach.[73] At the same time, it could be argued that the involvement of a valuation expert sufficiently safeguards the exiting shareholder's interests, hence justifying that access to private information is denied, similar to the reasoning applied in the *Fuikebrug*, *Boonstra Beheer*, *Xeikon*, *Mecus v. Helisa et al.* and *Bakker Beheer v. Haasnoot Beheer* cases.[74]

Ultimately, I expect the answer to this question to depend on the safeguards offered to the shareholder in the relevant exit process. If it is sufficiently safeguarded that the relevant valuation expert is independent, has the required expertise and will have full access to all information required to value the shares, there will generally be no need for shareholders to also obtain access to that same information to verify the

---

the procedure in which they value the shares are often referred to as an 'independent expert procedure'. The shares are typically bought by one or more of the other shareholders and/or by the company itself to be held in treasury.

71. *See* Rotterdam District Court (summary judge) 6 Sep. 2023, ECLI:NL:RBROT:2023:8406.
72. *See* Rotterdam District Court (summary judge) 6 Sep. 2023, ECLI:NL:RBROT:2023:8406, para. 4.2 (informal translation by author).
73. *See* The Hague District Court (summary judge) 15 Nov. 2023, ECLI:NL:RBDHA:2023:17634, paras 4.6 et seq. Among other grounds, the relevant claim was brought by the relevant shareholder 'to better prepare himself for the discussion about the value of his shares in the Holding, a discussion that he believes should be held in the short term' (para. 4.6, informal translation by author). The court ultimately ordered that the shareholder's advisors are granted monthly access to the company's books and records. Interestingly, while these discussions appear to be framed in the context of plaintiff as shareholder, it is not entirely clear whether plaintiff was (also) a director of the company. The facts underlying the judgment suggest that this may have been the case, which would mean that the relevant person would in principle have access to such books and records anyway as a director (Art. 2:10 DCC), although that argument may not have been raised in litigation.
74. Cf. Limburg District Court (summary judge) 2 Feb. 2023, ECLI:NL:RBLIM:2023:816, in which the plaintiff sought, among other things, an order requiring the company to provide to an independent valuation expert all information required by such expert to perform their valuation. The court did not substantively rule on that claim.

valuation expert's findings. Whereas the independence, expertise and access to information of court-appointed valuation experts are safeguarded by law, such safeguards may not always be equally as strong as contractual mechanics. This is a factual assessment to be made on a case-by-case basis.

[C] Preliminary Conclusions

A number of preliminary conclusions can be drawn from the above case law. First, this case law suggests that an exiting shareholder's interest in being able to ascertain the value of their shares may indeed constitute a reasonable interest that can justify access to private information. I would argue that the interest in being able to make an informed exit from the company is inherently linked to that person's capacity as a shareholder. That being said, it could also be argued that such interest is not linked to that shareholder's position *within* the company, in which case such interest could arguably be viewed as a personal interest of the shareholder that is not related to their capacity as a shareholder.[75] This would arguably mean that such shareholder's interest in obtaining private information to value their shares may not constitute a reasonable interest and hence cannot be relied on in support of an inspection request. I believe, however, that the approach taken by the Dutch courts is fair and just.

Second, this case law confirms that there is no general shareholder right to private information of the company required to value shares. Only in exceptional cases where there is a concrete need to protect the shareholder against potential harm resulting from an information asymmetry an ad hoc information right may be triggered. Such a situation is likely to only arise if the exiting shareholder is an 'outsider' that is not privy to the private information of the company and engages with an 'insider', such as a shareholder having board representation or the company itself, on the terms of the exit. In these cases, a duty of care may arise requiring that the company ensures, within reasonable boundaries, a level playing field. Other situations are unlikely to trigger such duty of care. Exploring (for example) a third-party sale is unlikely to trigger such duty of care, as both parties would be outsiders and so there is no information asymmetry against which the shareholder must be protected.

Third, this case law confirms that the existence of an information asymmetry in the context of an exit process does not justify shareholder access to private information per se. Instead, the (potential) impact of that information asymmetry should be

75. I understand that a similar discussion takes place in German doctrine on whether invoking the inspection right of §51a of the *Gesetz betreffend die Gesellschaften mit beschränkter Haftung* (hereafter: 'GmbH Act') to obtain information used for to value shares means that such request is made for a purpose that is not related to the company (a '*Gesellschaftsfremde Zwecke*') within the meaning of §51a(2) of the GmbH Act. Teichmann notes that this answer is generally answered in the negative. *See* C. Teichmann, 'Information Rights of Shareholders in German Company Law', in: R.S. Thomas, P.S. Guidici and U. Varottil (eds), *Research Handbook on Shareholder Inspection Rights: A Comparative Perspective*, Cheltenham (UK) / Northampton, Michigan (US): Edward Elgar, 2023, p. 130: 'According to the general opinion, the purpose of the request by a shareholder for information is legitimate if it concerns the calculation of an appropriate price for the shareholder's own shares (...). The request for information cannot be refused with the argument that it serves purposes unrelated to the company (...).'

considered in view of the safeguards – if any – offered by the (envisaged) exit process. The more safeguards there are to alleviate the impact of an information asymmetry between the parties, the less 'additional' protection a minority shareholder would need by being granted access to private information of the company. In other words, such safeguards may preclude a shareholder's (otherwise legitimate) interest in verifying the valuation used in the exit process and/or the information underlying that valuation. This holds especially true if the shareholder agrees to the appointment of the valuation expert and the valuation process or in the case of a court-supervised process.

The above case law provides limited guidance as to what safeguards would be relevant to such assessment. I expect that the principal safeguard will be the independence of the valuation expert. Such independence will be assumed if the relevant expert is appointed by a court but can also follow from factors such as the professional capacity of the relevant expert and applicable independence requirements.[76] Any reputable valuator will generally be assumed to have the required expertise, also depending on the complexity and scope of the relevant valuation. Additional safeguards can be provided by, for example, a fairness opinion or a report verifying the process and data used by the valuation expert.

Safeguards pertaining to the valuation process itself, especially where it concerns the valuation expert's access to information, can also be of relevance for this assessment. A valuation expert will inherently need to rely on information provided by the company for its valuation.[77] Any potential conflict of interest between the company and the exiting shareholder may give rise to concerns as to the valuation expert not being duly informed. The exiting shareholder may argue that it needs access to private information to ensure due and fair provision of information to the valuation expert.[78] I believe that this may not justify access to such private information of the company per se. Typically, the valuation expert's access to information is safeguarded by contract or, in the case of statutory exit proceedings, by law. In such cases, save for manifest

76. For example, accountants in the Netherlands are subject to certain independence requirements and similar requirements typically also apply in other jurisdictions. If a valuation is made by an accountant that is not affiliated to the firm(s) auditing and/or advising the company or the other shareholders, they can generally be assumed to be independent. The same applies, for instance, to so-called 'registered valuators' in the Netherlands.

77. *See* in the context of statutory exit proceedings Enterprise Chamber 28 Nov. 2023, ECLI:NL:GHAMS:2023:3011 (*Brouwer Bloembollen*): 'First of all, [the shareholder] argued in general terms that the expert did not check, or at least did not sufficiently check, the accuracy of the data he had received for the purpose of the valuation. Since most of that data came from [the company], the correctness of that data cannot be assumed as a matter of course and it would have been up to the expert to investigate that independently. The Enterprise Chamber overrules this objection. In principle, the expert may rely on the correctness of data such as annual reports, valuation reports, inventories and quotations, which are provided to him within the scope of his examination, unless he has sufficient concrete reason to assume – whether or not at the suggestion of the parties – that certain data may be incorrect, unreliable, incomplete or unusable' (para. 2.12, informal translation by author) and, in the context of statutory squeeze-out proceedings, Enterprise Chamber 30 Jan. 2024, ECLI:NL:GHAMS:2024:259 (*Boonstra Beheer*), para. 2.18.

78. *See, e.g.*, Rotterdam District Court (summary judge) 6 Sep. 2023, ECLI:NL:RBROT:2023:8406, as referred to in §14.02[C] above.

errors or omissions, I am of the view that parties will need to rely on the valuation expert's assessment as to whether they were granted sufficient access to information.

Finally, exiting shareholders may argue in proceedings on the valuation of their shares that they are not able to conduct a proper defence without access to private information of the company. Case law, including the *Boonstra Beheer* case discussed above, demonstrates, however, that shareholders have been able to successfully raise duly substantiated objections against the findings of the valuation expert(s) without access to private information and that such objections need to be addressed when determining the value of shares.[79] While such procedural interest is legitimate in and of itself, it may not necessarily justify access to private information of the company. This will require a highly factual assessment made on a case-by-case basis.

§14.05 A COMPARATIVE PERSPECTIVE BETWEEN THE NETHERLANDS AND DELAWARE

[A] Introduction

So, how do Delaware and the Netherlands compare when it comes to shareholder inspection rights to value shares? I would like to start with some similarities. In both jurisdictions, it is accepted that shareholders may have an interest in being able to determine the value of their shares, while companies have an interest in protecting their private information against disclosure to shareholders. This presents a legal dilemma that Delaware and the Netherlands both appear to tackle using similar strategies. Both jurisdictions (implicitly) employ a weighing of interests that aims to offer reasonable protection to the company while also allowing the shareholder to protect its legitimate interests. Neither jurisdiction allows for unrestricted inspection of private information; in both jurisdictions, inspection rights are limited in scope by the shareholder's legitimate interests. However, there are also fundamental differences that lead to a vastly different approach to shareholder inspection rights and shareholders' ability to value their shares. The three main differences appear to be related to the role and position of shareholders in both jurisdictions, the legal basis for the inspection right, and the thresholds applied when weighing the interests involved. Each of these differences is addressed below.

[B] Differences in Role and Position of Shareholders

First, there are differences in terms of the role and position of shareholders. In Delaware, shareholders are considered the owners of the company. Consequently, shareholders are deemed to be the beneficial owners of the company's books and

79. See Enterprise Chamber 28 Nov. 2023, ECLI:NL:GHAMS:2023:3011 (*Brouwer Bloembollen*), para. 2.6; and Enterprise Chamber 30 Jan. 2024, ECLI:NL:GHAMS:2024:259 (*Boonstra Beheer*), para. 2.12. In both cases, the exiting shareholders were able to raise duly substantiated objections against the valuation report, which were addressed by the court and resulted in an upward adjustment of the value of the shares as established by the valuation expert.

records. This implies that shareholder inspection rights are subject to a relatively low threshold and have a relatively broad scope, given that shareholders are effectively inspecting their own property. As a starting point, shareholders will thus be allowed to inspect a company's books and records to value their shares. Such an approach befits a shareholder-oriented corporate governance model.

In the Netherlands, however, shareholders are seen as members of the company to which they contribute risk-bearing capital. The company is seen as a strictly separate legal entity and Dutch company law does not view shareholders as beneficial owners of the company's assets. A company's books and records solely belong to the company and, in principle, only the board will have access to such books and records unless otherwise provided by law, constitutional documents or contract. As a starting point, there will be no such ground for a shareholder inspection right and companies have a legitimate interest in preserving the confidentiality of their private information.

This Dutch approach implies that shareholder inspection rights are subject to a relatively high threshold and have a relatively limited scope, given that there must be sufficient grounds to justify shareholder access to the company's books and records. Such access cannot be derived from a shareholder's underlying property rights but will generally need to be justified by that shareholder's reasonable interest in protection of its rights and position, among other things. As a starting point, shareholders will therefore *not* be allowed to inspect a company's books and records to value their shares. This befits a stakeholder-oriented approach to corporate governance.

[C] Differences in Legal Basis

The second difference pertains to the legal basis for inspection rights in the Netherlands and Delaware. Shareholder inspection rights are a well-established element of common law based on centuries of precedent. Such common law right has been codified by all US states, including Delaware. Moreover, a shareholder's interest in ascertaining the value of his shares has historically been accepted as a proper purpose, and so such claims in and of themselves should not be controversial. This provides for a clear basis on which inspection rights are based and offers comfort to shareholders, boards and courts as to the application of those rights.

This is quite different in the Netherlands, where the inspection right has no explicit statutory basis but would instead be based on what is essentially a broad and unwritten duty of care of the company vis-à-vis its shareholders. Moreover, this doctrine is still very much in development and guidance in case law is limited, especially where it concerns the use of inspection rights to value shares. These factors combined offer less comfort to boards, shareholders and courts when compared to Delaware.

[D] Differences in the Weighing of Interests

Finally, as follows from the above, there are vast differences between the parameters and outcome of the weighing of interests in the Netherlands and Delaware. Under

Delaware law, a low hurdle applies as shareholders are considered to be the beneficial owners of the books and records they seek to inspect. As a starting point, a shareholder's request to inspect books and records to ascertain the value of their shares must be granted. In such cases, a low threshold applies when it comes to setting aside a company's interest in preserving the confidentiality of private information. Inspection, in these cases, is the rule rather than the exception. The opposite applies in the Netherlands. Only in specific and exceptional cases will shareholders be granted access to the private information required to value their shares. These are cases in which shareholders are faced with an information asymmetry in an exit process and, absent other safeguards, levelling the playing field can help them protect their position and make an informed judgment.

It is interesting to note, however, that neither approach appears to have garnered notable criticism in legal literature. To my knowledge, the use of shareholder information rights to allow for the valuation of shares has not previously been addressed in Dutch legal literature and – as noted above – case law is limited. This suggests that, in practice, the inability to come to an informed valuation of shares held in a closely held company without the cooperation of that company's board generally does not lead to significant issues in Dutch corporate governance. Meanwhile, in the US literature and cases that I have come across in my research, it appears to be taken for granted that shareholders can invoke their inspection rights to value their shares. The relatively extensive access to private information required to value shares thus does not appear to have a significant negative impact on the companies involved.

§14.06 CLOSING REMARKS

There are vast differences between a shareholder's ability to gain access to private information of the company to value their shares under Dutch and Delaware law. Dutch law imposes a high threshold to access such information, whereas that threshold is significantly lower in Delaware. As a starting point, under Delaware law, access to private information is granted if the shareholder has a legitimate valuation purpose. Under Dutch law, limited case law suggests that this will only be the case if there is a concrete need to protect the shareholder's interests against an information asymmetry. However, the Dutch doctrine on shareholder information rights has not yet been fully crystalised. There has been significant development over the past few years and recent case law suggests that there may be more claims from shareholders seeking disclosure of private information. I expect that information litigation by Dutch shareholders will only increase as courts, legal practitioners and legal scholars continue to explore the boundaries of shareholders' right to private information.

The question may arise whether experiences from Delaware, suggesting that a lower threshold may not necessarily expose companies to disproportionate harm, could impact the threshold applied in the Netherlands. I believe that to be unlikely. The Dutch legal tradition differs greatly from that of Delaware where it concerns the position and rights of shareholders. This, combined with the lack of an explicit statutory basis for inspection claims, as well as the generally broad and unclear scope and sensitive nature of information required to value shares, may prompt Dutch judges to exercise caution in assessing such claims. Although Dutch courts tend to be pragmatic, I therefore expect that they will continue to apply a significant threshold to such claims aimed at ascertaining the value of shares. I believe that this would be a just and fair outcome in view of the Dutch corporate governance model.

CHAPTER 15

Developments in European Company Group Law, from Formalism Towards the Economic Reality

Bastiaan Kemp[*]

Statutory law treats the single operating legal entity as the default, whereas these days, the economic reality is that enterprises generally consist of a significant number of individual legal entities, sometimes even operating across borders. In this contribution, the development from a strict application of the more formal entity theory towards more room for the economic reality of the group is discussed. This development is, however, not without challenges, and those challenges are highlighted in this contribution.

§15.01 INTRODUCTION

The journal *European Company Law* (hereinafter: "ECL") is celebrating its 20th birthday. Over the years, ECL has developed into a leading journal in the field of European Company Law, with publications that inform its readers on important developments such as the takeover Directive, the case law regarding golden shares, the role of company groups in a cross-border context and the many (other) EU regulatory initiatives, including the Shareholder Rights Directive, the CSRD and the CSDDD. Much credit is due to Steef Bartman and Cees de Groot for being the driving forces behind the

* This contribution follows a lecture held in Dutch during a symposium on the "Corporate Group. Group Law in the corporate law of today and tomorrow" organized by the University of Utrecht in September 2023.

journal for almost 20 years. In line with two of Steef Bartman's primary research interests, I choose to write a contribution on stakeholders and purpose in the international group.

The role, rights and responsibilities of stakeholders and the company are in full development. Both on an international and national level, in Europe and in the United States, there are initiatives that generally aim for the interests of stakeholders to be considered more prominently, also within company law.[1] These movements also incite debate, both in politics, within the courtroom and—thankfully—within universities. As is the case with many discussions in company law, the focus of the debate on the role, rights and responsibility of stakeholders is mainly on the individual company, i.e., the enterprise being organized as a single company. Recently, the Dutch Supreme Court acknowledged that a significant part of (Dutch) statutory company law and thinking on company law is focused on the single company,[2] even though most companies are actually organized as groups, and many of these groups operate across borders with legal entities incorporated under different national laws. In the particular case that came before the Supreme Court, the question revolved around the legal responsibility of an indirect shareholder. Under Dutch law, shareholders of a company have the responsibility to act reasonably and fairly towards the company, other shareholders and other "institutional stakeholders."[3] The question before the Supreme Court was whether indirect shareholders under certain circumstances have the same responsibility. The Supreme Court answered this question in the affirmative and pointed out that even though section 2:8 DCC, the Dutch statutory provision on corporate reasonableness and fairness, is formulated in such a way that it focuses on the single legal entity, under specific circumstances, this provision also applies to the relationship between companies and their institutional stakeholders in an organizational group.[4] This demonstrates that the assumed "default position" of the individual legal entity, as applied in most jurisdictions, is not always in line with economic reality[5]

1. *See* for an overview of this development: Lucian A. Bebchuk & Roberto Tallarita, *The Illusory Promise of Stakeholder Governance*, 106 Cornell Law Review, 9 et seq. (2020); Jill E. Fisch & Steven Davidoff Solomon, *Should Corporations Have a Purpose?*, 99 Texas Law Review, 1309 (2021); Bastiaan Kemp, *The Role of the General Meeting in Corporate Governance, in Instruments of EU Corporate Governance* (Hanne S. Birkmose et al. eds., Wolters Kluwer 2023).
2. HR September 22, 2023, ECLI:NL:HR:2023:1283 (*Funda*).
3. The term "institutional stakeholders" is used for persons that fall under the scope of section 2:8 DCC and therefore have the obligation to act reasonable and fair towards each other and the company. *See* for more detail on this term: Jan B. Huizink, *GS Rechtspersonen*, Art. 2:8 DCC n. 6 (Wolters Kluwer 2023).
4. *See* para. 3.7 *supra* n. 2: "The circumstances of the case may therefore mean that, in addition to the persons mentioned above in the first sentence of this recital, the scope of Article 2:8(1) of the Civil Code also includes the legal entity organisationally related to the legal entity mentioned in that first sentence and those who are involved in the organisation of the latter legal entity by virtue of the law and the articles of association."
5. *See* more detailed on this development, also in its historic context: José E. Antunes, *Liability of Corporate Groups* 13 (Kluwer Law and Taxation Publishers 1994). *See* more detailed on this development, also in its historic context: J.E. Antunes, *Liability of Corporate Groups* (Kluwer Law and Taxation Publishers 1994), p. 13.

and therefore the legal reality as it should be. Enterprises are generally structured not through one individual legal entity but through various legal entities that may be located in different jurisdictions. When these enterprises cross borders, the stakeholders of the company are confronted with different legal systems that can prescribe other values.

The challenges of acting in company groups, especially when acting across national boundaries, are well known. Challenges and potential solutions have been noted for years and there have been various attempts to solve or at least mitigate these challenges. An early example is the attempt by the European Commission to largely harmonize European group law through the Ninth Company Law Directive. After that attempt failed, there have been efforts to argue for softer minimum harmonization inspired mainly by the recognition of the group interest and the French Rosenblum doctrine, including the Forum Europaeum on Group Law (2000), the Reflection Group on the Future of EU Company Law (2011), the Proposal of the Forum Europaeum on Company Groups (2015) and the Informal Company Law Expert Group (2016).[6] The same is argued for in the European Models Company Act (2017, EMCA), which is a model law designed by academics as a free-standing general company statute that can be enacted by Member States either in its entirety or by the adoption of selected provisions.[7] Chapter 15 of the EMCA provides for regulation of groups of companies, including the recognition of the group interest.

Any harmonization, however, currently seems unachievable. The most probable explanation for this seems to be twofold. First, the proposals for the aforementioned Directive were heavily inspired by German company group law,[8] while many Member States did not (and still do not) have a specific and statutory group law. When looking at the way states regulate company groups, four approaches can be identified.[9] The first is states with a global and comprehensible group law, such as Germany, Portugal and Brazil.[10] The second category of states has a partial or selective regulation on company groups, which covers certain parts of the group without aiming to regulate it in a comprehensive manner. This is, for instance, the case for Italy. The third category of states has a more flexible case law, where the group interest is, at least to an extent, recognized. This is applied in France with its famous 1985 Rozenblum judgment,[11] as well as in the Netherlands, Spain and the Nordic countries. Lastly, there are those states with no specific provisions on the group interest, of which the United Kingdom is the most prominent example.

With all these different approaches to regulating company groups, it is not surprising that it is challenging to harmonize company group regulation on a European

---

6. *See* for an overview: Adriaan F.M. Dorresteijn et al., *European Corporate Law* Ch. 10 (Wolters Kluwer 2022); Stefan Grundmann, *European Company Law* 762 et seq. (Intersentia 2012).
7. Paul K. Andersen et al., *European Model Company Act (EMCA)*, 1st ed. 2017 1 (Nordic & European Company Law Working Paper no. 16-26).
8. Antunes, *supra* n. 5, 286-287.
9. *See* Andersen et al., *supra* n.7; Rafael M. Manovil, *Groups of Companies: A Comparative Law Overview* 21-26 (Springer 2020).
10. *See* for a description: *ibid.*, 21-25.
11. Cour of cassation, Criminal Chamber, February 4, 1985.

level. The second reason is that the subject is strongly tied to the traditionally difficult-to-harmonize topic of corporate governance, a subject which Member States are largely unwilling to harmonize within the EU.[12] There are also discussions as to whether it is actually necessary to harmonize parts or whole of corporate governance or whether regulatory competition should be facilitated,[13] although it could be argued that in case of cross-border company group law, there are relatively strong reasons for harmonization. Nevertheless, there is no material harmonization of company groups law and therefore it remains a patchwork of rules under European and national law on specific subjects. These subjects are not always in the field of traditional company law but also, for instance, in the field of competition law and labor law.[14] At the same time, from within the patchwork, it is possible to discover certain broader developments.

This contribution will focus on the aforementioned developments. First, the development of the entity theory and its application in two classic judgments from the English and U.S. courts will be discussed. Then, the development towards an approach that is more focused on the economic reality of company groups and parts of the enterprise theory is described. Finally, a number of aspects of this development are noted that warrant particular attention. The aim is to give a bird's eye view of these developments, point out certain overarching trends and discuss their implications.

§15.02 THE ENTITY AND ENTERPRISE THEORY

[A] The Entity Theory

In the entity theory, it is assumed that the various legal entities within the group should be strictly separated from each other when they jointly operate an enterprise.[15] As part of this theory, the purpose, responsibility and protection of individual stakeholders is primarily determined by the individual legal entity to which the stakeholder is directly affiliated. This theory fits well with the way in which modern companies were originally developed in the 19th and early 20th centuries. While difficult to conceive today, when modern companies were first used, the norm was the individual legal entity with multiple shareholders that operated a single enterprise. Only around the

12. Klaus J. Hopt, *Corporate Governance in Europe: A Critical Review of the European Commission's Initiatives on Corporate Law and Corporate Governance*, 12 New York University Journal of Law & Business no. 1, 139-213 (2015); Dionysia Katelouzou & Konstantinos Sergakis, *When Harmonization Is Not Enough: Shareholder Stewardship in the European Union*, 22 European Business Organization Law Review, 203-240 (2021), footnote 14.
13. *See* for a helpful overview of this debate: Marcel Kahan, *The State of State Competition for Corporate Law, in: Corporate Law and Governance* (Jeffrey N. Gordon & Wolf G. Ringe eds., Oxford University Press 2017); *see* specifically for Europe: Stefano Lombardo, *Regulatory Competition in European Company Law* (ECGI Working Paper Series in Law no. 452/2019).
14. Manovil, *supra* n. 9, 31-32.
15. Mariana Pargendler, *The New Corporate Law of Corporate Groups* 6 (ECGI Law Working Paper no. 702, 2023).

start of the 20th century did the first company groups start to emerge in Europe and the United States.[16]

The entity theory has led to interesting case law by courts that applied the theory relatively strictly. A famous example demonstrating this is the American case of *Walkovsky v. Carlton.*[17] This case revolved around Carlton, who was the owner of a taxicab company. Carlton had structured his enterprise in such a way that individual taxis were housed in ten different subsidiary companies, while Carlton directly led the entire enterprise. By structuring the taxicab enterprise in such a way, it was possible for Carlton to only insure his taxis with the minimum liability insurance of USD 10,000 for each taxi. As the reader will have anticipated, one of the taxis then caused an accident, as a result of which Walkovszky sustained an injury and damages. Walkovszky could, however, only claim compensation from the legal entity holding one taxi and the liability insurance of USD 10,000. Walkovszky believed that Carlton had abused the limited liability of the individual legal entities in his group in order to avoid having to pay actual damages in cases like this. Therefore, Walkovszky initiated litigation before the New York State Courts to claim damages from Carlton in person as the ultimate beneficial owner of the taxicab company. Judge Fuld, the president of the New York Court of Appeals—being the highest court of the state of New York—held for a majority of the court that Carlton could not be held liable by Walkovszky. An enterprise may, according to Judge Fuld, be structured in such a way that the company holds only minimal assets and the injured party has to accept this:

> The law permits the incorporation of a business for the very purpose of enabling its proprietors to escape personal liability [...] but, manifestly, the privilege is not without its limits. Broadly speaking, the courts will disregard the corporate form, or, to use accepted terminology, "pierce the corporate veil", whenever necessary "to prevent fraud or to achieve equity".
>
> [...]
>
> In the case before us, the plaintiff has explicitly alleged that none of the corporations "had a separate existence of their own" and, as indicated above, all are named as defendants. However, it is one thing to assert that a corporation is a fragment of a larger corporate combine which actually conducts the business. [...] It is quite another to claim that the corporation is a "dummy" for its individual stockholders who are in reality carrying on the business in their personal capacities for purely personal rather than corporate ends.[18]

Judge Fuld, however, does not hold this view for the full court. Interesting is the dissenting opinion of Judge Keating, who writes the following for the minority:

> The issue presented by this action is whether the policy of this State, which affords those desiring to engage in a business enterprise the privilege of limited liability

16. *See* for the Netherlands: D.J. Sannes, *De Rechtsverhouding van Moeder- en Dochtermaatschappij* 45-56 (Zutphen 1926). *See* for Belgium, Germany and Italy: Manovil, *supra* n. 9; *see* for the USA: Oliver E. Williamson. *The Modern Corporation,* 19(4) Journal of Economic Literature, 1537-1568 (1981).
17. New York Court of Appeals: *Walkovszky v. Carlton,* 18 N.Y.2d 414 (1966); *See*: J. Barneveld, *Financiering en vermogensonttrekking door aandeelhouders* Ch. 7.8.1.1. (Kluwer 2014).
18. New York Court of Appeals: *Walkovszky v. Carlton,* 18 N.Y.2d 414 (1966).

> through the use of the corporate device, is so strong that it will permit that privilege to continue no matter how much it is abused, no matter how irresponsibly the corporation is operated, no matter what the cost to the public. I do not believe that it is.[19]

It is, however, clear that the majority had a different view on the matter and that a relatively strict application of the entity theory prevailed in this case. The majority found that there should only be room to hold the shareholder responsible in case of abuse, and using the benefits of limited liability as provided by the law did not constitute such.

Another famous case on the entity theory and limited liability hails from the United Kingdom.[20] In this case, called *Salomon v. Salomon*, Mr. A. Solomon sold his then-solvent trading business to a limited company whose only shareholders were himself (for 20,001 shares), his wife, and his children (all for one share). The purchase price paid to Mr. Salomon consisted of the shares in the company and a number of debentures which formed a floating charge against the company's assets. The limited company subsequently went bankrupt. Mr. Solomon sued the company for payment under the debentures, which would have resulted in leaving nothing for the unsecured creditors. In reaction, the liquidator counter-claimed, wanting Mr. Solomon to pay back previously received amounts and cancel the debentures. The liquidator in essence argued that Mr. Solomon had breached his fiduciary duty and the formation of the company was intended to defraud unsecured creditors.

Both the trial court and the court of appeal held against Mr. Solomon. The court of appeal did so on the grounds that Mr. Solomon abused the privileges of incorporating a limited liability company. Judge Lindley LJ wrote:

> The company in this case has been regarded by Vaughan Williams J. as the agent of Aron Salomon. I should rather liken the company to a trustee for him—a trustee improperly brought into existence by him to enable him to do what the statute prohibits. It is manifest that the other members of the company have practically no interest in it, and their names have merely been used by Mr. Aron Salomon to enable him to form a company, and to use its name in order to screen himself from liability.
>
> [...]
>
> Mr. Aron Salomon's scheme is a device to defraud creditors.[21]

The House of Lords disagreed with this decision and overturned the judgment of the court of appeal. They looked more at the literal text of the Companies Act 1862 and held that there was no requirement that the shareholders should be independent of the majority shareholder.[22] The company was duly incorporated in line with the requirements of the act and therefore the company was validly incorporated.

19. *Ibid.*
20. *See* for more detail on this case: Marc T. Moore, *Salomon vs Salomon* (Faculty of Laws University College London Law Research Paper no. 19/2023); Philip Lipton, *The Mythology of Salomon's Case and the Law Dealing with the Tort Liabilities of Corporate Groups: An Historical Perspective*, 40(2) Monash University Law Review 452 (2014).
21. [1895] 2 Ch. 323.
22. [1897] AC 22, 29-32.

[B] Advantages of the Entity Theory

The entity theory is not only in line with how the company was traditionally viewed and applied; there are also a number of advantages to this theory. An important advantage noted in literature is that it allows for effective "asset partitioning."[23] This consists of three elements, namely: (a) entity shielding, as a consequence of which creditors of the shareholders cannot (directly) reach the individual assets of the company; (b) limited liability, as a result of which creditors of the company cannot claim (and reach the assets) of the shareholders; and (c) capital lock-in, meaning that shareholders cannot reach the individual assets of the company before the company is liquidated and the creditors are paid.[24] These elements help promote entrepreneurship and—at least that is the aim—taking responsible business risks and supporting the financing of the individual activities of the enterprise.

In most jurisdictions and for most situations, the entity theory is still the dominant theory or at least the starting point for legal analysis. In almost all cases, only the individual legal entity is primarily responsible for its own obligations, and only the individual legal entity can exercise the rights allocated to that entity. Under extraordinary circumstances, the law will move away from this starting point, which could be described as moving away from a strict application of the entity theory. It is possible to do so voluntarily, as is the case in the Netherlands under the so-called 403-statement. Such a statement can be issued in order for the subsidiary to be exempted from certain obligations to publish annual account statements, but only if the parent company declares that it will be jointly and severally liable for the debts of the subsidiary.[25] Another example comes from Germany under the so-called control agreement (*Beherrschungsvertrag*).[26] The control agreement provides the parent company the possibility to issue binding instructions to the subsidiary while at the same time creating the responsibility for the parent to compensate the subsidiary for obligations.[27]

23. *See* for more detail on asset partitioning: Thilo Kuntz, *Asset Partitioning, Limited Liability and Veil Piercing: Review Essay on Bainbridge/Henderson, Limited Liability*, European Business Organization Law Review (2017); H. Hansmann & R.C. Squire, *External and Internal Asset Partitioning: Corporations and Their Subsidiaries* (Yale Law & Economics Research Paper No. 535), *in The Oxford Handbook of Corporate Law and Governance* (Jeffrey N. Gordon & Wolf-Georg Ringe eds., Oxford University Press 2018).
24. Margaret M. Blair, *Locking in Capital: What Corporate Law Achieved for Business Organizers in the Nineteenth Century* (Georgetown University Working Paper no. 459984, 2004); George G. Triantis, *Organizations as Internal Capital Markets: The Legal Boundaries of Firms, Collateral, and Trusts in Commercial and Charitable Enterprises*, 117 Harvard Law Review 1102 (2004); Henry Hansmann, Reinier Kraakman & Richard Squire, *Law and the Rise of the Firm*, 119 Harvard Law Review 1335, 1338 (2006); Lynn Stout, *On the Nature of Corporations*, University of Illinois Law Review 253 (2005); Edward M. Iacobucci & George G. Triantis, *Economic and Legal Boundaries of Firms*, 93 Virginia Law Review 515, 520-521 (2007); Morgan Ricks, *Organizational Law as Commitment Device*, 70 Vanderbilt Law Review 1303, 1306 (2017); Giuseppe Dari-Mattiacci, *The Theory of Business Organizations* 23 (Amsterdam Law School Research Paper no. 2018-32).
25. Article 2:403 DCC.
26. *See* Adriaan F.M. Dorresteijn et al., *European Corporate Law* 305 (Wolters Kluwer 2022).
27. *See* Gerhard Wirth et al., *Corporate Law in Germany* 216 (C.H. Beck 2024); Manovil, *supra* n. 9, 332.

The "deviation" from the entity theory can also be nonvoluntary, for instance, in case a parent company has neglected its responsibility to intervene in the affairs of a subsidiary and a third party has sustained damages as a result thereof.[28] Especially in the latter, nonvoluntary, deviation from the entity theory, there have been many relevant developments over the recent years. The emphasis in this respect is mainly on liability, e.g., the possibility of not only holding the (local) subsidiary responsible for alleged negligent behavior but also the parent company or companies, which are often foreign-based. This is, however, not the only type of "deviation" where such a trend is noticeable. Also, when it comes to who has certain powers, there is a development towards breaking through the entity theory and looking at the group as a whole. An example where such a development is noticeable in multiple jurisdictions concerns shareholder information rights. In a large number of countries, shareholders have the possibility to make so-called books and records requests.[29] These can include far-reaching requests on the basis of which shareholders can obtain documents, including, in some instances, even emails between members of the board of the relevant company.[30] The right to make such requests is traditionally focused on the company in which the shareholder directly owns shares, and the statutory provisions allocating these rights to shareholders are generally also structured in such a way. However, as of the turn of the century, rights on books and records requests have steadily been broadened in scope in order to focus not only on the company in which the shareholder directly holds shares but also on its subsidiaries. For instance, section 220 of the Delaware General Corporate Law was amended in 2003 so that the shareholders of the parent have the right to inspect the books and records of subsidiary companies without having to prove fraud or abuse.[31] A similar development has taken place in Brazil, where the *Superior Tribunal de Justica* accepted a right to review the books and records of the subsidiary, despite there being no statutory right to this effect[32] and there being previous case law confirming there was no such right.[33] In the Netherlands, recent cases also confirm this position. The Enterprise Chamber of the Amsterdam Court of

28. *See* for an overview in various jurisdictions: Manovil, *supra* n. 9, 63-68.
29. *See* for a comparative perspective: *Research Handbook on Shareholder Inspection Rights. A Comparative Perspective* (Randall S. Thomas, Paolo Guidici & Umakanth Varottil eds., Edward Elgar Publishing 2023).
30. *See* for instance: Edward Micheletti & Jenness Parker, *Books and Records Demands*, Harvard Law School Forum on Corporate Governance, October 28, 2021.
31. *See*: Lewis S. Black & Frederick H. Alexander, *Analysis of the 2003 Amendments to the Delaware General Corporation Law* 5 (2003).
32. Superior Tribunal de Justiça, Fourth Chamber, Recurso Especial 1.223.733-RJ, Rapporteur Justice Luis Felipe Salomão, decided on April 7, 2011, D.J. May 4, 2011; Tribunal de Justiça de São Paulo, First Reserved Chamber for Business Law, Appeal 1005934-40.2015.8.26.0019, Rapporteur Hamid Bdine, decided on May 18, 2016; Tribunal de Justiça do Rio de Janeiro, Interlocutory Appeal 0003009-77.2014.8.19.0000, Twenty-Second Civil Chamber, Rapporteur Rogerio de Oliveira Souza, decided on March 18, 2014.
33. Superior Tribunal de Justiça, Fourth Chamber, Recurso Especial 1.223.733-RJ, Rapporteur Justice Luis Felipe Salomão, decided on April 7, 2011, D.J. May 4, 2011; Tribunal de Justiça de São Paulo, First Reserved Chamber for Business Law, Appeal 1005934-40.2015.8.26.0019, Rapporteur Hamid Bdine, decided on May 18, 2016; Tribunal de Justiça do Rio de Janeiro, Interlocutory Appeal 0003009-77.2014.8.19.0000, Twenty-Second Civil Chamber, Rapporteur Rogerio de Oliveira Souza, decided on March 18, 2014.

Appeal—the most important court for corporate governance-related disputes—accepted that the right of shareholders to obtain information also means that the shareholders should be able to obtain information on subsidiary companies. In the i3-ruling, the Enterprise Chamber noted the following:

> Depending on the circumstances of the case, section 2:8 of the Civil Code may imply that in closed relationships, the management board is obliged, either on its own initiative or at the shareholder's request, to exercise transparency even outside the context of the general meeting and to provide the shareholder generously with information about the company, its group companies and its affiliated enterprise.[34]

A similar expansion of the rights to consider the company group can be seen for other rights. Examples are the right to the double derivative suit, the right to approval of material transactions, co-determination rights and the allocation of knowledge within company groups.[35] These developments regarding the rights of shareholders demonstrate a trend away from a strict application of the entity theory, which would mean limiting rights to the direct legal entity that the shareholder is involved in and towards an application in which the economic reality of company groups is recognized.

[C] The Enterprise Theory

The opposite of the entity theory is the enterprise theory. As can be derived from the examples above, when the entity theory is considered to lead to unreasonable results because the economic reality is that the legal entity operates within a group of legal entities that together constitute a group, the enterprise becomes more important. This shift seems to be based on the idea that under those circumstances, focusing on the enterprise and the individual legal entities as a group constituting that enterprise instead of the individual entity leads to a more equitable result. Under the full application of the enterprise theory, it is assumed that the purpose, obligations and responsibilities of the company and the protection of stakeholders are primarily determined by looking at the enterprise and whether the enterprise transcends an individual legal entity.[36] This theory in its more absolute application would mean that one would establish rights and obligations not by considering the individual legal entities as incorporated, but the larger enterprise as an economic unit. This absolute application of the theory got some support from academics in Germany and the Netherlands after the Second World War[37] but has never become a default position under the national laws of developed countries, even in case of wholly owned subsidiaries with the same directors as the parent. Instead, what can be seen is that in

34. Gerechtshof Amsterdam April 6, 2023, ECLI:NL:GHAMS:2023:846.
35. *See* for more detail on various of these examples: Pargendler, *supra* n. 15.
36. A.A. Berle, *The Theory of Enterprise Entity*, 47 Columbia Law Review 3 (1947); Ewan McGaughey, *Enterprise Law and the Eclipse of Corporate Law* (March 6, 2023).
37. Carl P.M. Romme, *De onderneming als gemeenschap in het recht* (Urbi et Orbi 1946); Johannes Ph.M. van Campen, *Onderneming en rechtsvorm* (Dekker & Van de Vegt 1945); Thomas Raiser, *Das Unternehmen als Organisation* (Gruyter Verlag 1969).

very specific circumstances, based on the economic reality, elements of the enterprise theory are applied as an ideological basis when making exceptions to the entity theory and expanding rights and/or obligations to other legal entities that are part of the same group.[38]

There are various examples that confirm this development, a number of which have already been mentioned above. The most prominent and extensively covered example in recent literature is probably the proposed Corporate Sustainability Due Diligence Directive (CSDDD). From a functional perspective, the proposed Directive creates the possibility to completely ignore the limited liability of the direct and indirect shareholders for victims whose interests the proposed Directive aims to safeguard.[39] It is also interesting that in the latest draft version of the Directive, subsidiary companies had the obligation to abide by the parent company's due diligence policy in order to ensure that the parent company could fulfill its obligations under the Directive and the subsidiary needs to provide all the relevant information to the parent in order to fulfill these obligations.[40] These provisions seem to imply that the CSDDD, at least in part and specifically for in-scope companies, attempted to harmonize certain aspects of group law.

[D] Challenges when Considering the Economic Reality of the Group to Make Exceptions to the Entity Theory

At the same time, focusing more on the enterprise than the entity comes with various challenges. One of those challenges is which of the entities within the group that collectively constitute the enterprise can be held responsible by stakeholders. After all, under certain circumstances, it is reasonable to focus on the enterprise when determining who is to be held responsible for certain acts, but short of adopting the enterprise theory in full ultimately a "claim" has to be aimed at one or more individual legal entities. Which entities these are depends on the particular circumstances. In certain cases, the claim is aimed against the group holding as the entity that is ultimately responsible for managing the group. In this respect, one can think of the responsibility of the holding to manage the group, that—at least under Dutch law—can lead to the holding company having responsibilities to consider the interests of stakeholders in the subsidiaries.[41] In the Dutch district court judgment against Royal Dutch Shell, a similar (English law governed) responsibly is applied when the district court determined that Royal Dutch Shell, when setting its group policy, has to take into account that the CO_2 emissions of the Shell Group should be net 45% lower by 2030 than the level of CO_2 emissions in 2019. In certain cases, the focus is not only on the

38. *See, e.g.*, Pargendler, *supra* n. 15.
39. Alessio M. Pacces, *Civil Liability in the EU Corporate Sustainability Due Diligence Directive Proposal*, Oxford Business Law Blog (September 22, 2023), https://blogs.law.ox.ac.uk/oblb/blog-post/2023/09/civil-liability-eu-corporate-sustainability-due-diligence-directive-proposal.
40. Article 4a(2) points a and b of the CSDDD.
41. *See* for instance: Albert F. Verdam, *Bepaling van milieubeleid van ondernemingen*, 7360 WPNR (2022).

holding company of the group but also on other entities in the chain. An example of this is the Dutch Braskem case.[42] In this case, the Rotterdam district court accepted jurisdiction to rule on a liability claim against the Brazilian Braskem and its Dutch-based subsidiary holdings, while the court at the same time established that the Dutch holdings were not directly involved in the alleged unlawful acts. The court did this on the basis that the Dutch subsidiary holding could have known that they could be held jointly and severally liable under the Brazilian law governing the concept of indirect polluter.[43]

Another challenging question is which type of protection can be derived from the enterprise and from where that protection should be allocated. If the enterprise is active internationally (i.e., across borders) and operates in various countries, which legal system should determine the level of protection that a stakeholder should receive and where should that protection be enforced? This is a subject that leaves judges struggling. In more dated case law, it was generally assumed that the responsibility was with the subsidiary company itself and that only in extraordinary circumstances there was room to "break through" the individual legal entity and look at the enterprise and the other legal entities collectively constituting the enterprise. However, also here, courts over time are seemingly giving more room to the economic reality, mainly as part of the responsibility for the holding entity to manage the group. This development should be seen as part of the debate on how to deal with important challenges, such as those related to the environment and social inequality. On the one hand, this is achieved by applying local/national law on certain key entities in the group. This was the case in the aforementioned cases involving Shell and Braskem. On the other hand, it can also be achieved by directly applying the responsibility to manage the group to the holding company in the group. Such responsibilities imposed by different national laws can also contradict each other or otherwise deviate. The question is how to deal with such a situation. Under the proposed CSDDD, section 22(3) determines that civil liabilities arising out of the Directive shall be without prejudice to the civil liability of its subsidiaries. In other words, obligations under the CSDDD were to apply in addition to or on top of the obligations arising under national law in the jurisdictions that the subsidiaries operate in.

[E] A Spectrum Between the Absolutes of the Entity- and Enterprise Theory

There are many other examples and intermediate theories between the entity and enterprise theory and the way these theories are applied under national law. It is not the purpose of this contribution to discuss all these variations. Based on the above, it is, however, possible to make a few general observations on the two theories and their development over time. First, I would argue that there is a spectrum where the two theories in their most absolute form are on the fringes of the diagram:

42. Rechtbank Den Haag 17 May 2023, ECLI:NL:RBDHA:2023:7099.
43. *Ibid.*

Diagram: spectrum between entity theory and enterprise theory

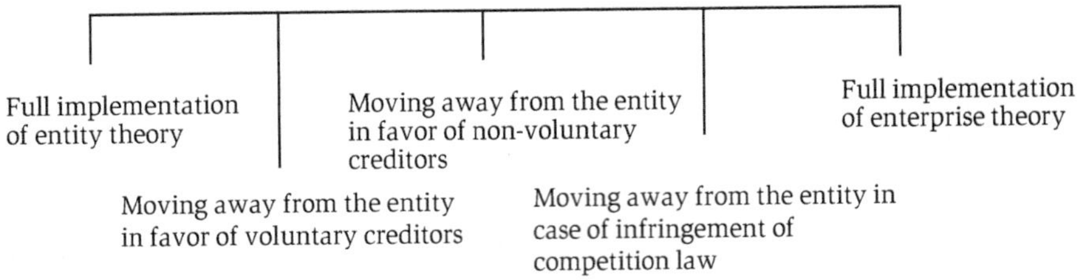

In practice, both theories are not applied in their most absolute form. Variations of both theories are applied that lie somewhere in between the absolutes, with the entity theory being more dominant under the default position and elements of the enterprise theory being applied under specific circumstances. Moreover, the intermediary variations are applied in a dynamic or flexible way. The theories and their intermediary variations are not universally applied in national and supra-national law for all issues but dynamically on the basis of the purpose of the specific regulation or situation. If the economic reality requires protection of stakeholders that reaches further than the individual legal entity, this may justify moving on the spectrum from the entity theory towards the enterprise theory. Fields in which such a movement has traditionally been visible are in co-determination rights and competition law. More recently, an important movement can be seen in relation to the protection of human rights and environmental laws. A subject where this movement is less visible is for shareholders and voluntary creditors. The latter can be explained by the fact that shareholders and voluntary creditors in many cases have (a) more influence on the structure of the group and their position within or towards that group and (b) a larger degree of choice whether they want to interact with the group.[44] The freedom of choice can therefore also be considered a relevant circumstance when determining whether the enterprise theory should be more influential or dominant in a certain field.

Lastly, the development from the entity theory towards more influences of the enterprise theory also fits the concept that economic reality plays an important role in shaping rights and obligations under company law. Nowadays, there is significant emphasis on the fact that the law should be in line with economic reality, and (excessive) legal formalism should be avoided if possible. This development is also visible in (Dutch) company law.[45] This concept has received increasing attention, at least in the Netherlands, with the Supreme Court citing the economic reality in multiple

44. Matthijs J.M. de Jongh, *Beperkte aansprakelijkheid van aandeelhouders*, 6 Rechtsgeleerd Magazijn THEMIS 298, 306 (2022).
45. Vino L. Timmerman & Bastiaan F. Assink, *Is de economische werkelijkheid een uitgangspunt voor het gehele ondernemingsrecht?*, 101 Ondernemingsrecht (2023); Bastiaan F. Assink, *De "economische werkelijkheid" in het Nederlandse ondernemingsrecht*, 7037 WPNR (2014); José M. Blanco Fernández, *De rechter en de economische werkelijkheid*, 21 Ondernemingsrecht (2015).

judgments in order to expand/clarify certain legal provisions.[46] The Dutch Supreme Court case referred to in the introduction of this contribution also emphasizes that statutory company law should be considered as part of the economic reality, and the economic reality is that most enterprises are organized as groups of individual legal entities. The entity theory is therefore still the default position, but given the economic reality of company groups, the exceptions to that theory based on the enterprise theory are becoming more frequent and far-reaching. The question is, what does this, combined with the fact that group law in most jurisdictions is not applied universally but dynamically, lead to. On the one hand, it supports the possibility of tailor-made solutions to specific problems and allows courts to create those solutions. At the same time, it creates a patchwork of regulations and rules, each their own set of conditions on—for instance—what constitutes control, what evidentiary presumptions apply (if any), to what extent active unlawful behavior from the parent is required, and if so, what constitutes unlawful behavior, etc. As a result, it is difficult to structure company groups in such a way that there is (legal) certainty on whether certain obligations will remain with the individual entity or break through to the group. This limits the possibilities of engaging in effective asset partitioning and creates uncertainty for existing company groups.

§15.03 CONCLUSION

Absent uniform group law, the dynamic regulatory approach has merits. It facilitates the use of tailor-made group law that provides a solution for specific circumstances. At the same time, it creates legal uncertainty, while legal certainty is important when structuring company groups. Therefore, it would be helpful to have more guidelines and uniformity on aspects that are relevant for moving through the aforementioned spectrum and the conditions that have to be met when moving to the enterprise theory. This can be formulated on a supra-national level because many groups operate across borders, and it would benefit those groups and their stakeholders if the guidelines are formulated in such a way that they can be used throughout the group. Previous attempts at this have failed, but given the challenges ahead, especially in the field of sustainability, as is also demonstrated in the proposed CSDDD, there is a realistic probability that this topic will again need to be addressed in the near future. Hopefully, and undoubtedly, *European Company Law* can contribute to this debate through publications in the journal.

46. *See*: HR February 4, 2005, ECLI:NL:HR:2005:AR8899 (*Landis*); HR March 29, 2013, ECLI:NL:HR:2013:BY7833 (*Chinese Workers*); HR September 22, 2023, ECLI:NL:HR:2023:1283 (*Funda*).

CHAPTER 16

A Tribute to Twenty Years Journal *European Company Law* and Its Founder Steef Bartman: An Interview

Bastiaan Kemp & Mieke Olaerts

Introduction

The journal *European Company Law* was founded 20 years ago by Professor Steef Bartman. As explained in the introduction to this book, reaching the venerable milestone of 20 years of *European Company Law*, as well as Professor Bartman's illustrious career, are a reason for celebration and for compiling this book. For this festive occasion, Bastiaan Kemp and Mieke Olaerts conducted an interview with Steef Bartman and Cees de Groot, Associate Professor at Leiden University, who was a managing editor of the journal for over 15 years and also greatly contributed to the journal. This contribution contains a reflection on the interview, providing insights into how the journal started, what the aims were at the initiation of the journal and providing some insight into the main developments in the area of European company law over the years, as seen by Steef Bartman and Cees the Groot.

How did the journal come into existence?

European Company Law was founded by Steef Bartman, who was at the time Professor of Company Law at Leiden University. Shortly after the launch of the journal, Cees de Groot, who at the time worked as an assistant professor at Leiden University, joined the team as editorial secretary, a position he held until the end of 2022.

Steef Bartman and Cees de Groot explain that at the time there was a demand in the market for a journal that focused on European company law. The journal should not only be interesting for academics but also be accessible to practitioners. Moreover, the journal should not solely focus on developments in European legislation and case law but also on developments in national law of the various European Member States, both stand-alone and from a comparative perspective. These characteristics still define the journal today.

At the time of its foundation, there were two journals that, at least in part, focused on European Company Law: the European Business Organization Law Review (EBOR, started in 2000) and the European Company and Financial Law Review (started earlier in 2004). These two journals aimed (and aim) to feature relatively elaborate articles that are mainly focused on academic discussions. Steef Bartman aimed for a different audience, with more easily accessible publications of high quality but at the same time providing for concise publications that make it easier for the reader to follow developments on comparative and European company law. The focus on practitioners also led to the so-called SCIP principle to which submissions for the journal should adhere. SCIP stands for: Scientific, Concise, Informative and Practical.

Steef Bartman was further triggered to start the journal by developments in European company law at the time, in particular, the developments and adoption of the 13th company law directive on takeovers. Steef Bartman recalls that there was a lot of criticism of this Directive at the time and this debate strengthened his conviction that it would be good to provide a platform for a broader discussion on the future of European company law.

The fact that the journal should not only be interesting for academics but also for practitioners can also be seen from the way in which the governance of the journal was structured. The journal had international law firms such as Allen & Overy, Baker & McKenzie and Loyens & Loeff contributing. Later, this format was discontinued and the journal is now structured around an academic editorial board. Practitioners also contributed to the journal in the form of country reporters. The first country reports were included in the very first issue of April 2004. It was a 23-page article on defensive measures against hostile takeovers and the impact of the 13th EC Directive, which included information on Spain, the United Kingdom, the Netherlands, Italy, Germany, France, Denmark and Belgium. The journal also featured regular country reports that highlighted general developments in relevant jurisdictions over the years.

Not only Steef Bartman and Cees de Groot have been consistent factors of the journal over the years; Kluwer has also been the publisher of the journal since the start and continues to support and publish the journal. Originally, the journal started with Kluwer (Netherlands). However, given the nature and audience of the journal, it was ultimately decided to move it to Kluwer Law International. Part of that transition was that also, given the success of the journal, the number of issues each year would be increased from four to six, which is still the number of issues that are published each year.

***European Company Law* was not only a journal; over the years, several conferences were organized under the *European Company Law* brand name. How did this come into existence?**

The journal was initially embedded at Leiden University and focused on a topic that was practised throughout Europe and comparative in nature. Therefore, Steef Barman believed it would be a good idea to also organize international conferences with colleagues from the Leiden research team and international academics. The first conference was organized in Leiden in September 2005. The list of speakers demonstrates the cross-border focus of Steef Bartman's ambitions. Speakers were John Birds (Sheffield), Luca Enriques (at the time Bologna), Loes Lennarts (at the time Utrecht), Kid Schwarz (at the time Maastricht), Christoph Teichmann (at the time Heidelberg), Beate Sjafjell (Oslo), Erik Werlauff (at the time Aalborg). The conference covered a wide range of topics and ultimately led to an edited book in 2006 with the title European Company Law in Accelerated Progress, which is also the first publication in the book series.

The conference was also the starting point for further collaboration between a number of Dutch universities on the subject of European Company Law, which were the University of Leiden, Maastricht University and the University of Utrecht. These universities became partners of the Centre for European Company Law (CECL) and were later joined by the Faculty of Law of Uppsala University, Sweden; the Department of Law of LUISS Guido Carli, Italy; and the Allerhand Institute of Advanced Legal Studies, Krakow, Poland. The CECL initiated six more conferences after the first one in Leiden. These conferences were held in Utrecht (Netherlands), Maastricht (Netherlands), Leiden (Netherlands), Uppsala (Sweden), Warsaw (Polen) and Rome (Italy). For the collaboration with the last three universities, Pavlos Masouros has also been a driving force.

What are in your opinion the most important developments in the area of European company law over the past 20 years, and what do you think the future in the area of European company law will look like?

In terms of developments over the years, several directives and consolidations have come in from Europe. These developments always provided for interesting topics to write on in the journal, such as the already mentioned takeover directive, the case law on golden shares and corporate mobility, and developments in national law, such as the application of arbitration in corporate law, on which *European Company Law* had a special issue comparing various national systems. By highlighting and debating these issues, *European Company Law* has been able to contribute to the development of these areas of European company law.

Taking a look at more recent developments in European company law, sustainability has obviously become a very important topic. In the past, the journal has had various articles and special issues devoted to this topic. It is also at the top of the agenda of the European legislator and therefore now dominates the European company law debate. The topic is here to stay and the journal is – in the view of Steef Bartman and Cees de Groot – perfectly positioned to provide an important contribution to the debate regarding the role company law can play when considering sustainability. One example of this is the need to inform both academics and practitioners of developments in legislation and case law in the area of corporate sustainability litigation, which is expected to become more and more prominent in the different European Member States. *European Company Law* can be an important platform to share information and thoughts on these developments in various Members States of the EU and how they relate to each other.

Another expectation is that traditional company law topics will in the future not be addressed on a European level in a more fundamental or all-encompassing way, as done previously with, for example, the takeover directive or the cross-border merger directive. Harmonization in those areas of company law seems to, at least for now, have reached its limits, and it seems politically difficult to make any significant progress in that regard.

Who, in your opinion, has had an important influence on the development of European company law over the years?

Steef Bartman and Cees de Groot mention that when it comes to European company law as an area of study, Jaap Winter has had an important influence. At the time when Jaap Winter was Professor of Company Law at the University of Amsterdam and partner at De Brauw Blackstone Westbroek in 2002, he chaired the High-Level Group of Company Law Experts who wrote a report with the title: A Modern Regulatory Framework for Company Law in Europe. The report of the high-level group of company law experts has had a significant influence on European company law reform for many years after its publication, provided inspiration for both research and developments in practice and is still regularly quoted in academic publications.

Another name that Steef Bartman mentions is that of Professor Marcus Lutter. Marcus Lutter was not only an expert of German company law but also a pioneer in comparative company law, as can already be seen from his habilitation thesis on *Kapital, Sicherung der Kapitalaufbringung und Kapitalerhaltung in den Aktien – und GmbH-Rechten der EWG*. He was also one of the founders of the German company law journal *Zeitschrift für Unternehmens – und Gesellschaftsrecht*. And for Steef Bartman, given his own interests, the work of Marcus Lutter on company groups in Germany provided an influential source of inspiration.

When thinking of persons who contributed to the *European Company Law* Journal itself, a lot of people come to mind that have played an important role. First of all, the members of the editorial board deserve praise, as well as all the authors who have been willing to contribute to the journal over the years. Pavlos Masouros and Thomas Papadopoulos greatly contributed to the journal and the organization of conferences and summer schools. Moreover, Steef Bartman and Cees de Groot also specifically mention the important contributions of scholars such as Eric Werlauff, who sadly passed away in November 2021. Eric Werlauff, Professor at the University of Aalborg, was always willing to write on interesting developments at short notice and did so for a considerable number of years. Another person to mention is Beate Sjåfjell, who Steef Bartman recalls being a very enthusiastic supporter of the journal from the very beginning. She also contributed significantly to the journal with a number of special issues (*see*, for example, Volume 11, Issue 2 of 2014 with Beate Sjåfjell, Tineke Lambooy and Jukka Mähönen as special editors for this issue) and has also been an important frontrunner in the debate on sustainability and company law.

EUROPEAN COMPANY LAW SERIES

1. Steef M. Bartman (ed.), *European Company Law in Accelerated Progress*, 2006 (ISBN 978-90-411-2529-3)
2. Karen Vandekerckhove, *Piercing The Corporate Veil: A Transnational Approach*, 2007 (ISBN 978-90-411-2591-0)
3. Beate Sjåfjell, *Towards a Sustainable European Company Law: A Normative Analysis of the Objectives of EU Law, with the Takeover Directive as a Test Case*, 2009 (ISBN 978-90-411-2768-6)
4. Cornelis de Groot, *Corporate Governance as a Limited Legal Concept*, 2009 (ISBN 978-90-411-2873-7)
5. Adriaan Dorresteijn, Mieke Olaerts, Bastiaan Kemp, Thomas Biermeyer, Marcus Meyer-Erdmann & Tomas Arons, *European Corporate Law*, Fourth Edition, 2022 (ISBN 978-94-035-3223-3)
6. Gert-Jan Vossestein, *Modernization of European Company Law and Corporate Governance: Some Considerations on its Legal Limits*, 2010 (ISBN 978-90-411-2592-7)
7. Catalin Stefan Rusu, *European Merger Control: The Challenges Raised by Twenty Years of Enforcement Experience*, 2010 (ISBN 978-90-411-3259-8)
8. Sabrina Bruno & Eugenio Ruggiero, *Public Companies and the Role of Shareholders: National Models Towards Global Integration*, 2011 (ISBN 978-90-411-3423-3)
9. Hanne S. Birkmose, Mette Neville & Karsten Engsig Sørensen (eds), *The European Financial Market in Transition*, 2012 (ISBN 978-90-411-3360-1)
10. Hanne S. Birkmose, Mette Neville & Karsten Engsig Sørensen (eds), *Boards of Directors in European Companies: Reshaping and Harmonising Their Organisation and Duties*, 2013 (ISBN 978-90-411-4141-5)
11. Christoph Van der Elst, *Executive Directors' Remuneration in Comparative Corporate Perspective*, 2015 (ISBN 978-90-411-5607-5)
12. Hanne S. Birkmose, *Shareholders' Duties*, 2017 (ISBN 978-90-411-6670-8)
13. Alan S. Gutterman, *Sustainability and Corporate Governance: A Practice Guide to Implementing a Sustainability Governance System*, 2018 (ISBN 978-90-411-9975-1)
14. Jan De Bruyne, *Third-Party Certifiers*, 2019 (ISBN 978-94-035-1091-0)
15. Hanne S. Birkmose, Mette Neville & Karsten Engsig Sørensen (eds), *Abuse of Companies*, 2019 (ISBN 978-94-035-0892-4)
16. Ivan Romashchenko, *Related Party Transactions and Corporate Groups: When Eastern Europe Meets the West*, 2020 (ISBN 978-94-035-1701-8)

17. Patryk Filipiak & Anna Hrycaj, *European Insolvency Proceedings: Commentary on Regulation (EU) 2015/848 of the European Parliament and of the Council of 20 May 2015 on Insolvency Proceedings (Recast)*, 2021 (ISBN 978-94-035-3410-7)
18. Alexandros Seretakis, *Regulating Hedge Funds in the EU*, 2022 (ISBN 978-94-035-3512-8)
19. Hanne S. Birkmose, Mette Neville & Karsten Engsig Sørensen (eds), *Instruments of EU Corporate Governance: Effecting Changes in the Management of Companies in a Changing World*, 2023 (ISBN 978-94-035-4162-4)
20. Bastiaan Kemp & Mieke Olaerts (eds), *Twenty Years of* European Company Law: *Developments and Challenges in European Company Law*, 2024 (ISBN 978-94-035-2118-3)

www.ingramcontent.com/pod-product-compliance
Lightning Source LLC
Chambersburg PA
CBHW071240230926
51849CB00001B/175
* 9 7 8 9 4 0 3 5 2 1 1 8 3 *